Secrets and Tips from Yesterday's Gardeners

Secrets and Yesterday's

Published by
THE READER'S DIGEST ASSOCIATION LIMITED
London • New York • Sydney • Montreal

Tips from Gardeners

Secrets and tips from yesterday's gardeners

Being outdoors on a late summer's evening, breathing in the heady aromas, watering our thriving plants and taking a quiet satisfaction in what we have conjured up from the earth: these are timeless moments, when the world stands still; moments when it is possible to imagine what it must have been like in our great-grandfather's garden, a million miles away from the noise and pollution, and the hustle-bustle of modern life; when it was easier to feel in tune with nature.

This is why more and more of today's gardeners are returning to the traditional practices of those simpler times, seeking alternatives to harsh chemicals and intrusive modern methods. In this book, we have gathered a vast store of old-fashioned gardening knowledge; down-to-earth tips learned through trial and error; secrets that have been passed down by word of mouth; wisdom born of a lifetime's patient observation. But because past generations were, above all, practical and forward-looking, we have not forgotten the latest scientific advances. Instead, we have brought together the best of yesterday and today. Dip into any page and you're sure to

discover countless useful nuggets of information. Some are grounded in science, others in common sense, some may surprise you – but they all work. In *Planning a traditional garden*, find out how romantic cottage-style planting works with nature to discourage pests or how you can create a haven for wildlife.

In *Flower beds and borders*, learn the secrets of using flower shapes and colours for the most pleasing effects then, at the end of the growing season, gather free seeds for next year's flowers. And see how something as simple as old newspaper can help to germinate and protect your seedlings. *Ornamental shrubs and trees* reintroduces you to some of the best of the old-fashioned roses, and rekindles our long-standing affection for climbers of all sorts as they scramble over trees and trellises. Be inspired to plant trees for future generations, and learn some of the tried-and-tested techniques that will help them to live a long and healthy life.

When it comes to growing fruit and vegetables, the experience of traditional gardeners really comes into its own. *The vegetable garden* and *Fruit from the garden* will tempt you to try the old-fashioned varieties whose superior flavours our grandparents would have savoured, plus some disease-resistant newcomers as well. If you've never grown your own peaches or figs, pumpkins or herbs, you'll find plenty within these pages that will inspire you to indulge in this very satisfying pastime.

Above all, yesterday's gardeners took pride in the sound cultural practices that freed them from reliance on toxic chemicals. *Garden basics* contains hundreds of practical tips, from combination planting and attracting birds and beneficial insects, to ensuring that plants are strong enough to ward off pests and diseases naturally. They make such good sense you'll wonder how we ever lost sight of this timeless wisdom.

Finally, to help you appreciate the rhythm of the seasons and take advantage of every precious moment in your garden, there is a *Gardener's calendar*, highlighting all those productive and enjoyable day-to-day tasks that send you to bed at night tired, but refreshed by your labours and satisfied by nature's bountiful harvest.

Contents

Planning a traditional garden

Designing your ideal garden

Although only grand houses had gardens that were formally designed, yesterday's gardeners knew the value of maximising every inch of their space. To do the same, familiarise yourself with your existing garden, then make a meticulous plan.

Making a plan

Getting started Before you begin, check with your local planning office to see whether your garden is covered by any planning regulations. Mature trees may be protected by a Tree Preservation Order and, if your house is a listed building or there is one nearby, you may encounter restrictions on layout and height in the garden. If you need to apply for permission to make changes, get started early.

What is your garden wish list? Think about what you want your garden to do. It should reflect your lifestyle, the people who will be enjoying it and the time you plan to spend in it, whether it is relaxing, playing or tending the plants.
▶ If you have small children and enjoy kicking a ball around with them, go for a lawn and edge it with borders of robust evergreen shrubs and grasses rather than delicate flowers.
▶ If you want to relax and entertain in your garden, lay a patio surrounded by fragrant low-maintenance borders.

Top tips for garden planning
It's best to plan your project on paper first. You can always refine your ideas by developing several versions, but date them so you know which one is current.
▶ **Map out the existing garden** Make sure you include everything in it. A plan made to a scale of 1cm:1m (1:100) is the minimum. If you can, particularly if your garden is small, use a scale of 2cm:1m (2:100).
▶ **Identify your boundaries** Mark whether they are fences, walls or hedging. Make a note of the

Have fun designing your garden with shapes cut to scale. Design kits are available, or you can make one up yourself.

hedging style (deciduous or evergreen, clipped or natural) and show the spread of the foliage.
▶ **Mark out the house** Include all major structures and any areas of hard landscaping. Then draw in details like paths, sheds, compost bins, pergolas, and water features.
▶ **Note the existing borders** Draw in flower beds, herb or vegetable gardens, and other large areas of planting.
▶ **Mark the orientation** Note down North and mark areas where shade is cast.
▶ **Remember services** Detect and note in red all electricity cables, gas and water pipes that already cross your land, as well as those you plan to put in. Keeping a record will save you from stumbling across any when digging at a later date.

Using a professional If you hire a professional to design your garden, insist on a written contract and ask for several references: and be sure to follow them up.
▶ Never let yourself be saddled with an idea you feel may be unsuitable. Choose a qualified professional who is willing to spend time in discussion with you at the planning stage and who will take into account your wishes and your needs. But remember, they're the expert, and listen to their advice.

Get your own qualifications You can, of course, also enrol on a garden design course to learn all the tips and tricks of the professionals yourself. Visiting local colleges, nurseries and gardens can help with inspiration and show you how the individual elements of a garden work together.

A full-size plan The best way to test your plan's suitability for the space available is actually to mark it out on the ground and live with it for a while.

▶ The simplest method is to use a hosepipe, length of rope or fluorescent spray paint to mark out the shape of the borders, lawns, play spaces and other large areas. Use stakes and twine to represent the exact shape and height of the hedges.

▶ Outline the paths with stakes and heavy string that is clearly visible – a coloured clothes line is ideal.

▶ To visualise a vegetable patch, lay down planks and use a rake to draw in the plant rows. You will need to be able to pull up a vegetable in the middle of the patch without having to tread on the bed.

Make a note of which direction your garden faces

This way you will see what you can plant and where: some plants love full sunshine, others prefer semi-shade and still others like evening sun. Don't forget to take into account the shadows thrown by hedges and large trees when planting, as they can be just as solid as the shadows created by buildings.

Plan your lighting in advance Start thinking about where to position any artificial lighting at the outset.

▶ A light at each entrance, and several positioned along pathways and on the patio, will aid visibility – and add life – at night and in the winter. It's a good idea to illuminate any steps, raised areas and doors leading into the house.

▶ Plan to have a number of lighted areas, not just one. It is much more effective to have several medium-voltage small lights rather than a single floodlight: the lights will not dazzle and, at night, your garden will feel lively and warm. A bulb brighter than 100 watts will accentuate the 'black hole' of unlit space behind and may also annoy your neighbours.

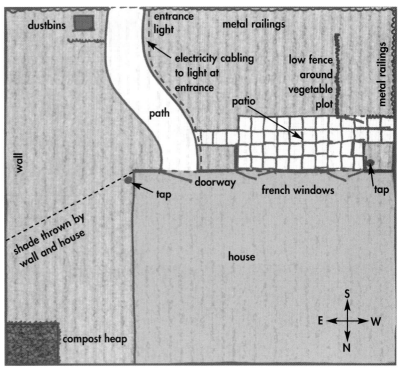

DRAW A PLAN OF THE EXISTING GARDEN STRUCTURE

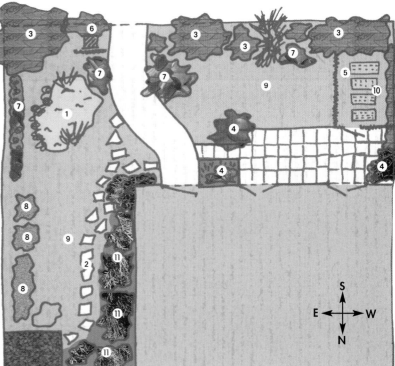

MARK IN PLANNED PLANTING AREAS AND NEW FEATURES

Draw in new features, *such as the pond* ❶*, walkway* ❷*, front hedge* ❸ *and the plants to surround the patio* ❹*.* **Mark out the boundaries** *of the vegetable garden* ❺ *and the screen for the dustbins* ❻*, then the flower borders* ❼*.* **In autumn,** *plant fruiting shrubs such as raspberries and mulberries* ❽*, sow the lawn* ❾ *and prepare the soil of the vegetable garden* ❿*.* **Note** *the areas of the garden that are in shade* ⓫ *and only use plants here that can tolerate this position.*

Measure a slope Use stakes and a spirit-level to calculate your garden's change in height over its length or width. This is really useful when planning a terrace or building steps. The incline of a slope is expressed as a percentage or a ratio. A slope with a gradient of 8 per cent increases by 8cm for every one metre in length, or by eight metres for every 100 metres.

What about the view? Don't forget to look beyond your garden to its immediate surroundings. There may be something you would like to hide from view – electricity pylons, advertising hoardings, buildings – or maybe you want to maximise a great outlook, if you have one.

Work out the size of a terrace or patio Calculate the size you think you need – and then add an extra 1.5 metres to each side. Size is difficult to judge exactly, so be as generous as you can when planning.

Planning for a water feature
Think carefully about the kind of water feature that is fitting for your style of garden.
▶ You may consider a raised or sunken pond, a waterfall or a self-contained fountain. The site itself will affect your choice: a running stream or waterfall is more natural on a sloping site, whereas a pond needs a level area where the ground is easy to excavate. If you have rock close to the surface or a high water table, a sunken pond will be impractical.

Planting near ponds
Deciduous trees and shrubs lose their leaves, pines lose their needles and bamboos renew their foliage over spring and summer, so avoid placing these plants close to a pond. For a shaded pond, surround with trellises covered with evergreen climbers.

▶ Remember to include electrical provision for a pump or lighting, if needed.

All mod cons If you want to keep a back gate locked, a bell might be useful, and, though a remote control system to open and close your gates may seem grand, it is practical and good for security. If you want to include either of these in your garden, plan and install them early on in your new design.
▶ Install sturdy, covered power points in the areas where you will most often use electrical equipment.
▶ Make sure you have an outside tap and plenty of water collection points (butts or tanks) distributed throughout the garden. This will make regular watering less of a chore.

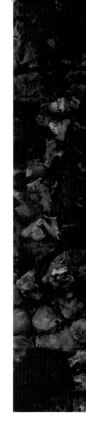

Make the most of your space

Create a window on the world A garden without a view can quickly become boring. If yours is enclosed by high walls, think about creating openings in them to give views onto the world outside. Inside the garden, establish some areas with low-growing plants to create a more open aspect.
▶ Openings also give an impression of space in a limited area. If your view is blocked, or is not a good one, consider painting a trompe l'oeil of an open gate, or of a window looking out onto a landscape.

Blurring boundaries Make your garden look bigger by planting shrubs at the end. They will disguise the length of a short plot by obscuring the boundary and merging into the plants of the neighbouring garden.
▶ Other garden 'defects' can also benefit from this trick. If you have a difficult corner, disguise it by planting a large, bushy evergreen there. Make a feature of a narrow spot by using foliage on both sides to create a leafy entry that opens out dramatically onto another part of the garden.

Change the perspective To prevent a long thin garden from looking like a corridor, avoid anything that encourages the eye to focus on the far end.
▶ Don't run a straight path down the garden's length. Instead, use stepping stones in a curved line, or place a trellis at right angles to the side boundaries part way down the garden and add a fountain and decorative foliage plants.
▶ Interrupt a long straight view by creating interest with hedges, mixed borders with contrasting heights, small trees or a summerhouse surrounded by shrubs and flowers.
▶ Try creating various levels – each higher than the last – running a winding pathway from one side of the garden to the other, and softening parallel walls with climbing plants.

Use an opening in a wall, fence or hedge to frame and draw attention to an eye-catching view.

▶ If your house is at the top of a slope, don't isolate it further by surrounding it with a bare lawn. Plant shrubs and perennials on at least two sides to unite the house with the garden and to soften the harshness of the position.

Hide an area from view A concealed space provides a parking area or hides your bins without spoiling the beauty of your garden. Plant a hedge or erect a fence then smother it with climbing plants to screen any eyesores.

Enlarge your garden with water However small, a water feature always makes a garden look larger, as water has the same reflecting effect as a mirror. If you have a small garden, site the water feature in the foreground, make it long rather than wide, and angle it in the direction of the garden's length.

Creating an illusion of depth
Install a mirror on a wall at the end of the garden, and frame it with dense foliage to mask its edges. Choose a shady spot where the mirror doesn't catch the sun and give a blinding glare.
▶ Stand a mirror on the bank of a pond, and the water will seem wider and deeper.
▶ Another way to create a feeling of depth is to make the pool narrower as it recedes from view. This makes it appear longer.

Consider planting a row of trees In a large garden, an avenue of trees is a handsome way to line a path, highlight a view or direct the eye towards a specific point such as the house, a bench, a pool or a statue. You could plant a single row that runs along one or both sides of a path or, if you really have space, a double row with the trees staggered.
▶ A line of trees is most effective if it is made with a single species. Before choosing which one, make sure you find out its height and spread when it is fully grown to avoid future overcrowding, and having to prune too often. You do not want to go to the effort and expense of planting trees and then have to remove them only a few years later.

Use levels to create space
In a very small garden, different levels not only add interest, they give you more space for planting. Don't let a lawn take up the centre of your garden – instead, create terraced levels, steps where you can cluster some pots, and rockeries against walls. Use containers of all kinds to increase your planting area.

Practical reminders for sloping gardens On sloping ground, plan to have winding paths and steps, which are both convenient and interesting. They will make your maintenance work easier and your garden look more varied.
▶ If possible, install your watering point, tap or water butt at the highest part of the garden. This will save you having to climb up the slope weighed down with a full watering can.

Paths with personality A garden path is an important design feature in most gardens. Avoid a completely straight one if you can – a curved or zigzagged path will create interest and can change the apparent shape of your garden. Avoid hard edges – instead, soften them with low-growing shrubs or perennials of varying shapes. If possible, avoid having the garden gate too close to the house – you may have to walk a bit farther but the effect the pathway makes will be much more attractive.

YESTERDAY & TODAY
Create a haven for wildlife
Hand a corner of your garden over to nature. Once established, it will require very little attention.
▶ Plant a mixed hedge of hazel, hawthorn and beech to attract birds and small mammals.
▶ Leave part of your lawn unmown, and supplement any daisies and clover you already have with plugs of ox-eye daisies and cowslips. These attract butterflies and just need a simple path mown through them for access.
▶ Leave a pile of old wood for insects, and allow nettles and brambles to provide habitats for wildlife.
▶ Grow a fruit tree or buddleja for bees, and underplant it with comfrey, dog-tooth violets and snowdrops.

15

Creating a garden, step by step

The balance between hard landscaping and planting has changed with fashion over the years, as have garden styles and materials. But it is always important to get the basic structure right before you put in any plants.

A traditional brick path, overgrown with plants, adds to the atmosphere of an old-fashioned cottage garden.

Starting points

What comes first? Start with the paths and any structures, then the areas around the house, as all the other parts of the garden will revolve around these. Feel free to develop your initial plans as you go along.

Commit yourself only to essential expenses Initially, the essential jobs are those such as levelling or shaping the site, adding drainage systems, incorporating compost into poor soil and digging any necessary trench networks. It is always worth taking the time to plan these thoroughly, rather than launching straight into large projects that may turn out to be unsuitable. For example, it would be a big mistake to start building an elaborate pergola only to find that it obscures a large part of the garden, or casts shade over the area where you were planning to put in a pond.

Protect your trees Before undertaking any major jobs, protect the trees you intend to keep. Stand 1.5m-long planks in a wigwam around the tree trunk and tie in position or, where less protection is required, use canvas or plastic covers (left).

Get an overview Start by clearing away any weeds from your site. Leave as many trees and shrubs as you can at this stage, unless they are a danger, or will be in the way. They may just need pruning rather than removing.

▶ Don't throw away stones, even small ones. You'll be glad of them later as a base for laying paths, for improving soil drainage, or creating a rockery or terracing.
▶ Hold on to any topsoil if the site has been stripped so you can put it back once the work is finished.

Do the digging jobs first There are specific safety rules governing how deep trenches must be for pipes and cabling. To ensure all the guidelines are adhered to, it's a good idea to use a professional. Get them in to dig the trench networks before you do any planting or lawn laying, making sure to keep well away from any planned or existing trees, or over the years their roots may lift the pipes or cables.

Cold weather work Autumn and winter are the best times of the year for large jobs. Professional landscaping firms are generally more available at this time of year, and the garden is clearer during this dormant period.
▶ After major landscaping, let the soil settle down for a week or two before continuing with the work, particularly if you have construction projects planned.
▶ Once all your structures are in place, dig in lots of manure to enrich your soil, adding horticultural gravel to heavy clay.

> ### WATCH OUT
>
> **Don't cover up manholes** Make a note of all the manhole covers on your garden plan and keep the plan safe. Even if you don't know what's below them, they are there for a reason, and you may need to use them some time in the future. You can conceal the covers by surrounding them with ground-cover plants, shallow-rooting shrubs or screening walls, or use special manhole covers into which you can set paving. Alternatively, sit an attractively planted container on top.

Prevent slipping Choose nonslip paving surfaces wherever possible – textured surfaces grip the best. Smooth paving becomes slippery when wet so only use it for covered areas.

▶ Moss and lichen can help to make your paths look weathered, but if you want to clean them, try a high pressure hose and a scrubbing brush before resorting to chemicals.

▶ If you have to use chemicals, check that they are suitable for your stonework before purchase. Some treatments for moss, for example, will permanently stain a patio.

Brick paths for old-world charm You can easily lay a simple garden path made from old weathered bricks.

▶ Level the ground, dig a narrow path to the depth of the bricks plus 15cm, smooth in a 15cm layer of coarse sand, then set in your bricks. Finally, brush in more sand to fill the joints. Experiment with traditional patterns – blocks or diamonds – to suit your house.

Safer slopes On gentle slopes try creating a 'donkey path' – shallow steps built with wooden logs. Drive wooden posts or steel reinforcement bars into the ground in front of each end of your logs to stop them rolling down the slope. Don't worry about banking up the soil or sand behind the logs; this will happen naturally over time.

Retaining earth on a steep slope For slopes with a gradient of over 8 per cent, build a series of low retaining walls using stones from the garden, or loose rubble to create terraces that follow the contour of the slope. The steeper the slope, the higher the walls should be.

▶ In a wild garden use wattle hurdling instead of walls. This rustic fencing is easy to make, which is why it has been so popular with country folk in the past. Sink 80cm-long stakes into the ground, 60cm apart, leaving 20–30cm above ground. Then weave willow or hazel stems between the stakes. The steeper the slope, the closer you will need to space the hurdles (between one and three metres apart).

Steps that are easy to climb Always build steps starting from the bottom and working up. Spend time working out the height and width of your steps. Risers (the step up) should be a minimum of 10cm and a maximum of 18cm high, and as a general rule the width of the tread (the step from front to back) plus double the height of the riser should total 65cm. So, to get a comfortable width for the tread of your steps, decide on the height of your riser, double it and then deduct this measurement from 65cm.

Laying an informal path

A practical and relatively inexpensive way of providing a walkway, individual stepping stones also have an enduring cottage charm. To lay the path you will need a solid rubber mallet, a spade, a trowel and some sand to stop the stones sinking. You may also need help to lift the stones.

1 Position the stones on the grass, cut around the edges of each one and carefully remove the turf.

2 Dig down 3–5cm deeper than the thickness of the stones. Spread a 5–8cm layer of sand in each hole and level.

3 Replace each stone carefully in its hole.

4 Using the mallet, drive the stones into the sand, wedging them in so that they are flush with the ground.

5 Fill in any gaps around the edges of the stones with a mixture of sand and soil, then pat down.

6 Sow grass seed in any bare areas in the lawn. Water with a fine rose until the new grass is established.

Modern lighting options

The latest choices in low-voltage lighting make it easy to illuminate your garden. Because there is less danger in accidentally cutting through a low-voltage cable, there's no need to bury the cables in deep trenches. You can lay the wires on the ground, concealed under foliage, and bury them lightly alongside paths. If you place spotlights at the base of trees and shrubs make sure there is no danger of the bulbs burning the leaves.

The width of paths Make sure your garden paths are wide enough for everyday use. On main paths, allow a minimum width of 1.5m (but preferably 1.7–2m) so that two people can walk comfortably side by side.

▶ Elsewhere, make sure that paths are wide enough to push a wheelbarrow along, and construct turning circles at convenient points so that you neither have to tread on your borders as you turn the barrow round, nor pull it backwards – which is bad for your back. In Victorian kitchen gardens, any paths and turning circles would have been large enough for a horse and cart!

▶ Access paths around planted areas and between hedges and beds only need to be 50cm wide. In the vegetable garden 20–30cm between beds should be sufficient.

Laying paths Any path that is likely to see heavy wear needs a good sub-base or foundation. Excavate the ground to firm subsoil, or until deep enough to take 10cm of hardcore and 5cm of sand as well as the surface material. Tamp down the soil and hardcore with a plate compactor, or use a traditional roller, then rake the sand level before adding paving or gravel.

▶ On paths that are used less frequently, a layer of sand should be enough to bed in paving stones. Dig to a depth equal to the depth of the paving stones, plus 5cm, pour in the sand and lay the paving stones on top, making sure they are level. Fill in the gaps by brushing fine sand over the path.

▶ To reduce the amount of weeding needed on bark or gravel paths, lay a semi-permeable membrane under the hardcore.

Experiment with colours The options afforded by colourful modern materials are practically endless and can be used to create mood or drama in the garden. Blue pergolas smothered with pastel-coloured flowers and grey foliage conjure up the sun-faded look of yesterday's gardens. Untreated wooden fences stained black contrast dramatically on a sunny day with evergreen plants and bright flowers. If used subtly, red or yellow bricks can create striking patterns in paths.

Avoid buying treated wood Organic and ecologically minded gardeners should steer clear of stains that stop wood from rotting – they are toxic and can contaminate plants and pond water. They also seep into the soil during wet weather. Ask questions when you're buying wood and avoid buying timber and furniture that comes from an unsustainable source.

▶ Build your own pergolas, fences and garden furniture from untreated wood, or buy from craftsmen who guarantee to work with this material. You can also use natural willow stems to make small woven fences.

▶ As a chemical-free precaution, sink pergola posts into a layer of sand, as untreated wood rots more quickly when it is in contact with the soil. Spiked metal casings are also available to protect posts sunk into the ground.

Order in new topsoil If the earth in your garden has been 'stripped' by building work you will need enough topsoil to provide a 30cm-deep layer for a lawn, 40cm for perennial plants and 60cm for shrubs and hedges. For trees that are planted individually, you will need 1–4 cubic metres of soil. Your builder or supplier will help you to work out the quantities you need.

▶ Any soil that has been moved or added will subside by approximately 20 per cent once it has settled and been watered. So take this into account and order extra, especially if you are intending to create raised beds.

THE BEST SPOTS FOR LIGHTING
When installing lighting in your garden, think about aesthetics as well as practicalities. Here are some suggestions for good lighting.
❶ *Under a feature shrub* ❷ *Between perennials and shrubs, to light up the display* ❸ *Level with the ground along the edge of a path* ❹ *Near the entrance to the vegetable garden* ❺ *In a patio corner* ❻ *Small lights to create atmosphere* ❼ *To highlight the pond.*

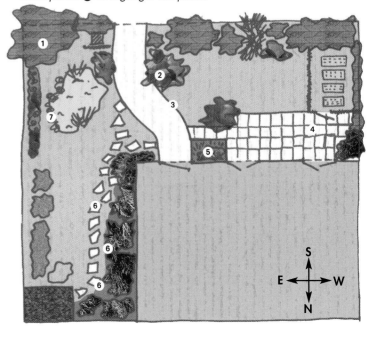

A pergola surrounded by plants should be made either from untreated wood or wood treated with a non-toxic product, to avoid polluting the garden.

Now you're ready to plant

Choose plants that will flourish The secret of success is to match plants with the type of soil and different conditions – sun, shade, moist or dry ground – in your garden. Take a close look at other gardens nearby to see which plants are doing well before drawing up your own planting list.

Try a 'dry run' at planting Once you have most of your plants and are ready for planting, check to see how they will look in position. Lay out the plants in their pots in the places where you intend to plant them, using tall stakes to simulate trees. Leave a space around the plants to represent the spread they will eventually achieve. Think about any shade they might cast, whether they will block any views and whether you're happy with the overall effect. Doing it this way means you can easily change your plans if you need to.

Start planting in early spring By this time, any organic matter you added over the autumn and winter to improve the soil should be broken down. Give priority to the plants that will form the basic framework of your garden, such as large trees, hedges and border plants, and ground-cover plants for rockeries and embankments.

Save yourself time Bygone gardeners had time to lavish on their gardens, but there are many low-maintenance shrubs and grasses that are just as appealing as herbaceous perennials and annuals. Plant your favourites near the house, so that you can enjoy them and look after them whenever they need it.

Establish 'the look' quickly Plant perennials that grow fast, such as asters, delphiniums, geraniums, gypsophila, lavender, bergamot and any of the polygonum vines. Consider putting in some of the most prolific old-fashioned ground-cover plants, such as aubrieta, dead nettle and periwinkle, which will speedily stop the ground looking bare.

▶ From the first year, sow fast-growing annuals such as mirabilis, nasturtium, cosmos and poppies to fill in gaps between young shrubs and perennials.

For hedges, consider costs and priorities For a trimmed and shaped hedge, choose very young plants, which you can buy cheaply and then shape as they grow. But if you want instant privacy, you need to buy plants that are 1.5–2m high, although this is an expensive option.

▶ A cheaper alternative is to use smaller plants and temporarily screen the areas you most want to conceal with a fence or a natural-looking bamboo or willow screen.

▶ Another interim solution is to plant a temporary hedge of quick-growing, tall herbaceous plants such as mallow alongside your small, slower-growing hedge plants. They will create a short-term, but decorative effect while you are waiting for the hedge to mature.

▶ Fast-growing shrubs such as ribes or *Berberis stenophylla* make excellent, natural-looking hedges.

Install the lawn last Make laying or sowing a lawn the last job you do so that you don't ruin the new surface by walking and barrowing over it as you develop other areas.

Edging a border with box

1 Box makes an attractive traditional edging for formal beds. First prepare the bed by digging the border well.

2 Stretch a piece of string 15–20cm in from the edge and follow this line when planting.

3 Position the individual plants 5–10cm apart then give each plant a good soaking at the base.

4 Box is a really slow grower. To help your plants to fill out and form a continuous hedge, clip lightly in May and September.

Flowers and colour all year round

The visual success of gardens has always depended largely on whether they provide colour and interest throughout the year. To achieve this, you need to plan a harmonious blend of evergreens and trees, flowering shrubs, bulbs, herbaceous perennials and annuals.

Interest through the winter months

Getting a good balance Winter is the time of year when you reap the rewards of careful planning. Aim for a third of the plants in your garden to be evergreens. Increase this proportion the closer you get to the house, and introduce a few fragrant plants that will flower at different times of the year so there is always colour and scent.

Beautiful catkins The award for the longest catkin goes to *Garrya elliptica* (left). Its slender silver catkins drape the branches in February and March and can reach 30cm on male plants. It prefers a sheltered, sunny wall.
▶ The willow *Salix caprea* displays golden, sweet-smelling catkins from February onwards.
▶ *Corylus avellana* 'Contorta', the corkscrew hazel tree, makes a magnificent and eye-catching show with its twisted branches and yellow catkins.

Choose colourful favourites for grey days The flowers of *Daphne mezereum* 'Grandiflora' are bright purple, appear from February to April (sometimes earlier) and have a wonderful fragrance. Beware of their scarlet berries, though, which are extremely poisonous.

Winter cheer The yellow flowers of winter-flowering plants will gladden the eye on the dullest day. Choose between *Jasminum nudiflorum*, which has no scent but is charming leaning against a low wall or wooden fence; *Hamamelis*, or witch hazel, which in addition to its highly individual bright flowers has a delicate scent; and *Chimonanthus praecox*, which flowers in mid winter and is also sweet smelling.

Combine warm, bright reds and yellows For the run up to spring, set off the traditional yellow forsythia with the orange-red *Chaenomeles japonica* or the deep rose-red *Ribes sanguineum* – their flowers go together beautifully and will last through the season to accompany your spring bulbs.

Grasses are striking in the frozen landscape Do not cut back wispy ornamental grasses such as pennisetum, miscanthus and cortaderia – they look stunning touched by a morning frost. Leave some herbaceous perennials standing, too. Their dead stems protect the dormant plants beneath from frost, and spikes of grasses, dried flower heads on hydrangeas and bergamot, and transparent pods of lunaria all add texture and interest to the winter garden.

THE GARDENER'S CHOICE

For a varied winter display ▶

To brighten up winter, plant plenty of evergreen foliage, as well as shrubs and trees with colourful stems and barks. Place winter flowers where you can appreciate them from indoors.

NOVEMBER
Flowers Aster, bergenia, small flowering chrysanthemum ❶, hardy cyclamen, Christmas rose (*Helleborus niger*), pansy
Foliage Aucuba ❷, evergreen bamboo, cineraria, Monterey cypress, gynerium, heather ❸, variegated sage, santolina
Fruits *Malus* 'Red Sentinel', pernettya, pyracantha ❺

DECEMBER
Flowers Christmas box, *wintersweet, Rhododendron dauricum* 'Midwinter', *winter heath*
Foliage Elephant's ear, ornamental cabbage, creeping juniper, rosemary, variegated holly 'Silver Queen'
Fruits Cotoneaster, holly ❹, hawthorn, snowberry

JANUARY
Flowers Birch, *Jasminum nudiflorum, Salix matsudana* 'Tortuosa', snowdrop, *Viburnum tinus*, witch hazel ❻
Foliage Corsican hellebore, box, lamium, New Zealand daisy, vinca, mountain flax, ivy
Colourful wood Chinese paperbark maple, dogwood
Fruits Cotoneaster, mahonia, skimmia

FEBRUARY
Flowers Chimonanthus, citrus trees, crocus, daphne, male dogwood, eranthis, garrya, willow, winter aconite
Foliage Variegated cherry laurel, blechnum, soft shield fern
Colourful wood Madrone, silver birch
Fruits Blue holly, elaeagnus

A succession of colour

The last frost Once this important date has passed you are safe to plant out less hardy varieties and annuals. As a rough guide, the last frost occurs at the end of April in the South West, in mid May in the South East, the Midlands and Wales, and at the beginning of June in Scotland and the North. But don't go by the calendar alone – keep an eye on the thermometer and the weather reports.

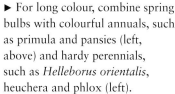

Small bulbs in spring The smaller bulbs will be the first to bloom. Bring your bare borders to life with snowdrops, winter aconites and *Iris reticulata*.
▶ For long colour, combine spring bulbs with colourful annuals, such as primula and pansies (left, above) and hardy perennials, such as *Helleborus orientalis*, heuchera and phlox (left).

Flowers to last throughout the summer For a new garden, you need species that provide a good season of colour and establish quickly.
▶ **Perennials** At their best in early and mid summer are the cranesbill geraniums Geranium psilostemon or G. endressii, scabious 'Butterfly Blue', Anthemis tinctoria 'E.C. Buxton', gaura, valerian and nepeta.
▶ **Shrubs** Make the most of the spectacular growth of the lavatera shrub and combine it with late-flowering spiraea and potentilla, which are good value and easy to find. While you are waiting for your evergreen trees and shrubs to bloom, create a little colour by sowing or planting out seedlings of green or bronze fennel.
▶ **Annuals** Plant old-fashioned favourites such as cosmos, nasturtium, nigella or other flashy annuals for instant colour and a denser volume of planting in your garden.

Remember autumn colour Flowers are bountiful in summer, but don't let late autumn be a low point. When planting, think about creating spots of colour for this season: dahlias, asters and *Anemone japonica* will give admirable support to the cooler tones of late fuchsias, buddlejas, *Tamarix ramosissima* and hebes.
▶ **Keep watering** Autumn colour will be even more striking if the summer has been dry. From late August, start watering the base of plants that are due to flower at the end of the season to make sure they don't dry out.
▶ **Colourful leaves** For beautiful autumn foliage try aronia, amelanchier, dogwood, cotinus, *Quercus coccinea*, maple, deciduous euonymus, witch hazel, liquidambar, nyssa, *Parrotia persica*, rhus, *Parthenocissus quinquefolia* (Virginia creeper), *Vitis coignetiae* and viburnum.

Early-flowering trees and shrubs	
Species	**Average month**
Crab apple, holly, pernettya, pyracantha and viburnum	November/December
Azara, beech, chimonanthus, daphne, hazel, honeysuckle, jasmine, mahonia, prunus, willow and witch hazel	January/February
Camellia, chaenomeles, flowering currant, forsythia, fothergilla, magnolia, malus and prunus	March

▶ **Decorative berries** For autumn fruits, grow ampelopsis, arbutus, hawthorn, *Colutea arborescens*, berberis, callicarpa, cotoneaster, *Euonymus europaeus*, holly, *Maclura pomifera*, physalis, ornamental malus, pyracantha, *Rosa rugosa*, koelreuteria, skimmia, symphoricarpus and viburnum.

At the height of summer, delphiniums, nepetas, achilleas and roses create a vibrant clash of colour.

A rock garden bursting with life

Rockeries go in and out of favour, but taking inspiration from elements of the natural landscape and re-creating them in your garden can be very effective. Find or construct a rocky slope, and you can add a brilliant array of alpine plants.

Sun-loving dianthus, stonecrops and primulas soften the craggy lines of a rockery.

Create an alpine corner

Creating the right conditions Rock plants love well-drained soil. They grow wild in high alpine areas as well as relatively low altitudes and the sun-baked stony soils of desert areas. Most of them need extremely dry conditions to thrive and will fail if the soil is too wet, so make sure that water does not sit on the ground. If puddles persist after it has rained, you will need to improve the drainage.
▶ Before placing your decorative stones, spread a drainage layer of broken bricks, gravel or stones 30–50cm deep, then cover this with inverted turves or grit and well-draining soil.
▶ Do not be tempted to create a rockery under a tree – autumn leaves will collect there and form a wet layer that will rot your plants. Tree roots could also dislodge your stones.

Start with a slope If you can make use of an existing slope in your garden it will make creating your rockery much easier.

Use an effective mix of garden plants to mimic the species you might find growing on a rocky outcrop in the wild.

A gentle, sunny bank sheltered from cold, drying winds and backed by a wall provides the ideal growing conditions for alpines. If you do not have a natural slope, create a gentle mound in a corner of your garden. Shallow slopes look far more natural than a sudden steep lump in an otherwise flat garden: as a general rule, for every 30cm the bed is raised, it must be 1–1.5 metres wide at the base.

Patience before planting If you are building a rockery from scratch, wait until the rocks and soil have stabilised in their new position before planting. Ideally, you should allow a winter to pass between building and planting up in spring.

Typical alpine plants Create a patchwork of low-growing perennials with stonecrops, houseleeks, mossy saxifrage, pasque flower, maiden pink, balloon flower, gentians, cranesbill, salmon primrose and fairy foxglove.

Provide volume Add high points and interest to a rockery with some dwarf conifers such as the mugo pine, common juniper or blue juniper and small shrubs such as hebes, brooms and heathers, which won't overshadow the perennials. Lavender, thyme, rosemary, rock rose and other scrubland plants will tolerate rockeries that become very hot in summer. Ferns and hostas are good for shady banks.

> ## WATCH OUT
>
> **Watch your back** If you build your own rockery, be careful how you carry the rocks. Raise them with a crowbar, always bend your knees and keep your back straight when lifting. Shift slabs zigzag fashion, pivoting them on their corners, and use a trolley or get help to carry larger rocks. Always wear steel-toecap boots and thick protective gloves.

Top tips for choosing rocks Locally quarried stones will look more natural and cost less than rocks brought from other parts of the country. Use a variety of sizes, but do not go any smaller than the size of a 5-litre bag of compost and do not mix two different kinds of rock.

▶ **Quality not quantity** The type and size of rock dictates how many you need: a few large, flattish stones look more effective than many smaller ones. Large stones are also more stable.

▶ **Avoid limestone** Water-worn limestone has traditionally been used for rock gardens, but it has become quite scarce and its collection has led to the destruction of valuable habitats, so try to find some other quarried rock to use.

▶ **Use sandstone** Look for slabs of recovered sandstone. Their irregular shapes give them a natural look. You can also buy artificial sandstone, which is less expensive.

▶ **Tufa for small plants** Keep tufa – a soft, pale rock with the consistency of chalk – for your more precious plants. Its porous nature means it's extremely free-draining and small plants can be grown in the cavities in its surface.

▶ **Avoid granite and flint** The size of the pieces, their shapes and resistance to erosion make them unsuitable for a rockery.

A natural effect Try to position rocks to mimic a natural rocky outcrop. Place them in steps, with the largest blocks at the base of the rockery.

▶ Keep the best pieces for the most visible rocky sections, particularly at the top. Bury your first blocks so that they seem to emerge from the earth naturally.

▶ Lay the rocks in horizontal layers to imitate the natural strata of the landscape. Make sure the 'grain' of each rock follows the same direction, but do not make them too regular.

▶ Start at the bottom of the slope and work upwards, laying the largest slabs on their flattest side first and inclining them slightly backwards for stability.

The right soil The best compost for rockeries is freely draining, made up of equal parts of a loam-based compost, garden soil and grit. Mix the ingredients thoroughly and then spread over the surface of the rockery to a depth of 20–30cm.

▶ Water helps the soil to settle by carrying fine particles of earth with it into crevices in between the rocks. Once the soil is in place, water it with a fine rose for about 20 minutes daily. The longer you do this, the quicker your rockery will stabilise.

▶ Bear in mind that digging up soil increases its volume, so allow for soil levels to drop over time.

When to water During their first year, protect your rock plants from drying out by keeping the soil just moist. You only need to water them properly in times of drought. When it is hot and dry, hoe gently around the plants to break up the hard crust, then water slowly and carefully to avoid dislodging the plants. Otherwise, just leave them alone.

Winter protection Cushion plants and silver foliage plants can be damaged by the cold and damp of winter. To protect them, cover them with a sheet of glass tied down over bricks or blocks of wood, or with a two-pane cloche. This will protect them from rain and damp but allows light and air in.

Well-fed plants To give plants a boost at the end of winter, add some soil enriched with bone meal – or leaf-mould and coarse sand – to the base of each plant. In spring, water once with a soluble general fertiliser.

Top up gravel Gravel spread between plants on a slope gets washed away by rain during winter, eventually exposing the soil below. Renew or replace this protective layer in spring.

Building a rockery

1 If your garden does not have a natural mound or sunny slope, build one up with broken brick, grit and soil.

2 Prepare a mix of garden soil, loam-based compost and grit, and spread it over the surface of the slope.

3 Position the first rocks at the base of the rockery; keep natural lines in the stone flowing in the same direction.

4 Place the next row using a stout stick or crowbar to move and raise the blocks.

5 Fill around each new row of rocks with compost, tamping it down well between the stones.

6 Tuck the plants into pockets of earth between the rocks. Cover bare earth around them with gravel.

Ideal growing conditions

Protect the delicate Do not put vigorous ground-cover plants such as aubrieta, alyssum and chickweed next to slow-growing alpine plants such as rock jasmine, gentian or stonecress. The ground cover will smother the alpines and demand endless pruning.

Planting secrets To give plants the best start, mix a dose of fertiliser with your planting compost and put a handful of sand under each plant's rootball.
► When you have filled the hole, remember to water the ground until it is saturated.
► After planting, spread a layer of gravel or coarse sand between the plants. This is not only attractive, it also stops weeds, reduces evaporation and surface compaction, and keeps standing water from rotting the base of the plants.

Acid and lime If you are lucky enough to have an old limestone rockery in your garden and you want to grow some acid-loving plants, put them high up in the rockery in pockets of ericaceous compost. If they are planted lower down they will suffer from the lime carried down by water draining away.

Plants to decorate a wall

Choose perennial alpine plants to fill the cracks in a vertical face or a dry-stone wall.

In full sun Alyssum, aubrieta, dwarf bellflower (*Campanula portenschlagiana*), catsfoot, Cheddar and cottage pinks (*Dianthus allwoodii*), crassula, *Gypsophila repens G. tenuifolia*, linaria, jovibarba, ptilotrichum, rupturewort, sea campion (*Silene uniflora*), seaside daisy (*Erigeron karvinskianus*) ❶, sedum (*Sedum oreganum*) ❷, sempervivum, stonecress, thyme (*Thymus doerfli, Thymus praecox*), wall rue and wallflower

In partial shade Phlox (*Phlox borealis, P. nivalis and P. subulata*), rock cress (*Arabis*), Rock jasmine (*Androsace*), saxifrage and whitlow grass (*Draba*)

A rockery in a pot If your soil is heavy or badly drained, or you only have a very small garden, you can still grow alpine plants in a raised bed or in a stone trough at least 30cm deep. Make a gravel drainage layer first, taking up at least a third of your depth. Then fill the bed or trough with a soil mix of equal parts loam and grit. Remember to raise your trough slightly to let water drain away freely.

Follow the example of traditional cottage gardeners and use old sinks and troughs for plants that like well-drained soil.

Using an alpine house

An alpine house is an unheated greenhouse, well ventilated with at least 25 per cent of the glass containing vents. It provides perfect growing conditions for alpines, protecting them from the cold winter weather.
► Grow alpines in terracotta pots rather than slow-drying plastic pots. Most species will grow well in loam-based compost mixed with equal amounts of grit, with broken crocks in the bottom of the pot. Top-dress each pot with gravel.
► To keep the plants cool, plunge them in their pots, up to the rims, in a bed of sand 15–20cm deep.
► Don't let the soil in the pots dry out. Remember to water not only the pots but also the sand they are buried in.
► From May to September, whiten the glass or erect a cloth awning over the plants to reduce the temperature and prevent the flowers and leaves from being burnt by direct sunlight.
► Remove dead foliage and flowers regularly to reduce the risk of fungal disease. Keep the glass and floor clean, and check your plants regularly.

An English cottage garden

Flowers and vegetables have been a feature of British gardens since medieval times. But it was the 19th-century cottage gardeners who, by necessity, became experts in combining flowers and vegetables attractively in their small plots. The practices they developed are just as relevant for gardens today.

Creating the look

A riot of colour The classic English cottage garden is a colourful mass of romantic informality characterised by old-fashioned flowers at the height of their glorious display in the summer months. This style is suitable for any garden, large or small, and can be tailored to complement your house whether it is old or modern. It can be low on maintenance too, with plants left to self-seed and tumble over pathways and edges.

Plant in layers To create the cottage garden style successfully, you need to think of your planting as a system of layers.
► Use a number of trees and shrubs for structure, and hedges to create frameworks – either around the garden as a whole or to define individual borders.
► Plant climbers to scramble through hedges and clamber up arbours, arches and walls.
► Use old-fashioned flowers and herbaceous perennials to make up the bulk of your planting.
► Include vegetables and herbs – important elements in a cottage garden – among or alongside your flowers.
► Fill gaps with annuals and bulbs for colour throughout the year.

Formal or informal? The prime feature of a cottage garden is 'controlled informality', but the layout of your garden can be a system of beds and borders in either regular or more relaxed shapes. Aim for an almost overcrowded effect in your borders.
► Edge rectangular beds with box hedging, or create kidney-shaped beds and plant them right up to your lawn.
► Set out plants in informal drifts and swathes, mixing species and colours to get a fantastic mass of flowers.
► Allow plants to grow and spread naturally, rambling over pathways and lawn edges.
► Repeat a number of key plants throughout the borders to link them together and give them rhythm.

Combination planting Mix flowers, vegetables, fruit and herbs all together in the same beds. This is what the original cottagers did to enable them to grow food for the table and experiment with an increasing range of flowers for colour.
► Include flowers such as marigolds and nasturtiums to repel pests that might attack your crops.
► Plant an apple or plum tree among ornamentals for their flowers as well as fruit.
► Grow your beans and gourds up rustic arches with other ornamental climbers to give surprise added interest.

Low maintenance A cottage garden doesn't demand a huge amount of time. No formal pruning is needed, and annuals self-seed and fill in gaps. Plants cramming your beds and borders will suffocate weeds and confuse pests.

Old-fashioned varieties Choose a selection of the following flowers to get the look of your cottage garden just right: hollyhocks, achillea, bellflowers, bleeding heart, foxgloves, lupins, delphiniums, wallflowers, fuchsias and mallow.

THE GARDENER'S CHOICE

Some old-fashioned settings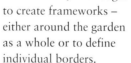

Fragrant path Massed ranks of pink peonies are held back from a path by an aromatic edging of lavender ❶.

Rustic centrepiece An ancient, weathered well sets a cottage style for the planting: salvias, petunias and a couple of cheeky tomato plants ❷.

Traditional herb garden A low box hedge neatly encloses the contrasting textures and shades of feathery fennel and a more formal-looking bay tree ❸.

Timeless rose garden Small-flowered roses and valerian combine in a gentle, informal planting that recalls the past ❹.

Colourful walls Mop-head hydrangeas accentuate the warm tones of the local stonework ❺.

Glorious jumble Asters, pieris, ferns and bergenia combine to create a typical, overgrown cottage garden setting ❻.

Cottage gardens

Flowers for cutting and scent One of the joys of a cottage garden is having flowers to bring into the house. Grow a variety of annuals and biennials as well as perennials in your garden, including:
► **Plants for drying** Some of the most successful are ageratum, calendula and statice.
► **Flowers for vases** Popular cut flowers include dahlias, lilies and gladioli.
► **Aromatic and honey-producing plants** Dianthus, sweet peas, honeysuckle and nicotiana attract bees to the garden.

Annuals for spring and summer Give instant colour to your garden and window boxes with annuals. Let them reseed and save yourself having to buy new plants again next year.
► In a shady areas use busy lizzies, mimulus, evening primrose, primula and pansies if your site is moist, or foxgloves if it is dry.
► For windy, exposed sites use cornflowers, honesty, poppies, rudbeckia, calendula and wallflowers.
► For containers try pelargoniums, osteospermums, lobelia, petunias and snapdragons, as well as nasturtium and sanvitalia for a trailing effect.

Old English garden styles Knot or parterre gardens have a formal, controlled planting style dating back to 16th-century England and Renaissance France. They give year-round structure as they are made up primarily of evergreen hedging.
► **To create a knot garden** Use dwarf evergreen shrubs such as box to form low hedges planted in intricate patterns and geometric shapes. Fill the beds between the hedges with an informal selection of the flowering herbaceous plants you might use in a cottage garden or with herbs. Dot topiary sculptures about to add height and keep the hedges trim.
► **For a parterre** (a French word meaning 'on the ground') Use the same pattern of low evergreen hedging as the knot garden, but fill in with simple low-growing or monochrome planting in the centre. Coloured or natural gravels alternated in the beds can also make a particularly striking effect. Incorporate columnar yew or cypress into the geometric design to complete the look.
► **Viewing the effect** Both of these styles will look great at ground level, but they really come into their own when viewed from the top of a slope or an upstairs window.

The Tudor knot garden was created with a complex pattern of rectangular, diagonal and circular hedges. Simpler designs can add structure and formality to a modern garden.

A secret garden Arbours and secluded spaces planted with scented flowers have been a popular feature of English gardens for hundreds of years. From the Dark Ages on, courtiers and wealthy families lived communal lives under the eyes of their family and retainers. Then, as now, the secret garden provided an intimate spot for quiet contemplation and privacy.

► **Define a corner** Screen off an area with trees or shrubs so that it is separate from the rest of your garden. Tall hedging is perfect as it means your secret cannot be seen at a glance. You could also use large-leaved plants for the same effect.
► **A dramatic approach** Make an opening in the hedge, or wind a path beneath low-hanging trees so that visitors discover your secret spot almost by accident.
► **A fragrant retreat** Introduce strongly scented plants to create a heady aroma in the enclosed space.

A Mediterranean garden In warmer parts of the country, add a touch of sunnier climes by growing lavender, African lily, Russian sage, roof iris and red hot poker, and training a vine or a wisteria over a pergola. Try sweet-scented jasmine in a sheltered spot; in winter, the long stems may freeze, but if the base is well-protected, it will regrow from below.
► To set off the bright colours of your flowers, grow plants with silver foliage, such as pearl everlasting (*Anaphalis*), rock rose, globe thistle, helichrysum, sage and thyme.
► To provide volume, contrast and evergreen foliage, plant some pointed conifers such as cypress or yew.
► Instead of the typically Mediterranean olive tree, which will die in freezing temperatures, plant a willow-leaved pear

(*Pyrus salicifolia*). It's fast-growing and hardy, and – from a distance – looks just like an olive tree.

▶ Oleanders freeze at −5°C. As a precaution, grow them in tubs that can be taken inside for winter. Use bay trees too, trimmed regularly into a cone or a ball shape on a stem. Cover the soil in the pot with a few handfuls of decorative gravel.

The secrets of composition Although borders in traditional gardens are relaxed and informal, you will create a more successful effect if you follow a few basic design principles.

▶ Think about the height of the plants you plan to grow in your borders. Keep taller plants such as veronica and salvia towards the back and gradually bring the height down as you get to the front. Here you can use low-growing and ground-cover plants such as geraniums and pulmonarias. You can also build up to tall plants at the centre of long borders to draw the eye, adding interest and drama.

▶ To soften the edges of your beds, use plants with a spreading habit, such as heuchera, erigeron, osteospermum and geum.

▶ Always plant individual species in odd numbers, in threes, fives or sevens. This is easier on the eye. Use a larger number of plants to create meandering drifts.

▶ Try to repeat species or particular colours in your borders to give them a sense of continuity and balance.

Top tips for the total look To complete whichever old-fashioned garden style you choose, you must use the right building materials and accessories. Any features must be in

A house front (below) covered in geraniums and, from left (above), Pelargonium grandiflorum 'Rosemary', Pelargonium 'Occold Shield', and 'Lady Plymouth' with scented leaves.

Cottage garden favourites

Dahlias With its many-coloured flowers that appear from June or July until the first frosts, the dahlia is the queen of the summer and autumn flower bed. Wait until the end of April before planting the tubers, 8cm deep for dwarf varieties, 12cm for more vigorous plants. Planting too deeply weakens the plants and reduces the number of flowers.

Hollyhocks Choose traditional varieties with simple flowers rather than the modern double blooms. As hollyhocks are biennial, sow seed you have collected in the autumn in a corner of your garden and move plants to their permanent positions the following year.

Peonies These plants are beautiful but sensitive – choose their location carefully, as they dislike being moved. Take care of their roots by digging them a large, deep hole with a generous drainage layer at the bottom and fill in with a mix of fibrous compost and sand. Peonies are slow to establish and may take three years after planting or moving to flower – but it is well worth the wait.

Foxglove This is a perfect self-seeding plant to use around your borders. Let their flower spikes surprise you as they pop up in the early summer. Combine them with decorative allium, larkspur and lupins to add statuesque drama at the back of a bed.

keeping with the style of your garden and should be chosen thoughtfully. Avoid modern, hard or urban materials and go for rustic, traditional styles instead. Anything weathered, antique, reclaimed or recycled would be ideal.

▶ **Walls** Build structures that are sympathetic with their surroundings. Echo the style of your house if you can, by using appropriate stone, slate or traditional brick.

▶ **Surfacing** Select materials that complement the other features in your garden. Traditional choices include gravel, cobbles and setts, as well as brick paving. Steer clear of concrete slabs but, if you have no option, try crazy paving.

▶ **Ground cover** Interplant paving or gravel with alchemilla, thyme, saxifrages and sempervivums.

▶ **Edging** Edge your beds and borders with wooden boards, old bricks set into the ground at an angle, or decorative Victorian edging tiles with scrolled or scalloped tops.

▶ **Fencing** Use post-and-rail fencing or wattle hurdles to create boundaries or define areas.

▶ **Containers** Use traditional unglazed terracotta for pots, or recycle old baths, sinks or buckets.

Add soothing water to your garden

Once, artificial ponds, lakes, fountains and cascades were possible only in grand gardens. Now anyone can easily devise a water feature to suit their garden and budget, and enjoy the enchantment, peace and serenity it brings.

A well-planned pond

The best site for a pond Your pond or pool should be visible from the house, but not so near that wildlife will be scared away.

▶ If the ground slopes, choose a lower corner of the garden: your pond will seem more natural here, as water naturally collects at the lowest level.

▶ A pond should be sited away from any fruit trees or plants that might be treated with chemicals.

▶ An open, sunny position provides the best conditions to grow most aquatic plants. Do not site your pond in a frost pocket or an exposed spot. This will restrict the plants you can grow in it and may mean that your pond will need protection over the winter.

▶ Only add fish if your pond is at least 80cm deep. Watch the water conditions in hot weather as the fish will suffer if the temperature gets above 25°C. If you need to reduce the temperature and top up the pond, add tap water that has been left to settle and warm up for a day.

A water feature on the terrace

If you don't have space for a pond, take a tip from yesterday's gardeners and improvise. Use a large basin, stone trough or half-barrel, or frost-proof pots.

▶ Plug drainage holes in pots with a silicone sealant and paint the inside of the pot with waterproofing paint.

▶ To prepare a half-barrel, fill it several days before you plan to plant it up so that the wood swells and becomes completely watertight.

A blend of herbaceous plants along the bank merge with flowering irises and floating water lilies to integrate this pond naturally into its environment.

▶ Choose water plants that like warmth, as such a small volume of water will heat up quickly. Try a miniature variety of water lily, which will flourish in less than 40cm of water. Add to it a heat-loving floating plant, such as a water hyacinth, and give the arrangement some height with a clump of plumed foliage, such as *Typha minima*, an attractive reed. Remember to include a plant that will generate oxygen under water, such as *Myriophyllum aquaticum*.

▶ In October you will need to bring your water hyacinth into shelter – a conservatory or heated greenhouse – for the winter, but other hardy species can be left in the water.

WATCH OUT

Beware of drowning Water attracts children like a magnet, and it is important to remember that a child can drown in as little as 10cm of water.

▶ Cover small ponds (under 10m²) with wire netting or a rigid grill – the vegetation will soon hide most of it. Surround larger water features with a metre-high fence with a gate that should always be kept locked. Disguise the fence with honeysuckle, ivy or clematis.

▶ Avoid steep banks, which make climbing out difficult for a person or an animal that has fallen into the water.

▶ Notify your insurer of your water feature.

▶ Guard against electrocution by placing electric cables in a sealed watertight casing.

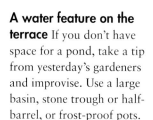

Water plants need sunlight Make sure that you site your pond where it will get at least five hours of light a day – if possible, the morning sun.
▶ Position it away from overhanging trees, which throw shade over the water. If you don't you will have to collect dead leaves and control roots that could pierce the pond's liner.

Provide a power point Plan ahead in case you want to install a pump to circulate the water and prevent stagnation. You can also light your pond at night and make it a feature of any evening parties.

Start in warm weather April to July is the best time to create your pond. The water will warm up quickly and create the perfect environment for your first water plants.

Choosing the shape of your pond If it is close to the house, it is best to choose a formal shape with simple lines. Farther away from the house or in a large garden, your pond can be a more irregular, organic shape, which will blend into the surrounding natural landscape.

Think big The bigger it is, the more natural your pond will look. A large area of water also has a more stable temperature, which is better for wildlife and plants. But a pond should take up no more than a third of the space in your entire garden.
▶ Aim for a minimum depth of 80cm so that plants and fish can overwinter without being stressed. The impression of depth can be exaggerated by using a dark-coloured pond liner.

Digging a pond yourself This is the most economical way to install a pond, and allows you to achieve the size and structure you want. A flexible butyl liner is the best material to use, as it can last for up to 50 years.
▶ A 1mm thick butyl liner is adequate for an average-sized pond. If the area is more than 100 square metres or if the ground is very stony, go for 1.5mm. To estimate the size of liner you need, first measure both the maximum length and maximum width of the hole you have dug. Then to each of these measurements add twice the maximum depth you have dug for your pond, plus 30cm. This will give you the length and width of liner you will need to buy, including enough to overlap the edges of the pond.

Things to consider when you're digging Check the rim of your pond is level all round using a spirit level; any differences in height will be very noticeable once the pond is full of water.
▶ Make shelves around the edge of the pond at least 30cm wide and at different depths. This will enable you to grow a whole range of water plants.
▶ Instead of carting them away, why not make a rockery with the earth and stones you've cleared when digging your pond?

Planning for overspills There are two things you can do to combat flooding. The first is to make one side of the bank lower than the rest so that any water overflows into an area of the garden filled with plants that can thrive in these boggy conditions, such as phalaris. Another is to install an overflow pipe into your main drainage system. Fix a grille to the mouth of the pipe to prevent vegetation causing a blockage.

Installing a pond

1 Mark out the shape of the pond on the ground. Tap in stakes every 30cm around the edge of the shape.

2 Excavate to the depth of your pond plus 15cm. Gently slope the sides and remove 15cm of turf all round.

3 Remove stones, spread a layer of fine sand, then cover with old carpet, strips of cardboard or newspaper.

4 Install the liner on a warm day so it will be flexible. Stretch it out from the centre, and secure edges with rocks.

5 Don't worry about wrinkles as the weight of the water will remove any creases. Run in water slowly to fill the pool.

6 Allow the liner to settle for several days after filling it. Trim the edges and conceal them with earth or stones.

Floating plants for ponds

Floating plants drift freely on the water and most need no soil since they take in nutrients through their trailing roots. Simply release these onto the surface and let them drift. They shade the pond and keep it from heating up too quickly in summer, and are friendly to fish which love to hide in their midst. Keep their growth in check so they cover no more than half of the pond, and overwinter tender species in a greenhouse.

PLANT		CHARACTERISTICS
	Water chestnut (*Trapa natans*)	Suitable for still, shallow pools. Helps to purify the water by consuming nitrogen. Annual, but reseeds itself.
	Water hyacinth (*Eichhornia crassipes*)	Spikes of pretty blue-lilac flowers in summer. Frost tender, so needs to be taken out of the pond for winter.
	Water lettuce (*Pistia stratiotes*)	Very attractive rosettes. Deciduous and frost-tender. Can be invasive.

Fish in the pond In addition to their visual appeal, fish such as the koi carp are great little gardeners for aquatic plants. They clean and trim ceaselessly and also keep down mosquitoes by devouring their eggs and larvae. However, fish soil the water with their excreta and stir up the mud at the bottom. If you do want to introduce them into your pond, take advice when you buy them on suitable numbers for your size of pond, and use a filter to keep the water clean and clear.

Introduce fish slowly Wait at least three months after filling your pond before introducing fish into it (ideally in spring).
▶ When you bring your fish home from the aquatic centre, do not put them directly into the pond. There will probably be a temperature difference between the water in the bag they were brought home in and the water in the pond. Float the bag in the pond, still closed, for a few hours to allow the water temperatures to equalise. You can then safely empty the fish into their new habitat.

A pond teeming with life

Hide the edges of your pond with plants The plants' roots will stabilise the ground at the banks. Mix flowering with foliage plants, and create interest by varying your species. The following plants like damp soil and will tolerate temporary immersion in up to 10cm of water:
▶ **Flowering plants** Marsh marigold (*Caltha palustris*), Japanese primrose, *Narcissus poeticus* 'Actaea', astilbe, iris sibirica, hemerocallis (day lily), *Hibiscus mascheutos* (rose mallow, with giant flowers), ligularia, lysimachia, mimulus.
▶ **Plants with decorative foliage** Carex, fern, hosta, miscanthus, *Petasites albus*, phalaris, rodgersia.
▶ **Keeping plants moist** During a dry summer, which will lower water levels and dry out the banks, pack a layer of grass clippings around your plants to keep them moist.

Star performers Floating plants that root in the water are the most decorative and wide-spreading. Of these, the water lilies (*Nymphaeas*) are the stars. They like an open, sunny site and still water.

Don't overdo planting Do not cover more than half the surface area of the water with plants. Leaving plenty of clear, reflective surface visible will make your pond seem bigger, especially in a small garden.
▶ Aquatic plants should never be packed tightly together. Make sure you plant them out according to the ultimate spread and depths given on their labels.

'Potting' aquatic plants The easiest way to grow aquatics is in special mesh baskets. Line with hessian, add 5cm of garden soil, then insert the plant. Fill in with more soil, firm well, then top-dress with gravel or pebbles and trim the hessian.

THE GARDENER'S CHOICE

Views of a pleasing pond ▶

A regular shape Perfect circles ❶ or straight sides ❷ work well for a small pond or for one close to the house and patio.

A fountain or cascade Spouts ❸, fountains and waterfalls ❹ oxygenate the water, helping to keep it clear. They are also decorative and soothing.

For a large pond Mass-plantings of the same species are effective around a large pond, if you have space. Ornamental foliage plants such as *Darmera peltata* ❺ are a good choice.

Pond in a pot A barrel or glazed bowl ❻ can add charm and interest to the smallest garden.

Water gardens

Marginal plants

With only their roots actually in the water, these shallow-water plants can tolerate periods of dryness when water levels fall. They conceal the edges of an artificial pond and attract a variety of wildlife, for which they provide a refuge. Restrict the spread of the most invasive of these plants by containing them in submerged baskets.

PLANTS	CHARACTERISTICS
Acorus (sweet flag), horsetail (left), rushes and scirpus	Tall, decorative clumps to give height and structure to the pool.
Aquatic mint	Thrives in moving water. Very fragrant.
Marsh trefoil	Pretty, star-shaped flowers. For acidic soil.
Pontederia	Abundant spikes of blue flowers in summer. Hardy.
Reeds and typha	Should be placed to the north of a big pool to protect other plants from the wind. Grow in baskets to limit their invasiveness.
Sagittaria (arrowhead)	Ideal in moving water. The underwater foliage produces oxygen in the water.
Water iris	Attracts dragonflies.

Create a calming background If your pond is small and your garden conditions permit, give the area an oriental feel by surrounding the pond with acid-loving shrubs and trees. Rhododendrons, Japanese maples *(Acer japonicum)* and azaleas will all look at home around water.

Wait to add the plants
If you have filled your pond with tap water, allow several weeks for the chlorine to evaporate before introducing the plants.
▶ Plant no later than August to give plants time to establish a root system before winter.
▶ Before adding aquatic plants, rinse them with tap water to wash off any pests and parasites.

Cleanse the water of your pond naturally Plants that develop under the surface are called submerged oxygenators. They are sometimes overlooked as they are thought to be less attractive than other aquatic plants, but they play a vital role in oxygenating the water. They also shade and nourish the animal life of the pond. However, they are often very fast-growing so plant only four or five. Stop them becoming invasive by thinning out in late autumn.
▶ **Ornamental oxygenators** Choose from myriophyllum; *Egeria densa*, which has decorative foliage; *Houttuynia cordata*, a water violet; *Stratiotes aloides*; and *Ranunculus aquatilis*, a water buttercup, which has clusters of small white flowers above underwater leaves.

Making a ballast If you need to plant something at a depth greater than 30cm, there's no need to get wet! Dig up a small clump of grass, wrap it around the roots of the aquatic plant you wish to position and secure it with a rubber band or wire. Throw it gently into the water where you want it to settle. The weight of the turf will make the plant sink to the bottom where new roots will spring up and anchor it.

Lower plants gradually Do not plunge plants with floating foliage straight into deep water. Introduce them over time by placing them on brick supports, which can gradually be lowered as the plant settles, and finally removed altogether. This way, the plants will adapt to the conditions of your pool, and the leaf stems will have time to grow to the required height.
▶ To place an aquatic plant far out in the pond, you will need someone to help you. Take a length of rope each and loop it through a handle on opposite sides of the basket, so each of you is holding both ends of your piece of rope. Then lower the plant gently into place and pull the rope back through the basket handles.

Maintaining your pond

Top tips for combating algae In high summer, when the pool is in full sunlight, algae can spread rapidly, turning the whole pond green.
► **Avoid algicides** They solve the problem only temporarily without tackling the cause.
► **Use natural remedies** Throw a handful of rye or barley straw into the water every 4–6 months. These encourage the development of bacteria that prevent thread algae growing.
► **Introduce floating plants** Frogbit (*Hydrochorus morsus-ranae*), water chestnut (*Trapa natans*) and water lilies will restore the biological balance and shade the pool, keeping the water at a constant temperature.
► **Don't over-feed the fish** Too much fish food pollutes the water. There is actually no need to feed in summer, nor in winter when fish are dormant.

Flushing out aphids

Water lily buds can become infested with aphids. There is no need to spray – simply drown the pests by using chicken wire to immerse the afflicted plant in water for several days.

A bad smell in the pond This indicates that organic matter is breaking down in the water, absorbing oxygen and causing poor development of plants and fish. It may even kill them.
► To prevent this, change one-third of the water, and lower the pH (the water's acid/alkali balance) by using proprietary pH granules. (In the past gardeners might have immersed a small cotton bag filled with peat.)
► Introduce oxygenating plants such as *Myriophyllum*, *Ceratophyllum*, *Anacharis* and *Potamogeton*.
► Use surface-floating plants, which will shade the pool and keep the water temperature stable.

Remove leaves In summer, clear all leaf debris from the pond. Then in autumn, lay poles over the pond and cover with a net. This will keep dead leaves from falling in. Clear away the leaves periodically and remove the net in spring.

Water your pond in summertime To top up any water lost through evaporation without scaring the fish, disturbing the plants or stirring up mud, gently dribble water in with a hose.

Shade for your pond Plant a tree nearby, but not overhanging, to give a few hours of daily shade in summer. This will help prevent overheating and slow the growth of the aquatic plants. Select trees such as alder or willow, and choose varieties under 10 metres tall. Avoid conifers, as any needles or resin that drop into the water will make it more acidic.

Tips for winter To prevent ice damaging the structure of your pond, float a ball on the surface. (A wooden log or some plastic bottles quarter-filled with gravel to weigh them down will also do the trick.) When the water freezes, pressure will be exerted on these objects, making them sink or burst, rather than on the edges of your pond.

► If you have fish in your pond make sure you give them air if the surface freezes by making holes in the ice. You can melt the ice by holding a saucepan of boiling water against it.
► Do not feed the fish in freezing weather as this will entice them to the surface – leave them in the depths to escape surface frost.

Removing algae Fix a piece of chicken wire over the tines of a garden fork to make an effective net for scooping up algae.
► Do not discard what you lift out. Instead, put it on your compost heap and use it to enrich the rest of your garden with its free and valuable nitrogen.

Dividing a water plant

1 Do this in the autumn. Begin by tidying up the plant and removing any old stems with secateurs.

2 Lift the clump from the water and take the plant out of its container. Leave it by the side of the pool to drain.

3 Divide the plant as you would any herbaceous perennial by inserting a spade through the cluster of shoots and severing it.

4 Pot each new plant in a basket of good garden soil, and add a generous layer of gravel to keep the soil in place.

A garden indoors

Thanks to the Victorian plant collectors, a huge range of exotic house plants is available today to create a bit of garden magic inside your home. Bright conservatories and sunny windows provide the perfect setting for a wonderful variety of foliage, colour and scent. However, house plants need special care and attention throughout the year.

An array of flowering houseplants, such as cyclamen, primula and hyacinth, will enhance any window sill.

Keep your plants healthy

Buying tips Try to buy plants that are in bud rather than those that are in full flower, so you can enjoy them for longer. Avoid pots with waterlogged or dried soil. Examine the underside of the leaves carefully: this is where various common pests such as whitefly and scale insects gather. If there are roots coming out of the drainage holes, this means that the plant is compacted – don't buy it. For advice on buying plants, see pages 260–261.

Settling in When you get a new plant home, don't put it with your other plants right away. Let it acclimatise in a draught-free spot out of direct sunlight. Keep an eye on it to make sure it has not brought any pests into the house.
▶ Most plants sold commercially are grown in composts which dry out quickly and don't hold nutrients. Repot new plants (see opposite) when you get them home.

Watering: don't be too heavy-handed More plants die from too much water than from too little. Let your plants almost dry out before watering and try to water in the morning, wetting the compost thoroughly. Water at the base of the plant with a watering can with a long spout. Stand pots on feet for good drainage, or if a plant stands in a saucer, pour away any water still in the pot saucer an hour after watering.

Let tap water stand before watering Tap water contains chlorine, which is harmful to plants. However, if you let water stand in an open container for a day, the chlorine will evaporate. The water will also rise to room temperature, which is better for roots.

Providing humidity Group plants on a tray half-filled with gravel or clay balls. Pour water into the tray, and keep it topped up so that the gravel stays wet. This will create all the humidity most plants need.
▶ Plants that need very high humidity can be mist-sprayed with soft water – use rainwater if your tap water is too hard. Spray sparingly on plants with hairy leaves, and avoid direct sunlight as water droplets cause scorching.

A plant for every situation

Full sunlight Beloperone, echeveria, *Euphorbia milii* ❶, *Hibiscus rosa-sinensis*, strelitzia, aeonium, *Solanum pseudocapiscum*, and most cacti are all suitable for a south-facing window.

Bright light Plants that can be placed at a south-facing window with a net curtain, or at an east or west-facing window, are azalea ❷, aeschynanthus, poinsettia, exacum, cyperus, phalaenopsis, codiaeum, hypoestes saintpaulia, streptocarpus and dieffenbachia.

Semi-shade Aphelandra, clivia, epiphyllum, primula, spathiphyllum, asparagus, schefflera, scindapsus, ferns such as nephrolepsis ❸, sparmannia and syngonium will thrive behind a north-facing or poorly lit window, or two metres from a well-exposed window.

Shade These plants need to be situated in the middle of a bright room or 1.5 metres from a north-facing window: cissus, philodendron, platycerium, tolmiea ❹, and adiantum.

Plants in terracotta pots These will need watering more frequently than plants in plastic pots, because water evaporates through the porous clay surface. For hanging baskets or pots that are difficult to reach, use plastic pots.
▶ Hanging baskets are difficult to water. The modern invention of water-retaining gel, which is mixed into the compost when you plant the basket, helps to reduce the frequency of watering.

Top tips for feeding House plants like fertiliser that is rich in nitrogen as it encourages leaf growth. Fertilisers rich in phosphorus and potassium will stimulate flowering.
▶ **Feed when active** Feed house plants once a week throughout their active growing period, which is between March and October. When the plant is dormant, feed it only once a month or not at all, depending on the plant. However, plants that flower in winter do not rest, so continue to feed them once a week.
▶ **Never apply fertiliser to dry compost** It won't soak through the soil evenly and can damage the roots.
▶ **Plan ahead** When potting on, add slow-release fertiliser balls, which last for five to six months, to the compost.
▶ **Encourage flowering** Give a specially formulated flowering-plant fertiliser to plants that bloom in winter and you will be rewarded with abundant flowers.

Clean and healthy Your plants' leaves need regular dusting to stop their leaf pores clogging up. Wash wide-leaved plants with a sponge or soft cloth soaked in clean water (left) and kept only for this job.
▶ Use leaf polish on broad-leaf plants only after you have dusted them. Be sparing: polish can block leaf pores.
▶ Dust cacti, succulents and downy-leaved plants using a dry, thin paint brush, a shaving brush (left) or a soft toothbrush.
▶ Shower plants with thin leaves such as ferns and asparagus regularly by spraying them with lukewarm water in the shower or bath. Make sure you let them drain off before putting them back in their place.

Provide the correct level of lighting All so-called indoor plants are natives of tropical and sub-tropical areas. Few are happy with very weak light but they also cannot tolerate strong direct sunlight in summer. In their natural environment these plants are protected from scorching by the leaves of the tree canopy.

Repotting a house plant

1 Immerse the pot in water so that the rootball is easy to remove, then gently ease it from the pot.

2 Lay a drainage layer at the bottom of the new pot with a couple of shards from a broken terracotta pot.

3 Next add a good layer of soil enriched with slow-release fertiliser.

4 Tease out the roots, then put the rootball into its new pot so that its soil is level with the rim base of the pot.

5 Fill around the rootball with compost, firming it down and adding some more soil if needed.

6 Water the plant well, allowing it to drain. Add more compost if necessary once the surface has settled.

▶ **Indoor light is not ideal** Indoors, light intensity diminishes very quickly as you move away from the window, even if your eyes do not perceive this clearly. Too little light makes leaves pale and stunted and the stems thin and weak.
▶ **Yellow leaves** If a plant doesn't get enough light, it produces less chlorophyll, causing it to yellow, wilt and lean towards the light. Change its position or give it daily bursts of artificial light. Any source is good, but the best are 'daylight effect' neon tubes or bulbs that can be used in conventional sockets.
▶ **Rotate your pots** Turn your plants by a quarter of a circle every week or so. This will encourage them to grow evenly and will prevent the stems from becoming straggly.

Indoor gardens

Use foliage plants to provide interest in otherwise dull areas.

▶ **Light balance** Young seedlings, cuttings, variegated plants and plants with coloured leaves all need a lot of light, but over-strong sunlight will damage the foliage.

▶ **Winter sun** Remember that in winter there is much less natural light than in summer and you may need to move some plants to a south or west-facing ledge to compensate for this.

Spring rain and summer sun

Take advantage of the first mild days of spring, when showers are expected, to take your house plants outside. The rain will wash the leaves and water them at the same time. If the sun comes out, leave them to drain off in a shady corner.

▶ Many house plants will enjoy spending the summer outside, so put them in a shady corner out of the wind. Even cacti and succulents like the sun.

▶ Wait until night-time temperatures no longer fall below 10°C before leaving plants outside.

▶ Give plants more water when they are outside, as the sun and wind have a drying effect.

▶ Remember to bring your plants back inside when the weather starts to cool.

Repot in spring For the majority of house plants, you can start repotting from the beginning of March, when the plants are just emerging from their winter rest period. Just remember never to repot a dormant plant.

▶ If a plant is potbound choose a new pot one size bigger than the old one; plants do not like being moved from a pot that is too small to one that is far too big.

▶ To stop the roots obstructing the drainage hole, put a piece of broken clay pot over it, with the concave side against the hole, then spread a 2cm layer of more broken pieces on top.

▶ Some plants, such as palms, don't like root disturbance and thrive with their roots confined. Don't repot them, just replace the old surface compost with fresh moist compost in spring.

▶ After repotting, wait a few weeks before feeding your plants.

The right time to stake plants Climbing plants will collapse without support, and the stems of very heavy flowers such as amaryllis and lilies will bend or break. Repotting is the best time to think about putting in stakes and mini-trellises, as you will not damage the roots or the bulbs. Drive the stakes deep into the soil so that the plant and its stake will not topple over.

Going on holiday? If you are going away for more than a fortnight in hot weather, prune at least a third of any hanging foliage from fast-growing plants and remove the flowers to reduce their need for water.

▶ To provide water while you are away, insert an upside-down plastic bottle filled with water into each plant pot or use small terracotta cones connected to a water tank. The water is slowly drawn into the soil.

▶ Don't leave your plants in a sink full of water, as you are likely to drown them. Put them on the draining board on capillary matting (available from DIY stores) soaked in water, or a heavy cloth with one end soaking in the sink. Plants can then absorb water slowly.

▶ Use self-watering planters with care. Unless your species need lots of water, use these planters only if you will be away for a long time. These systems keep the lower part of the compost constantly wet, which causes the roots to rot.

Don't ignore warning signs If the edges of leaves start to turn brown, the air in your room may be too dry. Spray affected plants regularly and put them on a tray covered with wet gravel or clay beads. If you cut off the brown ends of the leaves, make sure you always leave a thin strip of brown, as cutting the living leaf will scar it and dry it out even more.

▶ If a plant's leaves are rolling up over themselves, look as if they have been burnt in large patches or are slightly reddened, or if its flowers are fading quickly, your plant may be getting too much light. Move it to a shadier position or put a net curtain on the window so it's not in direct sun.

▶ If leaves are yellowing and falling off, the plant may be getting too much water or not enough light. Reduce your watering then, if it doesn't improve, move the plant. If it is a jasmine or a gardenia, the problem could be hard water. Water with rainwater instead of water from the tap.

Successful gardening under glass

Gardeners have used glasshouses to propagate and grow tender plants since the 19th century. These days, a conservatory is a relaxing haven for you to enjoy a range of unusual plants. If you just want to grow plants for the garden, a greenhouse – or even a cold frame – will provide the perfect conditions.

Red and yellow oleanders mix with a profusion of pelargoniums, set against luxuriant foliage and a vine.

A conservatory full of exotic blooms

An extension of your garden If you think of your conservatory as part of your garden, not an extension of your house, you may be less tempted to fill it with house plants and instead attempt to grow some more unusual plants in its enclosed and protected environment.

Siting your conservatory Unlike a greenhouse, which you can site in the best possible place, a conservatory is usually positioned on whichever side of the house it looks the best. Your conservatory will have higher temperatures than a greenhouse as it is sheltered by your house, and if it is connected to your domestic central heating system, you should be able to grow a good range of plants. Your problem may be keeping it cool, not heating it.
▶ Light levels are generally lower than in a greenhouse, though you will need to think carefully about ventilation and shading if your conservatory is in full sun.

Building materials PVCu is the most popular material today, but although it is inexpensive and almost maintenance-free, it lacks the traditional feel of wood. A wooden framework is decorative and helps to give a more natural look but requires regular maintenance, which the less-appealing and slightly cooler aluminium models do not.

Keep heating bills down To minimise the cost of heating, grow plants from a temperate climate such as bottlebrush, citrus and pelargoniums. These can be taken outside in the summer and brought back inside before the first frosts.

▶ Central heating and air conditioning dry the air and can encourage pests and diseases. Because a conservatory probably doubles as a living area, it is even more important to use organic and biological control methods rather than chemical ones than it is in a greenhouse. If you do have to spray take the infected plants and spray them outside. Make sure they are dry before you bring them back in.

Conservatory plants for the four seasons

By choosing plants that are at their best in different seasons, you can provide all-year colour and interest.

For autumn The following plants should give a seasonal display: calliandra ❶, datura, *Solanum jasminiodes*, asparagus, cyperus, bouvardia, turraea and bromeliad.

For winter These plants can be relied on to cheer up dull days: citrus ❷, poinsettia, wintersweet, *Monstera deliciosa*, pepperomia, tradescantia, African violet and kentia palm.

For spring Have your own colourful and sweetly-scented spring, starting early with camellia, banksia, *Pachystachys lutea* ❸, stephanotis, hippeastrum, brunfelsia, marguerites and acacia.

For summer Celebrate the opulence of summer with passionflower ❹, *Protea cynaroides*, hibiscus, acalypha, vine, lantana, glory lily and kohleria.

Make full use of vertical space Paint the walls of your conservatory a light colour as this helps to reflect the light and will set off your plants well.

▶ Train climbers such as plumbago and bougainvillea up wires attached to the wall to provide an attractive backdrop.

▶ Place moisture-loving plants on the floor and add some staging so plants that prefer drier air can be kept higher.

▶ If you include soil beds in your conservatory, you can grow really tall specimen plants with their roots in the ground, rather than being restricted to pots and other containers.

Create an atmosphere with furnishings Choose hard-wearing furniture with a tropical feel and make sure that the materials used will not be damaged by strong sunlight or a moist atmosphere. Wicker and cane are popular but they may not be as resilient to water or compost spills as wrought iron or wood. Outdoor garden furniture is ideal as it has been built to withstand the elements.

▶ Use tiles, stone or treated hardwoods on the floor. These will be easy to clean and will cope well with damp conditions.

Making a garden in a bottle

A bottle garden is a miniature hothouse that can make a great display of exotic greenery for your home, providing a complete self-sustaining micro-habitat for tender plants.

1 To make a miniature home for exotic plants, pour a bed of clay beads into a pot-bellied glass bottle, available from garden centres.

2 Add a thin layer of powdered charcoal and spread over it a layer of good house-plant compost.

3 Part-fill the bottle with the compost and put in the plants. Take care not to plant them too close together so they have room to grow.

4 Pour a little water down the sides of the bottle from time to time. This is one container display that requires very little watering.

Practical protection for tender plants

Choose the method that suits your needs There are three ways you can protect vulnerable plants. Use a cold frame to raise or harden off vegetables, biennials and shrubby cuttings before planting them out in the garden. Use cloches to cover and protect plants that are already in the open ground. But invest in a greenhouse if you want to free yourself completely from the mercy of the weather.

Small-scale greenhouse gardening A cold frame consists of a framework of wood, metal, concrete or brick, covered by panes of glass called lights. A portable frame in wood or metal is the most convenient type as you can move it in or out of the sun. Use a frame instead of,

or in addition to, a greenhouse to protect plants from the cold in winter, or to harden them off as seedlings.

▶ A cold frame is warmed only by the sun. But a heated frame provides added protection by means of soil or air-warming cables, which you can buy in kit form.

Protecting plants outdoors Developed by the French to protect plants from frost, cloches are still used today to speed up growth and extend the growing season in the vegetable garden. These glass or plastic covers are placed over young plants to keep out frost and cold

winds or can be positioned over an area of soil to warm it up a week before you sow or plant out.

A greenhouse for bumper results Plants will flower and fruit more profusely under glass than they would outside. You could either grow a whole range of plants or specialise in one particular type, such as orchids or cacti. Simply using your greenhouse for propagation will help reduce costs. Watching your seeds and cuttings grow into new plants for your garden is very satisfying.

Selecting a greenhouse Buy the biggest you can afford and have room for, as the more air circulation you have, the better the environment for your plants. The minimum practical dimensions for a traditional greenhouse are 2.5 metres long by 2 metres wide.

A greenhouse can be a permanent home to tender species as well as a place for forcing and overwintering others.

▶ Remember that, although wooden greenhouses look more attractive than PVCu or aluminium ones, they need a brick or concrete base and require treating every couple of years with wood preservative. If your wood is varnished or painted, you will need to sand it down each time before applying a primer and good-quality exterior paint.

You choose the site You can control the temperature, humidity and light levels more easily in a greenhouse than in a conservatory, so simply position it wherever it will get the most light. Always build on level ground in a sheltered well-lit spot away from trees or shade from buildings. Orientating your greenhouse north-south along its length will give you maximum light in the summer. An east-west orientation is best for overwintering plants or raising plants in the spring.

Where space is limited If you don't have room for any of the traditional models, why not try a lean-to greenhouse? These are built onto the side of a house or shed but make sure yours is not sited where most of the light will be blocked by the adjacent buildings.

A traditional free-standing greenhouse These have a central path with staging at the sides and at one end. Staging and shelving are useful whatever you choose to grow, as plants at waist height are easier to tend and water.
▶ If the glass goes down to ground level, you can grow ferns or plants in their dormant season beneath the staging.
▶ Use slatted or mesh staging if you plan to grow lots of plants in pots to stop water collecting beneath them.

The basic amenities To create the perfect growing environment for your plants your greenhouse or conservatory needs adequate ventilation and something to provide shade from the hot sun. Most greenhouses have some form of heating both for growing and protecting plants. A water supply will make irrigating much easier, and an electrical point will allow you to heat and light your space.

Your plants need air The amount of glass in your greenhouse that is given over to ventilators should equal at least a sixth of the floor space. Use hinged vents on the roof and sides and louvres in the sides below the staging.

Too much heat is a bad thing During the summer, you will need to shade your greenhouse or conservatory from the sun. The traditional method is to whitewash the outside of the glass with a weak mix of 1 part emulsion to 100 parts water. This is usually done in spring to last through the summer months. Although it is cheap and effective, it is not an attractive finish.
▶ Roller or concertina blinds are a better-looking option and are flexible, allowing you to adjust light levels according to the weather. Both automatic and manual systems are available.

Which shape of greenhouse?

Your choice of greenhouse will depend on how you plan to use it, the available space, and where it will be sited.

Traditional span ❶ These offer lots of growing space. Because the roof slants fairly steeply, make sure there is sufficient head room, particularly if you are buying a smaller model or if you want to grow tall plants on the staging.

Dutch light ❷ With their larger panels, they provide maximum light down to ground level and so are ideal for tall plants.

Lean-to ❸ If space is restricted, this is the best choice. It can also save you time and money as you can connect it to the electricity and water supplies in your house rather than laying new cables and pipes. Although it may be too small to work in, you can use all the vertical space to grow plants.

A good heat source Electric heaters are the most efficient and reliable choice if you have a power supply. Choose one that is thermostatically controlled so you do not waste heat. Fan or waterproof tubular heaters are best and should be fitted on the side of your greenhouse, just above the ground to prevent cold spots in the lower areas.

▶ A maximum and minimum thermometer is useful and fascinating. It allows you to check temperatures at night as well as during the day.

Insulation Double glazing is the most cost-effective way to insulate your greenhouse despite the initial expense. Thermal screens are a cheaper option, consisting of sheets of clear plastic or other transparent material. To conserve heat at night, stretch them horizontally between the greenhouse eaves – they will stop heat rising to the roof and away from your plants.

▶ Keep an unheated greenhouse frost-free and reduce heating costs in heated ones by insulating with clear bubble wrap. Cut sheets to size and attach them firmly to the framework of your greenhouse with suction pad fasteners or clips that fit into the frame. This will increase the range of plants you can grow and allow you to raise plants from seed. After several seasons' exposure to sun and dust, the plastic will become opaque and you will need to replace it to maintain light levels.

THE GARDENER'S CHOICE

Plants for greenhouse cultivation

Choose plants that you like and that suit the conditions you are able to provide. Try growing something useful for the kitchen as well as beautiful, sweetly scented species.

PLANTS FOR A COLD GREENHOUSE
Decorative Camellia, African lily, maidenhair fern, tolmiea, cyclamen and anemone
Practical Cucumbers, melons ❶ and peppers

PLANTS FOR A COOL GREENHOUSE
Minimum 2–10°C
Decorative Cape primrose, *Abutilon megapotamicum*, freesia, passionflower, angel's trumpets, dahlia ❷ and grape ivy
Practical Grapes and aubergines

PLANTS FOR A TEMPERATE GREENHOUSE
Minimum 7–13°C
Decorative Bird of paradise, African hemp, rose periwinkle, begonia ❸, *Protea cynaroides*
Practical Citrus, figs and peaches

PLANTS FOR A WARM GREENHOUSE
Minimum 13–18°C
Decorative *Ixora coccinea*, shrimp plant, wax plant, dumb cane, canna and cymbidium ❹
Practical Pineapple, bananas, ginger

Growing plants in your greenhouse

The right temperature for plants The type of plants you want to grow dictates the temperature of your greenhouse.

▶ A temperate greenhouse should have a minimum temperature in the range 7–13°C to enable you to grow plants from Australia, the Mediterranean, California and South Africa, such as proteas, cistus, olives and palms.

▶ A warm greenhouse will allow you to grow tropical and subtropical exotics, but temperatures will need to be at a year-round minimum of 13–18°C. These are expensive to run so think about having a warmer area within a cooler greenhouse or grow these plants in a heated conservatory. Partition off a section at one end of your greenhouse using a pair of sliding glass doors or vertical thermal screens. You can then heat this area separately with a thermostatic heater.

Propagating in water

This is one of the easiest and cheapest ways to propagate a large number of plants, such as cyperus.

▶ Cut off the ends of the leaves to a few centimetres from the centre of the head (top).

▶ Immerse the cutting upside down with its head in water (centre).

▶ Leave in a warm, light place and, in a few weeks, a mass of roots will have appeared (below). You can then plant your rooted cuttings in moist compost and grow them into adult plants.

The right conditions for propagating Plants are at their most vulnerable during propagation so their environment is really important. Make sure you have adequate ventilation and shading in the growing season to prevent mildew and dehydration. Heating is not necessarily vital but it will increase the range and numbers of plants you can grow, as well as the times of the year you can propagate.

▶ If you are propagating in the summer, a clear plastic bag placed over and under a tray of cuttings should be adequate for rooting softwood, tip or semi-ripe cuttings. However, if you plan to propagate large numbers of plants at other times of the year, it is worth setting aside a specific area of your greenhouse and buying some extra equipment.

Propagating plants in a greenhouse

The technique you use for taking cuttings depends on the type of plant you have chosen and the time of year. Choose only the very best specimens from which to take cuttings.

1 To take leaf cuttings, cut a leaf stalk 5cm from the leaf. Fill a seed tray with a suitable compost and firm it down. Insert the leaf stalk at an angle. Water and keep at about 20°C. Feed with liquid fertiliser as new plants emerge.

2 For begonias, in late summer cut a leaf 2.5cm from the base. Cut across the large veins on the underside. Lay the leaf, cut side down, in moist compost and secure it with pebbles. Keep covered at 20°C, until new plantlets sprout.

3 In spring, propagate perennials by cutting off 10cm shoots from the base of the plant at crown level. Plant them singly in 8cm pots in a greenhouse or cold frame. Keep moist and frost-free. Plant out in autumn.

Higher heat and humidity A heated propagating unit can be placed on a bench and connected to the electricity supply. For even better insulation, lay a polystyrene pad between the unit and the bench. A unit intended for use in winter or early spring should provide a minimum soil temperature of 15°C.
▶ Consider investing in a horticultural electric blanket to provide an even spread of base heat and high humidity.
▶ A mist system will help you root cuttings more quickly and in larger numbers – self-contained, enclosed units are the most convenient and least expensive. For large numbers of cuttings, invest in a purpose-built bench with soil-warming cables and a mist-propagation unit, which can be covered or open depending on the other plants you are growing.

Sprucing up On a warm, dry autumn or spring day, take out all the plants for an annual clean and maintenance check.
▶ Clean the glass inside and out, paying attention to the corners and places where the panes of glass overlap. Use diluted disinfectant and a stiff brush. Replace rusted metal and broken panes, and ensure vents are watertight.
▶ Regularly renew the gravel or matting on your staging or benches to prevent the build-up of pests and diseases.

Keep your plants healthy Plants need watering, feeding, misting and venting. If you plan to be away for any length of time, think about installing an automatic watering system.
▶ Keep plants clear of all dead leaves and flowers.
▶ Check buds, new shoots and the underside of leaves for pests and diseases, and act immediately if you spot anything. With bad infestations remove and burn the plants. Do not put them on the compost heap.
▶ Fungal diseases thrive in damp, still air so ensure good air circulation and water plants at the base rather than wetting the whole plant.
▶ Stop pests from getting onto the plants by using traps, barriers or repellents. Yellow sticky traps, which can be hung amongst the plants in the affected areas, catch pests and help you to identify and monitor populations.

Control pests naturally Avoid pesticides – they are harmful to humans, pets and beneficial insects too! Instead, use biological control by introducing a pest's natural predators or parasites. They generally need light and warm temperatures so it is best to use them in the summer months. They take time to work, so introduce them as soon as you spot a problem.

Container gardening

Gardeners have long used plants in containers to add an extra dimension to their gardens, whether formal or informal. They will brighten a window-sill or a balcony, and a large garden can benefit from the addition of plants in pots too: you can plant and replant them easily and move them about at will.

For maximum effect, group containers to show off contrasting textures and colours.

A garden in a pot

Make the most of your space Gardeners have always had to be creative to optimise their use of space, especially in smaller plots. To maximise your planting area, arrange pots at different levels: on the ground, on a pedestal, or on a wrought iron latticework shelf. You could also position pots at higher levels: hooked onto railings, fixed on a wall in metal pot-holders, or hanging from a canopy.

The best plants for containers

For a partly shaded corner Enliven dark corners with bright colours and foliage. Plants that prefer or tolerate partial shade are *Hydrangea macrophylla* 'White Wave', fuchsias ❶, myosotis, hostas, hyacinths, impatiens, begonias and periwinkle. Grow them in combination with hart's tongue fern, *Asplenium scolopendrium* or *Adiantum raddianum*.

On a balcony in full sun Choose marguerites, alyssum, cerastium, cornflowers, chrysanthemum ❷, morning glory (*Ipomea purpurea* or *Convolvulus major*), aubrieta, brachyscome, campanula, ceanothus, dahlias, eschscholzia, geraniums, verbena or zinnias.

In autumn or winter Asters, Christmas roses (*Helleborus niger*) ❸, violets, heathers and primroses will provide a cheering note on those dark and chilly days. Small bulbs such as crocuses, snowdrops, narcissi and *Ipheion uniflorum* look charming in shallow bowls grouped on a patio.

Preserve your privacy If you have a balcony, use plants to frame the view and provide a screen from the world outside. Grow climbing plants and evergreen bushes in a trough and hang window boxes and baskets around the windows. For the best flowering plants, consider wisteria, petunias and surfinias, marguerite or lobelias. To decorate a stairway, create a cascade of flowers by placing pots every two or three steps.

You don't have to be conventional For centuries, thrifty gardeners have used almost any unwanted containers to hold plants. Instead of buying special pots, you too can recycle salvaged items for planters. Plants will grow in anything that can hold compost and has drainage holes. Try galvanised buckets, old milk churns, saucepans or cans with holes pierced in them, either painted or left as they are. Architectural salvage – old chimney stacks, clay pipes and butler sinks – can be transformed into miniature gardens with old-world charm.
▶ Wooden half-barrels, wicker baskets and old wash boilers from scrapyards or antique dealers can also make attractive planters. Line them with plastic so your compost doesn't fall out, and make a drainage hole in the bottom of the liner.

What kind of soil? Don't use ordinary garden soil in containers. Your compost should be well aerated and moisture-retentive – the ideal type is a loam-based compost, which is slow to dry out but has good aeration and structure.
▶ Add grit, sand and gravel to your mix to make it more free-draining. For bushes, use rose compost. For acid-loving plants, use ericaceous compost. Grow annuals, biennials and perennials in multi-purpose compost. Bulbs, which draw on their own reserves, are content with any well-drained soil.
▶ Always ensure good drainage by adding broken crocks, polystyrene balls or stones to the bottom of your pot.
▶ To avoid the soil becoming too compact, which prevents water from penetrating to the roots, lighten it in large troughs with perlite or vermiculite.

Foliage for contrast To lighten your arrangements and give them volume, grow foliage plants, including trailing varieties, around the edge of the pot. Try growing assorted colours:
- **Grey** Artemisia, senecio, santolina, helichrysum.
- **Variegated** English ivy (*Hedera helix* 'Golden Ester') or Algerian ivy (*H. canariensis* 'Gloire de Marengo').
- **Purple** Sage, *Vitis vinifera* 'Purpurea'.
- **Bronze** *Carex comans* 'Bronze Form', fennel 'Purpureum'.
- **Yellow** Spear grass.
- **Black** Mondo grass (*Ophiopogon planiscapus* 'Nigrescens').
- **Bluish or blue-green** Blue fescue.

Rough up the surface Every couple of weeks, break up the crust of soil on the surface of the pots with a fork. This allows water to saturate the compost – your plants can die of thirst, even if watered, if the soil is impenetrable.

Feed your plants If you have not included a slow-release fertiliser in your potting mix, make sure that six weeks after planting you start feeding with a high-potash feed. For a natural fertiliser, try seaweed extract as a foliar feed.
- Every spring remove the top 2.5cm of compost from pots that are permanently planted and replace it with fresh potting compost mixed with a little fertiliser.

Wrapping up for winter In November, before the first frosts, arrange winter protection for less hardy plants that cannot be taken inside. To protect the stems, stick in four stakes around the plants, then cover this frame with horticultural fleece. Although it is expensive, fleece can be washed in a machine at 40°C and re-used for several years. Bubble wrap can also be used, but fleece allows plants to breathe, reducing the risk of rotting. To maintain a healthy atmosphere, half-open the wrapping on fine, sunny days.
- In April, remove the protection, watching the temperature at night. Keep more tender plants wrapped until mid-May.
- Bubble wrap, hessian or straw are ideal for wrapping up pots, and protect the roots as well as the pots themselves. Tie the insulation snugly around your pots but do not block drainage holes.
- You can bury pots up to their rims to provide protection from the frost during the winter months. Dig them up again once all danger of frost has passed.

Top tips for watering Plants in containers are more dependent on you for water than those growing in the ground. Remember that hot or windy weather will dry out pots quickly, so keep a watchful eye on them in these conditions and be prepared to water them several times a day if needed. Careful preparation of containers will help to conserve water.

- **Let in the rain** Check that there is nothing sheltering containers and window boxes from rainfall, and that the rain can penetrate the soil and will not simply run off the foliage.
- **Mulch to prevent dehydration** Protect large plants in pots from drying out by adding a layer of pebbles or glass beads on top of the compost.
- **Use ground cover** Grow ground-cover plants as an indicator of soil conditions at the surface of the pot. When they look limp you know that the top few centimetres have dried out, so the pot needs watering.
- **Watch for soil shrinkage** If soil shrinks so that it starts to come away from the side of the pot, immediately put the pot into water. Allow the plants to drink for up to an hour.
- **Soak new pots** Before you plant them, soak new terracotta pots in a bucket of water until bubbles stop rising to the surface. This will stop the pot drawing water from the soil, away from your plants.

May clearance In late spring, empty pots and window boxes onto a large plastic sheet and wash them thoroughly with dilute bleach. Replace the drainage gravel or chippings, and mix some fertiliser and compost into the soil. Refill the containers with annuals and bulbs ready for the summer.

To create an eye-catching focal point, choose an attractive pot and fill it with plants that trail and overflow.

A soft and springy carpet of green

A lawn typifies the traditional English garden. Whether it is a stretch of hard-wearing grass used by the family at weekends, or an impeccable striped green sward, it provides an open space to give pace to your garden, unifies the different sections and provides a foil for the colourful borders.

Establishing a lawn

Keep it simple Sharp corners and complicated edges will deteriorate quickly; the more straightforward the shape of your lawn, the longer it will last.

Easy care You can slope a lawn so that rain penetrates the surface rather than running onto the patio or paths, but don't sow grass on a slope of more than 25 degrees. Consider making a path from the place where your mower is kept to the lawn and put in edging to avoid mowing border flowers.

Seeds for success

A fine finish Grasses such as bents (*Agrostis*) and creeping red fescue (*Festuca rubra rubra*) are remarkable for their fine foliage, and form an attractive dense lawn. They can be mown frequently to the shortest setting on your mower.

A grassy path or play area Ryegrass (*Lolium perenne*), tall fescue (*Festuca arundinacea*), Kentucky bluegrass (*Poa pratensis*) and yellow oatgrass (*Trisetum flavescens*) are reasonably disease and pest-resistant and hard wearing. Perennial ryegrass grows quickly and stays green in winter.

Grass on dry ground Use hard sheep fescue (*Festuca ovina*), creeping red fescue (*F. rubra rubra*) or Chewing's fescue (*F. rubra-commutata*). In summer, creeping red fescue remains green the longest.

Grass in partial shade Ryegrass, creeping red fescue or rough-stalked meadow grass (*Poa trivialis*) can cope with some shade, although no grass will grow in complete shadow.

A well-kept lawn enhances the more obvious beauty of the beds; the lush green complements the variety of colours.

Give it an edge Edging your lawn helps to define paths and flower beds and keeps the whole effect neat and easy to maintain. Traditionally, edges were made of terracotta ropework tiles or bricks, but any suitable materials can be employed, from reclaimed building timber to log rolls.

To turf or sow? Sowing grass seed is the simpler and cheaper option when laying a lawn, but for quick results with less maintenance, lay turf. This can be done at any time of year, but avoid very wet, dry or cold spells.

Mix your seed Many types of grass seeds – *Graminaceae* – are used for lawns, and each species or variety has its own properties. Some may be quick to establish; others wear well or provide different colours and textures (see box, left). You need a mixture of different seeds to get an even lawn. Seed is usually sold ready-mixed, but make sure you shake it well before sowing to ensure an even spread.

When to sow a lawn The best time to sow grass seed is in autumn, when it can germinate and establish without competition from weeds. In mild regions, you can sow until the middle of November. Germination will be slower in spring as the soil is colder, but you can sow in March if the soil is moist and warm enough, and the air temperature has reached 10°C. If you wait to sow in the summer months from June to August, the seed will not be able to cope with the dry weather unless you water it with a fine rose once or twice a day.
► Check the seed packet to see how much seed you should sow, as different mixes have different rates of coverage. Mix with sand for even coverage and use more around the edges of the lawn, where it should be denser to cope with extra wear.

Preparing the site When the soil is dry, firm the area to be sown by treading the soil down evenly with your heels. Make sure there are no hollows that would make your mower scalp the turf. Do not do this when the soil is wet. Rake the soil to a fine tilth and leave it for a couple of weeks to allow weed seedlings to germinate. Then rake these away and level the soil again. A few days before you sow your lawn seed, rake in some fertiliser, for example blood, fish and bone meal, containing nitrogen, phosphorous and potassium.

► You can sow seed with a machine with a grass seed hopper, or by hand. Either way, scatter the seed evenly, half in one direction and the other half at right angles to this.

► If sowing by hand mark out your site into equal areas and weigh out how much you need per section.

► After sowing, rake the surface lightly. If the weather is dry, water the seed regularly to help it to germinate.

► Once the newly sown grass has reached a height of 5cm, cut it with a rotary mower with the the blade set to 2.5cm. This will encourage sprouting and thicken the grass.

Maintaining a lawn

Lawns need air To keep a lawn healthy, at the start of spring and in the autumn, get rid of any surface debris, then aerate and loosen the soil with a scarifier or spring-tined rake.

► The traditional way to aerate the soil is to use a garden fork. Drive it in using your foot, straight down and as deep

as possible, moving it from side to side to enlarge the holes. Then water the ground or wait for rain, and scatter some fertiliser. A good top dressing is four parts silver sand, two parts loam and two parts compost.

► A less labour-intensive, modern method is to walk the ground using spiked shoes, or use a spiked roller.

Rigorous checking It is important to give the lawn a quick check over before mowing. Examine the grass, removing any lumps of earth and picking up stones, branches, windfalls, or anything else that might damage the blades of your mower or spin off and break a window.

Brush away! Before cutting the grass, get rid of worm casts with a stiff besom – this is also a time-honoured way of scarifying lawns, so you can perform the two tasks at once. If left, worm casts will be trodden underfoot and become small areas of bare soil that will soon be colonised by weeds.

All about mowing At the end of March or the start of April, cut the grass for the first time with the blades set high. The next week move the blades a notch lower. Gradually decrease the cutting height down to 5cm. Never cut off more than the top third of the blades of grass. As a general rule you should cut your lawn weekly until the end of June, every ten days during July and August to 2–3cm, and once a week in September and October. Leave the grass fairly tall at the end of August to prevent moss from taking hold. The more a lawn is used, the longer the grass should be.

Sowing seed for a new lawn

1 Dig out your future lawn with a garden fork. Rake the site then tread down the soil firmly and evenly.

2 To give an even surface, you can also use a roller, particularly if your site is very uneven to begin with.

3 Mark out the site into areas and scatter seed evenly, half in one direction, half at right angles to this.

4 Cover the seeds by raking lightly. Net the area to deter birds and, if the weather is dry, water regularly.

► When you come back from your summer holiday, give your lawn a light trim, then cut it shorter after three or four days.

► After mowing, wait before applying fertiliser or weedkiller to the lawn. Leave it for two days if the grass is growing strongly, or four days if it is growing slowly.

► Always wait for the dew to disappear before you mow, otherwise the wet grass will clog the mower.

A quick driving lesson For a perfect striped lawn, use an old-fashioned cylinder mower with a roller. Cut the grass in parallel strips of equal width, being careful not to miss any section of the lawn. Mow up and down as you work across the lawn. The grass will soon begin to feel like velvet, with a traditional 'bowling green' appearance.

► For an even cut and to give you better control of your mower, always mow across a slope.

► To avoid damaging the mower, disengage the blades when pushing the mower along a path.

▶ Use a rotary or hover mower if you prefer a less formal cut, and for difficult areas such as banks. Long-handled lawn shears are also ideal for this purpose.

Water when the temperature is cooler Most established lawns should recover from periods of drought, but to maintain a high-quality lawn you need to water often enough to keep up an even green growth. On sunny days, droplets of water form tiny lenses that burn foliage. The best time to water a lawn is either in the morning or in the early evening, to prevent scorching and reduce evaporation. Check that there are no hosepipe restrictions before you water, and make sure

you water enough to moisten the soil to a depth of about 15cm. To check that the ground is wet enough, you can use a bulb planter to remove a small cylinder of earth from a little-used corner of the lawn, replacing it carefully afterwards.

Feeding the lawn Twice a year, in spring and autumn, after you have cut the grass, apply an NPK (nitrogen-phosphorous-potassium) fertiliser to your lawn, such as blood, fish and bone meal or municipal compost. Water the grass thoroughly to ensure that the nutrients dissolve into the soil without burning the grass roots.

▶ To revive a tired lawn, use a booster fertiliser, otherwise use a slow-release type or seaweed extract at the correct dilution.

▶ Do not apply nitrogen-rich fertiliser in the autumn, as too much lush growth late in the season can encourage diseases.

Top tips for beating weeds Regular mowing will protect your grass from invasion by certain weeds by preventing them from running to seed. If it is already too late, or if your lawn is infested with low-growing weeds that are unaffected by mowing, use the tried and tested method of removing them by hand. Although this can be hard work, particularly if your lawn is large or very neglected, this traditional method is the least damaging to the environment.

▶ **Manual removal** Dig out any long-rooted weeds such as daisies and dandelions with a long, narrow trowel – you will find the task easier if the ground is soaked first. Afterwards, tamp the soil down and sow some grass seed to repair any bare areas, making sure it is protected from birds.

▶ **Expose hidden invaders** If your lawn contains many weeds, rake the lawn before mowing. This exposes the stems of creeping weeds that otherwise lie flat and avoid the mower.

▶ **Use dyed weedkiller** If you have to resort to chemicals to tackle particularly persistent weeds, add some biodegradable dye to diluted weedkiller in your watering can to enable you to see where you've sprayed and avoid going over the same place twice. Work in calm, mild weather (14–25°C) and use a less concentrated solution on a young lawn.

▶ **Dealing with the hard cases** Couch grass is resistant even to weedkiller so you will need to dig it out with a fork. Make sure you remove all of the roots of this tenacious pest.

Repairing a bare patch The easiest way to repair a bare patch in a prominent place in your lawn is to cut out the damaged area, including a little of the good turf immediately around it, and replace it with a piece the same size from a less obvious part of the lawn. Then fill in the place you took the turf from with some garden soil and a top layer of sandy soil, level the area, reseed it and water.

Filling a dip Using an edging iron, cut a cross in the middle of the sunken area, then fold back the turf. Loosen the soil to aerate it, fill the hole with garden soil, replace the turf over it and put some sandy soil on top. Firm the area gently then sow seed to fill in any gaps, and water.

Laying turf in rolls or squares

1 Dig over your site and incorporate some slow-release fertiliser, such as municipal compost.

2 If your site is particularly hard to dig, use a mechanical rotavator, then level and firm the soil.

3 Rake the surface carefully: it should be perfectly flat. Lumps will cause bare patches when you mow the lawn.

4 Wet the soil with a fine spray to help the turf to bed in quickly. Make sure the ground is evenly moistened.

5 Unroll the turf or position the squares, following a straight line near by, such as the edge of a border.

6 Butt the joins firmly to avoid creating holes, and stagger the joints. Finish with another generous soaking.

Moss in your lawn?

Prevention is better than a cure and moss is normally an indication that your site is too shady, compacted, too wet or that you have mown the grass too severely. For a perfect lawn, you must get rid of moss, but avoid using iron sulphate, as it

acidifies the soil, stains flagstones and only works in the short term by burning the moss so you can scrape it away.
▶ If regular raking, scarifying and aerating fails to get rid of the moss, apply anti-moss fertiliser or chemical moss killer to the grass and remove blackened moss with a spring-tined rake. Do not throw the moss on the compost heap.

Goodbye moles! Moles are afraid of sounds and vibrations. If they disfigure your lawn to the point where you lose all hope of a peaceful coexistence, you can drive them away by deafening them with the sound of the wind. Push a cane into each molehill and put an empty plastic bottle on the end, or simply stick the bottle in the hole, with the mouth facing the prevailing wind.
▶ It is useful to remember that molehill soil is ideal compost for pots and containers.

Dealing with acid soil. If fungi develop in the grass, it means that the soil is too wet and too acid. Remove and burn the infected turf before it spreads further.
▶ To remedy acidity, dress the lawn with ground limestone or dolomite just before a wet spell in the autumn.

Creating an old-fashioned wild-flower meadow

Strip that turf! In an existing lawn with vigorous and competitive grasses such as ryegrass, you may need to take up the turf to give your wild flowers a chance. Just make sure you do not strip the topsoil with it. Because the meadow will not be mown as frequently as a conventional lawn, eradicating weeds before you seed is even more important.

Reduce soil fertility Do not apply fertiliser or remove any grass clippings for at least a year before you begin sowing your wild-flower meadow. This prepares the soil by returning it to a more natural state.

Get a head start Plant some plug or pot-grown wild flowers in the spring or autumn. These plants will give the meadow some cover while your seeds grow.

Sowing the meadow Use fine turf grasses such as bents and fescues, which won't compete with your flowers. Scatter your wild-flower mix in the early autumn or, if you live in a cold area, wait until the spring to give it the best possible start.

Let the site decide Choosing which flowers to grow depends on whether your meadow is in shade or sun or has damp soil. In an open sunny site, use ox-eye daisies, bellflowers, poppies, field scabious and cornflowers. In a damp site, plant common spotted orchid, ragged robin and meadowsweet.

Maintaining your meadow It may look wild but your meadow still needs regular attention, such as digging out any perennial weeds. It is best to cut a spring-flowering meadow from midsummer onwards to allow the flowers to seed. A summer-flowering meadow should be cut from the early autumn and in the spring when growth starts. Leave summer and autumn mowings to shed their seed before you collect them, but pick up the spring mowings straight away.
▶ When mowing a wild-flower meadow, remember that it needs to be left longer than a conventional lawn. Ideally, you should aim for a height of 8–10cm. If your mower will not adapt to this height and the area is fairly small, consider using a traditional method such as a scythe or lawn shears. A strimmer will also do the job.

For centuries, colourful wild flowers have added grace and a delicate charm to grassy areas.

Setting out your boundaries

To block an unsightly view, create shelter from a prevailing wind, or simply preserve your privacy – there are many reasons for enclosing a garden, and many ways of doing it. Whichever methods or materials you choose, you can find an attractive way of protecting your garden sanctuary from the outside world.

An old wall is a double blessing – it makes a handsome boundary and an excellent rockery at the same time.

Consider the options

How high can you go? Any wall or fence that is built or extended over two metres high will need planning permission from the local council. There may also be restrictions on height in the deeds to your house or in the local authority or highway regulations. Always check thoroughly before starting to build any walls or fences.

▶ The height of a gateway looks best if it is similar to that of the fence or wall. It extends the 'line' you have created, giving an impression of harmony.

Whose responsibility? If the supporting posts or wall piers are on your side, then the fence or wall probably belongs to you. If you are unsure, check the title deeds and plans of your property – a 'T' mark indicates that the fence or wall is owned by the person upon whose property the 'T' is shown. A 'TT' means that the boundary is shared. Title deeds or local regulations may oblige owners to keep boundaries in good repair, but otherwise there is no onus on you to repair a fence or wall: just neighbourly courtesy.

Creating a raised brick flower bed

In gardens that are flat and featureless, raised beds add an extra dimension. They can also be a boon to gardeners who find it difficult to bend to ground level to tend their plants. The good drainage raised beds can offer is an added bonus, particularly if you want to grow plants such as alpines that require well-drained conditions.

1 Mark out the area and calculate the number of bricks you need. Lay the first course on a thin layer of mortar spread on top of paving.

2 With a spirit level, check that the bricks are laid flat and adjust the thickness of the mortar if required. Leave gaps for drainage at intervals.

3 When you lay the second course, place the corner brick endways on, to make a strong bond.

4 Lay the top bricks upside down for a neat finish. Allow the mortar to set, then fill with a drainage layer and good-quality, free-draining soil.

Recycling is best Stone walls are not cheap to build. To keep costs down, it is worth looking around for quantities of old stones in local salvage yards.

Lay the foundations You will need to make a concrete footing for all walls, and this should be two or three times the width of your wall. About 40cm is deep enough for a simple, low wall. Put a layer of hardcore into a level trench, fill in with concrete and leave it to set for a couple of days.

Quicker bricks Using 'combination bricks', which look like several bricks stuck together, will make building a wall much easier and quicker. Some are regularly shaped, others interlock for greater stability.

Coping a brick wall To prevent water penetrating your wall and causing frost damage, put a coping layer (a line of 'roof' shaped bricks) on the top. It will also make the wall look finished. You can buy special curved coping bricks, but be sure to use ones that are wider than your wall so that they shed rainwater away from the bricks. Try pre-assembled coping in the form of sections of tiles or bricks already fitted together, and simply fix them to the top of your wall with cement.

What to do with a concrete wall A wall made of concrete blocks is one of the strongest and most compact types of wall you can have. However, it does not look very attractive.
▶ Cover it with trellis or evergreen climbing plants.
▶ Use a wooden cladding. Following the manufacturer's instructions, fasten the first row to the wall with screws. The following rows are overlapped and held in place with the special fixings provided by the supplier.
▶ Put the flat surface to good use and create a trompe d'oeil or false perspective effect. If you are artistically inclined you can paint one or, if you prefer, buy a ready-made trellis specially constructed to give this effect. If you add a judiciously placed mirror to an otherwise dull concrete wall you can give the appearance of space to your garden.

Fences are another option Fences require as much planning as walls, but are much less expensive. They are quicker and easier to erect, requiring little specialised knowledge, and it is easy to replace panels later if necessary. Fences create a less solid effect than walls and can be decorative features in their own right. Many different types are available, from wooden panels and willow hurdles to wire mesh.

What type of wall or fence?

A stone or brick wall The strongest and most solid way of enclosing your garden is a wall. However, they're expensive and you may need professional help to build and repair them.

Wooden fencing Traditional wooden fences consisted of stakes made from locally available wood or thin willow branches woven into wattle panels. Today, you can buy ready-made fencing panels, but beware of using panels that are too thin and so liable to blow over in the first gust of wind.

Hedges A hedge can provide an attractive enclosure, an effective windbreak and shelter for wildlife. However, some types demand high maintenance and take up a lot of space.

Trellis panels Light trellis or lattice can be used with wooden fencing to open up a view, provide a framework for climbing plants or reduce the effects of wind.

Cement blocks Small openwork blocks and cement panels can produce a similar effect to trellising. They are bulky and relatively expensive, but will last a long time.

▶ If you are putting up a fence, it's courteous to position the most attractive side – the one without the posts and cross supports – facing towards your neighbour. This arrangement also has the benefit of allowing you to maintain your fence from your own property.

Fencing takes two You'll need two people to erect a fence. It is not that the panels are particularly heavy, but they have to be held upright while they are fixed in place, and one of you needs to keep checking levels. Choose a calm day to work, as solid panels are difficult to handle in the wind.

Putting up a panel fence Dig a hole 75cm deep and the width of the post, plus another 20cm all around, and fill it with hardcore up to within 15cm of the top. Put in your first concrete post and check its height against your fence panel. Pack hardcore around the post and fill with concrete, firming it down and adding more concrete until the hole is filled. Keep checking that the post is vertical.
▶ Lay the fence panel on the ground to gauge the position of the next post hole.
▶ Place a gravel board between the two posts (to prevent the panels coming into contact with the ground and rotting), making sure the ground is level so that the board is straight.
▶ Slot the fence panel into the groove in the first concrete post, and put in your second post, slotting it over the panel.
▶ If you use wooden posts, you need to screw or nail the fence panels into position.

Making holes for posts A pick and spade often give the best results. Hole borers can also be used but the holes they make are not very big and stones or roots may deflect the borer.

Walls and fences

A living wall of turf

Use up spare turf to build a low retaining wall reminiscent of ancient times. First cover the turves to cut out the light or spray them with glyphosate, and leave them until the grass dies. Break them into strips 50cm by 30cm, and fold in half along the short edge, with the soil on the outside. Lay these pieces like bricks directly onto prepared ground, sloping towards the area to be retained. You can even use the pieces to cover an existing low wall you wish to disguise. When the wall is complete, plant up the joints with ferns, ivy and primroses, adding compost in any gaps and watering well. You can also add stones for greater stability.

Post holders As an alternative to digging a hole and filling it with concrete or stones, for wooden posts you could use metal post supports, known as fence spikes. The spikes must be driven into the ground perfectly straight, which is not always easy when the ground is stony or has roots growing across it. Make sure they are level before you put in the fence posts. Post supports are also susceptible to high winds so are really only safe to use in sheltered spots.

Waterproofing posts If your wooden posts have a flat end, shape the tops so that they come to a point, or make them rounded, so that water will run off and will not penetrate and rot the wood. Alternatively, fit ornamental caps or wooden coping to the top of the posts.

Not too thin There are several types of wooden fencing panels to choose from, but check the thickness of the wooden slats making up the panels. The wood will be exposed to the sun, rain and changes in temperature, and the thicker the wood, the longer it will last.
▶ If you buy wooden fence panels from a garden centre, check each one thoroughly. Avoid any that have broken, displaced or frayed slats. Buy panels in the same condition so that they all age at the same rate.

Paints and preservatives Modern wooden fencing panels, pre-treated with wood preservative, need little maintenance. You can leave your fence to acquire a natural grey colour over the years, or apply a coat of varnish or paint.
▶ Bear in mind that you will probably have to renew varnish or paint every three to five years, which is not always easy after climbing plants have grown up it. Wood stains are a lower maintenance way of colouring fencing.
▶ Don't use creosote on panels that are likely to come into contact with human skin, as it is now considered dangerous.

▶ If possible, use a water-based, non-toxic wood preservative on trellis or any other wooden fencing intended as supports for climbing plants, as this has few harmful effects.

Trellis as fencing You can use a trellis as light-weight, decorative fence that stands up well to the wind, as long as it is securely fastened to upright posts. It can also be used fastened to the top of fences, or secured to walls to support climbing plants.
▶ For a totally natural appearance, make your own openwork trellis from any locally available pliable branches.

Weaving a wattle fence

1 Use a string to mark the line of your planned fence. Drive in a stake at either end.

2 Position a stake every 30–40cm and use a mallet to drive them in.

3 Begin weaving the willow stems or other pliable branches around the stakes. Use sets of five or six together, keeping them flat.

4 Alternate the weaving to make the sets cross. At the ends, pull the pliable branches hard to tension the fence.

5 To secure the ends, bring them round the last post and push them through the weave. Cut off any extra.

6 The fence is finished. If you want to put soil against it, secure a protective barrier to it first.

This neatly painted picket fence covered in nasturtiums gives the garden an attractive rustic air.

Rustic fencing If you live in the country, unless you have young children or a dog, there is no need to use especially tall fencing or walls. A low fence will mark out your boundary and help it to blend in with your surroundings.
▶ To add a rustic look to a hedge while it is growing, you can make wattle hurdles (see left) or buy them ready-made.
▶ Picket fences, with their vertical, pointed wooden slats spaced evenly and fixed to horizontal rails, are traditional in country settings. They are popular in natural wood, or you can finish them with paint.

Dress up your wall or fence

Top tips for cloaking a fence Even if your fence already looks quite decorative, you may still wish to adorn it with some light climbing plants such as clematis or honeysuckle.
▶ **Add wires for support** Before your climbers start to grow, screw metal hooks or vine eyes into your fence posts or wall and stretch wire between them, keeping them taut so they can support the plants as they fill out and get taller.
▶ **Avoid ivy** All climbing plants whose tendrils can grow between the slats of a wooden fence can break them.
▶ **Use containers** Flowerpots and boxes can be suspended from a fence, but only hang them from the fence posts and not from the panels, which will not be strong enough to cope.
▶ **For good coverage** Fast-growing annual climbers will quickly cover a new fence and don't have strong suckers or tendrils that could damage it. Suitable plants are nasturtium, morning glory and sweet peas. For longer-term coverage, grow passionflower, jasmine or golden hops. If you have room, you could instead try some of the shrubs that are suitable for training up a wall, such as *Euonymus fortunei* 'Silver Queen', ceanothus, Japanese quince or *Cotoneaster horizontalis*.

Planting to disguise long, straight lines To shorten the appearance of a long, straight wall, break it up every two metres or so with a group of plants with unusual shapes or foliage. The more a line is divided, the shorter it will appear.

▶ For violet shades that produce a beautiful effect along a low brick wall, plant an edging of 'Johnson's Blue' geraniums, interrupted at regular intervals by bunches of mauve Siberian iris and a golden sedge with an upright habit.
▶ To complement most styles of fencing and a wide variety of flowering plants in the border, consider plants with grey leaves, such as lamb's ear and cinerarias, as well as aromatic herbs and species with purple or bronze-coloured foliage.

Choose an appropriate gate Always choose gates that are in keeping with the style of your boundary fence. It would look odd if you installed a massive oak gate in a garden enclosed by a simple fence. But don't be afraid to mix, say, a painted wooden gate with an old brick wall.

A rockery wall

Dry-stone walls have been a feature of the British agricultural landscape for centuries. If you are building one, to complete the traditional, long-established look, intersperse fist-sized blocks of polystyrene foam randomly between the stones. When the wall is finished, remove the pieces of foam and replace them with soil. You can then plant the pockets with rockery plants, such as aubrieta and saxifrages, which will add colour to the wall and make it a point of interest.

Use climbers or shrubs that can be easily trained up a fence to complement the weathered wooden panels.

Flower beds and borders

Colourful bulbs for spring

Spring bulbs awaken the garden from its winter sleep and usher in a new growing year. Whether they are naturalised in a lawn or displayed in pots, their colour delights the eye until the start of summer.

Best buys for bulbs

Go for quality Sound bulbs are essential for successful flowers. Choose your source carefully, avoiding places where the bulbs are exposed to humidity or excessive warmth.

Crocus will stud a lawn like jewels from the end of February onwards throughout early spring.

THE GARDENER'S CHOICE

For a continuous display

Plan a succession of bulbs to flower from the beginning of the year through to early summer. Spring bulbs come in many colours, ranging from fresh white, bright yellow and blue, to pretty pinks, rich violets and warm oranges. Don't forget these old favourites:

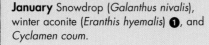

January Snowdrop (*Galanthus nivalis*), winter aconite (*Eranthis hyemalis*) ❶, and *Cyclamen coum*.

February Glory of the snow (*Chionodoxa*), crocus ❷, *Iris reticulata* and snowflake (*Lecojum vernum*).

March Striped squill (*Puschkinia*), windflower (*Anemone blanda*) and squill (*Scilla sibirica*).

April *Allium nigrum*, bluebell (*Hyacinthus non-scripta*), crown imperial (*Fritillaria imperialis*), dog's tooth violet (*Erythronium dens-canis*), grape hyacinth (*Muscari*) ❸, snake's head fritillary (*Fritillaria meleagris*), spring starflower (*Ipheion uniflorum*), star of Bethlehem (*Ornithogalum umbellatum*) and summer snowflake (*Leucojum aestivum*) ❹.

May *Allium neapolitanum*, *Fritillaria persica* and Dutch hybrid iris (*Iris hollandica*) ❺.

▶ Buy bulbs as early as possible, preferably in September. This way you will have the widest choice and the bulbs will be healthier than end-of-season leftovers.
▶ Reject bulbs that have started to grow (showing a hint of white roots or a light green bud) or any that show signs of bruising, mould or insect pests.
▶ Pick bulbs whose outer skins are intact, as they will be better protected from disease. A split skin might be a sign that the bulb has dried out during storage.

Feel the bulb A healthy bulb should be firm and fleshy. Reject any that are withered or dried out.

Large bulbs are best The greater the circumference of the bulb, the more nourishment it will contain for the bud inside, and the better the flower will be. Of course, larger bulbs are more expensive, but they are worth the price, especially if you want to grow them in pots or containers, where failed blooms would spoil the display.
▶ Hyacinths are the exception: keep the largest bulbs for growing indoors, as they produce heavy flowers that will not withstand outdoor conditions. For the garden, choose average-sized bulbs.

▶ To get good-quality flowers in the first year of planting, choose bulbs with a circumference of around 8cm for crocus, 28cm for hyacinths, 12cm for narcissus and 11cm for tulips.

Special offers can be tempting Bargain stocks of bulbs sold in bags often contain mixed varieties, predominantly the most common colours (for example, red and yellow tulips, or yellow narcissus). These bulbs usually differ in size, which means that they will not all flower at the same time and will not produce a uniform visual effect. The smallest ones may not even flower at all. Take advantage of special offers like this only if you are buying bulbs for naturalising.

Take care when you buy loose Bulbs sold loose are often high in quality and large in size. You can find interesting varieties, and buying in this way means you can select the exact quantities you want. But be careful – it is all too easy to go home with a mixture of varieties, as they can be difficult to differentiate. You could even end up with a mixture of species. If you are in doubt about the identity of any bulbs, plant them in rows in a corner of the vegetable garden and use them for cut flowers. Then any surprises will be pleasant ones.

Save money with multiflower varieties Some varieties of crocus, hyacinths, narcissus and tulips produce several flowers per bulb. By choosing these varieties, you can increase the impact and length of their flowering period, as the individual blooms do not all open at the same time.

Five months of brilliant bulbs For a continuous display of bulbs throughout the spring, plant a range of species and varieties. Begin with snowdrops, then move on to crocus, hyacinths, narcissus and tulips, and try some unusual species too. By mixing the earliest and latest flowering varieties, you can enjoy a succession of flowers from January until June.

▶ Bring spring indoors by growing bulbs for cutting. If you have space, plant some in an out-of-the-way corner of the garden, and stagger them so you have cut flowers all spring.

Bulbs in your garden

A natural effect Plant bulbs in drifts about 30cm wide, letting them meander between flowering shrubs and clumps of perennials. The spring growth of the other plants will hide the yellowing foliage of the bulbs after they flower.

▶ Try to mimic the way bulbs grow in the wild by scattering them at random over a patch of ground before planting, rather than arranging them in rigid rows.

▶ Leave a space of two or three times the width of the bulbs between each one. Unlike other plants, which can look cramped when planted closely, bulbs look best in tight groups.

In the sun but sheltered Most bulbs like to be planted in well-drained soil, exposed to the sun, but sheltered from cold, drying winds. Certain bulbs, such as snowdrops, *Eranthis hyemalis*, *Cyclamen coum*, *Anemone nemorosa* and erythronium, also grow well in semishade, close to deciduous shrubs or trees.

Planting bulbs in baskets

Planting bulbs intended for display in a lawn into baskets, instead of directly into the lawn, has a number of advantages. It prevents the bulbs spreading into areas where they are not wanted and you can lift them and refresh the soil for the next year, or even change the bulbs completely.

1 Cut out a piece of turf the same size as your bulb basket and dig down to the depth required for your bulbs.

2 Arrange your bulbs in the basket, making sure they are evenly spaced, then place it in the hole.

3 Fill the hole with fine soil and replace the turf. After flowering, remove the basket and store the bulbs indoors.

Spring bulbs

Settle in the bulbs If possible, plant bulbs as soon as you buy them, or store them in a cool, dry place. The still-warm soil at the beginning of autumn is perfect for planting, but by late autumn it is very cold and often waterlogged.

▶ From the end of August, you can plant out anemones, ranunculus, freesias, scilla and ornamental allium. You can also put in some of your narcissus so that they will flower early at the beginning of spring.

▶ Make sure you plant out any members of the *Fritillaria* family before the end of September, as the bulbs will lose their freshness after that. Any that are still unplanted by October will probably be dried out. If you have inadvertently left it this late, try rehydrating the bulbs by soaking them in water for 24 hours before planting them.

▶ Wait until mid-October to plant out tulips. If you plant any earlier and the autumn is mild, they could start to show premature shoots, which would be very sensitive to frost.

Fritillaria and lilies like deep planting Unlike most bulbs, *Fritillaria imperalis* and lilies (except *Lilium candidum*, which requires shallow planting), should be planted a good 20cm deep.

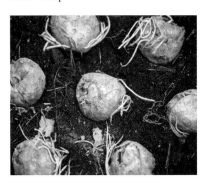

▶ When planting, tilt fritillaria bulbs so that they are not upright. If water soaks directly into the central growing point, the bulb will rot. You can identify the growing point of the bulb as it shows traces of the previous year's stem.

Cyclamen prefer the surface Plant cyclamen close to the surface of the soil. If they are buried too deep, they will not grow well and will not flower. Mulch them with leaf-mould.

Which way is up? Bulbs should be planted with their tips uppermost. If you are unsure which end is which – and anemones can be particularly confusing in this respect – it is best to lay them on their sides at the bottom of the hole.

Planting a bed of bulbs

1 Choose an open spot that has nothing else planted in it. Mark out the edges of the flower bed.

2 Remove the surface soil from this section to a depth of about 20cm.

3 To assist drainage spread a thin layer of coarse sand (not building sand) over the entire surface of the bed.

4 Lay out the bulbs, pointing upwards. A mix of colours is appealing but avoid a haphazard effect.

5 When all the bulbs are in position, scatter fine soil around them with a trowel.

6 Replace the topsoil you removed at the beginning, covering the bulbs completely and firming down.

The right bulb in the right spot ▶

Ensure that bulbs reach their maximum potential by planting them in the most suitable place.

Shady rockeries *Scilla sibirica* ❶, *Chionodoxa lucilliae*, and *Crocus chrysanthus*

Cool, damp places *Fritillaria meleagris* ❷ and English bluebell (*Hyacinthoides non-scripta*)

Colourful spring beds *Tulipa* Brilliant Star ❸, *T. tarda* or the water lily tulip (*T. kaufmaniana*)

Under shrubs and trees *Anemone blanda* ❹, *A. nemorosa* and winter aconite (*Eranthis hyemalis*)

Unheated greenhouses *Ipheion uniflorum* ❺, *Hyacinthus orientalis*, and *Narcissus* 'Paper-White'

Lawns *Narcissus* 'Carlton' ❻ *N.* 'February Gold' or *N.* 'February Silver'

Spring bulbs

Use a natural fertiliser If you do not have very rich soil, place the bulbs in a 2cm-deep bed of good compost or add a little bone meal. This means you will not need to use chemical fertilisers, which often contain too much nitrogen and encourage foliage growth while weakening stems. Don't use fresh manure, as this will rot the bulbs.

Good bedfellows Spring bulbs go well with country garden flowers such as forget-me-nots, primula, pansies, viola, wallflowers and foxgloves.
▶ For the beauty of their evergreen foliage, also mix bulbs with perennials such as saxifrage, carex or *Phlox subulata*.
▶ In beds, the giant forget-me-not (*Brunnera macrophylla*), with its heart-shaped leaves, is an excellent partner for early-flowering bulbs, while the feathery inflorescences of lady's mantle (*Alchemilla mollis*) accompany late-flowering bulbs particularly well.

Plant en masse To make a bold splash, create a bed using just one variety of bulb, all in a single colour. You will need to plant at least 20 bulbs, or even 50–100 if the area is large. For a more subtle but still dramatic effect, use different shades of the same colour, making sure that the bulbs will all bloom at the same time.

Hide dying foliage Once their display has finished, spring bulbs become rather unsightly. To hide their yellowing leaves and the empty space that follows, partner early-flowering bulbs with plants with thick summer foliage. In sunny spots, use hardy geraniums, *Nepeta* x *faassenii* 'Six Hill's Giant' and valerians. For semishade, use hosta, ferns and lamium.

Naturalising bulbs in your lawn Grass is the perfect setting for certain bulbs. Over the years, they adapt so well that they become naturalised, reproducing and forming ever-larger clumps of flowers. Once the flowering period is over, however, you must wait at least seven weeks to mow the lawn, leaving

Spring bulbs, such as narcissus, flourish in the dappled light beneath a cherry tree in blossom.

the foliage to build up food reserves in the bulb for next year's flowers. Get round this by planting bulbs in areas that you can develop as natural meadows, or around trees. Or choose bulbs that flower early in the season so that you can mow the lawn that much sooner.
▶ If you have a sprinkler system on your lawn, avoid planting spring bulbs there. Frequent watering during their summer rest period will rot the bulbs.
▶ The spring bulbs that naturalise best in lawns are *Anemone blanda*, *Eranthis hyemalis*, *Fritillaria meleagris*, crocus, snowdrop, bluebell, grape hyacinth, summer snowflake, *Ornithogalum umbellatum*, *Scilla sibirica* and *Tulipa sprengeri*. Many species of narcissi also lend themselves to naturalising and are readily available, especially *Narcissus* 'Actea', *N. cyclamineus*, *N.* 'February Gold', *N.* 'Golden Harvest' and *N. pseudonarcissus*, the wild daffodil.

Protect tender new growth From early winter onwards, it is not uncommon for the tender shoots of bulbs such as anemones and tulips to start nudging through. Protect them from slugs and snails by surrounding them with ash or sharp gravel known as horticultural grit.
▶ If the climate where you live is rather harsh, protect your bulbs in winter with a layer of leaf-mould. As well as being a good heat insulator, the leaves will absorb excess winter moisture, which could rot the bulbs.

Divide at the right time Clumps of spring-flowering bulbs can be divided and replanted as soon as the leaves start to die back. However, the snowdrop (*Galanthus*) should be divided straight after flowering, before the leaves start to die back.

Can you move bulbs?

The usual advice given is never to move bulbs that are in flower. This is sound advice, but does not apply to snowdrops (*Galanthus*). Flowering clumps of snowdrops can be moved and replanted elsewhere. If the soil is very dry, water around the bulbs generously to help them to make new roots.

Bulbs make beautiful cut flowers

Using a sharp blade, cut your flowers early in the morning or late in the evening. Take as few leaves as possible to avoid weakening the bulbs.

▶ **Keep them cool** Place the flowers in a bucket of cold water for several hours – they will soak up the water and will keep longer. But if you've ever wondered why tulips bend and droop in a vase, this is because they have become waterlogged. They need only a little water to keep them at their best.

▶ **Separate narcissus** Keep them in their own bucket of water overnight so that they release their toxic sap, which is harmful to other flowers and makes them fade. They can be mixed with other flowers the following day. To be on the safe side, change the water every morning.

▶ **Encourage larger flowers** Spray with a foliar feed as soon as the flower buds appear.

Scattered on the lawn Scatter several handfuls of bulbs over a mown lawn and use a bulb planter to plant them where they fall. Replace the plug of soil and turf extracted by the planter.

▶ To plant small bulbs such as crocus and fritillaria in a lawn, use a sharpened spade or edging iron to mark an 'H' on the lawn, approximately 30cm wide and tall. Cut the turf to a depth of about 8cm and carefully roll it back. Loosen the soil and push in the bulbs. Cover them with fine soil, gently re-lay the turf, firm down and water to get rid of any remaining air pockets.

For a striking display of bulbs in a pot, arrange them very close to each other.

Growing bulbs in pots

Clay or plastic? Clay pots dry out more quickly so use them for bulbs that like well-drained compost, such as tulips and iris. Keep plastic pots for species that grow under trees or prefer damp conditions, such as fritillary and snowdrops.

Plant close together If you are planting bulbs of the same variety, go for a massed effect and pack them in tightly.
▶ Choose a pot that is at least 15cm deep and as wide as possible, so that the pot doesn't hinder the bulb growth.

Planting in stages For a container that's bright with blooms from the beginning until the end of spring, plant bulbs with complementary flowering periods, such as narcissus, tulips, grape hyacinth and crocus. The largest bulbs need to be planted at the greatest depth, so place narcissus at the bottom of the pot, followed by a layer of compost. Then space out the medium-sized tulip bulbs around them, making sure they are not directly over the ones beneath. Cover with a layer of compost, then finish off with the small grape hyacinth and crocus bulbs, with a final 2cm layer of compost on top.

Water wisely and well Water regularly but moderately, giving a little more during and after the flowering period. As bulbs hate stagnant water, stand pots on saucers filled with clay beads or gravel so that the pot drains well.
▶ For lots of flowers, use a potting medium that consists of coir (or a similar peat substitute), loam and coarse sand in equal parts. Only use fertiliser after flowering has finished.

Forcing bulbs indoors

Enjoy winter flowers

Forced bulbs can produce lovely flowers as early as Christmas. Of course, you can find forced bulbs in the shops, but it is easy and satisfying to force some yourself.

▶ Some bulbs respond better to forcing than others. Hyacinths, small tulips, crocus and grape hyacinth are all good choices for this method.

Start with good bulbs

Take special care to choose good-quality bulbs for forcing. Then, in either September or October, depending on the species, place a layer of clay beads at the bottom of a terracotta pot with a drainage hole, or in a special bulb pot. Fill it with two-thirds fine garden soil and one-third coarse sand or bulb compost. Push the bulbs lightly into the soil, setting them close together. Cover with bulb compost, and water lightly to prevent air pockets.

Continue by keeping bulbs cool

To help forced bulbs make roots, keep them in a cool, dark place for at least two months.

▶ Dig a small trench on the north side of a wall or fence, and place the pots in it. Replace the soil around the pot, cover with a few centimetres of sand and finish off with straw.

▶ If you have a cellar with a winter temperature of 4–10°C, or a frost-free garage, you could also keep your pots there.

Follow with gentle acclimatisation

At the end of their two months' hibernation period, move the pots from their resting place into a cool room (at 10–15°C) for a few days. Then place them in a warm, well-lit location. Three or four weeks later, you will see the first flowers appear.

▶ Extend the flowering period by moving the pots to a cool room or a frost-free porch at night.

Hydroponics made easy

If you grow a hyacinth or amaryllis bulb in a narrow-necked vase filled with water, leave a space at least the width of a finger between the base of the bulb and the liquid. The humidity in the air pocket encourages healthy root growth and the gap prevents the bulb rotting.

Chinese style

The Chinese method of growing bulbs on fine gravel lets you appreciate the root growth as well as the beauty of the flowers. The white narcissus 'Paper White' or the yellow 'Grand Soleil d'Or' will give the best results.

▶ Choose a transparent glass bowl 10cm deep and fill it with alternate layers of sand, gravel and clay beads. Make a bed of compost over these layers and position the bulbs close together on top. Support the bulbs by spreading a layer of fine gravel around them, letting the tips show through. Finish by carefully filling the bowl to within 1cm of the base of the bulbs with water containing crumbled charcoal, which keeps the growing medium sweet.

Life after forcing

Although you can't force the bulbs again, you can get them to flower in the garden in subsequent seasons. Remove the faded flowers – but not the foliage – and feed the bulbs with a flower fertiliser every other watering. When the leaves begin to yellow, stop watering and feeding. Then plant hardy bulbs such as hyacinths, narcissus and crocus in the garden, and repot less-hardy species such as amaryllis in new compost.

▶ You can even replant bulbs grown in water, but be patient. They usually take two or three years to flower again.

Growing hyacinths in water

1 Select a light position for the glass holder, and fill it with water up to the neck.

2 Choose a good-sized, healthy bulb and place it in the neck, top uppermost.

3 The water should be 1cm below the bulb so that it does not rot.

4 The bulb will put out roots into the water and produce leaves and a flower.

Caring for bulbs when flowering is over

Nourishing foliage Once your bulbs have finished flowering, remove the faded blooms to prevent seeds from forming, which exhausts the bulbs. Don't remove any foliage, as the bulbs need their leaves to restore their strength for flowering in the following year. You can help them by watering regularly and feeding with bone meal or organic fertiliser to provide the necessary nutrients.

▶ While the foliage is still green, it is a good time to dig up and divide dense clumps of small bulbs such as anemones, winter aconites, crocus and snowdrops.

▶ Only once the foliage has become yellow and dry should you cut it. Trim close to the ground, and mark out where the bulbs are so that you don't accidentally disturb them when weeding or digging the garden.

Prevent dryness Water narcissus and wild daffodil bulbs during the autumn if it is very dry. The flower buds are formed during this period and a lack of water will dim the beauty of their springtime show.

Keeping disease at bay A light sprinkling of flowers of sulphur before the summer rest period will protect your bulbs from disease and mould. You can also use it before planting – put the bulbs in a paper bag with the powder and shake vigorously. You should be able to buy flowers of sulphur from garden centres and chemists.

Summer hibernation If you prefer to remove bulbs once their flowers have faded to avoid the sight of yellowing foliage, lift them carefully with a fork, keeping the soil around the bulb.

▶ Dig a trench in a semishaded little-used corner of your garden and put a plastic net or wire mesh at the bottom, letting it overlap the ends of the trench.

▶ Set the bulbs in the trench and cover with soil, leaving the foliage exposed.

▶ Water thoroughly during dry spells. Once the foliage has shrivelled and faded, the bulbs can be lifted for storing. Simply pull out the net, shake off the soil and remove the dead leaves.

▶ Dry the cleaned bulbs in a well-ventilated place for a few days, then place them, uncovered, on a bed of sand in shallow boxes.

▶ Store them in a dry, dark and cool room or garage until replanting in autumn. Never store bulbs that are damp or have dead or damaged skins.

Beware of rodents If you are worried that your stored-away bulbs will be attacked by rodents, place the bulbs in old tights or stockings with some dry sand. Rats and mice hate synthetic fibre and are unlikely to attempt to nibble through it. Even so, check the bulbs regularly and remove any that show the slightest signs of rot or damage.

A water-free diet for your tulips Originally from mountainous regions of the Middle East, tulips like hot, dry summers in well-drained soil. These are difficult conditions to provide in mixed beds, so it is best to lift them as soon as the foliage has yellowed and store them in a warm, dry place all summer before planting out again in the autumn. To avoid this time-consuming chore, plant them under fruit trees, which dry out the soil in summer.

Storing bulbs

1 After the foliage has dried completely, dig up the bulbs and place them on a layer of dry sand in a crate.

2 Space them out well to ensure none are touching and sprinkle them evenly with flowers of sulphur.

3 Cover the bulbs with another layer of sand until only their tips are showing.

4 When the bulbs are covered up to their tips, store them in a dark, cool, dry place, safe from rodents.

Bulbs for a spectacular summer

Working their magic on your garden from May through to October, summer-flowering bulbs provide a splash of colour even when perennials have begun to fade. Plant them in spring or autumn, to display in beds or to complement other flowers, shrubs and trees.

Planting and tending tips

Healthy purchases Buy your bulbs as soon as they appear on garden-centre shelves or market stalls. This ensures that they will have less chance of being damaged by poor storage.
▶ Although the largest bulbs are not guaranteed to produce the best flowers, don't buy bulbs that look unusually small or poorly developed in comparison with the normal-sized bulbs of the species. They may not have grown properly or they may have some type of disease. Choose bulbs that are plump, firm and uniform in appearance. They should not be marked and their skin should not come away easily.
▶ If gladioli corms are pink because they have lost their papery brown tunic, don't buy them. They have been handled roughly and may be damaged.

The best soil Most bulbs like light, well-drained soil. If your soil is heavy and has a tendency to become waterlogged in winter, improve it by digging in sand or gravel, then plant the bulbs on a layer of gravel to provide further drainage. You can also plant them in a rock garden covered with gravel.
▶ Soil that is too light and porous for other plants is ideal for growing bulbs. Plant them on top of a layer of garden compost or well-decomposed organic matter.

Plant lilies in threes For a beautiful show from the first year on, plant large lilies in soil enriched with plenty of organic matter such as leaf-mould. Plant them in groups in flat-bottomed holes measuring 50–60cm in diameter. In each

Dahlias flower all summer. They look lovely in flower beds but also last well as flowers in arrangements.

hole, first add a handful of coarse sand for drainage then place three bulbs in a triangle and firm them in. This formation guarantees an attractive arrangement.

UNDER GLASS

Get ahead of the season

Plant summer bulbs early in pots and keep them under glass. They will be ready to transfer to the garden as soon as your spring-flowering bulbs have finished.

Gladioli In April, plant gladioli individually in 10cm pots. Place in a cool, frost-free greenhouse or porch and water well. Within a couple of weeks a green shoot will appear. Make sure they receive plenty of light, and during May you will be able to plant them out in their final position.

Tuberous begonias Commonly used in hanging baskets, pots or troughs, begonias can also be started off in April under glass. Put them in their final positions once the spring nights are frost-free.

Freesias At the end of April, tender bulbs such as freesia or ornithogallum can be planted in pots and given a start in the greenhouse. Move them out into the garden or outdoor containers when all risk of frost has passed.

Autumn-flowering bulbs

▶ **Autumn crocus** (left) Plant around the base of shrubs and at the bottom of slopes. They will then peep through grass or other foliage and make room for themselves between clumps of perennials. The flowers will appear before the leaves, which follow in early spring.

▶ **Crocosmia** (left) Easily grown and excellent as cut flowers, these liven up herbaceous borders from July to September. Plant them in a warm sunny site, in well-drained sandy soil. They are hardy in all but the coldest areas, where lifting and storing may be necessary in October.

▶ **Kaffir lily** (left) In full sun or half shade, the lily will produce fiery red, pink or white flowers that will still be in full bloom in November. It requires cool soil in summer and should be divided in April.

▶ **Belladonna lilies** (left, below) If planted against a south-facing wall and given frost protection, *Amaryllis belladonna* produces numerous fragrant trumpets in late summer. These are usually pink or, in the case of some hybrids, white. The leaves follow shortly after the flowers have faded and last throughout the winter.

Deadheading dahlias Remove the dead flowers from plants such as dahlias, crinum and amaryllis and they will grow back even more vigorously. When deadheading dahlias, cut off the flower and its stem just above the first pair of leaves. In the case of plants that bear flowers at the top of a floral spike, such as gladioli, remove individual flowers as they die by pinching them off at the stem beneath the flower. Cut the spike off at its base when all the flowers have died.

Tender or half-hardy plants Gardeners who live in milder regions may be able to leave dahlias in the ground once they have finished flowering. However, in most areas, the tubers must be lifted and stored in a dry, dark and frost-free room, garage or cellar, because the fleshy roots are very sensitive to moisture in winter. Other bulbs such as freesia will also not survive a very wet or frosty winter in the ground.

How deep should you plant?

Planting depths given on packets or in books relate to the depth of the soil between the tip of the bulb and the soil surface, not to the depth of the hole. As a general rule of thumb, bulbs should be planted at a depth equal to at least twice their height. However, if your soil is very light, then plant them at a depth equal to three times their height.

▶ Gauge the correct depth at a glance by using a trowel that you have marked with graduated measurements.

Divide and multiply

New bulbs for free If a clump of bulbs becomes very congested, gently uproot it after flowering and divide it. This will give the mother bulb a new lease of life and generate a flush of new shoots. Shake the soil off gently and remove the young bulbs. These offsets should come away from the original bulb easily. If they don't, it is because they are not yet mature – in which case don't force them or you may end up damaging the plant. Replant the mother plant and its offshoots immediately.

Another method of multiplication Some varieties of allium and lily, such as 'Enchantment', produce bulbils that appear on stems or in leaf axils in the summer. Carefully remove them, dust with flowers of sulphur and put in a plastic bag with damp moss. Keep them cool but frost-free. In the spring, plant them in small pots filled with multipurpose compost, and place them in a sheltered spot in half shade.

▶ Wait a year before replanting them in the garden and they will flower better.

▶ Gladioli, crocus and crocosmia also produce offsets around their corm. Remove these and replant in a small box kept somewhere cool and sheltered. Water in spring, then put the young plants in the ground. Crocus corms will flower the following year whereas gladioli take two to three years.

Be gentle with young plants Use a dibber or small bamboo cane to set your new plants into a box of fresh compost or directly into the garden. The roots are fragile and the aerial shoots are easily broken if you are too heavy-handed, but a dibber will make holes of the right size, into which you can easily insert the plants, firming lightly to remove air pockets.

Overwintering dahlias

1 Cut the stems 15cm from the ground and dig up the tubers. Label the plant if you have more than one clump.

2 Allow the tubers to dry for several days, then clean them gently with a brush, removing most of the soil.

3 Sprinkle the tubers with flowers of sulphur to prevent fungus growing during storage.

4 Trim all the stems again,10cm from the tubers, to complete the preparations.

5 In a clean box, position the tubers. Cover with sawdust or dry sand to the base of the stems.

6 Ensure all the tubers are labelled and put the box in a cool, dark, well-ventilated, frost and vermin-free place.

Solving common problems

Chemical-free pot traps Earwigs are one of the worst enemies of bulbs, damaging their flowers and leaves. Instead of spraying them with insecticide, try a simple, chemical-free trap. Cook a jacket potato, carefully scoop out most of the contents, leave it to cool and then place amongst your plants. The earwigs will climb into the jacket shell to feast. All you have to do is remove the potato jacket with its occupants – but do it gently, because these small pests are quick to escape.

Dealing with virus Lilies are prone to virus. Once a plant is affected, there is no cure. Look out for symptoms – deformed leaves and twisted or missing flowers – and insects like aphids and greenfly, which spread the virus. Uproot an infected plant immediately and destroy it so that it cannot infect the others.

Watch out for soft rot If irises show signs of rotting at the base of the outside leaves, check your soil is draining properly. If the soil is too wet, damaged rootstock can be invaded by bacteria, which attacks rhizomes and leaves, causing them to rot. You can smell the decay. Destroy the plant immediately, then lighten the soil to improve drainage for any other irises.

Beware of scorching Iris rhizomes protrude above the soil's surface and, because they are exposed, they are prone to damage. When mulching or top-dressing with animal manure, avoid covering them with organic material, even if it is well decomposed, as this will cause scorching.

Beautiful flowers at stake The weight of large dahlia blooms often causes the stems to bow down to the ground and snap. Three bamboo canes, inserted in the ground in a triangle around the clump and ringed with string or raffia two-thirds of the way up, will hold the foliage and flower stems together. Position stakes before planting to avoid damaging the tubers.

Disbud your dahlias To get the biggest blooms, remove secondary flower buds, leaving just one bud on each stem. If you are worried about losing your only flower in bad weather, disbud every other stem to still enjoy a dazzling display.

Bank up your gladioli If you cannot stake gladioli or plant them in dense groups, build up a small mound of soil at their base to support them or plant them in a sheltered area.

Showy bulbs at their best ▶

Dahlias ❶ The large-flowered hybrids are striking everywhere but are particularly effective in big flower beds.

Cyclamen (*Cyclamen neapolitanum*) **❷** These beautiful bulbs are easily naturalised in most settings and will form a magnificent carpet of flowers under the foliage of trees.

Irises ❸ and Madonna lily (*Lilium candidum*) **❹** Imposing, elegant blooms will grace formal flower beds in very late spring and early summer.

Gladioli ❺ Because their upright habit can make them difficult to combine with other bedding plants, gladioli look best when grown for cutting or displayed in beds on their own.

Nerine ❻ With its long-lasting pink flowers nerine is an attractive sight in autumn. They do well next to a warm wall.

Bulbs for every setting

A splash of colour beneath the trees Autumn crocus and cyclamen are excellent for creating a carpet of flowers under tall trees. They naturalise readily and will eventually cover the ground entirely, which is a definite advantage in areas where grass struggles to grow.

▶ Autumn-flowering crocus such as *Crocus speciosus* look good with creeping bugle. Plant in spring for autumn flowers.

Dividing rhizomatous irises

To ensure they continue to flourish, irises need to be divided every three years after they flower, in July or August.

1 Dig up the rhizomes carefully, using a fork to lift as much of the root growth as possible.

2 Take out the rhizomes intact, brush them off and cut the stem into 10–15cm sections with a sharp knife.

3 Each division should have several roots and leaves, or a bud. Trim the leaves to half their length.

4 The rhizomes can rot where they have been cut. Avoid this by spraying the wound with flowers of sulphur.

5 Replant the rhizomes. In heavy soil, leave the tops exposed; in light soil, plant just below the surface.

6 Space them 25–50cm apart, depending on the variety, and water each divided plant thoroughly.

Lilies for damp shade Lords and ladies (*Arum italicum*) should be planted in autumn. A handy filler for a shady area, this lily needs no maintenance and is very robust. It will naturalise spontaneously and regrow year after year, spreading its beautiful green foliage marbled with white, which is renewed in November and lasts throughout the winter. As an added attraction, its flowers are replaced in August and September by clusters of berries (right) which turn bright red.

▶ The sensational arum lily (*Zantedeschia aethiopica*) (right) is not just beautiful but useful too. It can actually improve the drainage of excessively wet soil. Plant it in spring around the edges of ponds or in flower beds and borders in cool places. Its large white trumpets bloom from May to late July. Divide it in autumn and it will regrow from the rootstock. Cut the foliage back to the ground and add a mulch.

Planting in crevices Autumn-flowering crocus can grow through the dense foliage of rock-garden plants such as aubrieta, and in the small crevices of dry-stone walls. Plant them in a little soil and cover with gravel. The autumn-flowering snowdrop (*Galanthus reginae-olgae*) will also thrive at the top of dry, sheltered rock gardens.

Discover irises All irises prefer a sunny position and can be grown from rhizomes or bulbs. Rhizomatous types prefer drier soils: damp soils encourage disease. Although their flowers are beautiful, they can be untidy when not in bloom. The dwarf forms of bulbous iris flower in early spring, while the taller Dutch or English varieties flower in late spring and early summer, and provide excellent cut flowers.

Grow crocosmia for late colour The scarlet, orange or yellow hues of crocosmia will brighten up even partially shaded sites, if they are well-drained and sheltered. These plants are prolific and spread rapidly. Divide them in spring.

Planning a fragrant garden Plant the hardy regal lily (*Lilium regale*), which tolerates all growing conditions, at the entrance to your garden. For sweet scents in late summer and autumn, opt for *Lilium speciosum*, a large Japanese lily which is also highly perfumed, but needs to be planted in a sheltered position safe from the first frosts.

Star performers for summer Lilies and allium get top billing for performance and versatility. Hardy and easy to grow, they will grace flower beds, borders, pots and even the vegetable garden. All lilies prefer light shade, though Martagon lilies will naturalise in large spaces and meadows. Allium flourish in full sun in any type of well-drained soil and prefer to be planted in autumn. The giant garlic (*Allium giganteum*), though a popular choice because it looks so spectacular, can grow to a height of 1.8m, so if your garden is exposed and windy, it is better to choose a shorter option.

Shade-loving lilies Many lilies, such as *Lilium superbum*, flourish when lightly shaded by trees, allowing the plant to have its head in the sun but its roots in cool ground. If you don't have trees with light foliage, plant your lilies with perennials that will provide protective cover as they grow.
▶ Ensure that your lilies thrive for many years without artificial fertiliser by preparing the ground well for them. Add leaf-mould to the soil, plus some sand if the ground is heavy. Mulch with well-decomposed compost every autumn.

A lasting bouquet Gladioli are perfect cut flowers and can last up to 12 days in a vase if you follow two basic rules. The first is to pick the flower spikes when the buds at the base of the stem are just starting to open. The second is to remove the two unopened top buds and pinch off dead flowers every day.

Late bloomers Some bulbs can be planted in July to flower from August to October. This is the case with *Amaryllis belladonna*, colchicum, *Crocus speciosus* and nerine.

Summer stunners Make room in your garden for dahlias. There are so many hybrids and colours available, flowering from July to October, that there is one for every occasion. Combine them in groups of three or five with other late bedding plants. The dwarf species are ideal in path-side borders, flower beds and containers of all types, and

DID YOU KNOW?
Bulb, corm, tuber or rhizome?

Bulbs
Lilies and allium have 'true' bulbs ❶. These are formed of fleshy scales surrounding a central bud and attached to its base. Most bulbs should be planted with the tip upwards.

Corms
Gladioli and crocus grow from a corm ❷, which outwardly resembles a bulb. This is a thick modified stem, without scales, on top of which there is a flowering bud. Every year the corm regenerates by creating a new storage organ at the top. When planting always ensure that the bud is at the top.

Tubers
Begonias and cyclamen are tubers ❸. They take the form of a flattened cake with very small buds on the surface and are planted lying flat with the buds facing upwards.

Rhizomes
Irises (except for bulbous irises, which are grown from bulbs, as their name suggests) have a rhizome ❹, a fleshy creeping stem, which spreads by growing horizontally along the surface of the soil. The buds can be seen along the top of the stem and the roots along the bottom.

large-flowered dahlias look good along walls. Give your vegetable garden some old-fashioned charm, by planting rows of dahlias there to provide spectacular flowers for cutting.

Window dressing
Summer bulbs are ideal for planters and window boxes. All they need to flower is some compost mixed with sand. Plant them singly in pots three or four times their size in diameter or combine them with a flowering annual or a deciduous perennial in a larger tub. Tuberous begonias (left) mix well with other summer plants.

Summer-flowering bulbs bask by a sunnny wall.

A flush of flowers until the first frosts

Familiar to every old-fashioned gardener, annuals and biennials never fail to delight. These abundantly flowering, short-lived plants bring brilliant colour to trellises, arches, banks and flowerpots. They are easy and inexpensive to grow, and their innocent charm will take you back to a simpler time.

The art of sowing

A good start Conditions in the first two weeks after sowing will determine an annual's strength and beauty for the rest of the summer. To help seeds germinate quickly and plants to develop strong roots, sow them in mild weather, on moist, well-prepared soil. If the ground is poor and the weather too warm, the seeds will produce spindly and feeble plants.

For continuous flowers
Annuals have brief lives and need to be replaced at the end of their flowering period. For a regular supply of plants sow seeds in trays at intervals of two to four weeks, starting in April. Some gardeners use this method to replenish their borders several times a year.

Be patient! Most annuals can be sown in April or May and will flower later in the summer. Some, such as marigold (*Calendula*), can be sown in autumn and after mild winters will often start to flower in March. But be patient and choose the right time to sow – a plant sown in April will often overtake the same plant sown a month earlier, and may give a better display of flowers.

Biennials for spring colour From July to August sow daisy, campanula, viola, polyanthus, forget-me-not, foxglove, wallflowers and other biennials. Plant them out into their flowering positions in October. They will spend the winter producing leaves, and flower the following spring.

A clever mix of annuals and biennials gives a dazzling display for very little effort on the part of the gardener.

Hardy choices for beginners Some species put up with all manner of mistreatment and still germinate well. If you are new to gardening, start with these tolerant favourites.
▶ **Cosmos** From June to the end of October, its graceful white, pink or deep red flowers are carried on long slender stalks 80–150cm high. The foliage is delicate and feathery.
▶ **Scarlet runner beans** As well as producing edible beans, this annual flowers from July to September, thus earning its place in many cottage gardens, where it was traditionally grown up chestnut poles. Its foliage is abundant, it puts out white or bicoloured flowers and the plant will climb to 1.8–2.4m.

UNDER GLASS
Give your plants a head start
If you live in cooler regions, start sowing a few seeds during the autumn and winter in a cold greenhouse or cold frame. Sow large seeds individually in plug modules and smaller seeds in pots or seed trays, then prick them out into individual pots later. Be sure to label all your seeds. You can also buy established plug plants from specialist nurseries or garden centres. Wait 24 hours after receiving them, then prick them out into trays or individual pots. Grow them on in frost-free conditions for about four weeks before planting out.

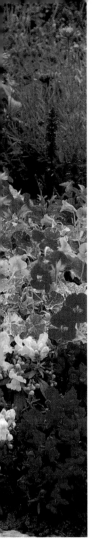

► **Lavatera** From July to October, graceful, pastel-coloured cups stand out against the blue-green foliage of the mallow. Clusters of stems that can reach 60cm in height make a handsome, branching clump.

► **Marigold** The marigold (*Calendula*) is a favourite in the country garden for its pretty orange-yellow, sometimes pink-tinged, single or double flowers. The plants flourish for many months, even managing a few flowers in most months of a mild winter.

Avoid seed mixtures Assortments are a bad idea invented by seed merchants. The pack may contain an odd mix of varieties called 'scented', 'wild', 'for shade' or 'for dry ground'. Often, the pack doesn't provide specific information on each variety, so you won't know the correct conditions for successful planting. The result tends to be disappointing, with one or two prolific varieties taking over.

Don't use fresh manure Even if it is well decomposed, fresh manure contains too much nitrogen for seeds. This makes the plants produce too much leaf and stem growth, at the expense of robust flowers. Sow on ground that was manured two years previously, or follow a centuries-old gardening practice and enrich the soil with a green crop such as mustard or clover.

Buy some plants in plugs Some plants are difficult to grow from seed. Plugs are a better option for gerbera, calceolaria, Bells of Ireland (*Molucella*), lisianthus and aster (*Callistephus*). Verbena, petunia, busy lizzie (*Impatiens*) and *Begonia semperflorens* are often available as young plants.

Newspaper encourages germination Seeds sprout more easily when they are covered in daytime with damp newspaper, especially in very hot weather. Keep the paper in place with tent pegs or markers stuck in the ground. This covering will also prevent the birds from pillaging your seeds.

Cool-loving plants Digitalis and primula seeds like to be covered with a fine layer of organic matter, such as leaf-mould or garden compost, which keeps the soil cool and damp. Professionals use vermiculite, a light expanded mineral.

Sow an annual border from the centre out

To sow a large bed without compacting the freshly dug soil, start in the middle. Stand on a plank and move it outwards towards the edges as you work. Rake over the flattened strips of soil left by the plank each time you reposition it.

► If you are growing annuals for cutting, sow seeds in rows. Sow four rows, then leave a space before sowing another four, and so on. The spaces will serve as paths so that you can pick the flowers without trampling on them.

Annuals for summer display

Many plants can be cheaply and easily raised from seed, under glass or in the ground.

UNDER GLASS
February–March Antirrhinum ❶, begonia, cosmos, dahlia, gazania, gerbera, impatiens, limonium, morning glory (*Ipomoea*), petunia, salvia ❷, sweet pea and thunbergia.

March–May African and French marigolds, everlasting flowers (*Helipterum*), nasturtium and tagetes. Plant out from the end of May to the beginning of June. Mimulus, lavatera and nemesia ❸ should be kept under glass until all danger of frost has passed.

In autumn Hardy annuals, such as sweet alyssum, candytuft, Californian poppy, cornflower, clarkia, larkspur (*Delphinium*), linum, marigold (*Calendula*), nemophila ❹, nigella, poppy (*Papaver*), rudbeckia, scabious, silene and sweet pea. Transplant the plants when they reach 3–4cm in height, planting them directly in place. They will need to be in a sheltered corner of the garden. In spring these young plants will have a very feeble root system. Do not move them again or you might lose two-thirds of your crop.

IN THEIR FINAL POSITION
March–April *Gaillarda*, Californian poppy, *Chrysanthemum carinatum*, clarkia ❺, cornflower, everlasting flowers (*Helipterum*), lobularia, and marigold (*Calendula*).

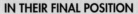

In May Convolvulus, cosmos, everlasting flowers (*Ammobium*), godetia, love-in-a-mist, nasturtium, Virginia stock and zinnia.

Planting out a seasonal display

The best time to plant April's sudden showers and temperature variations rarely spare young plants. Frosts threaten all but the hardiest of seasonal floral displays, right through until May. Many of the plants we grow as summer annuals are tender or half-hardy perennials – for example, antirrhinums are fairly tolerant of frosts and often survive through the winter in sheltered locations. Except for hardy annuals and in all but the very mild areas of Cornwall, Devon and Dorset, wait until May before planting out.
▶ Wait until mid-May to plant out pelargonium, impatiens, salvia, begonia, tagetes, verbena and other tender annuals, even if – which is not unusual – your garden centre has been selling them for several weeks.

For a winter garden In September or October, it is best to plant out biennials such as violas and daisies, which will first flower in the next month, and then again from April to June. For continual flowering from autumn until the end of spring, go for the pretty *Viola* 'Ultima Coronation Robe,' the superb velvet and deep red blooms of 'Scarlet Dynamite', or

Blue salvias and rudbeckias, sown under glass in March or April, can be planted out from the end of May through to early June. Here they complement the tall sunflowers.

the large black-spotted yellow flowers of 'Fama'. The pink or white daisy – *Bellis perennis* 'Galaxy' – will also flourish throughout the winter.

Colour for early spring Autumn is the time to plant forget-me-nots (*Myosotis*), wallflowers (*Cheiranthus*), primulas and other biennials that will bloom when the hard frosts are over.
▶ These early-flowering biennials are ideal companions for spring bulbs. Group them with narcissi and tulips in your early borders for welcome colour at the end of winter.

Stake out tall plants Give larkspurs and other tall annuals support as soon as they are planted in the garden. Place twiggy branches from hazel or birch trees among the young plants and the branches will support the growing stems as they rise through them. You can also use canes for support – fix growing stems to them either using traditional means such as soft string or raffia, or with modern metal or plastic ties. Make sure you do not tie so tightly that growth is restricted.

Work in cool conditions In fine weather, do not plant during the hottest time of the day. To keep small plants from drying out as soon as they are put in the ground, work in the morning before 11 o'clock. Better still, wait until the end of the day, after 5 o'clock. The plants will then benefit from the coolness and humidity of the night.

Potting up young plants or plugs

1 Water the tray before removing the plants. Use a pencil to push up the root ball from the bottom.

2 Make a small planting hole in the compost, and position the plant so that its neck is level with the soil.

3 Fill the space around the roots with fine compost, and use your fingertips to firm the soil around the stem.

4 Water carefully to avoid disturbing the plant. Then, seal in the moisture with a mulch of fine gravel.

Welcome sunshine While most annuals are generally undemanding about their soil so long as it is well drained, they do need a sunny situation. Several can cope in lightly shaded corners though, including nasturtium, campanula, euphorbia, impatiens, mimulus, nemophila, creeping zinnia (*Sanvitalia*) and catchfly (*Silene*).
▶ Group together plants with the same requirements, such as impatiens, digitalis and torenia. These will all flourish in semishade, in a cool, well-drained soil.

Plan before planting Fill a bottle with sand and gently pour it out over the soil to mark out the boundaries of your planting scheme.
▶ Line up the plants, in their pots, in staggered rows, every 15–30cm depending on their spread to decide on the final positions before planting.

Plug plants make it easy To save some time or space, or to replace seedlings that have died, you can buy plants in plugs at garden centres or by mail order. These young plants, grown from seed, will be around 3–5cm high and not yet flowering, making them smaller and cheaper than plants sold in pots. They come in blister packs of five delivered in protective wrappings, or in module trays of 30–50. Because their rootsystem is fully developed, they will not suffer from transplanting and their recovery time is very fast. Plant them directly into window boxes, tubs or hanging baskets.
▶ To help them to gain strength, you can plant plugs in pots or in boxes before bedding them into their final positions several weeks later.

A good soak for a quick recovery Half an hour before planting out, immerse plant packs in a bucket of water until all the air has stopped bubbling out of the soil. Thoroughly water the hole in the ground before putting in the plant.
▶ Water around the plant until the soil is saturated. Turn the rose of the watering can upwards for a gentle shower that will not loosen the soil.

Not too deep The planting hole should be deep enough to allow you, after placing the plug, to add a small handful of fine topsoil, which reduces the danger of the plug drying out. The neck of the plant should be level with the soil surface to ensure moisture will be absorbed when the plant is watered.

A rainbow in the garden

Annuals and biennials come in nearly every colour imaginable. Combine flowers and foliage to make eye-catching combinations, to complement and contrast, and to provide a theme for your planting schemes.

Blue Ageratum, felicia, forget-me-not (*Myosotis*) **1**, ipomoea, linum, lobelia, love-in-a-mist, nemophila and nicandra

Green Bells of Ireland (*Molucella*), euphorbia **2** and mignonette

Yellow or orange Golden eye (*Bidens*), calceolaria, chrysanthemum, coreopsis, eschscholzia, evening primrose (*Oenothera*), everlasting flowers (*Helichrysum*), gaillardia, glaucium, limnanthes, marigold (*Calendula*) **3**, mimulus, nasturtium, nicotiana, portulaca, rudbeckia, sanvitalia, sunflower, tagetes, thunbergia, tithonia, ursinia, viola, wallflowers (*Erysimum*, *Cheiranthus*) and zinnia

Pink or fuchsia Ageratum, antirrhinum, aster (*Callistephus*), bellis, clarkia, cleome, cosmos, dahlia **4**, *Dianthus barbatus*, dimorphotheca, everlasting flowers (*Helipterum*), geranium (*Pelargonium*), gomphrena, heliotrope, hollyhock, impatiens, lavatera, malcolmia, matthiola, mirabilis, nicotiana, petunia, *Phlox drummondii*, portulaca, silene and sweet pea

Red Bellis, celosia, gerbera, godetia, linum, lobelia, monkey flower (*Mimulus*), nemesia, poppy (*Papaver*) **5**, and wallflower (*Cheiranthus*)

Violet Brachycome, campanula, cornflower, convolvulus, gilia, honesty (*Lunaria*), ipomoea, larkspur (*Delphinium*), lisianthus, lobelia, pansy, petunia, phacelia, salpiglossis, scaevola, torenia, verbena and viola **6**

White African daisy (*Arctotis*), begonia, campanula **7**, cosmos, dimorphotheca, gypsophila, everlasting flowers (*Ammobium*), lavatera, linum, love-in-a-mist (*Nigella damascena*), nemophila, nicotiana, salvia and viola

Grey and silver Cineraria (*Senecio*) **8** especially varieties such as 'Silver Dust' and 'Cirrus'

The secrets of composition

Vary the height Mix three or four different heights to give a border structure, with low-growing annuals at the front and taller plants at the back of the bed.
▶ **First row (10–20cm)** Sweet alyssum (*Lobularia*), gazania, limnanthes, lobelia, Virginian stock (*Malcolmia*) and sanvitalia.
▶ **Second row (20–50cm)** Ageratum, antirrhinum, arctotis, star of the veldt (*Dimorphotheca*), felicia, gomphrena, impatiens, love-in-a-mist, nasturtium, petunia and salvia.
▶ **Third row (50cm–1m)** Cornflower, clarkia, mallow (*Lavatera*), gypsophila, everlasting flower (*Helichrysum*), larkspur, lisianthus, nicandra, nicotiana and papaver.
▶ **Fourth row (over 1m)** Amaranthus, cleome, cosmos, sunflowers and *Verbena bonariensis*.

Simple splashes of colour Plant together annuals or biennials of the same type – the same height or flower shape, for example – in a group approximately one metre square. Start simply, restricting yourself to just two or three different colours at first. Some gardeners don't like to mix flowers of different yellow hues, or oranges with reds or yellows, or reds with blues. Others might find the result very pleasing.

Planting bulbs in a mixed bed

1 Set out the plants at the correct planting distances, and plant them in firmly.

2 Place bulbs between the plants, spacing them evenly. Dig holes with a bulb planter or trowel.

3 Plant bulbs at the required depth. Push them gently into the soil at the bottom of each hole, pointing upwards.

4 Firm the soil lightly and water if it is dry. Insert a label to remind you of what has been planted.

A curtain of flowers To hide an unsightly wall, train morning glory (*Ipomoea*) or another quick-growing climber up a piece of garden twine. At a convenient height, stretch a horizontal piece of twine between two nails set 1.2m apart, and insert two more nails along its length to hold it firm. Every 15cm along this main cord, knot in vertical cords, leaving them free to trail to the ground. Place annuals in pots at the base. They will grow rapidly up the twine, and your wall will soon disappear behind an abundantly flowering curtain. Morning glory also has the advantage of attracting hoverflies, whose larvae feed on aphids.

Valuable space-fillers In their first year of planting, shrubs and perennials will not fill all their allotted space. Use annuals to fill the gaps in your borders while waiting for the other plants to reach full growth.

Hidden guttering Since they live no more than three to six months, climbing annuals do not develop woody stems that might damage guttering, so you can safely use them as a concealer. They will scale a drainpipe in several weeks but you will need to take them down at the end of the season and start again the next year.

Seaside garden Take inspiration from the local wildflowers. *Oenothera biennis* frequently grows wild in sandy terrain on the coast and, with its pretty yellow flowers, it is perfect for a semiwild garden redolent of the sea. In fact, it will grow anywhere: just scatter the seeds in a sunny place and enjoy the profusion of flowers all summer.

Flower-dressed tree trunks
If your tree trunks are not too thick, train convolvulus or cobaea around them. These elegant annuals have bell-shaped flowers of blue, violet, pink or white and can climb to a height of six to eight metres.
▶ Morning glory can also be trained up the trunk of a tree, although the shade will reduce its flowering.
▶ Even if it doesn't reach its normal height in such a spot, a bright red tropaeolum (right) also gives a sunny effect.

Plant a floral carpet Choose low-growing annuals with interesting foliage or habit to make a living mosaic. Outline the shape of your design by planting two staggered rows around the edge. Make sure you allow for enough plants – you will need 12–16 cineraria for each metre, for example. Then, to complete the effect, fill in your 'frame' with a block of a single variety or mixed plants in a geometric pattern.

A sober-looking wall can be given summer charm by a row of pink hollyhocks (Althaea rosea).

▶ **Flowers for colour** *Ageratum houstonianum, Begonia semperflorens,* lobelia, lobularia, tagetes and viola.
▶ **Foliage** *Senecio cineraria* 'Silver Dust' for grey, and beetroot (*Beta* 'Bulls blood') for purple. Feverfew (*Tanacetum parthenium* 'Gold Moss') or 'Plenum' has striking gold foliage with small white flowers.

Cover a sunny trellis To smother a fence, pergola or trellis in a season, consider ipomoea, sweet pea and other fast-growing climbing annuals. Plant these creepers in deep, rich soil to increase their vigour.
▶ Canary creeper (*Tropaeolum peregrinum*) flourishes from June to October with bright yellow flowers 2–3cm in diameter. It climbs to a height of 2.5–4 metres.
▶ Black-eyed Susan (*Thunbergia alata*) is another vigorous climber, presenting abundant yellow or orange flowers with a black eye from July to October.

To brighten up paving Here and there, scoop out the soil in the gaps between paving stones, bricks or flagstones. Replace it with a mixture of multipurpose potting compost or garden soil with added coarse sand or grit, and sow daisies or other small plants.

Popular wall flowers To soften a low, sunny wall, sow annuals and biennials in the crevices or on the top. Antirrhinum, Californian poppy and wallflowers will all thrive in this hot, dry situation. Fill the spaces between the stones with sandy soil supplemented with bone meal, or a mixture of equal parts of soil, coarse sand and leaf-mould. Use a small fork to squeeze the planting mixture into the gaps and water liberally until the soil is soaked before sowing.

Living wigwam Make a circle of bamboo canes about one metre in diameter. Push the canes into the ground to a depth of 40cm, leaving a space about 50cm wide between two of the canes for the door. Bind the canes about 15cm from the top with raffia or wire. Then sow runner beans or sweet peas at the foot of the canes. Water the plants regularly, and as they grow up the bamboo canes, the sides of your wigwam will begin to take shape.

A scented terrace To fill your patio or terrace with fragrance from June to September, plant different species of stock (*Matthiola*) and tobacco plant (*Nicotiana*), whose scent is especially attractive at night.
▶ Morning glory (*Ipomaea*) has astonishing red and yellow 'ears' that give out a very sweet smell in the evening. The plant is capable of covering any kind of fence or other support within a couple of months.

WATCH OUT

Toxic annuals Some wild or cultivated annuals and biennials are poisonous, and they are all the more dangerous when they spread through a garden. Contact with the sap of euphorbia or with the leaves of nicotiana and *Heracleum mantegazzianum* can cause skin allergies. It is dangerous to eat the seeds of sweet pea, larkspur or *Solanum capsicastrum*. The seeds, bark and leaves of the castor oil plant are all more or less toxic, but the strongest concentration of poison is in the seeds and the attached oil gland. Take them off and destroy them before maturity if you have small children or animals.

Getting the most from your plants

Water and hoe regularly Watering is indispensable, especially immediately after planting and during hot summer weather. Every two or three days check the compost in pots and containers to see if it has dried out.

▶ To avoid disturbing young plants, use a watering can fitted with the finest rose, and take care to hold it quite high above the plants.

▶ If watering with a hose, use a rose attachment and point the rose upwards over the plants. This prevents damaging the plants by watering with too much pressure.

▶ Hoe the ground regularly to get rid of weeds that will compete with your plants. Mulching well will also help.

Pinching out for strength

Encourage your young plants to develop into sturdy, bushy specimens by pinching out the tips of the growing shoots. Grasp the tip between your thumb and index finger, above a leaf or a pair of leaves. This light pruning will delay flowering slightly, but it will be all the more abundant when it does start. Regularly pinch out clarkia, cosmos, godetia, sweet pea and heliotrope.

▶ The fragile stems of rudbeckia, aster and campanula are vulnerable in wind. Pinching out the tips restricts their development and helps them to remain upright.

The right natural fertiliser To boost the flowering of annual climbers, feed them every two weeks with bonfire ash or an organic fertiliser high in potash suitable for roses, geraniums, raspberries or tomatoes. Avoid nitrogen-rich fertilisers as they encourage leaf development rather than flowers.

Watch out for spontaneous reseeding Since they reseed themselves generously, marigolds, forget-me-nots and other annuals or biennials are favourites with those who love cottage gardens, but they can wreak havoc in more formal schemes. Control their spread and prevent seed from developing by removing flowers as soon as they have finished. In some cases, it is best to remove the whole flowered stem or even the plant. As these plants are produced from a cross, their seeds may give rise to plants very different from the mother plant.

▶ If you want an orderly garden, it is probably a good idea to avoid the Californian poppy, coreopsis, larkspur, limnanthes, linum, marigold, nasturtium and nigella, or at least keep them firmly in check.

Natural profusion If you like the informal jumble of a cottage garden, allow your annuals and biennials to develop and scatter their seeds before pulling them up. Forget-me-nots, foxgloves and honesty will spread themselves in semishade, while evening primroses will do the same in sunny places.

Prolong flowering

Remove spent blooms to prolong flowering and prevent your annuals and biennials from exhausting themselves by producing unnecessary seeds.

▶ Many annuals will flower vigorously for a fortnight, then dwindle to a few scattered flowers. Prune the stems that have finished flowering to stimulate further growth.

▶ Cut hollyhocks back to the base of their stems as soon as they have finished flowering. They will grow back and flower again over several years. If allowed to seed, a plant may not grow back the following year.

▶ Prune the principal stem of foxgloves as soon as they have finished flowering. New flower spikes, smaller but still worth having, will spring up from lateral stems.

Back from summer holidays If you find your window boxes or other containers dried out on returning from holiday, refresh them with plants that can cope with early autumn chills, including felicia, marigold (*Calendula*), aster, *Begonia semperflorens*, nicotiana, rudbeckia, zinnia and salvia.

Show no mercy after the first frosts Pull out annuals – including climbers – as soon as their foliage begins to wither. To cheer up your empty pots with an immediate splash of colour, replenish them with violas, polyanthus or heathers, which will last through the winter.

A winter overcoat To protect biennials over winter, cover them with straw, wrap them in horticultural fleece (below) or cover them with cardboard, which can be taken off in the middle of the day to give the plants light. To minimise the danger of frost damage, you should also reduce watering. You can discard the winter protection when the weather gets warmer and danger of frosts has passed.

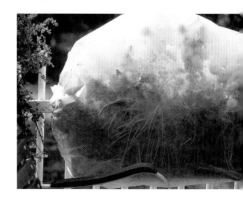

Harvesting seed is easy once flowering has finished.

Collecting seeds for next year's plants

Use a cone of newspaper ... To gather seeds from your garden, roll up two sheets from a broadsheet newspaper to make a large cone with a wide opening at the top. Fold and secure it at the bottom to keep the seeds in place. Shake the plant over this cone, then fold over and seal the top and label with the name of the plant.

Paper bag ... Put a paper bag over flowers that have finished blooming and secure it by binding round the stem of the plant with a piece of string, raffia or wire. Once the stems have dried out, cut just below the tie, turn the bag upside down and shake the plant so that the seeds fall into it. Label the bag immediately.
▶ Never store seeds in a plastic bag – it will not let air through and the seeds will rot.

... or an umbrella To gather the maximum number of seeds in record time, shake seed-bearing stems above an up-turned open umbrella.

Drying is essential To reduce the risk of mould, air-dry seeds thoroughly on newspaper before storing them.

Safe, dry storage Old tablet bottles are perfect for storing seeds. The drying agent in the cap will protect them from damp. You could also use old film canisters, or put the seeds in envelopes or paper bags and peg them to a line in a dry, well-aired space such as a garage.
▶ Collect the little bags of absorbent silica gel that come with electrical or computer equipment. Drop them into the tightly sealed boxes in which you store your seeds.
▶ To keep off weevils and rodents, add a mothball to the storage container.

Use a fine mesh sieve For fine, small seeds such as antirrhinum and petunia, put the ripe, dry flower heads into an old kitchen sieve. Rub gently over the mesh, and the seeds will fall through. Some will be spoiled by this treatment, but there are so many that you can afford to waste a few.

Check the cupboard Don't store seeds in an MDF cupboard as MDF emits formaldehyde, which shortens the life of seeds.

THE GARDENER'S CHOICE

Seeds for collection

Many common garden plants set plenty of seed, which is ready for collection when the pod or seed head dries out. Always collect seed from the best specimens only.

Hardy annuals Plants in this group that produce an abundance of seeds include forget-me-not (*Myosotis*), honesty, love-in-a-mist (*Nigella damascena*), marigold (*Calendula*) and poached egg plant (*Limnanthes douglasii*). Seeds from these plants are easy to collect before they fall and can be sown where you want to grow them, or given to gardening friends.

Annuals or biennials Wallflowers (*Erysimum*), pansies, poppies, nasturtium (*Tropaeolum*) and nemesia all set good quantities of seed, which can be sown when required.

Perennials Seeds of primula and cyclamen are best sown as soon as they are ripe, when they will germinate quickly. If stored and dried, germination takes a long time. Lupins, Welsh poppy (*Meconopsis cambrica*) and evening primrose are often short-lived and are best started from seed every few years.

Sweet peas These plants also readily set seed, but remember that the offspring will not be exactly the same as the parent plant. This is particularly true when growing hybrid plants, which often have specific colours and forms only when the same parents are used. This plant variability is caused by cross-pollination by flying insects, such as bees. However, this has often resulted in the accidental production of a new improved variety, so there is no harm in seeing what comes up.

Beds and borders in bloom

Inspired by the cottage garden, where ornamental plants had to jostle for space with vegetables, the most pleasing flower beds are usually dense and varied, and so have a long flowering period. They may look natural, but in fact they need careful planning to avoid dead spots, colour clashes or plants swamped by taller neighbours.

Rosa 'Florian,' evening primrose, phlox and dahlias make a traditional mixed border for the summer.

A well-planned bed

Round or square? The formality of straight lines or the charm of curves? It's up to you to choose. A combination of the two – a basic rectangular shape with curved edges, for example – gives excellent results.

Allow for space A garden you are happy to be in is one where you feel you have room to breathe. Do not try to plant every bit of ground, for an overgrown atmosphere can be oppressive. The planted areas – hedges, shrubs and trees, flower beds and borders, and plants in containers – should take up no more than 50 per cent of your garden. Keep the rest unplanted and reserve it for lawns, paths, steps, terraces and patios to give a feeling of spaciousness.

Make a sketch If you have a large flower bed or border in mind, draw up a plan of the proposed bed, taking the spread and height of each plant into account. Colour your plan, using the colours of the plants you are intending to use to give you a good idea of the overall effect.

Marking out borders You can mark out any shape you want with sand. Just scoop up a handful of dry sand and let it trickle out between your fingers in a thin, even stream to act as a nontoxic, temporary guide for digging. All traces will soon disappear afterwards.

▶ To mark out a circle or semicircle, tie a length of string to a bamboo cane. Fix a bottle filled with sand to the other end of the string, pull it tight and 'draw' your curve with the sand.

▶ To help you mark out the corners of a rectangular bed, use an old wooden vegetable crate as a guide. This will help to ensure your right angles are accurate.

Plan a few surprises Break up the symmetry of flower beds and borders by planting a tree or a bush at one end but not at the other. Strong elements such as climbing and taller plants lend greater weight to their particular part of the border and give a pleasing sense of drama.

Get off to a good start Although they look tempting, do not buy young plants in flower. Choose healthy, compact plants with vibrantly coloured leaves and well-branched stems. The base of the stem should be strongly attached to the root mass, not loose, and the rootball should be damp to the touch. Reject plants with either dry or saturated compost.

Choose quality, not quantity The beauty of a flower bed does not rely solely on the number of plants it contains, but on the harmony of their colour and shape, and the balance of textures, heights and flower sizes that you use. The most successful arrangements comprise no more than about half devoted to flowers, combined with small shrubs or plants with attractive foliage.

Great heights Lend interest to your summer borders by adding some large greenhouse or conservatory plants such as fuchsia, angel's trumpets (*Brugmansia*), oleander (*Nerium oleander*) or long-stemmed verbena. Plunge the pots into the middle of the flower bed – remember that they will need to be watered regularly – or put the plants directly into the soil. Don't forget you'll need to take the plants back inside in autumn.

Experiment with shape and texture

For the middle and back rows in the border, choose plants that are interesting or unusual, whether bushy, climbing, globe-shaped, upright, slender, erect or bristly – there is a great variety from which to choose.
▶ Plant compact perennials such as yarrow (*Achillea ageratum*), wood spurge (*Euphorbia amygdaloides* 'Purpurea') and day lily (*Hemerocallis*) among plants that are leafy or that have tall flowering heads, such as iris, allium, giant feather grass (*Stipa gigantea*) or *Verbena bonariensis*.

A parasol for shade-loving species Many border plants – hostas, ferns and some euphorbias – do not like full sunshine. To protect them, grow them under a tree or shrub, such as a lilac or a Japanese angelica tree (*Aralia elata* 'Aureovariegata'), a beautiful shrub three to six metres high that can even be grown in a tub.

Top tips for a four-season border To keep your flower bed or border interesting as the months go by, stagger the flowering times, combine deciduous plants with evergreens, and plant species with berries, autumn foliage or decorative branches, as well as perennials and winter bulbs.
▶ **For berries** Try beauty berry (*Callicarpa bodinieri* 'Profusion'), spindle tree (*Euonymus europaeus* 'Red Cascade'), *Skimmia japonica* 'Reevesiana', snowberry (*Symphoricarpos orbiculatus*) and crab apple (*Malus sieboldii*).
▶ **For autumn foliage** Plant smoke bush (*Cotinus coggygria*), American smoke tree (*Cotinus obovatus*), *Fothergilla major*, spindle tree, purple chokeberry (*Aronia* x *prunifolia*) and Japanese maple (*Acer palmatum*).
▶ **For decorative bark** Consider red-barked dogwood (*Cornus alba*) and ornamental raspberry (*Rubus cockburnianus* or *R. biflorus*), both with decorative branches.
▶ **Winter evergreen** Try Christmas rose (*Helleborus niger*), pansy (*Viola*), heather (*Calluna*) and primula.
▶ **Winter bulbs** For a good display in winter, plant crocus, snowdrop (*Galanthus nivalis*), dwarf iris (*Iris reticulata*), narcissus, striped squill (*Puschkinia libanotica*) and glory-of-the-snow (*Chionodoxa*).

Bedding plants The term 'bedding plants' can be applied to annuals, biennials and half-hardy or tender perennials (a name applied to perennials used as annuals and pulled up at the end of the season, such as geraniums). They include marguerites, lobelia, petunia (right), busy lizzie (*Impatiens*) and golden eye (*Bidens*) and are used to embellish flower beds and borders for just one season, from spring until the first frosts. You can buy them as plugs or young plants instead of growing them from seed.
▶ Do not keep bedding plants beyond October or November when they stop growing. Just pull them up and compost them.

Indispensable foliage

Here is a selection of the best grasses and decorative foliage plants for your flower beds.

DELICATE FOLIAGE
Fennel (*Foeniculum vulgare* 'Purpureum'), wormwood (Artemisia 'Powis Castle') ❶, rosemary-leaved willow (*Salix rosmarinifolia*), male fern (*Dryopteris filix-mas*) and lady fern (*Athyrium filix-femina*)

TO GIVE MOVEMENT
Quaking grass (*Briza media*), pony tail grass (*Stipa tenuissima*), fountain grass (*Pennisetum setaceum*) ❷, blue fescue (*Festuca glauca*), zebra grass (*Miscanthus sinensis* 'Zebrinus'), lyme grass (*Leymus arenarius*), and weeping sedge (*Carex pendula*)

TO ADD HEIGHT
Pampas grass and burning bush (*Bassia scoparia*) ❸, and the climbers birthwort (*Aristolochia clematitis*) and the golden hop (*Humulus lupulus* 'Aureus')

TO SOFTEN BRIGHT COLOURS
Silver-grey leaves Woolly lamb's ears (*Stachys byzantina* 'Silver Carpet') ❹, cineraria, curry plant (*Helichrysum italicum*).
Golden leaves Bowles golden sedge (*Carex elata* 'Aurea'), hakone grass (*Hakonechloa macra* 'Aureola')
Blue leaves *Euphorbia myrsinites*, hosta 'Blue Blush' or 'Hadspen Blue'.
Bronze or purple leaves New Zealand flax (*Phormium tenax* 'Bronze Baby'), *Heuchera micrantha* 'Palace Purple', *Sedum telephium maximum* 'Atropurpureum' and purple bugle (*Ajuga reptans* 'Burgundy Glow')

Compose your display

A layered effect A flower bed should be made up of three or four plant layers, getting gradually taller towards the back. This way, the bed will have interest and structure when viewed from the front. Heights of the individual layers, working from the front, can be from 10–30cm, 30–70cm, 70–120cm, and over 120cm in height. Make sure your arrangement contains a good variety of plant types in each of these layers.

A restricted colour palette Create a bold effect by using no more than one or two dominant colours in your beds. You can add a third colour if it is white or black (dark violet, actually, as black flowers do not occur in nature). Choose monochrome and complementary colours, such as those in the following suggested schemes.

▶ **Fruits of the forest** Combine these deep pink and white flowers in full sun on dry soil: *Achillea millefolium* 'Cerise Queen', *Verbena bonariensis*, bear's breeches (*Acanthus spinosus*), ice plant (*Sedum spectabile* 'Brilliant') (left), shown here matched with the chrysanthemum *Dendranthema* 'Rakhel', and fleabane (*Erigeron karvinskianus*).

▶ **White and peppermint** Jack-in-the-pulpit (*Arisaema sikokianum*), lesser periwinkle (*Vinca minor* 'Alba'), plantain lily (*Hosta sieboldiana* 'Elegans'), Mexican orange blossom (*Choisya ternata* 'Aztec Pearl'), bee balm (*Monarda* 'Snow Witch'), cosmos and spider flower (*Cleome hassleriana*) (left) make a striking display in partial shade on moist soil.

▶ **Blue and green** Deep shade is often very moist. The blues and greens of bugle (*Ajuga reptans*), plantain lily (*Hosta* 'Bressingham Blue'), lady's mantle (*Alchemilla mollis*), giant forget-me-not (*Brunnera macrophylla*) (left) and blue corydalis (*Corydalis flexuosa*) are a successful combination.

A sympathetic backdrop Shrubs or a thicket of bamboo make a good backdrop for a bed. So do climbers such as golden hop, jasmine and clematis, and giant perennials such as plume poppy (*Macleaya cordata*). Climbers have the added advantage of occupying very little ground space, which makes them particularly useful if your bed is narrow or if your garden is short of space.

For a natural look Establish your flower bed as an extension of some other existing feature in your garden. Merge it into another group of plants such as a hedge or a bed of shrubs. Or back it onto some hard landscaping such as a pathway, some steps, a low wall, a pergola or patio. A bed in the middle of the lawn will always look artificial.

*Create tiers of plants in deep borders: dwarf zinnias at the front, then African marigolds (*Tagetes erecta*) and cornflower (*Centaurea cyanus*), with clumps of dahlias as a backdrop.*

A decorative mulch In addition to preventing the growth of weeds, retaining moisture in the soil and slowing erosion caused by heavy rain, a mulch can be decorative too. Spread between the plants, a layer of coloured gravel or pebbles hides the bare soil and accentuates the flowers and foliage.

Raising interest Do you wish your flat garden was more interesting? A raised flower bed can give your favourite plants a higher profile. Build low walls (15–20cm high) on a concrete foundation buried about 10cm below the surface. Use concrete, brick or stone for the walls, depending on your surroundings. Fill the bed with a mixture of garden soil and compost, coarse sand or gravel. Overlapping beds of different heights can look good bordering a terrace.

▶ A raised flower bed gives height to any planting schemes featuring perennials, bulbs, annuals and biennials.

THE GARDENER'S CHOICE

Flowers with a lovely scent

Plant these flowers at the front of the border, under a window or wherever you will be able to savour their fragrance.

In spring *Dianthus superbus*, wallflower, tulip, hyacinth (*Hyacinthus orientalis* 'Delft Blue') and paper-white narcissus (*Narcissus papyraceus*)

In summer Madonna lily, acidanthera, chocolate cosmos (*Cosmos astrosanguineus*), lavender, sand pink (*Dianthus arenarius*), sweet alyssum, tobacco flower, mignonette and night-scented stock (*Matthiola longipetala*)

In autumn Sage, blue spiraea (*Caryopteris x Clandonensis*), butterfly bush and chaste tree (*Vitex agnus castus*)

In winter Sweet box (*Sarcococca hookeriana*) and garland flower (*Daphne odora* 'Aureomarginata')

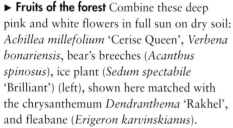
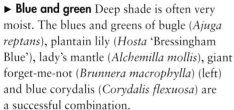

▶ For anyone who has trouble bending down to ground level to weed and plant, raised beds can make gardening less of a trial. If you make the walls 50–60cm high and 25–30cm thick, you can even sit on them while tending the garden, making it an altogether more relaxing experience.

Planning a raised flower bed When selecting plants for a raised bed, make sure it is deep enough for them. Allow a depth of about one metre for a tall shrub.
▶ If you need to use soil that is very different from that in the rest of the garden, for example if you need to use ericaceous compost for an acid-loving plant and your garden soil is chalky, cover the bottom and inside walls of the bed with a porous membrane to prevent the soils from mixing. Do not forget to provide drainage – cover the bottom of the bed with a 10cm layer of gravel.

Improve the contours of your garden Give your garden height and enhance the scale of your plants by building up a mounded bed. On a free-standing mound, put the tallest plants in the middle, with the smaller ones spreading down to the edges. If you create a slope against a wall, your tallest species, positioned at the back, will have even more impact.

Top tips for edging There are several good ways to separate flower beds from the lawn or paving that borders them.
▶ **Construct a hard edge** Wooden boards, bricks or buried slates will hold back plants that tend to escape from the border into the lawn, such as plants with rhizomes.
▶ **Plant a border** Box, cotton lavender, geranium 'Johnson's Blue' or lady's mantle all have evergreen foliage.
▶ **Use ground-cover perennials** Elephant's ears (*Bergenia*), lesser periwinkle (*Vinca minor*) or Japanese spurge (*Pachysandra terminalis*) will merge together to hide the bare earth.
▶ **Grow grassy plants** Planting Golden pearlwort (*Sagina subulata* 'Aurea') between paving stones at the edge of the border will create a natural, softening effect.

Keep gravel tidy If you want to create a gravel path alongside a flower bed, make sure the bed is slightly lower than the path to prevent soil, bark or other mulch material from spilling over onto it.

An access path If you create a rectangular border of hardy perennials, put a path in front of it, however narrow. This will give you access for maintenance, allow spreading plants in the front row to spill over attractively, and ensure a smooth transition to the lawn that makes mowing easier.
▶ For really large beds, arrange a narrow path 40–50cm wide along the back of the bed to make access easier.

Natural mulches

Mulches can be used to prevent moisture loss from the soil, suppress weeds and to protect plants from winter frosts. They can also act as an ornamental setting that complements the colours of the plants, or to provide long-term nutrients that are released when it rains, or when the bed is watered. Some types also give protection from slugs and other pests that are deterred by dry, sharp surfaces.

MOISTURE RETENTION
Grass clippings ❶ Although not very decorative, this is the most easily obtainable of all the mulches. It provides good moisture retention and some nutrients.
Crushed bark ❷ This is more decorative than grass clippings, but it can be expensive. It also acidifies the soil so use it only around acid-loving plants. It comes in various sizes: use the coarsest for large beds and at the base of trees or bushes.

Pine needles ❸ Pine needles retain moisture, although they are slow to break down and release nutrients. They too are very acidic, so they can harm non acid-loving plants.
Woodchips ❹ These make a good, moisture-retaining mulch for the base of perennials and small annuals. They are fairly readily available, although a cheaper option would be to chip your own prunings.

PROTECTION FROM SLUGS
Cocoa bean shells ❺ These are almost rotproof and fine enough to give good cover. They deter slugs, but unfortunately can be very harmful to dogs if they eat the shells.
Gravels ❻ For an ornamental covering, use one of the many types of gravel available in garden centres and from quarries. For protection from slugs and snails for hostas and other vulnerable plants, sharp-edged gravel or crushed seashells or eggshells are best, although shell will gradually make the soil more alkaline, so it is unsuitable for plants that prefer acidic conditions.

IMPROVING THE SOIL
Garden compost To add a balanced, slow-release fertiliser to your soil, in late spring spread ordinary, well-rotted garden compost around the roots, making sure it is clear of the stems. Compost also improves the general condition of the soil, making it easier to dig and more pleasant to work with.
Manure If you have access to farmyard manure, you have another invaluable aid for soil improvement. Most forms are useful but must be well rotted.

Flowers that last and last

Mainstays of the old-fashioned flower border, herbaceous perennials regrow from their rootstock in spring after they have been cut back, so you don't need to replant every year. Some perennials are evergreen, and you can enjoy their attractive foliage all year round. Choose these to keep your beds interesting when everything else has faded – a few of them flower even in the depths of winter.

Well-planted perennials

Keep your distance Plant labels and seed packets usually indicate how many plants you can grow in a square metre, enabling you to work out how many you will need to fill your flower bed. Increase rather than decrease the recommended spacing between plants to permit adequate air circulation and allow plenty of room for the plants to spread naturally. It is important that you keep in mind the final height of the plants when planting them out in a bed – you are aiming to keep them in the right proportion to their eventual width.

When setting out plants, make sure they are properly spaced.

Perennials are ideal for softening the edges of paving and brickwork, giving a weathered, old-world air to the garden.

Gain a season The traditional advice is to plant perennials in spring, but if you put them in at the beginning of autumn they will have time to settle in before the cold weather begins and hard frosts set in. Protect very young plants beneath a mulch of dry leaves or fern fronds, or cover with sacking when there is a frost. By spring, the rootstock will already be established and new growth will begin sooner. The new shoots will grow quickly and the numbers of flowers will be greater in the first year of flowering.
▶ If you are gardening in a harsh climate or in heavy soil that becomes waterlogged in winter, it is still advisable to plant in spring. Tender Japanese anemones or grasses may not survive if planted in autumn.
▶ Be careful not to make a depression around autumn-planted perennials, as water will collect there, and this can be harmful in the winter cold.

Buy well-developed plants To speed up the time it takes for plants to settle in, buy established specimens in large pots. They will be between one and three years old, or older if the pot is large, and take much less time to develop dense growth than young or bare-root plants.
▶ Before buying any plant, check that it is in good condition and that the rootstock is sprouting a number of young shoots.

At arm's length When you create a bed of mixed perennials, consider its dimensions from a practical as well as an aesthetic point of view. You must be able to reach all the plants in a flower bed for pruning, clearing and cutting flowers for bringing indoors. For this reason, the length of your outstretched arm is the best yardstick for determining the width of a flower bed. If you can reach the bed from behind as well, then you can allow two arm lengths.
▶ The longer the flower bed, the more effective it will be. Bear in mind, though, it's better to repeat sequences than to plant too many different species. Three to five species is enough for a single-depth border five metres long. You will need twice as many if the bed is double depth.

Try out new plants If you want to experiment with an unfamiliar plant, try planting two or three in different locations around your garden. After a year, you will be able to see where it flourishes and can move the other plants to the best location.

Plant a vertical garden Make the most of nooks and crannies in low dry-stone or old brick walls and create a miniature vertical garden.
▶ Fill gaps with a moistened mixture of soil and compost and plant using plugs or even seedlings. Choose species that will tolerate dry soil and poor conditions, such as erigeron and saxifrage, and they will take root and multiply without any help from you. Water them only in hot weather or long periods of drought to prevent them drying out completely.
▶ Plant trailing species on top of low walls. Choose species that need the minimum of nutrition, such as sedum and

Cold shock treatment

Some perennial seeds need a cold period to emerge from their dormant state and begin to germinate. This principle, called stratification, involves exposing the seeds to cold temperatures to encourage germination the following spring. It works particularly well for campanulas and primulas.
▶ In autumn, sow seeds in small pots filled with a mixture of soil and sand, and cover with a layer of fine gravel. Stand the pots in the garden, in a trench filled with sand to allow for good drainage.
▶ You can also put the seeds in the refrigerator for two to six weeks before sowing them in spring.
▶ Watch carefully for germination in spring, and prick out in new pots as soon as the seedlings can be handled.

YESTERDAY & TODAY

A lively old friend

Mint – an old favourite in the flower border as well as the herb bed – is a natural insect repellent. But it will invade your whole garden in no time if the soil and location are to its liking. A traditional way of keeping mint in check is to plant it in a pot and sink the pot into the soil to prevent it from overpowering other plants in the flower bed.
 But be aware that the creeping rhizomes can still sometimes climb over the rim of the pot or out through the drainage holes at the bottom. If you want a large clump of mint, transplant several plants into a very large pot and grow it on the patio.

cerastium. You can choose from a wider range of plants if you're prepared to add a little compost from time to time. In that case, try sea thrift (*Armeria maritima*) or aubrieta.

Water before planting

Soak planting holes and wait until the water has drained away before planting. This will make it easier to work the soil and the roots of your plant will be in less danger of drying out. Water or, preferably, soak new plants before transplanting them. The freshly watered compost will hold together better and the roots will quickly re-establish.

▶ If the weather is wet and your soil is already waterlogged, wait until it dries out a little before planting. Meanwhile, stand your plants outside in the rain.

Gravel lightens the soil If you have heavy, damp or perpetually waterlogged soil, add gravel to improve it. Spread a 10–15cm layer of gravel – the depth depends on how heavy your soil is – on top of the bed. Decide where you want to place your perennials and plant them, adding compost around the plants. The gravel will gradually sink into the soil, lightening its structure.
▶ To prevent the root collar of alpine plants from rotting in winter, surround the stem of each plant with a 5cm layer of gravel or loose chippings.

For thrifty, patient gardeners Seeds cost less than plants, but even the fastest-growing perennials take two years to flower from seed, while the slowest, like peonies, can take six to eight years. The best plants to grow from seed are those that are difficult to find in the nursery or garden centre, or plants that are expensive to buy in large numbers if you are planting a new garden.

▶ Seeds should be sown in early summer in a shady out-of-the-way corner of your garden or in a cold frame. Sow thinly, adding organic matter and sharp sand to improve the soil.

A good mix of plants

At home in moist soil With their bright, varied colours, primulas are probably the prettiest perennials for moist soil. Many of the 600 varieties of primula listed grow well around ponds and in damp ground. *Primula bulleyana*, one of the most spectacular, comes in every shade of yellow, orange, salmon, red and purple, and flowers from May to July. *Primula japonica*, the Japanese primrose, flowers in midsummer and boasts white, pink or red flowers.

Insect-repelling plants Aromatic plants, such as mint, lemon balm, thyme, sage and artemisia, keep annoying insects at bay with their strong fragrance. They also make attractive borders for flower beds and around the kitchen garden. Sage wards off flies when planted near carrots, geraniums keep mosquitoes away, and lavender and lemon balm repel midges.

Tried and tested colour combinations The wide variety of perennials available allows you to be creative in your use of colour. A useful tip is that perennials in dark, vibrant colours are enhanced by paler shades of the same hue.
▶ **Single-colour plantings** These can be dull so widen your range of colours for a better effect. Introduce green and silver shades to whites, add violet to blues, pick out yellows with pale lemon or heighten them with gold. Temper warm reds, which can be garish, with a more elegant crimson.
▶ **One prevailing colour** Use a single colour per season as the main shade in multicoloured flower beds to avoid jarring, especially over large areas.
▶ **Bold colour mixes** If you like mixing red and orange, use them in delicate flowers, as this lessens the clashing effect.

Labour-saving treatment for slopes Grassy slopes, which are hard to mow, can be planted instead with ground-cover perennials, whose roots also keep the soil from sliding. Hypericum is one of the best plants for this purpose, along with oregano and agapanthus in mild climates. Epimedium, dead nettle and creeping bugle are unbeatable under trees.

Planting a herbaceous perennial

1 If it is dry, soak the plant in water while you dig a hole twice as large and deep as the rootball.

2 Add some garden compost to the bottom of the hole, and mix it in. Add some slow-release organic fertiliser.

3 Water the planting hole. This helps your plant settle in and is essential if the soil is very dry in hot weather.

4 Place the plant in the hole with the top of the rootball level with the ground.

5 Replace the soil around the rootball, firming it down to remove all air pockets. Water well.

6 When the water has soaked in, spread a thick layer of mulch to preserve moisture around the roots.

THE GARDENER'S CHOICE

Cottage garden favourites ▶

Golden marguerite ❶ and gaura ❺ *Anthemis tinctoria* and *Gaura lindheimeri* 'Siskiyou Pink' last well as cut flowers.

Primula ❷ *Primula bulleyana*, one of the most charming species, likes being in damp soil near water. *Primula sieboldii* has a bright white centre and deep pink petals and enjoys a slightly acid, damp soil.

Corydalis ❸ *Corydalis flexuous* grows best in partial shade and acid soils. Try *Corydalis ochroleuca* in a well-drained spot, perhaps tucked against a wall or on a slope.

Bee balm ❹ *Monarda didyma* likes its roots to be cool and its head in the sun. *Monarda* 'Prarienacht' has purple-mauve flowers and distinctively veined leaves.

Foxgloves ❻ All *Digitalis* thrive in the shade. *Digitalis lutea* has been grown since the 16th century; it is only 60cm tall, with pale yellow flowers.

Perennials

Borders of colour Lupins are popular perennials, largely due to the fact that they thrive in the English climate, but also because of their striking shape and colours.

▶ *Lupinus* 'Lulu' (left) is a hardy perennial which can be grown from seed and will flower in the first year. Reaching a height of 60cm, it is shorter than other lupins and is therefore known as a dwarf lupin. Despite its size *Lupinus* 'Lulu' is a splendid plant with a good colour range and is ideal for herbaceous borders in small gardens.

▶ The sowing period for lupins is January to July if they are to flower in the first year. Seeds should be sown in pots or trays and covered with a little compost.

▶ Lupins need full sun to partial shade, and actually prefer sandy soil to a rich soil, as the latter encourages soft growth.

A scented garden There are many scented and perfumed perennials. Choose phlox, sweet rocket (*Hesperis*), wallflowers, carnations, romneya and violet for a garden filled with fragrance. Aromatic plants like mint, lemon balm, anthemis, monarda, sage, verbena and santolina form a fragrant background to which you can add new plants every year. Lavender, although actually an evergreen shrub rather than a perennial, is one of the most popular scented plants and is fairly easy to grow. Position fragrant plants along garden paths so that you can savour them as you pass by.

Classic restraint, with a twist A flower bed made up of only one or two species is easy to maintain, but your garden could look static if this is the only style of planting it contains. There are several ways to add interest to these beds.

Patches of cool blue delphiniums contrast well with warm yellow achillea and other bright meadow flowers.

Dividing a clump of flowering perennials

1 Dig up the crown with a fork, lifting the rootball without damaging the roots. Shake to remove the soil.

2 Divide the clump into at least two sections, using your hands for small plants or a fork for larger ones.

3 Immediately replant these sections, selecting those with healthy roots and removing the middle sections of plants that are getting old.

4 Replace the soil removed from the hole and firm well with your hand for small plants or with your foot for large perennials. Then water.

▶ Give pace to your flower bed by introducing a few lupins, delphiniums or tall campanulas at irregular intervals.

▶ Experiment with colour by adding contrasting touches. Introduce a bright shade if the flower bed is dark, white if blooms are red, and blue or deep violet if the bed consists of warm pink, orange, salmon or yellow.

▶ Combine these two approaches for an even more striking effect. Plant several midnight blue delphiniums in a large flower bed of yellow achillea, or let some crimson lupins emerge from a carpet of blue geraniums.

Compact borders save time Perennial borders can be a good idea for gardeners who are pressed for time. Opt for compact species that retain their regular shape over the years with little maintenance. The best species, from the smallest to the tallest, are perennial candytuft (*Iberis sempervirens*), which is covered in white flowers in the spring, bellflowers (*Campanula carpatica*, C. 'G.F. Wilson', C. *portenschlagiana* or C. *poscharksyana*), oregano (*Origanum vulgare*), carnations (*Dianthus plumarius*) and common rue (*Ruta graveolens*), with its dense grey-blue foliage. Other taller species include geranium varieties such as *Geranium sanguineum*, *G. renardii* or *G. pratense*, common bistort (*Persicaria bistorta*) and catmint (*Nepeta nervosa*).

Single-colour beds can be cool and sophisticated, like this silver border of centranthus, foxglove and stachys.

Reduce your workload Cut down on maintenance by planting perennials in large patches and restricting the number of species used. This means in autumn you can cut back the dying plants all at the same time, using a pair of shears to work quickly across the entire bed.

The hardiest perennials

Perennials thrive in difficult conditions, and they are remarkably long-lived. Here are some of the most robust.

In poor, dry soils Valerian, erigeron, gaura, antennaria, potentilla, anthemis, achillea, hollyhocks, wormwood (*Artemisia*) and centaurea

In shady areas Foxgloves (*Digitalis*), astrantia, lady's mantle (*Alchemilla*), lungwort (*Pulmonaria*), euphorbia, aconites and giant forget-me-not (*Brunnera*)

In chalky soils Achillea, limonium, chrysanthemums (*Leucanthemum* and *Dendranthemum*), anthemis, centaurea, hellebores, helianthemum, gypsophila, gaillardia, valerian, aubrieta, asters, bergenia and arabis

In acid soils Corydalis, potentilla, Pasque flower (*Pulsatilla*) and lily of the valley (*Convallaria*)

Long-flowering perennials Achillea, anthemis, penstemon, verbena, cranesbill (*Geranium*), gaura, bee balm (*Monarda*), diascia, bellflowers (*Campanula*), centaurea, coreopsis, gaillardia, nepeta, potentilla and delphinium

▶ Wait until winter has passed, however, to cut back tender perennials such as verbascum and salvia. The dead stems protect the crown during bad weather and can also look very attractive covered with hoarfrost in winter.

Successful transplants Most perennials can be easily transplanted, so long as you prepare the planting area with a compost mixture and are careful not to damage the roots when you move them. The dormant season is the best time to do this. If you don't have the chance to do this in the autumn, avoid the cold weather and wait to transplant until early spring, just before regrowth begins.

Moving home-loving plants Hostas, peonies and hellebores do not like being moved and take a long time to become established. If you have to move them, make sure you take up the entire rootball and water frequently during the first year until their roots have spread. Flowering after transplanting is unpredictable however, so be patient.
▶ Be careful not to bury peony buds too deeply. Make sure they are planted just below the surface, or there is a chance that they will never flower.

With a mixed all-yellow border your single-colour bed will be vibrant and exciting and never lack impact.

Always wear gloves
Never handle spurge (*Euphorbia*), common rue (*Ruta graveolens*) or giant hogweed (*Heracleum mantegazzianum*) with bare hands. They are poisonous and can irritate the skin. It is essential to wear gardening gloves when planting, cutting, dividing or transplanting these species. In fact, it is a good idea to protect your nails and hands with gloves when planting or tending any perennials.

Perennials for the vase Many perennials will last well as cut stems in a vase. Pick them in the morning, just after they open and before the sun is too high. The best species for cutting are agapanthus, anthemis, astilbe, bee balm (*Monarda didyma*), centaurea, chrysanthemum (*Leucanthemum*), coneflower (*Echinacea*), crocosmia, delphinium, dicentra, epilobium, gaura, gypsophila, heliopsis, liatris, peonies, phlox, primula, rose campion (*Lychnis*), salvia, golden rod (*Solidago*), sunflowers (*Helianthus*) and valerian.
► If you like arrangements of dried flowers, then grow anaphalis, achillea, Chinese lantern (*Physalis alkekengii*), camomile, globe thistle (*Echinops*), honesty (*Lunaria annua*) and statice (*Limonium*).

Prolific perennials
Spreading, creeping and self-seeding perennials will cover walls, banks and other large areas in just a couple of years.

Helianthemum This spreading plant rapidly carpets large areas of sandy, well-drained soil, as long as it is in the sun.

Bellflower *Campanula portenschlagiana* and *C. carpatica* (left) will cover low walls and edge paths in record time.

Geranium All types of hardy geranium spread quickly, including *Geranium macrorrhizum*, *G. pratense*, *G. sanguineum* and *G. endresii*. They can be invasive in small gardens.

Foxgloves If you are not careful, foxgloves (*Digitalis*) will run riot in sun or shade. A single plant can seed itself over an entire garden. To restrict it to one area, cut the flower stems before they have completely shed their flowers and the seeds will not mature.

Top tips for staking Tall plants, or those with heavy flowers, often need staking to keep them upright.
► **Peonies and delphiniums** (right) Insert twiggy branches from hazel or silver birch into the soil around the clump and slant half of them inwards to support the centre of the plants. You can also buy cages or linked stakes, through which the plant will grow.
► **Delphiniums** (right) Insert a single, sturdy stake in the ground near the base when planting, being careful not to damage the root system, and attach the stem to the stake as it grows. The fastener should be flexible so it does not impede the growth of the stem.
► **Maintaining an edge** For discreet staking along the entire length of the border, put in a thin wooden stake at each end of the bed and extend raffia, string or green plastic garden twine between the stakes (right). The support will soon be hidden by the foliage.
► **Clumping perennials** Insert three or four bamboo or plastic stakes in the ground around the clump and tie a length of string or raffia around them, about halfway up (right, below). You can raise the height gradually as the clump grows.

Hosepipe damage It is surprising how much damage you can do to flower beds by dragging your hosepipe behind you when you water. Avoid this when setting out your beds by putting in some small wooden stakes to guide your hose safely past vulnerable plants.

Opt for easy-to-grow species Heuchera, elephant's ears (*Bergenia*), santolina, silene, salvia, phlox, lychnis, campanula, aquilegia, Hattie's pincushion (*Astrantia*), hellebores and tradescantia are all relatively undemanding.

Flower beds with good edges Protect your grass and make it easier to mow by creating a paved path about 30–50cm wide along the edge of your flower beds. The bushy foliage of the border plants will soon spill over to soften the edges: much better than them spreading onto the lawn, getting in the way when you are mowing and killing the grass.

Give your perennials a longer flowering season

Plant protection

Glass cloches are expensive, but they are ideal for protecting young seedlings from late frosts and delicate early blooms, such as hellebore, from the weather. If you use cloches, remember that condensation and sunny days can cause temperatures to soar in these miniature glasshouses.

▶ Empty plant pots provide excellent protection for delicate perennial rootstocks. Choose those with a diameter twice as large as your plants, fill them with dry leaves or straw and turn them upside down over the crown. Frost-resistant terracotta pots are least likely to blow away, but plastic pots are much cheaper.

Two flowerings are better than one Some perennials, such as hardy geraniums, delphiniums and lupins, can flower twice each year if you take the trouble to cut them back as soon as their first flush has finished. Water the freshly pruned plants liberally and feed with organic fertiliser.

Late-flowering perennials continue the pageant of summer and autumn colour right up until the harsh frosts begin.

Taking herbaceous perennial cuttings

1 Cut 15–20cm sections from the year's young shoots or from stems with no flowers.

2 Recut just below a node at the base of a bud, and remove all the leaves below.

3 Replant the cutting in a mixture of sand and potting compost, then water liberally.

4 Keep the cuttings warm (15–18°C) under a fleece or plastic sheet suspended by stakes.

▶ To phase the flowering of nepetas, asters and summer phloxes, cut back every other plant to about half its height in late May. This will also improve the stability of tall asters and help keep them from flopping over. Dividing plants is another way to produce a lot more flowers and helps to maintain healthy all-round plant growth.

Holiday clearing If you are going away in summer for more than two weeks, remove all the blooms from your plants, even those that have not yet faded. This prevents them from going to seed and exhausting the plants in your absence.

A little boost Since perennials remain in place for many years, give them a healthy supply of organic material when you first plant them. They will recover from their move quickly and establish themselves with renewed vigour. Before setting the plants in, mix leaf-mould, garden compost or any well-decomposed organic matter into the soil at the bottom of the planting hole. In spring, spread sifted garden compost around the base of the plants to stimulate regrowth.

Annual cutting back At the end of the year, cut back ground-cover perennials to keep them thick and encourage young shoots to grow more vigorously. With bushy species, such as cotton lavender and thyme, cut back stems to two-thirds their height after flowering, or at the end of winter.
▶ To ensure that clumps of plants continue to grow and regenerate, cut back one out of every three plants each year. This maintains their appearance while encouraging regrowth.

Overwintering geraniums and pelargoniums Also known as cranesbills, hardy geraniums such as *Geranium grandiflorum* (left) can stay in the garden without receiving any special attention during the winter. Bedding geraniums from the *Pelargonium* family (below left), however, are a different story. They are called tender perennials because they continue to grow all winter in frost-free climates, but they are often treated as annuals in harsher areas. If you enjoy these vividly coloured flowers, make sure you prepare them for overwintering by the end of October. You can use several techniques for this.

▶ **Pelargoniums grown in pots** Bring them inside just as they are. In spring, you can put the plants back outside, cut the stems to two-thirds of their height and trim off the dry leaves. Your scented pelargoniums will retain their bushiness and keep growing year after year. Alternatively, in autumn, cut the stems back to 10cm above soil level, remove any remaining leaves and bring the pots in out of the frost.
▶ **Pelargoniums in the ground** Lift the plants in October, pot them up and put them in a greenhouse. Keep the foliage dry and water them as little as possible – the compost should be allowed to dry out between waterings. In spring, put the plants back outside.

Dressing pelargoniums for the winter This technique rejuvenates older plants. Dig them up and 'dress' them by cutting off the stems, leaving only about 15cm with no leaves, and trimming the dried roots. Then place the plants at well-spaced intervals in boxes of dry sand that just covers the roots. Keep them in adequate light in a cool but frost-free place until late winter when you will see new shoots appear. Repot the plants so they can start growing again.

Layer your carnations Carnations often die out after three years of growth, but regular layering provides young plants that will gradually replace the old ones. Once plants a year old

To 'dress' pelargoniums before overwintering them in a greenhouse, cut back their stems and dried-out roots.

or more have flowered, take a side stem with no flowers and bend it down so that it touches the soil. Trim off the leaves, leaving several at the end. Make a narrow slit in the side of the stem and insert this section in the soil, using a small hook to hold it down. Water with a fine spray. After six weeks roots will have formed, and it should be possible to separate the new plant from the mother plant with a sharp knife and transplant it. This technique is ideal for carnations in borders.

UNDER GLASS

Spring cuttings from chrysanthemums

It is easy to take cuttings from this popular perennial by removing young shoots in spring, when new growth emerges from the base of the plant. This is the perfect opportunity to prepare a large number of new plants, which will add a splash of colour to areas that may be lacking in young flowers later in the year. You can also take cuttings from delphiniums and lupins in the same way.
▶ Remove young shoots that are about 5cm long, including a small part of the old main stem. Trim off all the lower leaves, leaving a few at the tip, and make a clean cut across the bottom of the cutting. Replant in small pots filled with cutting compost. Water and keep warm in a greenhouse or cold frame, though placing a plastic bag over the pot also helps. Repot individually after the cuttings have taken root, then plant them out in the garden.

By combining propagation techniques, you can quickly and inexpensively achieve the look of a long-established garden.

▶ **Root cuttings** Dig up a plant during its dormant period, and remove a few root sections as thick as your little finger and 7–10cm in length. Replant the mother plant as soon as you have taken the cuttings. Make a slanted cut along the narrowest end of each cutting: this is where the new roots will grow. Plant each cutting upright in compost and sharp sand, cover with approximately 2cm of compost and finish with a layer of sand. Finally, place under a cold frame or in a frost-free greenhouse or porch for the winter. In spring, you will see the first shoots emerge.

▶ **Self-seeding** Lupins and aquilegia are also difficult to divide, but they usually seed themselves around the mother plant. When the plant has shed its flowers, simply leave the stems intact and let nature take its course. Transplant the new seedlings if you wish.

Harvesting seeds Collect seeds when the seed pod comes to maturity, but before they are dispersed naturally. To avoid missing the right moment, gather the seed pods when they are changing colour and drying out, or cover them with paper bags in order to catch the seeds as soon as the pods open. Shake the paper bags over a piece of paper to ensure that all of the seeds fall out, then leave the seeds to dry in a sheltered place.

Divide and rule When perennials are well established and happy in their environment, they have just one goal – to grow taller and bigger. This means that sooner or later they will have to be divided, before the most vigorous, such as hardy geraniums, alchemilla and artemisia, overwhelm the less robust plants in your flower beds.

▶ There are two key periods for dividing perennials. Divide spring perennials in June or July and summer-flowering or autumn-flowering plants in March. Water them well in the weeks following division and, if necessary, remove some of the leaves to limit water loss.

▶ Never transplant a perennial without dividing it first.

A new lease of life As they get older, herbaceous crowns become less vigorous, which means they often lose their central leaves. Give them a new lease of life by lifting them and cutting away the oldest parts of the plant, leaving the younger, outer sections intact. Proceed as if dividing the clump normally but, instead of splitting the plant into smaller pieces, clean it by removing old and damaged roots. Without allowing the roots to dry out, replant immediately in well-loosened soil, then firm it down to remove any air pockets, and finally, water liberally.

Difficult to divide Japanese anemones, acanthus, thistles and oriental poppies do not divide well because they have only a few fleshy roots, known as taproots. To get new plants you will have to take root cuttings.

Thinning out, disbudding and pinching

Thinning out Perennial seedlings should be thinned out when the plants have reached a height of about 10cm. Remove one out of every two or three plants, depending on their mature spread, and either discard or transplant them.

Disbudding Disbud perennials with large flowers, such as chrysanthemums, to produce a showy single bloom. Wait until most of the side buds have emerged along with the central bud, then remove all but the central bud. The resulting flower will be magnificent.

Pinching The opposite of disbudding, this technique forces the stems to branch out and produce a greater number of flowers. Pinching works well on perennials that branch easily, such as rudbeckia and helenium, and is best done when the plant has reached a third of its height. Nip out the top 3–5cm of the stems with your fingers or secateurs.

Beautiful long-lasting foliage

Ornamental foliage plants adorn your garden for much longer than flowers. They brighten up shady spots, carpet the ground beneath trees and shrubs and in Victorian times were used in gravel gardens. Some of them are evergreen perennials, and others take on striking tones for winter.

The long, arching sprays of miscanthus form an elegant contrast to the upright clumps of rosemary around them.

Large-leaved plants

A magnificent show These shade-loving giants flourish in cool positions and spread rapidly, which makes them useful as ground cover where nothing else will grow. But it is important not to let their roots dry out in summer.
▶ In shady places, opt for ligularia, filipendula, petasites, rodgersia and macleaya.
▶ Gunnera, acanthus and ornamental rhubarb (*Rheum palmatum*) will tolerate sunshine and shade.
▶ Hostas will develop into large clumps in east-facing gardens, which enjoy sunshine in the mornings and shaded warmth in the afternoons.

Controlling slugs and snails These pests are very partial to hostas. Put an end to disappearing seedlings and leaves shot with holes by spreading a thick layer of wood ash, sawdust, sand or sharp gravel around the base of the plants in spring. Slugs hate anything that sticks to their mucus or slime.

Finding a sheltered home for a rodgersia This plant has magnificent leaves similar to, although much bigger than, those of the chestnut tree. It likes very wet, even waterlogged, soil and a sheltered position. To give it the protection it needs, pick a position beneath deciduous trees where it will flourish. You will need to water its foliage when the weather is very hot and make sure the soil does not dry out completely.

Taming the gunnera A work of art in its own right, the gunnera has rounded, lobed leaves one to two metres wide and leaf stalks two to three metres tall! Plant it in the spring, in moist or wet soil and full sun, ideally near the margins of a pond. In other locations, be sure to water it regularly.
▶ Allow a space of three to four metres between the base of each plant. The gunnera takes root quite slowly and does not like being moved.
▶ In late autumn, fold the leaves down over the plant. In cold areas, supplement this protective covering with a thick layer of dead leaves kept in place with conifer branches.

Keeping giants in check In small gardens, plant clumps of large-leaved perennials in big containers and plunge them into the soil. This will keep them from growing too big. You can also gradually uproot stems that are too invasive, particularly those of the winter heliotrope (*Petasites japonicus*). These plants spread by creeping rhizomes and eventually cover vast areas. Others, such as cow parsley, multiply by seed. Cut off flower stems before they produce seed heads to keep them from spreading across your garden.

Coloured leaves

Attractive ground cover Plant species in eye-catching colours beneath trees. Dead nettle, periwinkle, persicaria and creeping bugle lose no time in covering the ground. You only

need four to six plants per square metre because they spread by runners or rhizomes. The brighter, variegated varieties, such as spotted dead nettle *(Lamium maculatum)* (left) or variegated hostas, are your best choice.

Beware of sun scorch

Avoid planting species with gold-coloured foliage in full sun. These may burn because they are more sensitive than those with green foliage. Plants with grey, crimson and bluish foliage, however, will flourish in bright sunlight and are unharmed by it.

Revive your borders Bergenia adds beauty to borders and tolerates shade, full sun and all types of soil. Its red and purple colours are even brighter in poor soil.
▶ The only drawback is that this plant spreads continuously by rhizomes. Divide every two or three years in late summer and replant only the newer outer sections.

Attention-seeking grasses

Ornamental specimens The large *Gramineae* family encompasses all plants with long, narrow leaves, including cereals and the grass grown on lawns and in meadows. Various interesting grass varieties have been selected for the garden, generally for the colour, shape and unusual appearance of their leaves, although occasionally for the shape of their seed heads. Planted in isolated clumps, they provide an elegant focal point while, en masse, they form an attractive backdrop for flowering perennials.

▶ Wait until early spring to cut back dead foliage: in addition to being ornamental – many species remain colourful in winter – it protects the plant from the cold.

Perfect for dry areas

Two wonderful grass genera are ideal for a position in full sun with porous, sandy soil: *Pennisetum* and *Stipa*. The many species and varieties suit a variety of situations, and their ornamental seed heads look

wonderful in flower arrangements. The bright reddish *Imperata cylindrica* is a spectacular grass but unfortunately is only suitable for parts of the country with mild climates.

Grasses are good for rock gardens Ensure your rock garden looks attractive even in winter by planting ornamental fescue grasses here and there, including *Festuca eskia*, *F. glacialis*, *F. glauca* or *F. valesiaca*. These slender-leaved species grow in clumps that reach a height of only 15cm and remain ornamental throughout the winter. They are low maintenance, needing only an annual trim.

An alternative lawn In moist areas holcus (*Holcus mollis*) is a good alternative to a regularly mown lawn. Mow it just before flowering to ensure that its white foliage streaked with green remains thick and dense.

Colourful and evergreen

Crimson and purple have a mellowing effect, yellow adds zest, while white lifts and softens contrasts. Scatter evergreen perennials throughout your beds and borders, and winter will not seem so long and bleak.

A splash of crimson or purple Species that don't need much maintenance when it's cold include *Heuchera* 'Palace Purple' and 'Chocolate Ruffles', purple sage (*Salvia officinalis* 'Purpurascens'), *Persicaria microcephalia* 'Red Dragon' ❶, bergenia, various types of sedum that carpet beds, tubs and low walls, and the outstanding creeping bugle (*Ajuga reptans* 'Atropurpurea'), which spreads very quickly.

Stately spurge This sculptural plant ranges from dull blue-green to bluish in colour, including *Euphorbia characias* ❷, *E. polychroma* and *E. myrsinites*, which is good for ground cover. The most interesting euphorbia, known as chameleon spurge (*Euphorbia dulcis* 'Chameleon'), changes colour throughout the year and turns a rich purple in the winter.

Winter flowers and foliage Hellebores make an excellent choice. The Corsican hellebore (*Helleborus argutifolius*) ❸ is the most spectacular with its large, bluish jagged-edged leaves and creamy green flowers.

Sun-drenched flower beds In sunny borders, the creamy yellow foliage of oregano (*Origanum vulgare* 'Aureum') will certainly make an impact.

Foliage plants

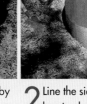

Quick growth If you have cool soil, fill out your borders quickly by planting miscanthus. This is a fashionable grass, particularly the variety that has striped foliage (*Miscanthus sinensis* 'Zebrinus'), and it forms tall ornamental clumps. Use it as a focal point or as an attractive windbreak at the back of a border.

Distinctive ground cover Plant ophiopogon at the base of containerised perennials and shrubs for an attractive way of concealing the edges of the tubs. *Ophiopogon planiscapus* 'Nigrescens', an unusual-looking plant with narrow black leaves that form dense waves across the ground, retains its intensity all year round. It looks like a dwarf grass at only 15–25cm tall, but it is in fact a member of the lily family, and you can use it anywhere, even in small pots.

Grasses to stabilise slopes Choose aquatic grass (*Glyceria maxima*) for the edges of a pond or river. It stabilises sloping ground and tolerates its roots being submerged in 20cm of water. This hardy plant grows to a height of 80cm and spreads rapidly by rhizomes.

Grasses for wet soils Most varieties of evergreen carex, molinia (*Molinia caerulea*), and graceful tussock grass (*Deschampsia cespitosa*) form dense clumps that eventually cover heavy, wet or boggy soils.

Places where nothing will grow *Hakonechloa macra*, one of the most ornamental members of the *Gramineae* family, is a good choice for shady town gardens and areas under trees, since it forms a dense carpet of variegated leaves. The deciduous foliage of luzula, part of the rush family, does wonders at the foot of trees where nothing else will thrive. *Luzula nivea* produces frothy white heads in midsummer.

Bamboo for a different kind of hedge Plant clumps that are already quite tall and are producing new shoots. These emerge from the ground in spring, attain the height of last year's stems, then grow higher. The new stems increase the height of the clump every year, until your selected species reaches adult size. Make sure you choose a species suitable for its position in the garden. If the clump becomes too bushy, cut off peripheral shoots as soon as they emerge from the ground.

Exotic windbreaks Medium and large bamboos form excellent windbreaks, whether you plant groves, isolated clumps or hedges. Create a noise-reducing screen by planting two rows of species whose slender stems are completely covered in leaves, such as *Phyllostachys flexuosa* and *P. nigra*.

Natural wonders Dwarf bamboo species cover slopes, stabilise loose soil and tolerate areas where grass would require too much attention. Clip the smallest varieties, such as *Pleioblastus pygmaeus var. distichus*, twice a year. Leave the others to grow thicker unaided. Their irrepressible vigour makes them ideal for inaccessible areas.

Elegant screens For a balcony or patio, choose frost-hardy bamboo varieties that will not exceed three metres high. Species with moderately vigorous rhizomes are also suitable if planted in sturdy tubs made of wood, brick or concrete. Their rhizomes are so strong that they can split plastic tubs.

Bamboos in pots provide excellent patio screening.

Use ferns to carpet damp ground or to relieve gloom in the shady areas beneath trees.

Fabulous ferns

Heat insulation Gather the dry fronds of ferns in autumn by cutting the stems just above ground level with a pair of secateurs. Always wear good gardening gloves, because these fronds are sharp. Tie them into bundles with string and stand them around your shrubs and perennials to protect them from frost. You can also use them as mulch for the vegetable garden (left).

▶ Cover trimmed rootstocks of perennials that die back in winter with a blanket of dead leaves. Over these, lay a circle of ferns, their fronds overlapping and pointing towards the centre. Bend the end of each stem and push it into the ground around the edge to anchor it in place.

▶ Do not remove too much of the dead foliage from ferns in autumn. This protects the rootstock during the winter. Cut back in spring or, in the case of evergreen ferns, only remove any damaged leaves.

For shady spots The Victorians were enthusiastic growers of many ferns, even building dedicated ferneries to provide ideal growing conditions. As ferns originated in dark prehistoric rainforests, they like shade, even dense shade. They thrive in a north-facing position in continually wet soil where other plants fail and make ideal ground cover under trees, along with hostas, irises, day lilies, lady's mantle or elephant's ears.

Set in stone Evergreen ferns are ideal for planting in the crevices of stone walls in the shade, beside steps and between the stones around ponds. Choose the Hart's tongue fern (*Asplenium scolopendrium*) with its slender green fronds, *Onoclea sensibilis*, whose delicate, pale green fronds dry out in winter, or maidenhair ferns such as *Adiantum capillus-veneris* and *A. venestum*.

▶ Very cool soil is good for the ostrich fern (*Matteucia struthiopteris*) or the lady fern (*Athyrium filix-femina*), which rapidly grows into clumps almost one metre in diameter.

▶ The hardiest and least labour-intensive fern of them all is the male fern, *Dryopteris filix-mas*, which will grow anywhere. It tolerates chalky soils and even drought.

Perfect in pots Grow ferns in plastic pots so that they retain the moisture they love. To make a plastic pot look more attractive, conceal it in a larger, decorative terracotta container like an old urn. Put some gravel at the bottom of the outer container before inserting the plastic pot. If your terracotta urn is not large enough for this, line the sides of it with a plastic sheet and transplant the fern directly into it, leaving the bottom open for drainage. Once you have planted the fern, cover the surface of the soil with pieces of bark or other mulch to keep the compost moist. Remember to keep the pot well watered.

Sowing ferns

1 Fern fronds bear cases that release a fine powder of spores when mature. Release these by rubbing the stem.

2 Fill a container with fine compost. Water liberally and firm down the compost with a small piece of wood.

3 Sow the spores. In several months, each spore will germinate to form a tiny green platelet, the prothallus.

4 Transplant prothalli into small pots, and they will each produce a new fern.

Pests and diseases of ornamental plants

Decorative plants are grown for their appearance, and pests should not be allowed to spoil this. However, many ornamentals are prone to disease.

Bulbs and roots

BASAL ROT

▶ **Symptoms** Leaves turn yellow and the plant's roots or bulb give off a characteristic rotten smell. The underground parts lose colour and rot, and the outer skin withers. The rot is caused by a number of fungi and bacteria belonging to the *Erwinia*, *Fusarium* and *Verticillium* species.
▶ **Plants affected** Most plants that grow from a bulb, rhizome or tuber.
▶ **Treatment** These persistent soil-borne diseases are difficult to combat and spread quickly. It is best carefully to pull up and destroy affected plants as soon as symptoms appear. Disinfect or discard infected soil. Replant with plants other than bulbs until the infection naturally disappears, which can take several months. Prevent rot in overwintering bulbs and tubers by dusting with sulphur.

BLUE MOULD

▶ **Symptoms** Reddish brown marks appear on the bulb, followed by a covering of bluish spores. The bulb then starts to rot. This is caused by a pinkish fungus belonging to the *Penicillium* species, which primarily attacks bulbs in storage but can also affect those in the soil.
▶ **Plants affected** Most types of bulbs including crocus, iris, tulips.
▶ **Treatment** Dust bulbs with sulphur as a preventive measure, then store in a dry, well-aired place that will not be affected by frost. Destroy bulbs as soon as the first symptoms appear.

CABBAGE MOTH The caterpillar of this moth particularly attacks the roots of China aster, French marigold (*Tagetes*) and pelargonium. See page 205.

CROWN GALL This bacterial disease is common in chrysanthemum, cineraria, pelargonium, phlox and sweet pea. See page 150.

HONEY FUNGUS Caused by the *Armillaria mellea* fungus, this disease attacks the roots of trees, shrubs and flowering plants, such as the abutilon and the peony. See page 150.

NARCISSUS FLY

▶ **Symptoms** Bulbs rot in the ground, or produce twisted leaves with no flowers. This is caused by the larvae of narcissus flies, which lay their eggs in the soil around dying leaves in spring. The larvae hatch and burrow down into bulbs to feed for a year or two. Adult flies look like bees and are seen around bulb foliage.
▶ **Plants affected** Narcissus, amaryllis, snowdrop, snowflake.
▶ **Treatment** Avoid this pest by planting firm, healthy bulbs at the correct depth. Dispose of soft bulbs. Feed bulbs after flowering with a fertiliser high in phosphate and potash. Sprinkle crushed garlic around dying foliage as a deterrent.

NECK AND ROOT ROT

▶ **Symptoms** The stem goes soft and the rest of the plant withers and dries up. When violets are affected, purplish spores grow on their roots, which then rot and crumble. This rot is caused by a variety of fungi including *Pythium* and *Verticillium*, which grow vigorously in wet weather.
▶ **Plants affected** Sweet alyssum, busy lizzy, lobelia, lupin, carnation, French marigold (*Tagetes*), pelargonium, pansy, petunia, sweet pea, sage (*Salvia*), verbena, violet.
▶ **Treatment** Remove and destroy affected plants. Replant with nonsusceptible types and change the planting scheme every two years. Apply sulphur dust around the roots when planting, or at the base of the stems of healthy plants in infected areas. In bygone days, gardeners treated plants with horsetail decoction and stinging nettle extract to protect plants at risk.

VINE WEEVIL

This little weevil, whose larvae are more harmful than the adult insect, attacks a large number of flowering plants, such as begonia, fuchsia, busy lizzy (*Impatiens*), pelargonium and primula. The natural control is a parasitic eelworm (nematode) which is drenched onto the soil and plant roots. The nematodes parasitise the weevils. See page 153.

WHITE ROT

▶ **Symptoms** On bulbous plants, white rot appears first at the base of the bulb, and then the leaves turn yellow. On ornamental plants with roots, oily traces appear on the leaves followed by a white, downy layer. The plant rots and dies. This rot is caused by the *Sclerotinia sclerotinium* fungus.
▶ **Plants affected** Many types of flowering plants, but most commonly antirrhinum, China aster (*Callistephus*), cornflower (*Centaurea*), crocus, delphinium, gladiolus, iris, lupin, sweet alyssum.
▶ **Treatment** Remove and destroy affected plants and disinfect the soil. The disease can be active for up to four years in the soil, so do not replant with susceptible species. Dust the roots with sulphur when planting and feed with liquid nettle manure to toughen the growth and increase resistance to the disease.

Stems

DAMPING OFF

▶ **Symptoms** The seedlings seem to be growing well when, suddenly, their basal stems turn reddish and then black. The young plants wilt and die. Also known as black rot disease, this is caused by numerous fungi – *Pythium, Phytophthora, Fusarium, Rhizoctonia* – that penetrate the young plants.
▶ **Plants affected** Seedlings.
▶ **Treatment** Use only fresh growing compost and store it in a cool, dry area out of direct sunlight. Before use, disinfect all tools, pots and trays that are to be used for raising seedlings and cuttings. Use a copper fungicide at the first sign of attack.

EELWORM

▶ **Symptoms** Infected stems twist, swell and burst open. The leaves yellow, wither and become stringy. When bulbous plants are affected, the bulb turns soft and powdery and the plant eventually dies. This is caused by a number of microscopic eelworms (nematodes) that live in the soil and on plants. Eelworm can also carry plant virus diseases.
▶ **Plants affected** Chrysanthemum, hyacinth, narcissus, phlox, snowdrop.
▶ **Treatment** Pull up and burn the diseased plants, then remove the contaminated soil. If you notice the symptoms in

your garden, lift and treat your bulbs by soaking them for two hours in water at a temperature of 40°C to prevent the disease from spreading. Plant French marigold (*Tagetes*) close to bulbs or vulnerable plants as a deterrent.

Leaves

BACTERIAL CANKER

▶ **Symptoms** Circular spots appear on leaves, surrounded by a ring of yellow that is punctuated by little black raised points. These circular spots are sometimes semitransparent before they turn brown or black. As the canker spreads, the leaves dry up and the plant dies. Also known as bacterial spot, it is caused by numerous bacterium – *Pseudomonas, Erwinia, Xanthomonas* – that enter the plant through wounds.
▶ **Plants affected** Antirrhinum, delphinium, prunus species.
▶ **Treatment** Affected plants need to be pulled up and destroyed. The only remedy is to prevent the disease by using disinfected soil, and taking care not to cause damage to plants when transplanting them.

BLACKFLY

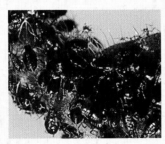

▶ **Symptoms** The plant's growth slows and, if the infestation is large, its shoots wither and curl up. This is caused by the insect *Aphis*

fabae, which is 2mm long with a black body. Blackfly pierce the tissue and suck sap from the young leaves and stems, weakening the plant.
▶ **Plants affected** Most ornamentals and vegetables.
▶ **Treatment** Apply an approved spray to the infested areas as soon as the pest is noticed. Garlic infusion and stinging nettle extract (see page 255) were used by earlier gardeners. Alternatively, introduce ladybird larvae into the garden or build a ladybird shelter to encourage these friendly insects to stay in your garden permanently.

BOTRYTIS

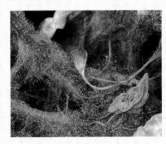

▶ **Symptoms** Also known as grey mould, botrytis attacks buds, leaves and fruits. The buds are covered with a whitish powdery layer, which prevents them from opening. The leaves turn yellow and wither. Fruits change colour, go soft and fall. When the plant is shaken, it will give off a white dust. Botrytis is caused by the fungus *Botrytis cinerea*, which attacks any plants that are damaged and weak.
▶ **Plants affected** Many ornamental species as well as fruit and vegetables.
▶ **Treatment** If the outbreak is serious, remove and burn affected plants (do not put on the compost heap). This disease can be prevented by good nutrition and air circulation around plants. Do not crowd plants together, remove

infected growth as soon as it appears and spray with an approved fungicide.

CABBAGE MOTH The
caterpillar is a greenish pest that eats the leaves and shoots of pelargoniums, stocks and many other flowering plants. See page 205.

CAPSID BUG

▶ **Symptoms** There are so many holes in the leaves that they seem to have been riddled by a volley of lead shot. The buds can also be affected, so that they fail to develop. There are raised brown marks on the fruits. Capsid bugs (*Lygus*) eat the leaves and inject a toxic substance into them, so destroying the cells.
▶ **Plants affected** Many plants including chrysanthemums, geraniums, sage (*Salvia*).
▶ **Treatment** Only in severe attacks, spray with an approved insecticide such as pyrethrins and derris.

CYCLAMEN MITE

▶ **Symptoms** Tiny insects (*Tarsonemus pallidus*) infest the growing tips of cyclamen. They live and feed inside the leaf and flower buds causing the stem and leaves to become scarred and distorted into spoon-like shapes. Flowers fail to open.
▶ **Plant affected** Cyclamen.
▶ **Treatment** No preparations are available to control these mites. Burn infected plants.

Pests and diseases

FLEA BEETLE

▶ **Symptoms** Round holes appear in the leaves. These then turn a whitish colour and dry up. The plant may die if it is a heavy infestation. Flea beetles belong to the *Altica*, *Phyllotreta* and *Psylloides* species. They thrive in warm, sunny weather in spring and summer. Beetles jump off when an infected plant is shaken.

▶ **Plants affected** Aubrieta, nasturtium, stock (*Matthiola*), sweet alyssum.

▶ **Treatment** Protect young plants by covering them with fleece until the growth is mature and less prone to attack. If necessary, spray with an approved treatment and feed to aid recovery.

FROGHOPPER

▶ **Symptoms** Bright yellow or white streaks can be seen on leaves. They are unsightly but do not actually damage the plant. During the nymphal stage, froghoppers hide inside a froth known as cuckoo spit. This pest belongs to several species of sap-sucking insect.

▶ **Plants affected** Busy lizzy, chrysanthemum, foxglove (*Digitalis*), marigold (*Tagetes*), primrose, sage (*Salvia*), tobacco plant, verbena.

▶ **Treatment** Pick off these insects by hand. If there are vast colonies, spray using an insecticide with a base of pyrethrins or bifrenthrin.

Apply a foliar feed at regular intervals during the summer to encourage new growth to repair the damage.

FUSARIUM WILT

▶ **Symptoms** The plant seems to lack water even when it has been given the correct amount. Its leaves wither, go yellow and dry up. Sometimes they turn pinkish and the base of the stem turns black. The roots could also be affected. This wilt can be caused by several fungi belonging to the *Fusarium* species. Damage occurs quickly in hot or humid weather.

▶ **Plants affected** Antirrhinum, aster, carnation, China aster (*Callistephus*), chrysanthemum, cineraria, sweet alyssum (*Lobularia*), sweet pea.

▶ **Treatment** Pull up and dispose of affected plants and disinfect the soil. Replant with nonsusceptible plants and dust roots with sulphur when planting. Ensure good hygiene to prevent the spread.

GERANIUM RUST

▶ **Symptoms** Yellowish marks appear on the surface of the affected leaves and brown spores on the underside. They are caused by the *Puccinia pelargonii zonalis* fungus, which grows in wet weather.

▶ **Plants affected** Pelargonium. Other types of rust, varying in colour, affect carnation, chrysanthemum, gypsophila, hollyhock, mallow, sweet william and all of the Malvaceaea family.

▶ **Treatment** During damp periods, spray affected plants several times at fortnightly intervals with products containing, for example, mancozeb, or use stinging nettle extract or a horsetail decoction (see page 255).

GREENFLY

Although these aphids often affect fruit trees, they can also be found on all species of ornamental plants. They are usually most active quite early in spring. See page 252.

LEAF MINER

▶ **Symptoms** Leaves are mined by curving tunnels. If you place a leaf up against the light, you will see larvae in these tunnels. The tiny larvae belong to the *Agromyza*, *Lyonetia* and *Phytomiza* species, which hatch from eggs laid in the leaf by adult flies. Severe infestations can result in the leaves dying. These flies can produce two or three generations in one year.

▶ **Plants affected** Columbine (*Aquilegia*), chrysanthemum, cineraria, delphinium, gerbera.

▶ **Treatment** Pick off badly affected leaves or squash the larvae in their tunnels between your fingers. If the problem spreads, spray the foliage with an approved systemic treatment and repeat until it has been controlled.

LEAF SPOT

▶ **Symptoms** Round spots with yellow edges, which spread and turn black, can be seen on the surface of the leaves. The leaves then dry up. Stems and also roots, especially tubers, may be affected and rot. These symptoms are caused by the fungus *Alternaria*, which develops in summer and autumn when the atmosphere is very humid.

▶ **Plants affected** Many different plants are affected by this disease.

▶ **Treatment** This disease can spread rapidly, so at the first signs of attack, spray with a copper-based treatment and repeat. Foliar feeding in the summer aids recovery.

LILY BEETLE

▶ **Symptoms** Bright red beetles with black heads and long bodies produce dark-coloured larvae in early summer. Both adults and larvae rapidly devour all parts of lily plants and must be controlled quickly.

▶ **Plants affected** Lily, fritillaria.

▶ **Treatment** Deter the beetles from climbing up the lily stems by coating them in vaseline. Remove from the leaves and destroy the adults and larvae. Alternatively, spray with an approved treatment.

MEALYBUG

▶ **Symptoms** Tiny soft-bodied insects can be seen on the undersides of leaves and at leaf axils (where the leaf stalk joins the stem). Fluffy white wax is excreted to cover the mealybugs and their eggs, so the foliage becomes sticky.

▶ **Plants affected** Plants in greenhouses, such as abutilon (when they are known as *Hesperides* lice), pelargonium, fuchsia (known as floury mealybug).

▶ **Treatment** Introduce *Cryptolaemus montrouzierei*, a predatory ladybird, on large plants and *Hypoaspis miles*, a predatory mite, on small ones.

SHOTHOLE Shothole is caused by a number of fungi, bacteria and virus diseases. Spots appear on the leaves, which then turn brown and eventually fall out, leaving the shothole peppered appearance. This symptom can be found on a wide range of plants. See page 251 (Coryneum blight).

SLUGS AND SNAILS

▶ **Symptoms** The edges of leaves, sometimes even whole leaves, have been eaten. A slimy trail indicates their presence. They come in many colours and sizes, and wet weather makes the situation worse as plants tend to rot.

▶ **Plants affected** Most garden plants, seedlings.

▶ **Treatment** Collect these pests by torchlight at night when they are most active and visible. Place traps at intervals around the garden and empty frequently. Tip the slugs into polythene bags, tie the tops and put them in the waste bin. Use the traditional barriers of sharp sand, ash or one of the modern granular equivalents around plants at risk. Copper rings,

tape and sprays were also used in bygone days and are still available today. Encourage slug and snail-eating wildlife into your garden – frogs, birds and hedgehogs all eat many slugs and snails. To control slugs in the soil, drench areas with a parasitic nematode that invades the pest and quickly kills them.

SOOTY MOULD

▶ **Symptoms** The upper side of the leaves becomes sticky and blackish, as if soot has fallen on it. Sooty mould is caused by a fungus that grows on honeydew excreted by sap feeding insects. It does not threaten the plant's life, but slows its growth by blocking out air and light.

▶ **Plants affected** All ornamental species attacked by sap-sucking insects.

▶ **Treatment** Wipe the leaves to remove the mould if practical, and spray the foliage with an approved systemic treatment to control the pest.

TORTRIX MOTH

▶ **Symptoms** The leaves curl up and show signs of having been eaten, as do the buds and stems. Several leaves may have been joined together by silky threads to form a 'nest'. The holes are made by the caterpillars of the tortrix moth (*Cacoecimorpha pronubana*). The caterpillars are green and 2cm long, and roll up in the leaves to protect themselves while feeding.

▶ **Plants affected** Carnation, some perennials, indoor plants and shrubs.

▶ **Treatment** Cut off the leaves bearing caterpillar 'nests' and burn them. Spray the plant with *Bacillus thuringiensis* or an approved product containing derris or pyrethrins.

VERTICILLIUM WILT

▶ **Symptoms** Despite being correctly watered, the leaves start to wither. They then turn yellow and dry up. The disease next affects the stems and then the roots, which lose colour. This wilt is caused by *Verticillium* fungi, which cause the plant to wither by blocking the circulation of the sap.

▶ **Plants affected** Antirrhinum, bellflower (*Campanula*), carnation (*Dianthus*), chrysanthemum, cineraria, gerbera, pelargonium, poppy, sage (*Salvia*).

▶ **Treatment** No chemicals can combat this fungal disease. Pull up infected plants and burn them; do not put disease-infected plants on the compost heap. Disinfect all tools that have had contact with infected plants, and replace any soil in which they have been grown.

WATER LILY BEETLE

▶ **Symptoms** Numerous oval-shaped holes appear between leaf veins. The pest occurs generally in spring or summer. Sometimes the perimeter of the hole dies and rots. This is caused by *Galerucella nymphaeae*, a yellowy brown beetle. Both the adults and the larvae eat the leaves.

▶ **Plant affected** Water lily (*Nymphaea*).

▶ **Treatment** It is not possible to use insecticides because they would harm the fish. Instead the beetles and larvae have to be picked off the leaves by

hand. Alternatively, shake the leaves so that the pests fall into the water and drown or get eaten by fish.

WHITEFLY

▶ **Symptoms** A cloud of whiteflies fly off as soon as the plant is moved. Swarms of them can be found both outside and in greenhouses. They secrete honeydew on the leaves, causing a black mould to develop. Whiteflies (*Trialeurodes vaporariorum*) lay their eggs under leaves. From the eggs emerge larvae (scales), each with a covering of white waxy film that makes them look like mealybugs. These larvae live on the underside of the leaves and suck sap, which gradually weakens the plant.

▶ **Plants affected** Many plants in the garden including abutilon, busy lizzy, fuchsia, gerbera, pelargonium and many more.

▶ **Treatment** In a greenhouse, use yellow sticky cards, to which the whiteflies get stuck (this also enables conclusive identification of the problem). It is also possible to purchase 'scales' of *Encarsia formosa*, a tiny parasitic wasp that preys on the larvae. The temperature must be above 10°C for this wasp to survive. Outdoors, spray with pyrethrins or insecticidal soap in mid-summer, paying particular attention to the undersides of the leaves. Repeat these treatments until cleared.

Ornamental shrubs and trees

The beauty of roses

No flower is more a part of the quintessential English garden than the rose. Over the centuries, gardeners have celebrated it, nurtured it and developed hundreds of new disease-resistant, repeat-flowering varieties. But the old roses have never fallen out of favour, for their charm is unsurpassed.

Planting a new rose

Companion planting Plant your roses close to the herb garden to benefit from natural pest control. Herbs such as thyme, lavender, rosemary, lemon balm, chives and tarragon repel many garden pests.
▶ Chives help roses to combat powdery mildew because, like garlic, onion and leek, they contain sulphur compounds that are a natural enemy of this fungus.

Special varieties for poor soil Even gardeners with difficult conditions can grow roses. Choose varieties that have been bred or hybridised to tolerate adverse conditions and even chalky soil. Some rose growers actually toughen up their plants by growing them without fertiliser and pesticides, and by rationing water. This creates plants that are much better able to grow in poor environments.

The soft colours of sweetly scented old roses fit perfectly into a traditional cottage garden setting.

▶ Don't forget that you can improve the soil to encourage a tricky specimen to flourish. Choose a site that has not been previously used for roses, dig in plenty of well-composted manure or garden compost to boost the organic content of the soil and feed the rose well at planting. Once established, dose regularly with a dedicated rose feed and mulch with well-composted manure or lawn clippings.

The best time to plant Planting in autumn gives the roots time to establish before spring and ensures that the plants will flower better. Protect the crown and the roots of a new rose by applying a layer of straw.
▶ Roses planted in early spring will be less likely to suffer from frost damage than those planted in autumn, but they may need to be watered more often until they are established. In areas where the weather is harsher, plant in spring, but in milder regions, you can plant in spring or autumn.

Wait before buying Be careful not to buy bare-root roses too early in the autumn. If they are lifted before time they may start to sprout if the weather turns mild, and these shoots will be susceptible to frost. For the best results, wait until the natural resting period in late autumn or early winter, when the plants have shed their leaves and are dormant. Look out for new stocks of containerised roses from mid-October, or if the weather is mild, wait until mid-November, when plants are less likely to regrow before spring.

Roses and lavender make a delightfully fragrant pairing and the lavender keeps the aphids at bay.

Containerised roses are thirsty If you buy roses in pots, plant them immediately after buying. If you can't, then make sure you keep them well watered.

▶ Submerge the container in a bucket of water for half an hour before planting.

▶ Roses planted in the spring are more vulnerable to drought than those planted in autumn. Keep them well watered and in dry weather water thoroughly on alternate days.

Let the sun shine in Don't forget the golden rule: roses love sunshine. For the best results plant them in a site where they will get as much sun as possible.

Not too dry, not too wet Roses do not thrive in wet or waterlogged soils. If you have heavy soil, then improve the drainage before planting your roses. Avoid areas close to walls or fences as these may prevent rain from reaching your plants.

▶ Don't plant your roses near a downpipe or they may be drowned by excessively wet soil.

Avoid wet weather for planting If it has rained continually since you bought your roses or if there has been a hard frost, wait for the weather to improve before you plant them. Choose a spot at the base of a north-facing wall or somewhere sheltered from the sun and dig a trench with a sloping side.

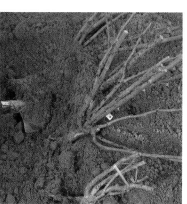

Spread out the roots, lay them against the slope and cover with soil up to a third to a half of their stems (left). Make sure that two plants do not overlap.

▶ When the weather improves, prepare your site, dig up the roses, and plant them in their final positions. Do not leave the bare roots in the open for more than an hour.

Self-sufficient roses If you want your roses to be resilient, then plant them in the autumn and water just once in the first year. Allow nature to do the rest. The most vigorous plants will survive and thrive without a lot of time-consuming care.

▶ In a prolonged dry spell in any season, water copiously once or twice – even the hardiest roses can die of thirst.

Tidy roots Before planting new roses, tidy up dense and tangled root balls. Use sharp secateurs to remove some of the overgrown roots carefully. This allows the remaining roots space to grow quickly into the new surrounding soil.

Banana skins Old-fashioned gardeners say that banana skins improve the colour of many garden flowers. Use fresh skins, or dried and crushed ones, and bury them beneath your roses.

▶ Rich in potassium and starch, which turns into sugar, banana skins also make a good natural additive to compost. Just mix together and dig in to enrich the soil before planting.

Wait before training climbers When planting climbing roses, tie the stems loosely to the trellis and wait several days until the soil has settled around the new plant. When the ground returns to its original level, refasten stems securely.

Planting a bare-root rose

1 Dig a hole 40–50cm deep and loosen the sides and bottom with a fork. Mix a dedicated granular rose fertiliser into the soil in the planting hole before you position the rose.

2 Untangle the roots, cut off any that are damaged, and trim the others back to one or two-thirds of their length. Cut back stems to a third of their original length and remove any that are dead, diseased or crossing.

3 Dress the roots by soaking them in a bucket of water and soil, with the addition of cattle dung, if you can get some. Coating the roots in this solution will keep them from drying out when they are planted in the earth.

4 Build a small mound of earth, place the rose on it and spread out the roots. The neck of the plant should be just below the surface of the soil. Fill in the hole and tamp down with your foot or hand, then water.

Choosing the perfect roses for your garden

A red, red rose Choosing red roses can be quite difficult. For example, some red blooms can look streaky or even faded depending on the light. Choose dark red varieties, such as 'Royal William' or 'Velvet Fragrance' for positions in full sun and lighter reds, such as 'Alexander' or 'Loving Memory', for bright areas that are not so sun-drenched.

▶ Set off brightly coloured red roses against a dark green backdrop such as a shrubby hedge or a painted trellis.

▶ Some red roses can look almost black in very bright sunlight. If this is the effect you are after, plant roses that are purplish red or crimson in hue, such as 'Deep Secret' or 'Guinée'. Truly black roses have not yet been developed.

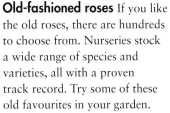

Old-fashioned roses If you like the old roses, there are hundreds to choose from. Nurseries stock a wide range of species and varieties, all with a proven track record. Try some of these old favourites in your garden.

▶ **Bush and shrub roses** 'Ballerina' (top), light pink; 'Buff Beauty', yellow and buff; 'Cardinal de Richelieu', purple; 'Fantin Latour', soft pink; 'Hansa', bright red; 'Mrs John Laing', a delicate pink; 'Mme Caroline Testout', satin pink; 'Félicité Parmentier', pinkish white with bluish leaves (second from top); 'Reine des Violettes', rich purple, fading to lilac; 'Variegata di Bologna', unusual crimson-striped white flowers.

▶ **Widespread ground-cover** 'Max Graf' (third from top), bright pink.

▶ **For pots** 'Little White Pet'.

▶ **For hedges** 'Stanwell Perpetual' and 'Roseraie de l'Haÿ' (below).

▶ **Climbers and ramblers** 'Blush Noisette', delicate pink; 'Cécile Brunner', pink; 'Dorothy Perkins', light pink; 'Félicité et Perpetué', white.

Late colour If you want a low-maintenance shrub rose with glorious autumn hips to brighten your garden at the end of summer

YESTERDAY & TODAY

Roses through the ages

Today the rose is among the most popular garden flowers, but it was traditionally valued more for its healing properties than its beauty. Pliny listed more than 30 medicines that could be derived from roses. *Rosa gallica officianalis* is thought to be the medicinal rose cultivated by the Romans and was later adopted as the Rose of Lancaster. The flowers were used by the Greeks, Romans and Egyptians in perfumes and oils and were thought to ward off the plague. The Victorians used rose petals in jellies, sandwiches and even in rose petal tea.

Garden lore says that you should plant a rose in any month that has an 'r' in it, but for the sake of your new plant, avoid the very bitter winter months.

then consider *Rosa glauca*. It has beautiful blue-grey leaves, a mass of pink single flowers and bright red hips.

Top tips for choosing roses Roses are versatile plants, but some are more suited to particular situations than others.

▶ **Species roses** These are vigorous plants found in the wild or bred close to the wild species as hybrids and are often used to brighten boundary hedges or in natural plantings.

▶ **Old roses** Their gentle colours, sweet scent and the varied and appealing shapes of their blooms make them perfect for cottage, country or period gardens.

▶ **Hybrid tea roses** Highly scented and good for cutting. Team with old-fashioned flowers to soften their bright colours.

▶ **Floribunda roses** Ideal for creating blocks of colour in mass plantings. Their long flowering season suits a mixed border.

▶ **Modern shrub roses** Bred to combine all the best features of roses – fragrance, beauty and disease-resistance.

▶ **Climbing and rambling roses** Use to clothe arches, obelisks, walls and trellises, or train along ropes for swags of flowers.

▶ **Miniature roses** Ideal for growing in pots or at the front of a mixed border.

THE GARDENER'S CHOICE

Roses to suit every taste ▶

Cover a wall If you want to grow roses over a large structure, plant 'American Pillar' ❶ or 'Handel' ❷.

Colour through winter *Rosa moyesii* ❸ is one of the ancestors of modern roses. It has ornamental hips.

A vigorous rambler *Rosa filipes* 'Kiftsgate' ❹ flowers profusely over a short period in early summer. Its branches will reach a height of 9m and will spread up to 6m across.

An old rose 'Variegata di Bologna' ❺ is a hardy Bourbon rose that oozes charm. It needs tying to supports.

Flowers till autumn 'Centenaire de Lourdes' ❻ is a wonderful floribunda with a long flowering period.

Fill your garden with the scent of roses

Ground-cover roses Low-growing roses are widely available with many different varieties from 30cm to 1.2 metres high. These plants spread outwards rather than upwards, and some form wonderful carpets of flowers. Many can also be used to create hedges up to 1.2 metres high and lose no time in covering banks, rock gardens and other inaccessible places. They can also form decorative mounds that can be used to hide unsightly garden features such as old tree stumps and manhole covers.

▶ Ground-cover roses usually need little care and attention and are extremely hardy. This is particularly true of 'landscape' roses, a category bred for ornamental use in towns, parks and roads. Make the most of their sturdiness to protect vulnerable areas of your garden – for example, use a thorny variety like *Rosa* 'Paulii' to stop animals getting into your flower garden.

▶ To keep the roses in their horizontal state, shear them regularly. Don't worry about cutting off buds as new flowers will soon follow.

THE GARDENER'S CHOICE

Mix and match roses

Spring display Roses can be preceded in spring by a display of primulas, columbines, anemones and hellebores.

Herbaceous perennials ❶ Extend the rose flowering season by planting agapanthus, aster, campanula, geranium, hosta, iris, lilies, oenotheras and salvia.

Decorative herbs Fennel provides an excellent backdrop for shrub roses, and tarragon looks good under bush roses.

Spring and summer irises These tall plants create bold contrasts. Choose colours that highlight your roses, for example purple irises look stunning with yellow or orange roses.

Interesting shrubs Many shrubs make good companions for roses, including *Viburnum carlesii* and *V. mariesii*, hydrangea, honeysuckle, weigela, oleander, ceanothus, eleagnus, abelia, hibiscus and clematis.

Attractive borders Plant an edging of dwarf box (*Buxus suffruticosa*), blue or white lavender, or nepeta to give your rose beds the perfect finish.

Climbing roses work their magic: the very prolific 'Wedding Day' cascades over trees, walls and pergolas.

Cascading roses If you want to train roses over a high wall, choose vigorous varieties such as 'Madame Alfred Carrière', which is white, flushed with pink. 'Wedding Day' and 'New Dawn' bloom profusely and will cascade over pergolas or gazebos. 'Aloha', an elegant, old-fashioned-looking modern rose, is very fragrant and can be trained as a short climber.

Potted roses: think big If you are growing roses in containers, make sure you use large pots that won't restrict the roots. As a rough guide, plant standard roses in pots that are at least 50cm in diameter and 60cm deep. A bush rose – a hybrid tea or floribunda – will need a pot that is 40cm in diameter and 50cm deep. Miniature roses will thrive in smaller containers, around 30cm deep.

▶ Don't forget that these sizes are for young plants. As your roses grow they will need to be transplanted into progressively larger containers.

Surround your ponds Ramblers and ground-cover roses create an effective and attractive barrier around water. Plant them in large groups around the edge of a pond – in pots or in

the ground about 40cm apart – to prevent children from leaning over the water or discourage pets from jumping in. Roses will also attract a variety of birds and wildlife to the water, making your pond a natural haven.

Cover trees with blooms Rambling roses look fantastic clambering through the branches of old fruit trees. They extend the trees' season of interest and add a splash of flowers at eye level. Old trees also provide robust support for flowering stems laden with blossom.

▶ Choose vigorous varieties: 'Rambling Rector' climbs to about ten metres with canes spreading around five metres in a single season, 'Bobbie James' reaches over six metres and the sweet-smelling, pink-flowered 'Paul's Himalayan Musk' is also recommended.

▶ *Rosa longicuspii* and 'Sir Cedric Morris' are two varieties that will flower prolifically, producing hips in late summer and reaching a height of seven to ten metres. For a little more colour choose the blush-pink-flowered 'Kew Rambler', with branches spreading to over eight metres and wonderful rose hips.

Make beds more interesting A bed that is home only to roses can look sparse for much of the year, when the roses are not in flower. To add some interest and 'clothe' the bare lower stems of large-flowered roses, plant perennials such as alchemilla, dwarf potentilla, nepeta, sage and artemisia. Hostas are also a good choice, especially those with variegated or blue-tinted foliage.

Autumn roses

Modern rose varieties include an increasing number that reflower in late summer and remain in bloom until the end of October. They are available in all colours.

Red 'Alec's Red' ❶, 'Ena Harkness' and 'Tess of the D'Urbervilles' are good reds.

Pink 'Anne Boleyn' and 'Queen Elizabeth' ❷ produce pink flowers.

Orange and yellow 'Rusticana' has orange flowers, while 'Golden Wings' ❸ is a light buttery yellow.

White 'Anita Pereire' ❹ boasts pure white flowers until the first frosts, even in rainy areas, and 'Glamis Castle' reflowers with prolific white blooms.

Foliage Some species and hybrid roses are grown for the appeal of their feathery foliage and attractive hips, in addition to their flowers. Varieties in the Rugosa and Pimpinellifolia families have many tiny leaves which turn from lustrous bronze to orange, even red, in autumn, and many also produce glossy hips. Roses with both ornamental foliage and hips include *Rosa rugosa* and *Rosa glauca*.

Weed suppressors Covering the bare soil in a rose bed with ground-cover plants will also smother the weeds. Lavender bushes make an attractive combination with roses. The silvery grey foliage is a wonderful foil to the colours of the blooms, and the fragrance also repels some garden pests.

Planting containerised roses for instant impact

1 For the best results plant roses in autumn or early spring. Choose plants that have at least three healthy, well-balanced branches.

2 Before planting, water the rootball thoroughly. Either soak the pot in a bucket of water, or pour water directly into the top of the pot.

3 If the roots are pot-bound, tangled and dense, then carefully tease them apart and thin them out if necessary.

4 After planting and watering, spread a thick layer of mulch such as bark around the base of the shrub to keep the soil moist.

Get more from your bushes

Leave the soil neat and tidy Old-fashioned rose gardens were often rather drab: they were regularly hoed and weeded and the ground was left completely bare in a determined effort to avoid the invasion of aphids and other pests. Nowadays rose beds often contain other plants for added interest. But that does not mean you can slack on keeping the beds tidy. Garden pests can and will attack discarded plant material as well as a variety of weeds, so be sure to remove any waste and weeds, especially after pruning.

Top tips for training roses Keep on top of training your climbers and ramblers. Tie them in and tidy them regularly as they grow, which will boost flowering and make maintenance easier. If you don't, the branches will become tangled and you may lose track of stems that should be pruned or removed.

▶ **Trellises and pergolas**
Check regularly to ensure that new shoots have not grown through to the underside of the structure. Ensuring that a plant is growing on one side of the structure only will make it easier to take the plants down if you need to do any repairs. It will also make maintenance work and annual pruning and removing dead wood simpler.

▶ **Horizontal wires** Use these to train roses up walls. Separate the upward-growing stems when you tie them in and gently curve them, which will generate a greater number of flowers on each stem.

▶ **Vertical training wires** For tall climbers and ramblers on high walls, vertical wires offer support. On a house front, if you want to train roses up to the first floor, position wires between ground-floor windows and fix the central stems to them. Then you can spread the central stems and train the canes horizontally below the first-floor windows.

Prolific flowers Climbing roses will flower more profusely if you bend their supple stems as they grow by attaching a weight to them, such as a small pot. For the best results, train the stems horizontally as much as possible. If you are growing a rose over a column, arch or pergola, choose small-flowered species as they will adapt more easily to the required shape.

No more chemicals Reduce your reliance on chemicals by pruning out rose stems and tissue affected with mildew instead of spraying them. Remove any leaves affected with the blackspot fungus and burn them to destroy the spurs. Stems severely affected with aphids and leaf-rolling sawfly should also be removed and destroyed.

Pegging roses to produce more flowers

This technique is suitable for hybrid roses that tend to grow long shoots with flowers only at the ends. By restricting growth, pegging encourages stems to produce more flowers.

1 In late autumn, clear the soil at the base of the rose and remove any dead leaves.

2 Cut off at ground level any stems that have flowered during the current season and any that may hinder arching.

3 One by one, gently bend long, non-flowering stems until their tips are touching the ground. Space them evenly around the clump.

4 Hold them in place with hooks or pegs made of supple hazel or bamboo, at least 60cm from the base.

5 Leave the bent stems pegged like this until the following autumn.

6 As the current year's new shoots emerge from the bent branches, the plant will start to look like a pincushion.

A sunny wall is an ideal spot for a climbing rose, which can be trained to enhance a feature like this window.

Caring for roses

Winter snows In snowy weather, the stems of shrub roses tend to splay outwards, creating a hollow centre. Hold the branches together and give the bush extra support by winding string or raffia several times around the middle of the shrub.

Frost protection In autumn, when you have finished pruning, spread a thick layer of garden compost around the base of each plant. Then bank up the earth around the base to a height of 20–30cm. It should be removed at the start of the fine weather, around April or May. This is not only a good way to protect young plants from winter frosts, it also slows down the development of dormant buds and prevents premature regrowth during early mild weather.

Good timing for treatment If you have to treat your roses, choose a day when the weather is calm and not rainy or windy. This ensures that treatments are applied exactly where required and are not blown onto nearby plants or washed into the soil. Apply any garden treatment during the early morning or evening, out of the heat of the sun.

Power shower Cuckoo spit, a frothy lather found nestling in leaf joints, contains the pupae of insects that are more unsightly than harmful to roses. But if you don't like the look of this spittle, remove it by spraying with a jet of water from the hose, avoiding the rose flowers themselves.

The right time to water In the summer, water your roses early in the morning and never in the middle of the day. Do

not water roses in the evening of a very hot day as this will promote diseases such as black spot, which develops in hot, wet atmospheres, and powdery mildew, which occurs when roses are grown in soil that is too dry.

▶ Apply water around the base of the plant (right). Avoid using a fine spray, as roses weighed down with water will not last long. Overwet leaves may also burn in the sun from the magnifying effect of the droplets.
▶ Water the soil thoroughly before spreading liquid manure around the base of the plants, or do this after it has rained.

Combatting rose sickness If a rose dies unexpectedly, pull it up with its rootball and remove the soil where it was planted to a depth of 50cm. Replace with fresh compost before planting a new rose into the hole. Ideally, leave the site clear for at least three years before replanting with roses. Whenever you transplant a rose, remove the old soil from around the roots and use fresh compost in the new planting hole.

Aphid decoys Plant nasturtiums around a rose bed. They will attract colonies of aphids to their stems and leaves, which can be cut off and destroyed. The nasturtium plants will quickly recover, and your roses will have been spared.

Holes in your rosebuds This is a sign that small caterpillars are living in your rose and that the flowers may soon be entirely eaten away. There are two natural solutions: simply remove all the affected buds, or plant shrubs and flowers that attract birds alongside your rose bushes. The birds will eat the caterpillars and keep them off your roses.

Unhealthy foliage Chlorosis, the rapid yellowing of foliage, is usually caused by a shortage of iron, which can mean that your soil is too alkaline. Without touching the roots, dig a trench all the way round the rose at a distance of about 40cm from the base, and fill with ericaceous compost. Feed annually with this compost and plenty of organic matter.

Prevent powdery mildew Whitish, floury marks on leaves and buds are the symptoms of this disease, which often appears in hot, dry weather. Roses with deep roots can withstand it, so the best way to prevent powdery mildew is to water infrequently but profusely to encourage the plants to push their roots deep into the soil.

Fight fungal disease Treat your roses to a tonic of sulphur, a powder contained in most rose feeds. It helps to unlock inaccessible nutrients in the soil, gives your roses a boost and helps to combat black spot and powdery mildew. Roses grown in more industrialised areas tend to be free of black spot.

Pruning and trimming for bigger, better flowers

Well-pruned roses When pruning your roses, systematically remove all dead, diseased, stunted, damaged or broken wood. The pruning wound should be very white. If it is brown, cut slightly lower down into living stems. Remove any stems that rub together, cross over each other or look as if they are likely to cross in the future.

Aim for open growth Open up the centre of the plant as much as possible and cut off any suckers growing below the graft union, removing them at the stem (see below). Retain only healthy stems and cut them back to a good length for the shape of your bush.

Removing suckers

Suckers are stems that grow from the plant base beneath the graft union. A sucker tends to be bright green and has seven leaves. These shoots are from the rootstock, so are different from the rose you are growing. Remove them or they will drain the rose's energy to the detriment of the rest of the plant.

1 Dig carefully around the base of the rose with a spade to uncover the point where the sucker is attached. This will be beneath the graft union.

2 Cut the sucker as close as possible to the stem from which it is growing, taking care not to damage the stem. Never remove suckers from above ground.

3 Carefully replace the earth and water well. Keep a close watch on your rose so that you can take action if another sucker begins to grow.

When to prune You can prune your roses between the end of winter and early spring, even if the plant has already started to sprout some small new leaves. Don't worry about removing some new growth: these shoots will grow back even better.

Pruning standard roses To preserve a well-balanced shape in the first year, prune two-thirds of all the main stems in the crown and remove any excess stems in the centre. In subsequent years, remove secondary stems level with the main stems and trim the others to half their original length.

▶ Slope the angle of the cut away from the bud (the high side of the cut should be above the bud) to prevent water from collecting in the bud and causing it to rot. Leave at least 5mm between the bud eye and the cut to avoid damaging it.

▶ Prune weeping standards lightly and not until after they have flowered.

Encouraging growth along the right lines Look closely at a rose stem and you will see that the buds are alternately arranged along its length. When pruning a rose, make an angled cut just above a bud that faces in the direction you wish the shoot to grow. Normally this will be an outfacing bud – pruning to one of these opens up the centre of the rose bush and allows in light and air.

Deadheading Spent blooms look unsightly and provide a refuge for pests. Remove them daily or as soon as possible.

▶ **Large-flowered roses** Cut off spent flower heads just below the second pair of leaves, level with an opening bud.

▶ **Cluster-flowered roses** Remove individual flowers just beneath the corolla as they fade. Then when all the flowers have died, cut off the whole cluster following the instructions for large-flowered roses.

▶ **Spectacular new blooms** Deadheading in the correct way for your type of rose gives the stems a new burst of energy. The bud nearest to where you cut off the bloom will develop and produce new flowers.

▶ **Prevent hips forming** Unless the hips are particularly attractive, do not allow them to form as they will divert vital energy away from the plant and will prevent the formation of further flowers that season.

Enjoy bigger blooms by cutting off all buds except the terminal bud at the end of a stem.

Opening buds by hand If a hot, sunny spell follows hard on the heels of wet weather, rosebuds can become dehydrated. After becoming stuck in the damp and then burned by the sun, the outer petals form a sheath that stops the bud opening. Gently remove the outer petals by hand to allow the inner ones to unfurl. Do this as soon as possible to prevent the plant from losing every single flower.

Handle with care Tetanus is a serious and sometimes fatal disease. It is caused by a bacterium that lives in the soil and also in animal intestines. Make sure your antitetanus vaccination is kept up to date and always wear protective gardening gloves, especially when pruning. Even a tiny wound, such as a thorn prick from a rose, can become infected with the tetanus bacterium.

Get bigger flowers You can encourage a large-flowered rose to produce even bigger blooms by removing all the buds adjacent to the main bud at the end of a stem and retaining only the end bud. This rosebud will take advantage of all the sap and bloom magnificently, although you will have fewer flowers. Do not use this method on young or newly planted roses as you will not get enough flowers for a good display. Instead choose plants that have already reached a fair size and are producing numerous healthy stems for this type of pruning.

DID YOU KNOW?

To prune or not to prune

Although pruning bush roses, standard roses and climbers will generate new shoots, you can also let them keep their natural shape. As a result they will produce more foliage and slightly fewer flowers, but will only require a little maintenance pruning about once a year to remove dead wood and any unhealthy, deformed or crossing branches. You will also occasionally need to cut out some centre stems to open up the plant to improve air circulation.

Hedge roses that are difficult to reach at the rear of the flower bed, as well as climbers on fences and walls, will benefit particularly from this treatment. Standard roses, however, demand regular pruning to preserve their shape or compact habit and keep the stem free from shoots.

Too early to see the buds If the buds are too small to see, prune the stem to the required height and wait for the nearest buds to show. As soon as you can see the buds, pick the one you wish to encourage and prune above it with an angled cut. Do not wait too late in spring or the bud will not develop.

Beautiful stems Standard roses should be staked during their first two years: this will help them to take root more securely and develop a better shape.

▶ Disbud the main stem regularly. Because the graft union of a standard is at the top of the stem, shoots of the rootstock may appear along the trunk.

Tidying up at the base Dead stumps at the base of a plant will harbour disease and encourage rotting. Remove these carefully with a sharp, clean pruning saw, to reveal a smooth surface where rain cannot collect. At the same time, get rid of other debris and plant waste from around the base of the plant.

Pruning repeat-flowering roses

1 In year one, cut back main stems to 12–15cm for bush roses. Don't prune shrub roses, climbers or miniatures yet.

2 To prune, make a slanting cut, just above an outward-facing bud eye.

3 From year two, remove excess shoots in the autumn or early spring. Moderately prune vigorous outer stems.

Growing new roses from old

New roses the easy way You can propagate many roses from cuttings, but don't expect more than an 80 per cent success rate, especially for climbing roses. You would be pruning the stems anyway, so it's worth having a go.

▶ In September, choose some green healthy canes that have already become woody. Take some 20cm sections, by cutting just above a bud eye at the top and just below a bud eye at the base. Remove the lower leaves.

▶ Fill several 3-litre flowerpots with a mixture of horticultural sand and soil, in a ratio of 2:1. Push the cuttings into this mixture with the buds pointing upwards until only the top half of the stems are showing. Keep one variety to each pot and label well. Place in a shady spot in the garden.

▶ Water and keep moist until autumn.

▶ Over the winter protect the cuttings by burying the pots in a trench in the garden (left) or bringing them into a frost-free place in full sunlight.

▶ In the spring, when the weather is fair, dig up the trench or take the pots outside. Water, then transplant the rooted cuttings into your flower beds in April.

Natural rooting hormone In the summer, choose a favourite rose and cut off a vigorous non-flower-bearing stem that has not yet become woody. Remove the lower leaves with a knife, leaving a small part of the leaf stalks. Cut a cross in the base of the stem and insert a grain of wheat in the crack. Soak the stem in a glass of water overnight, and plant into a pot filled with a mixture of equal parts horticultural sand and soil. This treatment will help the plant become established.

Hardy and smothered in blooms throughout the summer, most floribunda roses are easy to propagate.

Keeping your graft under wraps Standard roses are grafted at the top of the main trunk. This graft is exposed to the cold and can be susceptible to frost. In winter cut back the stems at the top of the rose by about half their length and wrap the graft union to protect it.

▶ A simple way of making a graft cover is to cut the sleeve off an old jumper, slip it over the graft and fill with moss or straw. Gently pat down this protective layer then cover with a plastic bag to keep the rain out.

Bouquet cuttings If you like a rose you are given as a cut flower by friends, ask them to take a cutting for you in the autumn. Or you could try taking a cutting from the stem yourself. Don't try to take cuttings from florist roses. These are special varieties of roses, bred for greenhouse production, and will not normally thrive in a garden.

DIY ramblers Save money and bulk up your garden plants by layering any of your roses that have long, flexible stems. In spring, choose a healthy rose stem that is close to the ground. Leave it attached to the plant, but lay it horizontally on the soil. Remove the leaves where the stem touches the ground and carefully make an incision in the bark on the underside of the stem at this point. Cover with a few centimetres of soil, leaving the tip of the stem exposed. Peg the stem down with wire (right) and keep it well watered. In autumn, check to see that it has rooted into the soil. You can then cut the new rose from the mother plant with secateurs and plant it elsewhere in the garden.

▶ To ensure you obtain strong-growing, bushy plants from your cuttings, be patient and do not allow the new rose to flower in its first season.

Enjoy the versatility of roses

Ornamental hips Some varieties of rose produce attractive fruits that appear in late summer and will last until winter, even longer in the case of some species. Instead of cutting off the dead flowers, gently pull off the entire corolla to remove the petals, leaving the core intact.

▶ This is difficult to do with ramblers and roses that form dense hedges. Remove the petals where you can, but elsewhere the hips will develop unaided.

▶ Roses with ornamental hips include species roses such as *Rosa rugosa* and several old roses such as 'Fru Dagmar Hastrup'. *Rosa pomifera* produces hips shaped like small apples and *Rosa glauca* develops bright hips in bunches. *Rosa moyesii* produces very long hips shaped like plump bottles, which look attractive for months.

The sweet taste of roses Although rose hips – the fruit of roses – are edible, they rarely feature in modern recipes. This is a shame because they are rich in vitamin C and have a pleasant, delicate taste.

▶ Make rose jelly and rose jam by picking the hips after the first frosts so that they are softer. Crush them in a vegetable mill and filter the pulp to remove the seeds and hairs. For each cup of rose hip pulp, add half a cup of sugar to the strained liquid. Cook and stir the mixture until it thickens, then pour into sterilised jars and seal them.

▶ Rose petals are also edible and can be used in salads, in desserts such as candied rose petals and rose sorbet and in savoury dishes such as lamb tajine and meatballs. Gather petals in the morning from newly opened, fragrant flowers.

▶ Rose hip tea, rich in vitamin C, is an age-old preventive for colds, made by infusing hips in boiling water for several minutes. Strain to remove the hairs and sweeten to taste.

Freshly cut flowers

Choose rosebuds that are about to open or blooms that opened the night before. Take fairly long stems and cut just above a bud that is about to regrow.

▶ Before cutting roses, assess the general appearance of the plant so that you avoid creating an unbalanced shape.

The right tool for a clean cut Rose stems must be cut cleanly, not crushed. Use bypass secateurs, which give a very clean cut, in preference to a pair of anvil secateurs.

To enjoy a display of ornamental hips and provide winter food for the birds, don't deadhead your roses.

A long-lasting vase of roses After cutting, strip off some leaves as they will rot in the water. Also remove the thorns as these small wounds will help the stems draw up more water.

▶ Keep roses looking good for an extra two days by helping them draw more water. Cut the stems at an angle or make a vertical cut in the base of each stem. If your roses are drooping, stand the stems in hot water for a few seconds.

▶ Do not stand the bouquet in direct sunlight, and top up the vase every day with a third of fresh water. Remove flowers as soon as they begin to fade.

▶ Some people add an aspirin to the water and swear that this keeps their roses fresher for longer.

An old herbal remedy Rosewater has soothing properties and is particularly effective in eye compresses. Make rosewater yourself by adding 500 grams of freshly picked rose petals to one litre of previously boiled, cooled spring water. Leave the liquid to infuse for three or four days in a covered container, filter, then pour into a stoppered glass bottle and keep it somewhere cool.

Name your own rose If you are keen on hybridising your own roses and feel that you have created a new form that you would like to register and name, then contact the Royal National Rose Society in St Albans, Hertfordshire. They will grow the rose for three years on your behalf to ensure that it is stable and, if it is, they will then register it with the International Registration Authority for Roses and with the American Rose Society. They will also be able to advise you on obtaining a Plant Patent to protect your rights in your new rose, which is very useful if it becomes popular.

Glorious garden shrubs

Shrubs are the backbone of a garden's structure, giving shape to old-fashioned herbaceous borders and providing dramatic focal points. From the pretty flowering shrubs of the cottage garden to stately Victorian evergreens, there have never been so many to choose from.

Choose well, plant well

Getting them off to a good start

When you buy a container-grown shrub, it will probably have already spent some time in its pot, and the ball of compost around the roots may have dried out completely. If you plant your shrub in that condition, its roots will remain desiccated – even copious watering will not revive it and it will not survive. As a precaution, before planting immerse the rootball and its container in a bucket of water for at least 15 minutes, until bubbles stop coming to the surface.

Getting down to earth

Before choosing shrubs, assess your soil and test its acidity or alkalinity with a DIY kit from the garden centre or by having it analysed by a lab.

Type of soil	Suitable shrubs
Dry earth for most of the year	Kerria, tamarisk, *Viburnum opulus*, sea buckthorn, *Genista hispanica*
Moist or damp soil for most of the year	Amelanchier, elder, hydrangea, *Nandina domestica* (heavenly bamboo), mahonia
Acid soil	Camellia, rhododendron, *Kalmia latifolia* (calico bush), azalea, *Pieris japonica*, hydrangea
Chalky soil	Cotoneaster, deutzia, forsythia, philadelphus

Cotinus coggygria *is an eye-catching shrub remarkable for its magnificent foliage, especially in autumn.*

Lots of water Immediately after planting your shrub, give it 10–15 litres of tepid water, even if it is raining. This isn't just an old gardener's tale, but a necessity to help the plant to bed in and let the rootball make good contact with the soil.
▶ If the water does not soak in fast, create a small basin by building up a ridge of soil around the plant. Fill it with water and let it ebb away, then repeat until your can is empty.

Keep an eye on the roots Shrubs are almost always sold in containers. Check the root system to make sure that it will flourish once you get it home.
▶ Turn the plant over to check that the roots are not poking through the drainage holes (right) which is a sign that it has spent too long in the pot. Don't be afraid to take the plant out of its container (right). It should have several white roots all around the rootball. If it doesn't, the plant has been recently repotted and you will be paying unnecessarily for a large pot.

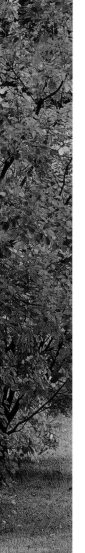

Look after bare-rooted plants Some shrubs are not sold in containers, but have been lifted from the soil where they were raised, so that their roots are bare. They should be planted in winter while they are dormant. Avoid frosty weather when planting and do not plant in frozen or waterlogged soil.

▶ Before planting a bare-rooted shrub, prepare the roots. This is called 'dressing' them. Cut off any broken or damaged roots, trim the larger ones, but do not touch the little ones, as these are the ones that take up water from the soil.

▶ To plant, follow the same procedure as for a containerised plant. So that you do not plant too deeply, lay the handle of your spade across the planting hole. The neck of the shrub – the spot between the roots and the trunk that you may be able to identify by a soil mark made when it was in the ground – should be at that level.

Mistakes to avoid To give your shrubs the best chance, avoid these common pitfalls.

▶ Don't plant them too close together. The shrubs will become overcrowded after two or three years and you will have to dig some up just when they are settling in.

▶ Don't economise by buying shrubs that are too small. It is better to buy a few large, good-quality plants and to enrich the soil correctly when planting.

▶ Avoid autumn feeding. This encourages the formation of soft and sappy new shoots that will only freeze and be damaged by frosts and cold.

Plant when it is cool, but never when it freezes
The best time to plant shrubs is at the end of autumn so they can settle in before the growing season in spring. In areas where winters are harsh, it is better to plant in spring. But whenever you plant, never put a shrub in the ground when it is freezing.

Growing acid-loving plants in the wrong soil
Don't try to grow acid-loving plants such as azaleas, camellias and heathers in alkaline soil by just filling a trench with ericaceous compost. These plants are not designed for such conditions, and you can't beat nature. Even though initially this method may work, it is only a temporary measure and creates an artificial environment that the plant will exhaust in two to three years before becoming stunted and sick.

▶ If your soil is already acidic but not a low enough pH for the plants you want to grow, then this method has a better chance of working. You may still need to lift the plant every few years and add more ericaceous compost to the hole.

▶ If your soil is alkaline but you are determined to grow an acid-loving specimen, consider growing it in a large pot filled with ericaceous compost.

Living with an alkaline soil Although an alkaline soil may restrict your choice of plants, there are many that tolerate it. They include cotoneasters, forsythia, the scented philadelphus and its relative, deutzia. Far less effort is involved if you grow only those plants that will enjoy your soil conditions.

▶ If your soil is very chalky, you could try modifying it over time by adding ericaceous compost or sulphur chips. But this should be done gradually, as a too-sudden change might endanger the plants that are already there.

Planting acid-loving plants in alkaline soil

To maximise your chance of success with a plant that is not suited to your soil conditions, use a lined trench. However, you will still need to renew the acidic mulch from time to time.

1 Dig a hole 1 metre deep – it might be helpful to hire a mini-digger. Line the bottom and sides.

2 Use a sheet of thick, permeable membrane, which lets water soak away but stops soils mixing.

3 Half-fill the hole with gravel, then part-fill with acid (ericaceous) compost, available at garden centres.

4 Immerse the plant's rootball in water for half an hour, then position it in the hole and fill with compost.

5 Firm in the plant and make a recessed area to retain water around the base. Trim the membrane.

6 Water well, then spread a layer of an acidic mulch such as pine bark around the base of the plant.

Garden shrubs

Making a case for shrubs

Shrubs are the perfect choice for small gardens, where there may not be enough room for trees. They are also quite at home planted in a tub on a patio or balcony. In a large garden, once they become established they are the ideal way to divide the space either as a hedge or a specimen plant.

Permanence They do not have to be replanted every year.

Year-round interest Shrubs with evergreen foliage remain neat and interesting throughout the year. Yew, box (left), santolina and rosemary are old favourites long used to give structure to a cottage garden.

Resistance Shrubs are much less susceptible to disease and cold weather than herbaceous plants.

Low maintenance Choose a slow-growing shrub that requires little pruning, such as *Syringa meyeri* 'Palibin'.

Planting in a lawn Any plant growing in a lawn will have to compete with grass for food and water. To reduce the drain on these resources, cut out a section of turf 3–4cm deep and as big as the plant's root spread where you wish to plant your shrub. This removes the grass that would otherwise grow right above your plant's roots. Plant your shrub as normal.

Tempted by a shrub in flower? Garden centres often entice gardeners to buy wonderful flowering shrubs in the middle of summer. It's risky trying to plant containerised shrubs when they are in flower, but if you can't resist, there are precautions you can take to ensure you get the best possible results.
▶ Plant your shrub in the desired location, but leave it in its container as long as it remains in flower, making sure to keep it watered regularly.
▶ When it has finished flowering, cut back the branches to half their length to reduce the foliage. Remove the plant from the container and plant it normally. Make sure it remains well watered right up until winter.
▶ Mulch around the plant with a thick layer of composted bark, which will keep the soil fresh and reduce evaporation.

The bigger, the better If you want to give your shrub the best possible start in life, then make the planting hole at least twice as wide as the diameter of the rootball. The shrub will establish much more quickly and perform to its full potential.
▶ Don't plant the shrub too deep: the top of the rootball should be at soil level after planting. Break up the soil at the bottom of the hole with a fork to make it easier for the roots to penetrate and get a good hold.

Colours and scents

Late-afternoon fragrance Flowers are often at their most fragrant around five o'clock in the afternoon. Plant them where you can appreciate the scent – near windows, next to garden seats and along the paths. Choose aromatic plants that flower in different seasons to keep your garden fragrant all year. Good examples include *Viburnum bodnantense*, lilac, honeysuckle, single-flowered philadelphus, choisya, lavender, daphne and *Mahonia* 'Charity'.

Shrubs as presents Give a shrub to friends instead of buying a bunch of flowers. It is a present that will last for years and will be a steady reminder of your friendship.

A cool blue summer
To bring a fresh feeling to your garden at the height of summer, plant shrubs with blue flowers such as blue forms of buddleja, hebe, ceanothus, hibiscus syriacus, caryopteris (right) and perovskia.
▶ These sun-loving species prefer a sheltered

site with well-drained soil, and in these conditions they are frost-hardy. For healthy plants, feed them with a complete fertiliser containing trace elements.

Autumn on fire Many shrubs have wonderful, warm autumn hues, changing to yellow, orange and bright red. The best colours are achieved after a good summer, one that is hot and dry, but not parched. For wonderful autumn colour choose plants such as *Amelanchier lamarckii*, *Acer japonicum*, *Cotinus coggygria*, *Enkianthus campanulatus*, *Euonymus alatus* and *Rhus typhina*.

Shrubs with showy flowers ▶

Summer scent Late-flowering *Buddleja crispa* ❶ has fragrant lilac-pink flowers in July. It is best grown against a sunny wall.

Acid or alkali Pink hydrangeas (*Hydrangea macrophylla*) ❷ like rich, alkaline soil, while rhododendrons ❸ need acid soil.

Early fragrance The early-spring flowers of the Mexican orange (*Choisya ternata*) ❹ have a delicious scent.

Bright spring flowers One of the classics, *Forsythia* x *intermedia* 'Spectabilis' ❺ makes a delightful hedge.

Blue cascades The fountain buddleja (*Buddleja alternifolia*) ❻ has overhanging branches that are covered in flowers in June.

Garden shrubs

Clematis clambers over the supportive framework of cotoneaster, bringing summer colour to the evergreen foliage.

Shrubs and climbers make perfect partners Some shrubs can be beautiful in one season but not very interesting the rest of the year. Try growing through their branches a climbing or rambling plant, which will appreciate the natural support and supply a touch of colour when the shrub is less attractive.

▶ Plant a flame creeper (*Tropaeolum speciosum*) at the foot of a pyracantha in April, and once the shrub has finished flowering, the red or orange flowers of the climber will stand out delightfully against its dark green foliage. Or plant an ipomoea, with its magnificent blue trumpets of flowers, at the foot of a variegated shrub.

▶ Clematis and climbing roses appreciate being planted close to shrubs and will clamber attractively through their stems.

The shrub as larder Birds are especially fond of shrubs with berries. By attracting birds to your garden, you will also reduce the number of pests, such as caterpillars and slugs. For year-round interest, plant a variety of deciduous and evergreen berried plants including elder (left, top) with scarlet berries in June and July, symphoricarpus (left) the snowberry, with white berries in autumn and winter, pyracantha, ivy, cotoneaster, *Euonymus europaeus* and callicarpa.

Under conifers Conifers create dry shade, which is a difficult environment for many shrubs to grow in. Prepare your planting area thoroughly and do not plant immediately underneath the tree. Try some of the following, according to your soil type: hydrangea, rhododendron, azalea, fuchsia, mahonia, euonymus, buxus, elaeagnus and aucuba. These should all adapt to the difficult situation.

▶ Make sure the shrub gets enough water. Conifers will compete for any available moisture in the soil.

Light in dark corners Lift a dull spot with variegated foliage. Elaeagnus, *Cornus alba* and sambucus are just three of the shrubs that have interesting variegated varieties. Lighter and brighter-coloured foliage may be more susceptible to strong sunshine so plant these shrubs in partial shade under trees, where they will enhance a dark corner.

Great all year round In any garden, it is important to strike a balance between deciduous and evergreen shrubs, as evergreens lend essential colour and structure to the garden in winter. Some gardeners advocate planting two-thirds evergreen to one-third deciduous shrubs to compensate for the long winter. There's a wide choice, including holly, mahonia, *Garrya elliptica*, *Viburnum tinus*, elaeagnus and *Euonymus europaeus* (above). Don't forget that, as these shrubs never lose their leaves, they will need watering all year round, until they are properly established.

Dwarf shrubs

Compact shrubs can be delightful planted in a garden border or in a rockery, but make sure that they do not become swamped by larger plants. They are especially useful for adding texture and height to low-growing beds.

Evergreen shrubs *Berberis* x *stenophylla* 'Corallina compacta', *Buxus microphylla* 'Green Pillow', *Cotoneaster microphyllus*, *Euonymus fortunei* 'Kewensis', *E. japonicus* 'Microphyllus Albovariegatus', *Ilex crenata* 'Golden Gem', *Pieris japonica* 'Little Heath', *Pittosporum tenuifolium* 'Tom Thumb'

Conifers *Abies balsamea* 'Nana', *Chamaecyparis obtusa* 'Nana Gracilis', *C. pisifera* 'Filifera Aurea', *C. lawsoniana* 'Gnome', *Picea mariana* 'Nana', *Juniperus squamata* 'Blue Star', *Pinus mugo* 'Mops'

Beautiful branches brighten up winter, from left: Rubus cockburnianus, Salix alba 'Vitellina', and Cornus alba 'Sibirica'.

Autumn does not mean the end of the garden
There are several shrubs that flower during autumn and even winter, including many varieties of *Erica carnea*, viburnum, hamamelis and garrya. Plant them close to the house so that they are visible from the main windows and you can enjoy them throughout the winter months.

Colourful branches in a bare landscape
In winter, once their leaves have fallen, whitewash brambles (*Rubus*), some dogwoods (*Cornus*), and many willows (*Salix*) have interesting white, yellow, orange or red stems, which contrast sharply with the grey wintry surroundings. *Cornus alba*, despite its name, displays fiery red branches in winter, while *Rubus cockburnianus* creates a Christmas-like atmosphere with its arching white branches, seemingly covered in frost.
▶ The most colourful branches will be those that have grown over the previous year. In spring remove the oldest stems from their base – those that have begun to lose their bright colour. This will encourage fresh new growth from the bottom, to form next winter's colourful stems.

Faded flowers
Don't be too hasty in pruning roses and hydrangeas. You'll miss the winter sight of red rose hips, and ice glistening on the frosty 'dried' flowers of hydrangea.

White weddings in spring
Unblemished white and soft pink flowers in spring are a pure delight. Enhance your garden with shrubs that bear blooms brilliant enough for a wedding display. Try a few of the more unusual ones such as *Cornus kousa*, *Exochorda* x *macrantha*, kolkwitzia, and *Viburnum plicatum* 'Mariesii' (below).

White blossoms festoon the branches of Viburnum plicatum 'Mariesii' early in the season.

The evergreen pieris not only produces a stunning display of red foliage in spring but also flowers profusely.

Shrubs that see red Some shrubs have beautiful young leaves that contrast with their older foliage. These are ideal for creating some midborder interest as spring progresses. The leaves of *Photinia* x *fraseri* 'Red Robin' and *Pieris formosa* 'Forrestii' are a spectacular red at first, before turning to a more subtle shade of green in summer.

Suitable for dry gardens When growing any plant don't try to fight nature. If you live in a dry area such as East Anglia, you may need to tailor the plants that you grow to the prevailing conditions. If the rainfall is minimal, grow plants that naturally occur in drier regions of Europe and the Mediterranean, such as broom, helianthemum, rosemary, tamarisk, santolina, gorse and yucca. Shrubs with silver or grey foliage are better adapted to hot and dry gardens.
▶ Be sure to plant these shrubs properly. Prepare the planting hole and add garden compost or well-rotted manure. Plant shrubs in the autumn, to allow the roots to establish over winter before the onslaught of summer. Water thoroughly at planting and at regular intervals until established.
▶ Remember that it is always better to soak the ground thoroughly but occasionally rather than water superficially on a daily basis.

Shrubs for nesting Birds are the gardener's friend, devouring a wide variety of insects and pests. Provide them with nesting sites and they will set up home in your garden.
▶ Birds particularly like evergreen shrubs, for guaranteed privacy, as well as shrubs with thick, prickly branches for protection. So try planting berberis, pyracantha, mahonia and holly, if possible in an isolated corner of the garden.

Keeping shrubs healthy

Green leaves on a variegated shrub? A branch bearing totally green leaves often develops in the middle of a shrub with variegated foliage. Remove the reverting shoot as soon as you spot it by cutting it out with secateurs right at the base of the branch it is sprouting from. If you don't take prompt action, your shrub may revert to a solid green all over and will be much less attractive.

The dangers of salt In coastal areas, sea spray and salt-laden winds can damage garden plants, clogging their leaves and stripping them of moisture. If your garden is in an exposed coastal location, choose plants that are able to withstand these conditions. Visit a local nursery for advice and take a look at what grows well in neighbouring gardens and in the wild. Plants such as pittosporum, rosemary, choisya, colutea, escallonia, hebe and broom normally thrive in coastal spots.

If your shrub seems rather tired There could be lots of reasons for this. To rescue your plant, try to identify the most likely cause and correct the problem.
▶ It may be that the soil and planting hole were not well prepared before planting. If the soil is not properly broken up this can lead to air pockets where the roots are unable to make good contact with the soil. The soil might be very poor quality or unsuitable for the type of plant you are trying to grow. In winter, try to lift and replant in good soil.
▶ The roots may have been damaged during planting or through staking too close to the shrub. If possible, lift the plant and cut out any damaged roots. Then replant with care (right), gently teasing out the roots by hand and laying them over a small mound of well-rotted garden compost in the base of a large planting hole.
▶ A cold snap or a period of drying wind may have affected the growth of your plant. Give protection or move the shrub to a sheltered spot.

Hebe andersonii variegata is a half-hardy evergreen shrub that prefers a sheltered position.

Top tips for poorly flowering shrubs
A disappointing display of flowers can often be easily remedied.

▶ **Have patience** The shrub may be too young. Some take several years to flower.

▶ **Give nourishment** Choose a fertiliser that is high in potash to encourage flowers. A nitrogen-rich fertiliser boosts leaf growth to the detriment of flowers.

▶ **Cover with horticultural fleece in winter** The flower buds may have been damaged by frost in spring.

▶ **Mulch the soil surface** It is essential to maintain humidity and protect roots from extremes of temperature. The shrub may have been too hot prior to flowering.

▶ **Prune correctly** Spring-flowering shrubs often suffer if they have been chopped back in a winter garden tidy-up. Pruning late in the season actually removes the shoots that form next year's flowers. Prune immediately after flowering, restricting winter pruning to a gentle trim.

▶ **Plant in a more suitable spot** The shrub may be in the wrong position, suffering from too much shade or sun, or it could be in a draught. Dig it up next winter and move it.

A bandage for rhododendrons
If frost has split the bark of your rhododendrons, the wound will be vulnerable to fungal diseases. Cover it with a medical bandage or hessian strip and leave it until a scar forms. Do not to wrap it too tightly around the stem, as this will create an unsightly bulge.

Dying of thirst in winter Dehydration isn't just a summer problem. Evergreen shrubs and conifers continue to need water in winter, even though their growth slows down. Water only when the temperature is above freezing, paying special attention to shrubs that were planted less than a year ago.

Prevent grass from growing under shrubs Mowing the grass around a shrub planted in the lawn can be problematic. The more grass is mowed, the quicker it grows, competing with the shrub for the available nutrients and water. Long grass may also harbour pests. Carefully cut away a circle of turf about a metre wide from around the base of the shrub and apply a thick layer of mulch.

▶ Mulch with a 5–8cm layer of cut grass, which will gradually break down into the soil. Spread it around the base so that it doesn't actually touch the stem of the shrub, and top it up every two or three months.

Producing healthy cuttings Many shrubs can be propagated using traditional techniques. Start by trimming the new shoots that develop at the base in summer. These are called lignified stems and are the best material for semiripe cuttings. Choose healthy stems and remove about 15cm of the shoot, cutting about 5mm below a node. Trim the cutting carefully so that the cut is clean and straight. This minimises the risk of disease attacking the cutting through a ragged edge. Remove the lower leaves carefully and cut out the shoot tip. Fill a pot with equal amounts of sharp sand and well-rotted compost, make a hole with a dibber and insert the cutting. Firm it in and water gently. Place it in a sheltered spot or cold frame to root, and plant the rooted shoot in the garden next spring.

To ensure the survival of your shrub, water it copiously just after planting, even if it is raining.

Pruning made simple

Top tips for pruning For the best results when pruning, make sure you use a quality pair of secateurs. To encourage flowers to grow, choose a pair of bypass secateurs. These have a scissor action for ease of use, which means they are gentler on the stems. Anvil secateurs, which have a flat jaw against which the cutting blade acts, minimise twisting, making them ideal for cutting out dead wood or removing undesirable growth such as suckers and thorns.

► **Position the cutting blade correctly** The larger of the two blades should always be closer to the part of the stem you are retaining (left, below). This will ensure that the cut is clean and neat so it will heal faster and reduce the risk of disease. If you cut with the smaller blade closer to the stem you are retaining, you are more likely to crush the stem tissue. It will take longer to heal and can dry out the stem.

► **Always cut to 1cm above a node** This stops the sap from flowing farther up the branch than it needs to and diverts it to the bud, which will quickly grow into a new shoot.

► **Use an angled cut on vertical branches** Prune all vertically growing branches with an angled cut to prevent water from stagnating on the wound. This speeds up the healing process and reduces the risk of disease. The slope of the angle should be away from the bud at the node, so that water will not run onto it. It is not essential to cut horizontal branches like this as water will run off them naturally.

► **Take note of the growth pattern before pruning** The branches of shrubs form one of two patterns, which determine where the pruning cuts should be made (see right). The branches either sprout in pairs from opposite sides of the stem joint, or from separate buds on alternate sides of the stem.

Bare stems: some serious pruning required Are your shrubs top-heavy with foliage and going bare at the base? If so the chances are they are not developing new stems from the base. In spring, when the first buds begin to shoot, cut out about one-third of the oldest branches down to ground level. This will encourage fresh growth from the base without seriously reducing flowering. Next year remove another third of the oldest branches to ground level and repeat for the third year, when you should have a completely rejuvenated plant.

Pruning a spring-flowering shrub

1 Prune spring-flowering shrubs such as forsythia just after they have flowered, when the leaves begin to appear.

2 Cut back old branches over 2cm thick. They generally have grey bark. They clutter the centre of the clump and do not flower well.

3 To let air and light into the centre and stimulate growth, cut back lateral shoots and any that are rubbing or growing inwards.

4 Cut back all other shoots to 50cm from the ground. The sap will flow to all the remaining buds and turn them into new branches.

Pruning a shrub with decorative stems

Shrubs grown for their attractive winter stems need to be pruned in early spring before they start growing in earnest. Cut back any stems that are more than two years old, right down to almost ground level. Alternatively, choose the oldest central stems and remove these. These older stems will have lost their vibrant

colours and will be dull brown or grey. Prune carefully with sharp secateurs to avoid damaging stems nearby.

► After pruning, fertilise the plant to encourage it to produce lots of new shoots, which will be brightly coloured. Carry on fertilising regularly throughout the growing season to ensure it produces lots of bright stems for next winter.

Rejuvenating a neglected shrub If you have inherited a shrub that is overgrown and needs restorative pruning, wait until it has flowered and then prune it hard before winter.
▶ Select the oldest branches and cut these back to the base using a pruning saw, being careful not to damage neighbouring branches.
▶ Locate the other branches originating from the centre of the bush and cut these back to their base, or just above a secondary branch that is growing outwards. Finally cut back all the other branches by removing two-thirds of their length (above). Remember to make your cut 1cm above an outward-facing bud to keep the structure of the shrub open.

Be bold when pruning Amateur gardeners are often afraid of hard-pruning shrubs, preferring to prune them lightly into neat shapes. This is more likely to ruin the shrub's natural appearance for it encourages dense and tangled growth that prevents flowers and leaves from growing in the centre. It is much better to remove the oldest branches, recognisable by their dark, often knarled bark. Cut them right back to the trunk, just before the growing season.

Eco-friendly tip Don't discard your shrub prunings; they make excellent natural supports for perennials and small shrubs. Alternatively you can put them through a shredder and mix them with equal quantities of green material in the compost heap.
▶ Once composted, which takes about three months, this will make an excellent mulch for your shrubs, retaining valuable moisture and adding to the fertility of the soil.

Pruning a standard forsythia With creative pruning, spring-flowering plants such as forsythia can be grown to look more like a tree than a shrub. As soon as it has flowered, choose the strongest branch and cut all the others right back to the base. Stake the main stem so that it is straight and supported. As shoots start to form on the main stem, remove those lower down to keep this area bare and trunk-like. At the same time allow those higher up to grow to form a bushy

Why you need to prune shrubs to make them flower
Spring-flowering shrubs normally flower on stems that are in their second year of growth. This means that to encourage plenty of flowers next year you need to stimulate the shrub to make new stems from the base this year. These new stems will mature and bear flowers in their second year.

Even though most shrubs will flower with no pruning, the plants will become woody and they may start to go bare at the base. For the best results, each year cut the oldest branches back as low as possible and just lightly trim the remaining branches, keeping the overall shape of the plant intact. Do this as soon as possible after flowering to allow enough time for the plant to generate some fresh stems that will flower next spring.

head. Next spring this top growth will flower, resembling a small tree. To encourage more flowers next year, cut these stems back hard after flowering to stimulate fresh growth.

Let shrubs become established Most shrubs don't require much pruning in the first few years after planting. At first, confine your efforts to removing any crossing branches that spoil the shape of the bush, and removing dead flowers. However, always cut out any damaged or unhealthy branches straight away, to prevent the spread of diseases.

Opposite or alternate buds? To decide how to prune your shrubs, look at the buds on their stems. If the buds grow in pairs, opposite each other, prune straight across above a pair of healthy buds. If the buds are arranged alternately up the stem, cut at an angle of 45°, just above a healthy bud, making sure that the lower point of your cut is just behind the bud, but not beneath it.

Pruning a summer-flowering shrub

1 *Buddleja davidii* responds well to pruning. When the flowers at the tips of the branches have died back, cut them off to encourage the remaining flowers to develop.

2 After the flowering season is over, cut the branches by about half and then in early spring prune hard, right back to the growth point of the previous branches.

3 Keep the centre of the shrub open to let in air and light. If branches are tangled and overgrown, cut back the oldest ones to the base. New stems will soon regenerate.

Living green walls and sculptures

A painstakingly clipped hedge or piece of topiary was once the hallmark of a grand formal garden. Cottage gardeners adapted the tradition to suit their more spontaneous style, and today we can borrow from the past to use shrubs of all kinds to create boundaries, backdrops and focal points of distinction.

An old-fashioned garden with formal hedges and topiary is a favourite gardener's fantasy. But even the grandest scheme can be the inspiration for less ambitious designs.

A handsome hedge

Buy bare-rooted plants Specimen shrubs are almost always sold in containers. This means they can be planted all year round – except during freezing, waterlogged or very dry, hot weather – with immediate results. If you are planning to grow hedges, however, it is much more cost-effective to buy younger plants with bare roots. These will need planting in the winter when they are dormant and your hedge may take a couple of years to thicken out, but it will establish quickly and work out much cheaper.

Use a mechanical digger If you have a long length of hedge to plant, you can save yourself some hard work by hiring a small mechanical digger to break up the ground. Plan to do your digging about a month before planting the hedge, add quality tree and shrub compost to the soil and then let it rest. The soil will settle down gradually during this period.
▶ When you are ready to plant the hedge, the earth should still be easy to work and you will only need to dig holes large enough for the rootball of each plant.

Mulching is essential Applying mulch to the base of a young hedge is essential to prevent the growth of weeds. Remove any perennial weeds and their roots, and then spread a generous 10cm layer of cocoa shell, chipped bark or well-rotted garden compost along the base of the hedge.

Make a path in front of your hedge Hedges need regular maintenance, so leave a path between a hedge and a flower bed. Make sure there is enough room to move about, possibly with a wheelbarrow, or even to erect scaffolding if the top of the hedge is too tall to reach from ground level.

Save precious space Although hedges offer many benefits, they are greedy for space so, in a small garden, they may not be the best solution. If you really want a living screen around the garden, consider erecting a trellis and growing climbers or, for a fruitful option, espalier and fan-trained fruit trees.

Fast growers There are some shrubs, in particular conifers, which will grow into a hedge fairly quickly. The disadvantage is that the vigour of these shrubs does not diminish once the hedge is established, which means you will have to cut them three or four times a year to keep them in check. The most rampant growers are the Leyland cypress (*Cupressocyparis leylandii*) and false cypress (*Chamaecyparis*).

Good hedges make good neighbours Until recently, property owners have been able to grow very tall hedges, regardless of their neighbours' wishes. The law is now changing to require owners to trim their hedges to a certain height. You are still within your rights to cut back any branches or roots that intrude into your own property.

A 'wild' hedge A natural or mixed hedge is composed of several different hedge plants and is not neatly clipped. It may not be as dense as a uniform evergreen hedge, but it looks attractive and needs less attention. You may need to curb the vigour of some plants to leave room for more timid ones.
▶ To get an idea of what grows wild in your area, take a look at local waste ground, where you are likely to find hazel (*Corylus avellana*), blackthorn (*Prunus spinosa*), hawthorn (*Crataegus laevigata*), elder (*Sambucus nigra*) and field maple (*Acer campestre*). Any of these can be used as the basis for

your hedge, combined with some favourite flowering or fruiting shrubs such as blackberry (*Rubus fruticosus*), dog rose (*Rosa canina*) and holly.

► If space permits, do what farmers do and take advantage of any strongly growing trees that the hedge throws up – let them grow to their full height as this will add interest.

A hedge to absorb pollution
If you want to reduce noise from the street and fumes from the traffic, choose dense evergreen hedge plants such as Japanese euonymus, cotoneaster, pyracantha, Leyland cypress or false cypress.

► Some deciduous hedges such as beech or hornbeam will also absorb sound, even in winter, as they hold on to many of their dead leaves during the colder months.

A protective hedge
One reason for planting a hedge is to deter both human and wildlife intruders, and plants with prickles and spines are particularly effective. Pyracantha, elaeagnus, berberis, blackthorn, dog rose, holly and hawthorn will all form a secure wall, either used alone or in combination, and they will be covered in flowers in spring and berries for the birds in autumn.

► To create a really impenetrable barrier, erect a sturdy wire fence before planting. Place your shrubs along this fence and after a few years they will cover the wire.

A new hedge each year
Ring the changes and grow annuals or herbaceous plants to create a different screen every year. Maize, sunflowers, Jerusalem artichokes and hollyhocks can all be sown or planted as young plants in spring to create a tall green, flowering hedge that will last from the start of summer through to the first frosts.

A hedge of roses
Several types of rose make fine, old-fashioned hedges, though they are bare in winter. The best all-rounders are the old roses, because of their dense foliage and long flowering period. Wild species roses such as *Rosa rugosa* were favourites in the cottage garden and make a tough hedge, producing an attractive display of hips in autumn.

► If you want a hedge smothered in flowers, remember to prune the stems to different heights to ensure that the flowers appear all over the hedge instead of just at the top.

A traditional laid hedge
Hedges made from interlaced willow stems were a feature of old-fashioned country life, being widely available and easy to make, and are regaining popularity in Britain.

► To create your own traditional willow hedge, 'plant' withies – rootless willow stems – at 20cm intervals, inclining them at an angle. Next, interlace another row next to it, inclined at an opposite angle. Then 'weave' alternate withies, one in front and one behind, to form a latticework panel, supported by posts if needed. Water the stems immediately and keep the soil moist.

► The branches, which are in effect cuttings, will root, and in spring they will sprout new leaves. Trim back excess growth in spring and autumn to reveal the living trellis beneath.

Planting a hedge through fabric
Various specialist fabrics are designed to suppress weeds yet let the rain permeate through to plant roots below. Known as landscape sheeting or mulching membranes, they keep the soil warm and damp and are ideal for use when planting a new hedge. Once the plants are in place, apply a mulch over the top and water well until the plants are established.

1 Loosen the earth in the plot to 40cm deep, add compost and level the surface. Dig a channel 10cm deep round the planting area.

2 Place the fabric over the plot, sliding the edges into the channels and holding them down with soil or pegs.

3 Use a knife to cut crosses where the plants will go. Fold their corners back and dig a hole large enough to take the rootball.

4 Set the rootball in the hole, fill with soil, press down, water, then replace fabric over plant base. Cover with an attractive mulch.

Hedges and topiary

A selection of suitable hedging plants

Key
E – Evergreen
Q – Quick-growing
SE – Semi-evergreen

Use the table and its key to choose the type of hedge that will suit your requirements and the conditions in your garden.

FOR SECURITY

	Harsh climate	Temperate climate	Coastal climate
	Hawthorn (Q)	All the plants in previous column	Gorse (E)
	Blackthorn		Sea buckthorn (Q)
	Dog rose		Hawthorn (Q)
	Rugosa rose		
	Holly (E)		
	Barberry ❶		
	Pyracantha (E)		

FOR SCREENING

	Harsh climate	Temperate climate	Coastal climate
	Japanese quince	Japanese spindle	*Elaeagnus* x *ebbingei (E/Q)*
	Thuja (E/Q)	Laurustinus (E)	Portugal laurel (E)
	Privet (E/Q)	Aucuba (E)	Olearia (E)
	Picea abies (E/Q)	Mahonia (E)	Pittosporum (E)
	Yew (E)	Photinia (E)	Escallonia (E)
	Spindle tree	Escallonia (E/Q)	
	Hornbeam		
	Beech ❷		
	Cherry laurel (E/Q)		

WINDBREAK

	Harsh climate	Temperate climate	Coastal climate
	Hazel (Q)	All the plants in the previous column, plus pollarded birch and bamboo	Atriplex (SE)
	Field maple (Q)		Tamarisk ❸
	Elder (Q)		Olearia (E)
	Laurustinus (E)		Pittosporum (E)
	Privet (E/SE/Q)		
	Lawsons cypress (E/Q)		

LOW DIVIDERS

	Harsh climate	Temperate climate	Coastal climate
	Box (E)	Lavender (SE)	Fuchsia
	Lonicera nitida (E/Q)	Cinquefoil	Cotton lavender (E)
	Lavender (SE)	Potentilla ❹	Lavender (SE)
	Rosemary (E/Q)		

NATURAL OR FLOWERING

	Harsh climate	Temperate climate	Coastal climate
	Japanese quince	Rock rose	Hydrangea ❺
	Deutzia	Broom	Escallonia (E/Q)
	Forsythia	Rose	Sea buckthorn (Q)
	Flowering currant	Abelia (SE)	
	Gooseberry	Sea buckthorn (Q)	
	Lilac	Bladder senna	
	Spiraea	Buddleja	
	Weigela	Lilac	
	Laburnum	Crab apple	

Brighten up a conifer hedge

A hedge made entirely of conifers can look fairly austere. Give it a touch of colour by sowing seeds of a deciduous flowering climber such as tropaeolum or cobaea at the base just after its spring trim.
▶ Using the secure support provided by the conifers, these plants will climb up into the hedge, brightening it up with a sprinkling of colourful flowers.

An easy-maintenance hedge

Rather than planting vigorous conifers that expand sideways and have to be cut back, plant a row of conifers with an upward-growing habit and a spread that rarely exceeds a metre. Try the Canadian thuja (*Thuja occidentalis*) 'Smaragd' or Irish juniper (*Juniperus communis*) 'Hibernica'. With these varieties, you will just need to give the tops a regular trim, but you won't have to worry about any sideways expansion.

A good windbreak

If you live in an exposed area, you may need a hedge to provide some protection from strong winds. The best sort of hedge to create an effective windbreak is one that filters the wind, rather than blocking it completely. A solid hedge could be damaged or even uprooted in very stormy weather, whereas a hedge that allows the wind through will reduce the impact of the weather by as much as 75 per cent.
▶ A windbreak will protect an area of ground equal to twenty times its height for every metre in length. This means that a hedge 1.8 metres tall and ten metres long will protect an area of 360 square metres: a considerable space. Check the height of the mature plants and how quickly they will grow when choosing the best ones to use. For suitable species for windy sites, see the Windbreak suggestions in the box (left).

Keeping hedges in trim

Trimming with care When using an electric hedge trimmer watch out for the cable at all times. For safety, pass it over your shoulder and behind you, well away from the cutting blades, to avoid cutting through it. Always use a circuit breaker when using outdoor power equipment.

Keeping safe Before use, make sure your hedge trimmer is in good repair.
▶ Modern machines require both hands to be on the machine to operate it: if you let go with one hand a blade brake stops the machine. Be extra careful when using machines that can be operated with just one hand.
▶ When buying a machine, make sure the blade ends are protected by blunt extensions so that if the blade falls onto your body it doesn't cut, it just bruises.
▶ Wear protective gloves and goggles, trousers, long sleeves and leather shoes.

A well-grown hedge If you want your hedge to be two metres high, don't wait until it reaches this height before trimming it, as this may make the growth towards the base sparse. Instead, trim the top of the hedge as soon as it reaches a metre in height. This will make it thicken out at the base. Allow the hedge to grow by a further 15–20cm each year until it has reached the desired height.

A gentle trim for the cherry laurel... The cherry laurel grows quickly and makes a thick evergreen hedge.
▶ Don't cut it with shears or a hedge trimmer, as slicing through its large glossy leaves will spoil its appearance. Instead, use secateurs, trimming individual branches to the required length one at a time.

... and for the pyracantha too During spring a pyracantha hedge becomes covered in tiny white flowers, then grows new foliage branches. Don't be tempted to cut it back with a hedge trimmer, because if you remove all the flowers, even when they have died, you will be deprived of the abundance of red or orange berries that appear in the autumn. Instead, cut back new branches one by one with secateurs, just to tidy up the appearance of the plants.

The best times for cutting a hedge Make the first trim of the year towards the end of spring, in May or June, then after the growth of summer, in September or October. Species that grow fast, such as Leyland cypress, should also be cut at the start of spring and during summer. Other hedges should be trimmed as necessary according to your preference and how quickly they grow.

Cut the sides at a slight angle When cutting a hedge, start at the bottom and work your way up. If you start trimming from the top the prunings will fall on the lower branches, making it more difficult to cut the hedge.
▶ For a well-presented hedge that is green from top to bottom, cut the sides at a slight angle, tapering inwards towards the top so that the top of the hedge is narrower than the bottom. With this shape, the bottom of the hedge will receive enough rain and more light.

A tool for a small hedge If you've got only a small hedge, consider investing in a battery-powered hedge trimmer. They are easy to use, cable-free and quick to charge, making cutting the hedge a real breeze. Generally these hedge trimmers have shorter blades than electric or petrol machines and are better suited to cutting smaller areas.

A hedge with a view Cut a round window or an arched doorway in a dense hedge to open up a romantic vista. This gives privacy and a view at the same time and was a favourite design trick of landscape gardeners of the past.

Cutting a hedge

1 A string tied between pegs will help you cut a straight line. Use secure steps rather than a ladder to climb on.

2 Never cut above shoulder height or stretch too far as you could lose control of your tools, or fall.

3 For hedges with small leaves use a hedge trimmer or shears. For hedges with large leaves cut branches one by one with secateurs.

4 Cut inside the line of the hedge so that the cut ends cannot be seen. Check frequently to make sure you are keeping a straight line.

Compost hedge clippings

Make the most of your hedge clippings by passing them through a shredder. If you place the shredder close to the hedge you can feed the clippings into it as soon as they are cut. Add the chippings to the compost heap to break them down before using as a soil conditioner or mulch.

▶ To catch the clippings spread a sheet along the base of the hedge. When you have finished cutting, the prunings can be bundled up and removed for shredding.

The ideal way to water a hedge Use a seep hose made of a special perforated material that lets water pass through its walls. This allows you to water slowly and gives the water time to penetrate the earth properly. It is ideal for watering the base of a hedge. Trail the hosepipe on the ground between the trunks or stems and attach one end to a tap. Check to see if you need a sprinkler licence for this type of watering product and make sure your tap is fitted with a double check valve to prevent backflow into the mains.

Spray conifer hedges Some conifer hedge pests thrive in very dry conditions but can be deterred by spraying water into the hedge once a week in summer.

A winter clean-up for bare hedges Tidy up a deciduous hedge in winter when the branches are bare. It is much easier to cut out the dead wood and tangled stems and remove any unwanted climbing plants such as bryony or brambles. Top up the mulch at ground level if it has become thin.

A dead conifer When one plant in a coniferous hedge starts to die while the others around it remain quite healthy, it may be due to the phytophthora fungus that affects conifers, particularly in damp or waterlogged conditions. Remove the affected plant completely with as much of the root and surrounding soil as you can. Burn all the plant material instead of composting it.

UNDER GLASS

A constant source of hedging plants

To get a good, thick hedge, you need a lot of plants. But this can be expensive. Grow your own by taking hardwood and semiripe cuttings and pushing them into pots filled with a loam-based cuttings compost such as John Innes No 1. Give them protection over the winter in a cold frame or cold greenhouse, keep a check on them and water sparingly until spring. Rooted cuttings can then be potted up and grown on until they are big enough to plant out in a hedge.

The fine art of topiary

An age-old practice Topiary dates back to ancient Rome and has been a feature in gardens ever since. A clipped geometric shape adds a formal, period feel to the garden, while a whimsical topiary bird or beast recalls informal country planting. Topiary is just one example of how traditional skills can be used decoratively in today's gardens.

The right structure To create a simple, straight-edged shape, place a frame made of thin bamboo canes over the plant before cutting it. Once you have trimmed the plant to the required shape you can take the canes away.

▶ If you want to create a more complicated shape such as an animal, or a clear-cut geometric design such as a pyramid, cylinder, ball or cone, make the shape first from wire netting. Fix over the plant, secure to the ground with short wooden stakes and trim any foliage that passes through the netting.

▶ Once in place, don't remove the wire structure: it will eventually be covered by foliage and disappear.

Topiary in pots Box topiary shapes in pots can make a stylish feature for the patio, beside a doorway or even on steps, and being slow-growing, they require little maintenance. When they are grown in containers, it is important to feed the plants well, because they derive all their nutrients from the soil in the pot. For box plants, add drainage material such as grit or perlite to the compost. A layer of gravel in the bottom of the planter, before filling up with compost, will also help to improve the drainage.

THE GARDENER'S CHOICE

The best plants for topiary

Box plants were frequently used for topiary in the past and remain one of the most popular plants for crafting into sculpted forms, but any of the plants listed will give good results.

Evergreen shrubs Box, *Lonicera nitida*, holly and privet will give year-round colour and form.

Deciduous shrubs Although hornbeam and *Berberis thunbergii* shed their leaves, they are worthy topiary subjects.

Conifers Yew is a traditional choice that is replacing privet as a cottage garden favourite. Juniper is also suitable.

Low plants For small living sculptures, try ivy, lavender or santolina trained over a frame.

Shaping topiary with a bamboo frame

1 Plant a young box shrub in a container. Box likes well-drained, even chalky, soil enriched with organic matter, and dislikes being directly in the sun.

2 Cover the plant with a bamboo frame made of canes. Be patient: box grows very slowly. Allow it to branch out and fill the frame completely.

3 Cut off all foliage outside the frame with shears, trimming monthly if necessary. Repeated cutting will encourage the plant to get more bushy.

4 Water regularly to keep the earth cool. When the shape is perfect, remove the frame. Break it and remove pieces to avoid damaging the plant.

The right time to cut topiary plants While the shape is still being formed, cut it once a year at the end of spring, removing half the previous year's growth. This will encourage secondary branches to develop, forming a dense growth. Once the desired shape has been obtained, the frequency of cutting varies according to the vigour of the species and the shape chosen – a complicated shape may need cutting every month to keep it precise. If an impeccable finish isn't important, cut once a year after the spring growth, and again after flowering in relevant species. Never cut once autumn has started because any new shoots will not have time to harden before the winter.

Topiary plants need nourishment To get the best from your topiary plants they need to be well fed, which encourages them to grow new shoots and dense foliage after trimming. Use an organic fertiliser high in nitrogen such as nettle mash.

For precision, use shears A hedge trimmer is too fast to use for accurate cutting, so use a pair of shears instead. They let you make a neat job of trimming and are also much easier to handle when dealing with complicated or rounded shapes.

▶ Invest in a quality pair and keep them in good working order with a sharp edge to the blade. If you cut a shrub with blunt shears you will maul its stems and cause lasting damage. This could result in yellow, brown and dead tissue that not only mars the look of the plant but can actually kill it.

A dying branch If one of your topiary branches turns brown and appears to be dying, cut it off at the base, into the healthy, living wood. If the plant is well fed and watered, new shoots should appear on the old wood to fill the hole, though sometimes it takes years to restore the original shape.
▶ This should work on most plants but remember that conifers rarely regenerate when cut back into mature wood.

Snow can be a problem

Snow can weigh heavily on plants and damage them. After heavy snowfall carefully knock the snow from the branches using a broom. You can also wrap them in early winter in horticultural fleece bound with string. It will then be easy to brush off any snow.

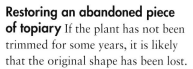

Restoring an abandoned piece
of topiary If the plant has not been trimmed for some years, it is likely that the original shape has been lost. Cut back hard in the first year to approximately the original shape, then trim more carefully for the next two or three years to obtain an even, precise surface and restore the original form. Feed the plant well to encourage plenty of new shoots.

Making a spiral

Yew and box are particularly suitable for creating a spiral shape. It is not very difficult but you will need patience, as it will take around seven years to obtain a neat shape. You need to start with a slender plant about 50–60cm high, staked to keep it upright. In the second year, cut it to a cylindrical shape, forming a column about 10cm in diameter, then cut it again at the end of the summer to the required width.

Repeat this process in the third year. When the plant has reached a height of about 1.2m, remove the stake and begin cutting the spiral shape with shears, starting at the base. Mark it out first using string or wire wound round the stem. Then gradually use secateurs to free the trunk from its stems and follow the shape around the plant.

Half way to paradise

We have the humble cottage garden to thank for our love affair with climbers. There, where space was at a premium, these charming plants clambered over walls and trees to delight the eye and lead it upwards. In the modern garden, we still appreciate their ability to transform the smallest space with their colourful flowers and heavenly scent.

Well-planted climbers

Always buy in containers In contrast to annual climbers, which are normally sold as seeds or as pots of seedlings, all shrubby climbers should be bought as mature plants in containers, or as small potted plants. These rooted plants

are in just the right condition to grow in your garden. Do not be tempted to buy climbers that are sold with bare roots.
▶ A healthy climber will have several stems growing from the base and its foliage will not be dry or discoloured.

When to buy Although plants in containers are available all year round, it is still best to buy a climbing plant in early spring or at the beginning of autumn. These are the best times to plant, which also means you will probably have the best selection of healthy plants to choose from.

Large-flowering clematis and a climbing rose – an old-fashioned marriage made in heaven.

Prices climb too Don't be surprised if you find buying climbing plants to be an expensive business. Some plants will cost more than others, depending on the size of the rootball and how many stems it has. Generally the older the plant the more expensive it will be. Some plants have been grafted onto a rootstock and then grown on at the nursery for several years, and the price will reflect this extra nurture.

Should you buy a large climber? Sometimes in garden centres you will find large climbers, two metres or more tall, sold in large pots and often already in flower. You can buy them with confidence, but for the best results grow them in a pot where they will create an immediate decorative effect.
▶ For the garden, it is better to choose younger, smaller plants in containers, no more than 1.5 metres tall. These will establish more quickly than larger plants, which may not flower for a year or two if planted out in the garden, and will grow so fast that in two years they will reach the same height as the larger climbers.

Planting out – spring or autumn? Plants in containers can be planted out all year round, except during periods of frost, flood or intense drought.
▶ If at all possible it is always preferable to plant out in autumn so that the roots have time to develop while the soil is

still warm from summer. They will also benefit from the winter rain.

▶ In heavy soil that stays wet all winter, it is better to plant out in spring.

Soak climbers before planting

Plants sold in pots are often grown in a soil mixture that is very difficult to make wet once it is dry, even more so after planting out. Always immerse the plant in a bucket of water at room temperature before it is planted. Soak it for at least a quarter of an hour, or until there are no more air bubbles rising to the surface of the water.

Close but not too close...
If you want to train a climber against a wall or tree, plant it 30cm away from the support. If it is any closer, any rain that falls will be deflected by the wall or tree, and the plant will not receive enough rainwater to grow. It will soon make the leap onto the support and start climbing.

Keep cool
Most climbing plants like to have cool roots. You can easily achieve this by covering the soil around the base of the plant with a thick layer of mulch. Make sure that the mulch does not build up around the stem of the climber or it may impede the circulation of air around the base.

▶ Provide shade by placing a tile or opaque screen at the base of the plant (left).

▶ Planting an evergreen close to a climber will also create beneficial shade for its roots.

Don't lay trellis flat against the wall
Whether you are using trellis, metal wire or fishing wire as a support for your climber, it is essential to leave 3–4cm between the support and the wall. This allows the stems of the plant to twist right round the support and also gives them some protection from the heat generated by the wall in summer. The best way to create this space is to place small pieces of wood or plastic spacers between the wall and the support.

▶ To make it easier to take the trellis down if you need to paint or repair the wall, do not fix it to the wall itself but instead attach it to hooks screwed into the wall. Then, when necessary, you can simply lift it up, with the plant in place, and lay it carefully on the ground beneath the wall.

Watering basin
Build up a small ridge of soil in a circle around the base of the plant, on top of the mulch, to create a watering basin. This will collect any water – when it rains and from when you water the plant – and direct it so that it penetrates the soil around and above the rootball.

▶ Keep the watering basin intact for at least the first year after planting your climber. However, if you live in a particularly cold area of the country, you may want to remove the watering basin in winter, to avoid creating a frozen puddle around your plant.

Soil conditions
Most climbers are tolerant of a variety of soil types. For the best results make sure you mix in plenty of well-rotted garden compost in the planting hole. Specialist tree and shrub compost may also help. This will improve the water retention of the soil, and add vital nutrients.

▶ In extreme alkaline conditions, wisteria plants may develop yellow (chlorotic) leaves. Try watering the plant with sequestered iron or by using an acidifying mulch.

Planting a clematis

1 Dig a deep hole a little in front of the support. Lay the rootball in it so that the stems lean towards the support.

2 Fill up the hole, covering the rootball and the first 5cm of the stem with a mixture of soil and well-rotted compost.

3 Water generously to get rid of any air pockets and give the plant the best chance of taking root.

4 Protect the base to help keep the roots cool. Clematis love 'a warm head and cool feet'.

Shrubby climbers for walls

North-facing

- *Pileostegia viburnoides*
- *Hedera helix* ❶
- Large, light-flowered clematis
- *Hydrangea petiolaris*
- *Parthenocissus tricuspidata*
- *Akebia quinata*

East-facing

- *Hedera colchica*
- *Lonicera japonica* 'Halliana'
- *Parthenocissus quinquefolia*
- Winter jasmine ❷
- *Clematis montana*

South-facing

- *Vitis vinifera* 'Purpurea'
- *Actinidia kolomikta*
- *Clematis armandii*
- *Solanum crispum* ❸
- *Trachelospermum jasminoides*
- Climbing roses

West-facing

- *Campsis radicans* ❹
- Passion flower
- Wisteria
- *Jasminum officinale*
- *Lonicera x tellmanniana*
- Summer-flowering clematis

Good combinations Whether they flower simultaneously or at different times, try planting two types of climbers next to each other. Roses intertwined with spring or summer-flowering clematis are a popular choice for an extended flowering season, but you could also try *Jasminum nudiflorum* with *Clematis armandii* for a real winter treat.

▶ Annual climbers such as tropaeolum, sweet pea and ipomoea, or even climbers usually seen in the vegetable garden, such as hops and scarlet runner beans, would make good summer companions for the evergreen ivy. Pick your planting partners carefully for the greatest impact.

Which climbers would enhance your garden?

Scented climbers If you like fragrant flowers, make space for *Clematis montana* 'Elizabeth' which smells of vanilla in spring, *Lonicera japonica* 'Halliana' and its entrancing scent that lasts all summer, *Jasminum officinale* a favourite for perfumes, cosmetics and aromatherapy, wisteria and, of course, climbing roses such as 'Compassion' which is salmon pink tinted with apricot orange.

Climbers that can withstand the cold If you live in a region where winters are very harsh and the temperature plummets to extreme levels, choose your climbers with care. Among the hardiest climbing plants are deciduous clematis, honeysuckle, wisteria, ivy, rose and parthenocissus.

▶ Plants do not really become resistant to cold until their second or third year in the garden, so don't forget to protect them from frost during the first few winters after planting, particularly at the base of the plant, where a generous layer of mulch would be beneficial.

A carpet of climbers Even without vertical support, climbers will continue to grow – horizontally. This means they can be used to carpet problem areas that are difficult to maintain or unpleasant to look at. Ivy is an excellent ground-cover plant that smothers weeds, while *Clematis montana* is ideal for creating a blanket of spring flowers over an unsightly boundary or shed. Trim the plants back with garden shears to keep them in good condition.

Cover a wall quickly Although ivy and parthenocissus can grow up to a metre in a year, to get quicker results, plant several of the same species of plant along the length of a wall.

Climbers for shady corners Some plants have variegated leaves, which can brighten up areas of the garden that are sheltered from the sun. A few to remember are *Actinidia kolomikta*, which displays pink and white young leaves in spring, and *Amelopsis glandulosa* 'Elegans', with lovely pink shoots and leaves splashed with pink and white.

▶ Use variegated ivies such as *Hedera canariensis* 'Variegata', *Hedera colchica* 'Sulphur Heart' and *Hedera helix* 'Glacier'.

Colourful climbers for every situation ▶

Cascades of flowers *Wisteria sinensis* ❶ has bright green leaves, the perfect foil for its clusters of lilac blooms.

Shady beauty The delicate blooms of *Clematis* 'Nelly Moser' ❷ appear at their best in partial shade.

A scented favourite The sweetly fragrant flowers of *Lonicera x americana* ❸ adorn this vigorous honeysuckle in summer.

Spectacular foliage The leaves of colourful climber *Actinidia kolomikta* ❹ are tipped with pink and white as they mature.

Shining trumpets The half-hardy *Mandevilla x amena* 'Alice du Pont' ❺ displays glowing, pink flowers in summer.

More than just flowers The glowing flowers of *Clematis* 'Bill Mackenzie' ❻ are followed by attractive, feathery seed heads.

Climbing hydrangea

The climber *Hydrangea petiolaris* (left) is the understated cousin of the flamboyant common hydrangea, with its large blue or pink inflorescences. It has flat white flowers that appear in June set against beautiful dark green foliage. This hydrangea likes a north-facing wall, but it needs light so avoid shade cast by neighbouring trees.

Fast-flowering wisteria

Some wisterias can take between ten and twenty years to flower if grown from seed, enough to try the patience of any gardener. To prevent this problem, avoid buying unnamed seedlings and try to buy wisteria that is already in flower at the time of purchase. Alternatively choose grafted plants – make sure this is specifically mentioned on the label – which will flower two to three years after planting.

▶ Do not give nitrogen-rich fertiliser to newly planted wisteria, as this encourages energy to be used for the growth of the stem and leaves, and can actually delay flowering.

Climbers are not suitable for all walls Be careful when choosing climbers to grow up a wall.

▶ **Walls with cracks** Avoid climbers such as parthenocissus, *Hydrangea petiolaris* and ivy that have adventitious roots and suckers (see panel, below left) if they are to be grown up a soft-stone or half-timbered house, or any walls with cracks. These plants will worm their way into every nook and cranny, weakening the joints and increasing the risk of damp.

▶ **Modern concrete walls** Although ivy can damage old walls whose stones or bricks need repointing, it is virtually impossible for it to get a hold on a modern, concrete wall in good condition, so a trellis may be needed.

Climbers under glass Lend a tropical feel to your conservatory by growing the exotic deciduous climber *Gloriosa rothschildiana* (right) up a support in a container. It has very unusual flowers with curved red and yellow petals in summer. Position it in full sun, but shade the roots with a generous mulch. It is very sensitive to the cold and its dried-off tubers must be kept under glass through the winter. But once it has been repotted and all danger of frost has passed, it can be moved to a sunny position outdoors. Remember to bring it in on cold nights.

Winter climbers Although most climbing plants lose their leaves when it turns cold, a few display lovely green foliage right in the middle of winter.

▶ One of the most attractive is *Clematis armandii*, whose white flowers appear for two months at the end of winter.

▶ Others to consider are akebia, *Lonicera japonica* and of course all the members of the ivy family.

Heat insulation Climbers can even help you run your home more efficiently. Evergreen climbers such as ivy can actually play a role in insulating your house. In winter, air cavities between the ivy and the outer wall form a useful insulating layer that helps to keep heat in. And in summer, the leaves block the sun's rays and help keep the house cooler.

DID YOU KNOW?

How plants cling on as they climb

Winding stems Wisteria, honeysuckle, phaseolus and akebia have stems that will coil around their support or other stems.

Adventitious roots Ivy ❶, campsis and *Hydrangea petiolaris* have clinging roots that develop on the stems when they are in contact with the support, especially if it is rough and damp. These roots have no nutritive function.

Stem tendrils Some parthenocissus and also passiflora ❷ have stem tendrils that will coil around any support – nails, the stalk of a nearby leaf, or a piece of metal wire. Clematis have twining leaf stalk tendrils.

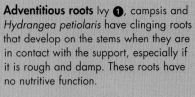

Suckers Other parthenocissus ❸ have stem tendrils that look like hands, with sticky pads, or suckers, at the end of each 'finger'. These suckers are very adhesive and can be extremely difficult to remove, even after you have pulled off the creeper.

Thorns Roses ❹ and rubus climb by scrambling up supports with their thorns. However, a certain amount of judicious training is usually required to ensure roses grow in the required shape.

Strong, shrubby climbers, like this wisteria, can be trained on a stake to look like a small tree.

Special effects for climbers

Train a climber to look like a tree Vines, *Hydrangea petiolaris* and wisteria can be planted in the garden and trained to grow into little trees. Plant them with plenty of space around them and drive a solid wooden stake into the ground near the base of the plant. Let the shoots run along the ground. Once the shoots are between one and two metres long, lift them up and wrap them around the stake. The branches will grow around it and thicken to form a straight tree-like trunk, while new shoots will grow from the top. You will need to be patient, but the final effect will be dramatic.

Flowering companions If one of your walls has been covered in ivy or parthenocissus for several years, give it new life with a flowering climber. Solanum and *Akebia quinata* will appreciate this sturdy natural support.

DID YOU KNOW?

Shades of the tropics

Most climbing plants originate from forests and wooded regions, often from the tropics. They take root in the well-shaded soil and climb up through the trees, flowering only when they reach the top. This undoubtedly explains why climbers particularly like to have their feet in cool, well-drained soil and their heads in the sun. It is also important to remember that climbers thoroughly dislike stagnant moisture or water.

WATCH OUT

Beware of poisonous climbers Certain climbing plants, such as wisteria, ivy, solanum and sweet pea, have poisonous parts that can be dangerous when eaten. If you have children, be careful what you plant, but also teach them to be wary of plants and never to eat anything from the garden.

Use a tree as a support If an elderly tree in your garden is not performing well, train a climbing plant up into its branches. This is ideal for old fruit trees that are past their best as they provide an excellent support for vigorous climbers. Honeysuckle, climbing roses, clematis and passion flower are all good candidates for this type of planting – in time your old tree will be covered in beautiful flowers again.

Use a mirror to create space If you have a small garden, try placing a large mirror in a corner behind a climber growing up a post or narrow trellis. The climber will not take much space to grow but will appear to double its size, and your garden will seem larger.

Superb autumn foliage
Some deciduous climbers display brilliant, fiery colours in autumn (right) that can rival others' showy flowers. *Parthenocissus tricuspidata* 'Veitchii' has blood-red leaves in October, while the large leaves of *Vitis coignetiae* turn wine-coloured several weeks before they fall.

Trailing climbers
Parthenocissus (right), ivy and passiflora will form a dramatic wall of colour. Just stretch a rope or chain between two structures such as a fence and a pergola, and these climbers will head for the new support. When they are unable to find anything vertical to cling onto, the young shoots will hang down, forming elegant green drapes in summer and a crimson curtain in autumn.

Caring for climbers

Blowing in the wind Be wary when covering wire netting with climbing plants. In many cases it is an ideal support for plants with twining stems or tendrils as it lets the air circulate. But the foliage can create a solid barrier to the wind, and in very exposed areas a violent gust could wrench out the supporting posts and blow the netting down.

Controlled freedom Climbers with stems that wind themselves around their supports sometimes also need to be fixed to them. However, don't strangle the stems by attaching them too tightly. Instead wind a flexible clip around the stem and fix to the support. Alternatively, tie garden string loosely around the stem and the support. You should be able to put your finger easily behind the stem where it is tied in.

Recycle old tights and stockings Wash and then cut the legs of old tights and stockings into 4cm wide strips that open out into a circular band. These can then be used as flexible ties to attach climbing stems to trellises and supports.

Layering climbers Producing new climbers by layering couldn't be easier. In spring, lay one of the soft shoots attached to the mother plant on the ground, and cover with a 5cm layer of compost so that several buds – but no leaves – are beneath the soil. Hold it in place with a wire hoop. The following spring, when it has rooted, take out the hoop, cut the shoot behind the new roots that have grown, dig it out and plant it in its new site. You might have to wait a year but the result is a free plant.

Climbers are a haven for small animals Climbing plants offer shelter, food and sometimes breeding sites for all kinds of creatures. Insects and spiders will be the first to arrive, and if you are lucky slow worms and lizards may follow, attracted by the natural supply of insect food. Then the birds will move in, finding in the foliage and elevated position both safety and privacy for their nests and young ones.
▶ Be careful when you prune or trim your climbers however, in case you disturb a nest of young or deprive birds of their safe home. Some birds nest as late as June or July.

Choose your climbing supports with care. Remember they must be strong enough to support the plant when fully grown.

Strong-armed wisteria Wisteria stems can grow as thick as a man's arm and wind themselves around their support with such force that they can bend it or pull it out, even if it is metal. Choose a sturdy support that is in good repair.
▶ Other climbers can also be very heavy, especially when they are well established or covered in fruit. Bear this in mind if you plan to erect a pergola and cover it with rampant growth.

Put delicate plants under straw matting If you have planted a climber against a wall and are not sure how well it will withstand the cold, protect it from frost by leaning straw matting against the wall so that it covers the plant. Insulate the roots with a mulch.

Flower power Feed your flowering climbers with an organic fertiliser that is rich in potash, such as cocoa shells or seaweed meal. This will encourage flowering and boost general growth. Pay particular attention to climbers growing in containers.

DID YOU KNOW?
My clematis is wilting...
Without warning, the flowers on one or more shoots of a clematis can turn black, dry out and die. This is called clematis wilt and is thought to be caused by fungus or bacteria present in the soil. There is nothing you can do to stop it, but you must act quickly and radically to save the plant. Cut the branches off completely, down to ground level, and clear the area around the base to a depth of around 10cm. Replace the soil you have removed with healthy soil from another part of the garden. If your garden has a history of this problem, try planting the clematis deeper.

Simple pruning tips

Prune before planting On climbers with adventitious roots, such as ivy, parthenocissus or the climbing hydrangea, only new young shoots will cling to a support. There is no point struggling to get the stems of a plant you have just bought and planted to adhere to a wall as they will not oblige. Cut back the stems to approximately 10cm from the rootball, above a bud, and the young shoots that soon begin to grow will automatically start to climb up the support.

Is pruning necessary? This depends on the type of plant. Many climbers will grow quite happily without pruning, but some need pruning to encourage plenty of flowers. If your plant is outgrowing its space or becoming unmanageable it is time to reach for the secateurs.

Pruning for better flowers If you note when your climbers flower and the type of stem wood on which the buds develop, you can prune them at the right time to encourage a spectacular display next year.

▶ **Spring flowers** Plants that flower in spring, such as *Akebia quinata*, *Clematis alpina* (below, top) and other early clematis, form their flower buds on the previous year's growth, which is ripened and woody. The buds rest during winter until the start of the mild weather when they open. If you prune these stems in winter you will remove next year's flower buds and miss out on a spring display. Wait until your plant has flowered then cut the flowering stems back hard to encourage new growth that will flower next spring.

▶ **Summer flowers** Plants that flower in summer, such as passiflora, climbing roses and large-flowered clematis like 'Mrs Cholmondeley' (left, centre), form their flower buds during spring, on fresh shoots that grow from the end of winter onwards. Don't prune the long shoots that appear in spring, as these are carrying the summer flowers. Instead, cut back the plant in winter or early spring to encourage the growth of new shoots.

▶ **Winter flowers** Winter-flowering plants, such as *Jasminum nudiflorum*, *Clematis armandii* (left) and ivy form their flower buds on growth made

When to prune flowering climbers

PLANT	WHEN	HOW
Passiflora	End of winter	To rejuvenate the plant, shorten all the secondary stems, which shoot from the older, main stems, to 5cm from the point at which they sprout from the main stem.
Grapevine	February	Cut off the young shoots from the previous year above the second bud.
Campsis	February–March	Cut back the secondary shoots close to their base.
Clematis	February–April	Prune early-spring flowerers after flowering, midseason flowerers in early spring, and late-season clematis in winter and early spring.
Repeat-flowering rose	March	Cut out all the weak, diseased branches. Shorten the strongest branches by two-thirds.
Non-repeat-flowering rose	July–August	Remove all the old stems after flowering.
Jasminum nudiflorum	April	Remove one of the oldest main branches at the base after flowering to encourage the plant to grow new shoots.
Wisteria	September–October	Once the main framework is established, cut off all the secondary shoots above the third bud in autumn.
Parthenocissus	October	To rejuventate the plant, cut back all the growth to ground level.
Honeysuckle	November–February	Remove the oldest stems in winter then prune back to the main stems after flowering.

during spring and summer. Prune them after they have finished flowering to encourage new shoots that will mature and ripen during summer to bear next season's flowers.

Prevent damage to roofs Ivy and parthenocissus can be very invasive on house walls and can even get under roof tiles, causing leaks. To keep their growth under control, cut them back once a year to 50cm below the level of the gutter.

Trim ivy Well-established ivy, and sometimes *Hydrangea petiolaris*, will become very thick and develop shoots that grow away from the wall. If they become heavy enough, they could even loosen the plant from the wall. Trim these protruding stems every three years with a hedge trimmer. Do this in August so your plants will be tidy for winter.

Supporting roles in the garden

Styles in trellising, pergolas and arbours have changed little in hundreds of years. Available in modern materials or traditional wood, there are options to suit every size and design of garden and every type of climber.

The versatile trellis

Spruce up a wooden trellis

An old trellis can be in poor condition, particularly if it has not been adequately treated against fungal rot and algae. Ideally it should be treated with a water-based preservative every two or three years, although this can be tricky once it is smothered with climbing plants.

▶ Untreated wood can be used for all manner of decorative purposes in the garden but, depending on the type of wood, it may deteriorate quite quickly.

▶ Once you have preserved your garden timber you can apply a whole variety of colour washes and finishes either to blend the trellis into the background or to add more colour and

The graceful leaves and blooms of laburnum add a charming, cascading effect to any garden.

contrast to the garden. Many of these colour washes are water-based and can be used in conjunction with a water-based preservative. Make sure you read the instructions carefully and do not use any preservatives harmful to plants.

Put spacers behind the trellis If you are fixing a trellis to a wall or fence to support climbing plants, use small blocks of wood to hold the trellis about 5cm away from the wall. This enables the plants to twine in and around the trellis more easily and so supports the plant more securely. It also improves airflow around the wall and the foliage of the plant, thus reducing the risk of fungus.

Natural sound-proofing Town and city balconies can be screened off using a trellis covered in evergreen climbing plants. Either buy ready-planted containers complete with trellis, or combine plants with a trellis of your choice, and in a short time you will have an attractive living screen.

▶ A wall of plants will also absorb a certain amount of air pollution and reduce noise from nearby roads.

Cover an unsightly water butt Make a screen or enclosure from trellis panels fixed to posts, then train vigorous climbers over it. To quickly cover an eyesore, choose plants such as clematis, golden hop, or, for a year-round disguise, ivy. These plants will not object to being pruned to ground level if major maintenance work or access to the tank is needed and will quickly regrow to create a thick screen.

Fixing removable netting to a wall

1 Fix specially designed clips, available from DIY and garden centres, to the wall at regular intervals.

2 Place the netting against the wall and press it into the clips, which will keep the netting away from the wall.

Train them well Before you tackle the task of training a climber, remember that the base of a support or a wall is often set in concrete, and it is almost always in a rain shadow. To make sure the roots get enough moisture, position the plant at least 30cm away from the support.

▶ Climbing plants are often sold with two or three stems attached to a thin supporting bamboo cane. After planting, carefully remove the bamboo cane, and gently position the stems against the support so that they will grow vertically, securing them with ties.

▶ A year later, the stems will have made new shoots. Separate these secondary stems and train them to fan outwards across the support at an angle of 45°.

▶ The following year the stems will have grown again and may even have developed lateral stems. Separate these and this time train them horizontally. Train the secondary stems at an angle of 45°, and so on each year.

▶ Remember to keep the plant ties loose and flexible, so that each stem is free to grow unhindered.

Create an illusion You can use a decorative trellis specially designed to alter the perspective of your garden and make a small space appear larger. A trellis with this 'trompe l'oeil' effect (left) draws the eye into it to create the illusion of a deeper space. It is most effective when attached to a wall.

▶ Remember, however, that if you train a plant over this type of trellis you will lose the illusion of distance that it creates.

Expandable trellis Some trellising is sold without an outside frame and can be expanded to fit the available space. The further you stretch the trellis, the more you open its structure.

Garden structures

Create a rose umbrella Train a climbing rose that has been grafted onto a standard rootstock to form a dramatic cascade of flowers (right). Simply fix an umbrella-shaped rose frame into the ground and arrange the trailing stems over it.

A covered wigwam If you have restricted wall space, you can still grow climbers on free-standing plant supports.

▶ Using tall bamboo canes, construct a wigwam in a bed or a large container of compost. This will support the more compact, slower-growing herbaceous clematis such as *Clematis* 'Arabella' or smaller climbing roses.

▶ For heavier, more vigorous clematis, roses or honeysuckle, use stronger supports made from wood or metal that you can anchor to the ground among other plants in the garden.

Lattice fencing Lattice fencing in a criss-cross pattern has a natural, rustic look and is an ideal support for clematis, honeysuckle and cultivated blackberry. Try using it to fence off different sections of the garden, such as the vegetable patch or the children's play area, as its open structure will make the whole garden appear larger.

Trellis panels for a terrace or patio If you can't dig down into the ground to fix supports for a trellis, don't despair. You can get special brackets that screw onto hard surfaces, into which the posts simply slot and are held in place with screws. The trellis can then be easily attached to the posts. If this is not possible you can also build 'shoes' from bricks cemented to the patio, which will hold the posts in position.

Easy-care trellises

Modern technology and innovative new materials have combined to create a wide range of recycled plastic trellising and garden supports. Many of these are designed to look like wood and need very little maintenance; they make an excellent alternative to timber trellising and are often available in a choice of colours. Metal trellis panels and screens are also available and may be more suitable for your needs. Look out for materials such as galvanised steel and painted aluminium which will not be affected by the weather. Visit your local garden centre to see what is available.

Attacking rust Some gardeners like the 'antique' effect of rusted metal in the garden. If you do not, and there is something corroding in your garden, rub it down with a wire brush to remove the loose rust and paint on a coat of an anti-rust product to form a protective barrier over the metal.

Recycled fishing line If your climbing plants are only growing up the vertical supports of your gazebo, use thick fishing line stretched horizontally across the arches, to train the plants along. The line is virtually invisible, and once the stems have reached the other side it can be removed. Just make sure it is not used where it could catch someone unawares.

Electricity pylons and poles Don't be tempted to cover them with climbers – it is not permitted.

Lattice or openwork panels are perfect for delicate climbers such as clematis as they let the light through.

Pergolas and arches

Origins of pergolas Gardeners have used pergolas, arches and arbours to add interest and height to gardens since the Romans, whose artwork depicts arching reed-trellis arbours adorned with vines and roses. The pergola is traditionally a wooden or metal structure that supports climbing plants, under which you can promenade or simply relax.

Build your pergola to last For a pergola to last, the base of its uprights must be kept dry and secure. Soak the post base in preservative and sink it into holes filled with concrete.
▶ You can also use metal brackets to hold the posts. These are easy to install, need no cement, and allow you to replace the posts easily. However, these brackets are difficult to drive into hard or stony ground.

A pergola with a roof For a shaded terrace next to the house, grow climbers over a pergola running alongside a wall. While you wait for the plants to cover the roof, use split bamboo panels for shade and protection from the rain.
▶ If you position a pergola next to a house, remember that the frame and plants growing up it can block out a lot of light from the windows in the winter. Avoid structures that are too heavy, choose climbers that are deciduous, and make the pergola high enough to let plenty of light into the house.

Decorate your pergola with pots Though wooden trellis panels and pergolas are intended to support climbing plants, they can hold baskets and pots too. This means you can choose plants to extend the flowering season or add colour.

Traditional materials for pergolas

Pine This wood is strong and easy to work with. The posts should be at least 11cm square and the horizontal crosspieces 6cm thick.

Chestnut Poles 2.5–3 metres long (right) are recommended for a light, traditional-looking arched tunnel.

Metal You can also use a metal framework, but avoid a look of scaffolding. Metal structures can create a traditional effect – not surprising, as iron has been used for garden furniture for over 200 years. You can now buy ready-made, decorative wrought-iron or aluminium arches, and position them one after another to create a formal pergola as long as you like.

Think big: the larger the pergola the more space there will be for plants to grow and display their colourful blooms.

Creating a covered walkway

For the best results a pergola over a path should be 2.5–3 metres tall and wide. If it is wider than it is high, you risk creating a 'tunnel effect'. Two people should be able to pass through easily side-by-side, and without ducking to avoid the plants: allow at least 60cm overhead.

Make your garden seem bigger

The arch of a pergola, inviting you to pass underneath, has the effect of dividing a garden in two. So, if you have a small garden, a pergola may help to make it seem larger, particularly if you position it so that it appears to hint at wider vistas beyond. On the other hand, it will also make a long garden appear shorter.

▶ In small gardens choose a pergola with a framework that is not too chunky, or one that is painted green to blend in with the background. In a large garden, you can afford to draw attention to its structure or colour.

Pergola and trellising kits

Even if you are not a DIY expert, you can still have a pergola. Ready-to-build kits containing posts, arches and struts in treated wood make it easy to design and construct your own pergolas, arches, fences and other garden structures. Select the individual elements you require and tailor them to suit your plan.

YESTERDAY & TODAY
Wood needn't always be brown

Make the timber in your garden work harder by giving it a coat of colour. There is a huge choice available, in both traditional 'heritage' colours and brighter, more modern hues, though tones of blue and green are always a good bet. A colourful trellis or pergola will add interest to the garden in all seasons, but they are particularly attractive in the winter when many of the plants have died back and the garden is bare.

The power of the wind

If you garden in an exposed, windy position, choose your pergola and climbing plants with care.

▶ A lightweight metal frame could twist and be damaged by wind, so build a strong wooden structure with posts set firmly into the ground.

▶ Plants with heavy growth also make a structure vulnerable, creating a solid barrier that is more likely to be damaged by gusts that would breeze through a less densely covered structure. If wind is likely to be a problem, choose lighter, annual climbers such as sweet peas, runner beans, tropaeolum and morning glory. Being deciduous, they are unlikely to have any leaves at all during the windiest months.

Assembling a pergola kit

1 Unpack and sort out all the components, including the posts, rafters, fixtures and fittings. Fix the first upright.

2 Secure it to the base using the metal fittings provided, and use a spirit level to ensure that the upright is vertical.

3 Erect the remaining posts, ensuring they are vertical, and add the crosspieces to stabilise the structure.

4 For speed, strength and efficiency use an electric screwdriver to fix the main crossbeams to the uprights.

5 Once the posts and crosspieces are in place, position the rafters, slotting them into the main frame.

6 Your new pergola will provide secluded, shaded living space in the garden.

Gentle giants and lifelong friends

It's impossible to imagine a garden without trees. If you have had the good fortune to inherit one from 50 or even a 100 years ago, you may have mused on its long life. When you plant a new tree, you are investing in future generations and continuing a precious tradition.

Buying a healthy tree

Consider the mature size and shape Never buy a tree without checking what height and spread it will reach at maturity, or at least after ten years' growth. This will help you choose the right tree – neither too tall nor with too wide a spread – for your garden, and the right place to grow it.
▶ Conifers and evergreens can cast a lot of shade, especially when the sun is low in the sky in winter. Due to the density of this shade and the inhospitable soil conditions created by the fallen needles of most conifers, other plants are unable to grow beneath them.

WATCH OUT

Transporting trees: beware of cold Tree purchases rarely fit easily into the family car and often end up poking out of the sunroof, tied to the roof rack or even sticking out of the open tailgate.

Be very careful that you don't cause the tree undue stress on its journey. The temperature of the exposed tree will drop by 1°C for approximately every six miles per hour of speed. So

if the car is travelling at 30mph per hour and the external temperature is 8°C, then the exposed branches are actually experiencing 3°C. Any faster and the real problems start. At 60mph this temperature would be –2°C. At that stage, especially if the journey is long, the roots will begin to freeze, and the tree will struggle to recover.

Wrap your tree well using plastic bubblewrap to cover any exposed areas during the journey and protect them from cold.

The attractive foliage of Robinia *'Frisia' provides a pleasing backdrop for a herbaceous border.*

Think local Garden centres and numerous flower shows unveil magnificent new species every season. But try to resist the fashion for rare varieties unless you are already an experienced and knowledgeable gardener.
▶ Visit the local nursery for the best choice of trees to suit your garden. It's always useful to know a plant's common name as this can give you a clue to its place of origin and thus to its ability to adapt to your garden. For example a Cape plumbago, a pineapple guava or an Italian cypress are likely to fare badly in cold British winters. Some trees, such as mimosa, are not fully hardy so are unsuitable for exposed sites but will grow well if sheltered.

Young trees establish quickly It's not always a good idea to buy plants that have developed into young trees. Those with a good-sized trunk and a spread of branches will already have spent several years growing in a nursery bed or a container, and transplanting them to your garden will cause them inevitable stress.
▶ If the tree has been field-grown, some of the root system may be left behind when it is uprooted, and the tree will have to regrow sufficient roots to anchor itself and absorb water and nutrients, while also adapting to its new environment.
▶ It may be better to spend less and buy a younger, smaller tree that will settle in more quickly. It will soon catch up with the older tree, whose energy will be concentrated on establishing a good root system instead of making top growth.

Study the catalogue

Trees are sold in two basic forms – as saplings or as standard specimens.

▶ **A sapling, or whip** A young shoot that has not yet achieved its proper formation is a sapling or whip. It can be as much as two metres tall. This is an economical way to buy a tree, but you will need to know how to prune it over the two or three years following planting, in order to obtain the desired shape.

▶ **A standard** A tree that has spent several years growing in the nursery and has been professionally shaped to display the canopy, or leaf surface area, that constitutes its structure. The trunk alone will be around two metres tall.

▶ Nurseries describe their standards in terms of girth or circumference, rather than diameter. This is shown by two numbers written on the label, allowing for a margin. So, a standard labelled 12/14 has a girth when sold of 12–14cm, measured at one metre above the ground. This measurement should not, of course, be taken to indicate the eventual circumference of the trunk once the tree has reached full maturity, as the tree is likely to continue growing for many years to come.

Flowering cherries and other spring-flowering trees are among the most popular, and many gardens have one.

Is it a tree or a shrub?

It can be difficult to define a tree. Broadly speaking, a tree has a trunk with branches that grow upwards from its crown. But some trees, notably conifers, grow branches along the whole length of their trunk: other trees have supple branches that bend down to the ground, called weeping or pendulous trees. The branches of others grow along the ground, with no trunk at all. Even height is no guide, as some trees peak at one metre, while some of the larger shrubs can, in maturity, reach three or four metres. If you are in any doubt as to the eventual size and suitability of your chosen tree, seek some expert advice from staff at a specialist tree nursery.

Buying on a grand scale

For instant impact you can buy semimature trees from specialist nurseries. These will have been grown in open ground for anywhere between five and ten years, sometimes longer. The time spent nurturing these trees is reflected in their price. They have to be dug up using specialist equipment, transported to their new home and then often lifted into place using a crane. Normally these nurseries cater for professional gardeners and landscape projects, but they are available to anyone prepared to pay the price.

Buying out of season

As long as a tree is containerised you can plant it at any time of year, but don't be tempted to plant a bare-rooted tree unless it is dormant.

▶ Even if a tree is container-grown it still needs regular care. If you plant in spring or summer, water regularly and ideally keep the soil cool, especially during hot weather.

Small is beautiful

If you have a small garden, and particularly if you have to plant trees near to buildings, restrict your choice to dwarf varieties or those that are particularly slow-growing. This will ensure that you are not in any danger of planting a tree whose roots will later undermine your house.

▶ If space is extremely restricted, consider using a small specimen tree in a large container, such as a half-barrel. You could try one of the smaller Japanese cherries or a bay tree (*Laurus nobilis*) – useful for culinary purposes as well as being an ornamental evergreen – but remember that trees housed in containers must be fed regularly.

143

Choosing a tree for your garden

Fast-growing trees Trees take many years to develop their mature size and shape. If you are looking for trees that are fast growing then consider some of these, all of which can grow a metre or more per year: Tree of heaven (*Ailanthus altissima*), maple, birch, hornbeam (*Carpinus*), poplar and paulownia.

Beautiful autumn foliage New England and Canada are famed for their bronze-red autumn foliage, and you can achieve the same effect in your garden.
▶ **Golden** Try the maidenhair tree (*Ginkgo biloba*) or the tulip tree (*Liriodendron tulipifera*) for golden autumn leaves.
▶ **Golden yellow to purplish-violet** The sweet gum (*Liquidambar styraciflua*) 'Lane Roberts' has dramatic autumn colouring.
▶ **Blood-red** The scarlet oak (*Quercus coccinea*) 'Splendens' or the red maple (*Acer rubrum*) have deep rich foliage.
▶ **Bronze** Don't forget about deciduous conifers such as the golden larch (*Pseudolarix amabilis*) or the swamp cypress (*Taxodium distichum*), whose needles turn an amazing bronze colour just before they fall.

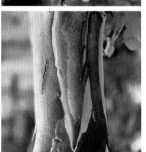

Decorative bark Everyone recognises the white bark of the common birch, but what about that of the Himalayan birch (*Betula utilis*), which is pale pink? Many trees are grown especially for their decorative bark, to brighten up the winter months.
▶ The plane tree is one example and so is the flowering cherry (*Prunus sargentii*). The Tibetan cherry (*Prunus serrula*) (top left) has walnut brown bark that peels off in horizontal strips to reveal shiny red bark below, and the paper-bark maple (*Acer griseum*) has cinnamon-coloured bark that detaches by rolling up on itself.
▶ Other magnificent examples of decorative bark include *Eucalyptus niphophila* (centre left) and *Betula nigra* (left).

Trees for screening In windy and exposed locations, trees can be used as an effective windbreak. Plant them densely to form a screen that will shelter the rest of the garden.
▶ Remember that it is better to filter the wind to diminish its force rather than to block it with a solid wall, which will create inevitable turbulence.

Blue shades Some conifers have grey-blue foliage – not only the Lawson cypress (*Chamaecyparis lawsoniana*) 'Pembury Blue' and the celebrated blue Colorado spruce (*Picea pungens*) 'Hoopsii' (right), but also the blue Atlas cedar (*Cedrus atlantica*) and the flaky juniper (*Juniperus squamata*) 'Meyeri'.

▶ The bluish colour of these conifers changes, depending on the intensity and amount of available light and the concentration of humidity in the air. It also varies according to the tree's general state of health.

Beware falling objects The fruits of conifers are cones. Some are striking, such as those of the Korean fir (*Abies koreana*), which produces violet-coloured cones from an early age, or those of the blue Arizona fir (*Abies lasciocarpa*), which are red and pendulous, measuring 7cm in length. Beware of parking or lying under the canopy of a tree bearing cones.

Trees for chalky soil... While an alkaline soil restricts the choices for your garden, there are many handsome species that tolerate it. Among the evergreens, choose holly, yew and juniper. Suitable broad-leaved trees include the whitebeam (*Sorbus aria*), beech, liquidambar and lime.

... and acid soil Most trees will grow in slightly acid soil, but some are rather more demanding and need a soil that is completely lime-free. These are notably the Judas tree (*Cercis siliquastrum*), red maple (*Acer rubrum*), Persian parrotia (*Parrotia persica*) and *Cercidiphyllum japonicum*.

Invasive roots Some trees have extensive roots that can lift paths and terraces, or possibly even crack the walls of houses. The poplar, weeping willow, chestnut, oak and cedar, among others, should not be planted close to buildings.
▶ You can help to prevent roots from reaching too close to paving and pipes, or even encroaching on shrubs and young trees, with a dedicated root barrier. Sink a rigid, plastic panel into the ground about two metres from the trunk. These are the same panels used to keep bamboo under control.
▶ Never plant trees with extensive roots near the vegetable or fruit garden where you will need to dig regularly.

Popular trees with charm

Trees are so varied that there is an interesting and attractive variety for any space you wish to fill, or any function you demand of it.

A conifer for your terrace

White spruce (*Picea glauca* var. *albertiana*) 'Conica'
Bosnian pine (*Pinus leucodermis*) 'Compact Gem'
Flaky juniper (*Juniperus squamata*) 'Blue Star' ❶

A weeping tree

Blue Atlas cedar (*Cedrus atlantica glauca*) 'Pendula'
Weeping ash (*Fraxinus excelsior*) 'Pendula'
Japanese pagoda tree (*Sophora japonica*) 'Pendula'
Willow (*Salix alba*) 'Tristis' ❷
Beech (*Fagus sylvatica*) 'Pendula'

An evergreen

Holm oak (*Quercus ilex*)
Holly (*Ilex aquifolium*) 'Argentea marginata' ❸
Magnolia (*Magnolia grandiflora*)

A tree with variegated foliage

Poplar (*Populus* x *candicans*) 'Aurora' ❹
Maple (*Acer negundo*) 'Variegatum'

A tree with purple foliage

Beech (*Fagus sylvatica*) 'Riversii'
Cercis (*Cercis canadensis*) 'Forest Pansy'
Prunus (*Prunus cerasifera*) 'Pissardii'
Maple (*Acer palmatum*) 'Atropurpureum' ❺

A scented tree

Eucalyptus (*Eucalyptus gunnii*) ❻
Paulownia (P. *fargesii* or P. *tomentosa*)
False acacia (*Robinia pseudoacacia*)
Manna ash (*Fraxinus ornus*)
Katsura tree (*Cercidiphyllum*)

A flowering tree

Red horse-chestnut (*Aesculus* x *carnea*) 'Briotii'
Judas tree (*Cercis siliquastrum*) ❼
Winter cherry (*Prunus subhirtella*) 'Autumnalis'
Tulip tree (*Liriodendron tulipifera*)
Flowering dogwood (*Cornus florida*)
Flowering crab apple (*Malus*) 'Evereste'

A tree with decorative fruit

Mountain ash (*Sorbus aucuparia*)
Mulberry tree (*Morus*) ❽ female specimen
Maidenhair tree (*Ginkgo biloba*) female
Oriental plane tree (*Platanus orientalis*)
Flowering crab apple (*Malus*)

Planting a tree

The best time to plant Deciduous trees are rarely grown in containers but usually cultivated in the open ground. Once their leaves have fallen, they rest during the winter. This is the best time to plant them so that they will be in good shape when the growing period begins again in spring.

▶ For the best results plant bare-rooted trees between November and February. Never plant in freezing temperatures and certainly never when the ground is frozen or waterlogged.

Planting a conifer Always buy conifers with a wrapped root-ball or growing in a container. Plant them as you would a bare-rooted tree, following these tips.

▶ Do not put an upright stake in the hole before planting.

▶ Soak the rootball in a bucket of water for about 15 minutes before planting.

▶ When the rootball is positioned in the hole make sure that the neck of the plant is level with the surface.

▶ Once planted, water well, with at least 10 litres of water.

▶ Keep the tree in place by attaching it to one or several stakes positioned away from the roots around the planting hole.

The autumn colouring of the tulip tree (Liriodendron tulipifera) is just as attractive as its earlier foliage.

Planting a bare-rooted tree

1 Dig a large, deep hole. Ideally make it 80cm square so that the roots will not grow round themselves if the earth is too hard.

2 Trim off broken, damaged or diseased roots just above the damage, cutting back into healthy tissue using a pair of secateurs.

3 Position the tree in the middle of the hole, laying a straight edge across the hole to make sure it is not too deep or too shallow.

4 Fill the hole with well-prepared earth. When it is half-full, gently shake the trunk so the soil settles around the roots then fill up and firm down.

5 Make a shallow trench around the tree and water. Fill the trench with water until the ground is saturated.

6 Fix two stakes, one on either side of the tree, 20–30cm away from the trunk, taking care not to damage the roots.

7 Attach each stake to the tree with a tree tie. Take care not to over-tighten and loosen off or replace the ties as the tree grows.

8 After watering, spread a layer of mulch, such as cocoa shells, over the planting site, on top of a covering of planting fabric if desired.

Dig, but not too deep When planting, a tree should be positioned in the soil exactly as it was at the nursery where it was grown, with the neck – the zone between the roots and the trunk, often visible as a watermark on the bark of the tree – just at soil level. To check this, lay the shaft of a rake across the hole. The 'neck' of the plant should be at the level of the shaft. If the hole is too deep, replace some earth until the tree stands at the correct level.

Watering basin When you have finished planting a tree and the soil has been replaced around its roots, there should be some soil left over. You can use this to create a watering basin, a small ridge around the tree on the surface of the soil. Try to give it a diameter that corresponds to the size of the rootball so that the water pools over the root hairs. The ridge will help to retain water in the correct area when you water the tree.

Top tips for planting a tree A tree should be planted for the long term and not moved again, so it's very important to give it every chance to settle in and get it off to a good start.
▶ **Heel it in** If you've bought a tree and find you can't plant it immediately, don't expose the roots to the air but take a tip from professional growers and 'heel it in'. Dig a hole 30cm deep with a sloping back, lay the tree on the ground with its roots in the hole, and cover them with well-tilled soil. The tree can spend several days, even weeks, like this before being planted in position.
▶ **Keep your distance** Whether you are planting a row of trees or a single one, the rule is the same: if the mature tree will be over two metres tall, the centre of the trunk should be at least two metres from any structure or large plant.

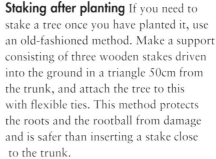

▶ **Dress the roots before planting** To stimulate the growth of new roots, before planting trees, pour a mixture of earth and water over the rootball (left). Traditionally this mixture was made using water, mud and cow dung.
▶ **Don't cut off the root hairs** Though you should cut off any damaged roots before planting, take care not to damage the smallest roots – the root hairs – as they are the ones that will draw water and nourishment from the soil.
▶ **Water immediately after planting, even if it's raining** The object is not so much to nourish the tree as to help the earth settle between the roots and to ensure good contact between the soil and the root system. Soak the planting area until the ground can take no more water.

Flexible staking Once you have planted the tree, fix it to a stake using a flexible tree tie to support it and to allow the new roots to establish themselves. This will allow for the movement of the soil as it settles around the base of the plant. Over the first few weeks the newly planted tree may subside by several centimetres as it beds down into its new position.

Advantages of staking A sturdy stake alongside a tree will support it when young but can also help to protect the trunk from the prevailing wind, whether cold or hot and drying, and from rain. It may also provide a little protective shade during the hottest time of the day.

▶ Be careful not to tie the tree too tightly to the stake, so that its growth is not hindered. Check tree ties regularly and loosen any that are too tight. Don't forget to remove the stake after about three years, when it will have outgrown its usefulness and can look unsightly.

Staking after planting If you need to stake a tree once you have planted it, use an old-fashioned method. Make a support consisting of three wooden stakes driven into the ground in a triangle 50cm from the trunk, and attach the tree to this with flexible ties. This method protects the roots and the rootball from damage and is safer than inserting a stake close to the trunk.

▶ Another method is to use an angle stake. This is a stake driven into the ground 1–1.5 metres from the tree. It is angled away from the tree and attached halfway up the trunk. Use proprietary tree ties to fasten the tree to the stake securely.

To attach a tree to a stake, use flexible ties available from garden centres or ties padded with foam rubber.

Trimming and pruning

Prune gently Trees can struggle to recover from harsh treatment – it's much more effective to prune them lightly. The objective when pruning is to preserve the overall shape of the tree and to open up the canopy by removing some of the internal branches.

When to cut a large branch At some time or other you may need to remove a large branch from one of your trees that has become a nuisance or has been broken by the wind. Do this in spring when the sap flow will accelerate healing.

No useless shoots Suckers are vigorous growing shoots that generally carry neither flowers nor fruit. They develop at the base of the trunk, on the trunk itself, and sometimes also in the middle of foliage or where there is a wound caused by the lopping of a branch. Cut them back as soon as they appear or they will drain the plant's energy.

Thin out a tree's lower branches You will find the light filtering onto the ground below very pleasing and it encourages plants to grow underneath.

Getting rid of spurs A spur is the remains of a branch that has not been cut close enough to the branch or the trunk that bore it. Apart from being unsightly, a spur inhibits the healing of the scar, dries out and rots, facilitating the onset of disease.

New styles for old trees Conifers sometimes age badly by losing their foliage at the base. You can revamp them with lopping shears and cut them Japanese-style, into cloud shapes. Cut away the side branches to reveal the trunk, retaining only the growth at the tip of the large leader branches, and trim these into ball shapes.

Removing suckers

1 Suckers are shoots that spring from a stump or a root and sap a plant's energy. To remove one completely, clear the earth around the base of the sucker.

2 Carefully cut the sucker back to the point where it grows from the main stem. Use sharp secateurs or a small pruning saw.

Cutting off a large branch

1 Make a notch under the branch. Cut a third of the way through the branch with a saw, working from underneath, 3–5cm closer to the tree than the place where you will make the final cut.

2 To help the cut to heal, you should always cut at right angles to the axis of the branch, as close as possible but not flush with the trunk.

Tips on ensuring a long life for your tree

When a young tree has not taken well Protect it from the sun's heat and from excess evaporation with a protective screen. Using three stakes as a framework, wrap the trunk with a protective sheet such as hessian or polythene, and spray the trunk and foliage with water in the morning and evening during hot weather. Keep the ground above the roots cool by spreading a layer of bark mulch or cocoa shells around the trunk. Check that the staking is adequate and that the cloth is tied neither too tightly nor too loosely.

Swift action needed for damaged trees A tree can be wounded in many ways. It may get a knock from a lawn mower or a car bumper, or a branch may be torn off by the wind, or lost from disease. Most wounds will heal naturally and do not require excessive attention. Torn tissue should be tidied and trimmed with sharp pruning tools to reduce the area of the wound and prevent access to pests and disease.

Keep an eye on scars The bark of a tree is rather like its skin. As soon as a wound appears through accident or disease, the bark will close over the naked wood. This is the tree's internal healing mechanism and is designed to prevent penetration by moisture, disease or parasites. Between the bark and the wood is a fine layer of tissue called the cambium, and as soon as the cambium is exposed to the air – when a branch is cut, for example – it begins to generate lots of new cells. These rapidly form a ridge around the wound and gradually cover it over until the wound is closed and healed. To speed up this process, keep the wound smooth and clean.

Give the trunk of an old dead tree a new lease of life by covering it with pretty flowering and foliage plants.

New life for old If a dead tree is spoiling the look of your garden, you can transform it into a stout support for a vigorous climbing plant. Try a combination of a climbing rose such as 'Seagull' and a *Clematis montana* such as 'Rubens', for instance. In the case of an isolated tree, consider planting wisteria or a climbing vine that will give you clusters of grapes, or insert small ferns such as *Gymnocarpium dryopteris* into the hollows of the trunk.

To remove a dead tree Forget the idea of attacking it with an axe. Begin by lopping off all the branches, then reduce the trunk to a manageable size. To remove the stump, don't resort to chemicals or burning, as previous generations might have done. Either hire a stump grinder or a winch, which you can use to pull the stump from the ground, or employ someone to do the job for you. Take advice from the hire shop and always use any safety equipment recommended.

Water generously Even though plants growing in dry soil can tolerate a certain amount of drought, they should not be left entirely to their own devices. As a plant establishes its root systems it is able to locate and draw up water from within the soil. In extreme drought its roots may not reach deep enough to find this precious resource so you need to give a helping hand. As a general rule trees that have been planted less than three years need to be watered copiously and often. Don't neglect your new trees, especially in summer.
▶ For a tree that is adapted to dry soil, choose a conifer such as the bristle-cone pine (*Pinus aristata*), juniper, the white spruce (*Picea glauca*) or *Pinus halepensis*. Among the broadleaved trees, eucalyptus and the false acacia are worth planting in dry conditions.

Drip-watering You sometimes see plastic pipes protruding from the ground beside trees in towns and cities. These pipes are pierced with holes and looped around the roots during planting, with the end left sticking out of the ground. The trees can be watered easily through the pipes to ensure water reaches right to their roots. This encourages roots of newly planted trees to establish themselves much more quickly.

Guard against lightning If your garden is home to an old, solitary tree that is in an exposed position, install a lightning conductor on your house. This will draw the lightning to the conductor and protect your tree from damage.
▶ The species most often affected by lightning are, in order of susceptibility, oaks, elms, pines, ash, willows, poplars, spruce and maples, especially if they are planted in sandy or normal soil. Chalky soil is not as conductive.

Treating a wounded tree

1 Clean the wound by brushing and scraping off the damaged wood to reveal the healthy wood underneath.

2 Remove dead tissue and pare the surrounding bark with a sharp, clean pruning knife until the surface is smooth.

3 Paint the wound and surrounding area with a wound-sealing compound, available from garden centres, to prevent disease.

4 A raised area will soon begin to form around the wound, protecting it further from infection and disease.

Pests and diseases of shrubs and trees

Controlling diseases on large trees and shrubs may sometimes require drastic measures. However, many species can support pest colonies without detriment.

Roots

CROWN GALL

▶ **Symptoms** This bacterial disease enters the shrub through a wound and produces whitish swellings (galls), on top of the roots or at the base of the trunk. These turn black and block sap circulation, leading to death.

▶ **Shrubs and trees affected** Cypress, euonymus (spindle), *Ribes sanguineum*, rhododendron, rose.

▶ **Treatment** There is no effective remedy for crown gall. As soon as the symptoms are recognised, dig up and burn affected plants. Replant new stock in another place. Prevent the disease by improving soil drainage around the plant and feeding with a high phosphate and potash fertiliser. Avoid root damage when transplanting.

FOMES ROOT AND BUTT ROT

▶ **Symptoms** Dark red-brown fungus grows on the trunk, or butt, of the tree at ground level. The lower surface is covered in minute pores. Fine white filaments appear under the bark, penetrating to the centre of the trunk. The needles on conifers turn yellow and the tree gradually dies.

▶ **Trees affected** Spruce, pine, elder, birch, oak, beech, larch.

▶ **Treatment** Dig up and burn the affected tree. Replace the soil before replanting.

HONEY FUNGUS

▶ **Symptoms** The foliage discolours, wilts and will progressively die back. The whole plant can die rapidly or hang on for years. Infected plants produce a white fungal-smelling growth beneath the bark at the base of the trunk. Black root-like 'bootlaces' grow on the outside of roots, which is how the fungus spreads to other plants. Clumps of honey coloured toadstools may also grow around infected plants.

▶ **Shrubs and trees affected** Most woody plants, climbers and some bulbs. Box, buddleja, caryopteris, chestnut, fir, holly, monkey puzzle.

▶ **Treatment** There is no fungicide to control this disease. Dig out and destroy infected plants immediately, removing as much root and infected soil as possible. Replant with disease-resistant annuals or perennials.

PHYTOPHTHORA (ROOT ROT)

A blackish liquid oozes from wounds at the base of the trunk. On digging the soil around the trunk, the roots show signs of fungal rot. See page 151.

Trunks and branches

ANTHRACNOSE

▶ **Symptoms** Infected branches shrivel. Cankers appear at the base of shoots and on the leaves along the veins, making the leaves appear burnt.

▶ **Shrubs and trees affected** Many shrubs and trees, such as cornus, plane, salix, walnut.

▶ **Treatment** Pick up all infected leaves, prune out seriously damaged branches and burn it all. Spray the whole plant with a copper-based fungicide and repeat according to manufacturer's instructions if the disease continues to affect the tree.

BARK BEETLE

▶ **Symptoms** The bark flakes off to reveal galleries that radiate from a central point where eggs were laid.

▶ **Trees affected** Most species, especially elm.

▶ **Treatment** Since the bark protects the larvae, treatment is ineffectual. Cut off affected branches or cut down and burn infected trees. As a preventive measure, ensure that your trees are healthy, and therefore less vulnerable.

BRACKET FUNGI

▶ **Symptoms** Fungi develop in clumps on the trunk and branches. The tree weakens and its branches become brittle.

▶ **Trees affected** Ash, beech, larch, oak, pine, plane, *Robinia pseudoacacia*, yew.

▶ **Treatment** Scrape off minor infestations with a knife. When established, the fungi will have penetrated the tissue, and felling is the only option.

CANKER

▶ **Symptoms** Swollen-edged cracks form on the bark. The bark tissue is exposed and oozes a whitish substance, or resin in the case of conifers. The tree then withers and dies.

▶ **Shrubs and trees affected** Ash, beech, chestnut, conifers, hawthorn, laurel, lime, plane, poplar, rose, sorbus, willow.

▶ **Treatment** Cut the diseased tissue back to healthy wood with a pruning knife, then burn the parings.

CORAL SPOT

▶ **Symptoms** Branches are covered with little orange-red pustules that rapidly multiply, eventually killing the plant.

▶ **Shrubs and trees affected** Most ornamental species.

▶ **Treatment** Prune out the affected growth to healthy wood, burn the prunings and sterilise tools after use. Clean up infected dead material around the garden, as this can be a source of infection.

FASCIATION

▶ **Symptoms** The affected stem thickens, enlarges and flattens, forming an undulating ribbon, sometimes with curling edges. The plant continues to grow and flower as normal. This is an accident of growth and not a disease.

▶ **Shrubs affected** Daphne, forsythia.

▶ **Treatment** There is no remedy. If too unsightly, simply cut off the affected shoot.

HORNET MOTH

▶ **Symptoms** Entries to galleries that leak sap can be seen close to the soil. Infected mature trees gradually wither; younger trees become brittle from ground level upwards.

▶ **Trees affected** Birch, ash, poplar, willow.

▶ **Treatment** Seriously infested trees should be felled. Keep down grass around the trunks as it makes a good place for the moth to lay eggs.

LONG-HORNED BEETLE

▶ **Symptoms** Sawdust at the base of trees beneath galleries bored out of the trunk.

▶ **Trees affected** Poplar, willow.

▶ **Treatment** Destroy the larvae by scraping the galleries with a steel wire. If infestation is too far advanced, fell and burn the tree.

NEEDLE DISCOLOURATION

▶ **Symptoms** Conifer needles turn yellow and then brown. Fungi gradually invade the whole branch and affected parts are black-spotted.

▶ **Trees affected** Conifers.

▶ **Treatment** Pick up and burn infected needles. Use a foliar feed throughout the summer to aid recovery.

PHYTOPHTHORA (ROOT ROT)

▶ **Symptoms** A blackish flux appears at the base of the trunk. The leaves turn yellow, then brown, and the shoot tips wither. Finally the shrub dies.

▶ **Shrubs and trees affected** Aucuba, catalpa, cornus, holly, elm, skimmia, rhododendron.

▶ **Treatment** There is no cure. Remove and destroy the plant and infected soil. Improve the drainage and avoid damage to roots when transplanting.

WITCHES' BROOM

▶ **Symptoms** Small clusters of dense and stunted shoots appear at the tips of branches, causing the foliage to yellow. If shaken, a white dust drops off.

▶ **Trees affected** Birch, carpinus.

▶ **Treatment** This disease is more unsightly than dangerous. Cut off 'brooms' and burn the branches to prevent spores spreading.

Leaves

BLACKSPOT

▶ **Symptoms** Dark brown spots appear on the foliage. The spots grow larger and finally join together. At the same time, the leaves turn yellow and fall, leaving the stalks entirely bare.

▶ **Shrub affected** Rose.

▶ **Treatment** Collect up infected leaves, prune out heavily diseased wood and burn. In the spring, spray the whole rose plant and the surrounding soil with an approved fungicide and repeat as directed.

BOTRYTIS This disease attacks flowers as well as leaves and fruits. It affects mostly weak, damaged shrubs. See page 97.

BROWN-TAIL MOTH

▶ **Symptoms** Grey caterpillars with red marks form colonies in woven silky nests that hang in trees and hedges.

▶ **Shrubs and trees affected** Many types of trees and shrubs including apple, cherry, hawthorn, lime, plane.

▶ **Treatment** Prune out the overwintering nests of caterpillars (wear gloves and take great care to prevent contact with caterpillar hairs, which are highly irritant). When the caterpillars are active in spring, spray with *Bacillus thuringiensis* or an approved insecticide.

BUFF-TIP MOTH

▶ **Symptoms** Branches suddenly look bare as the leaves have all been eaten.

▶ **Shrubs and trees affected** All deciduous species.

▶ **Treatment** When the caterpillars become active, spray with *Bacillus thuringiensis* or an approved insecticide containing derris or pyrethrins.

CAPSID BUG All ornamentals are vulnerable. The plants look as if they are riddled with lead shot. See page 97.

DUTCH ELM DISEASE

▶ **Symptoms** This disease caused the disappearance of most elms in southern England, Wales and the Midlands and has spread into Scotland. The leaves change colour, turn yellowish and dry up. First the branches, then the tree withers and dies. The bark is covered in brown blotches and peels off. A cut branch will reveal a brown ring at the centre.

▶ **Tree affected** Elm.

▶ **Treatment** There is no remedy. Only cutting down and burning affected trees will limit the spread of the disease.

ELM LEAF BLIGHT

▶ **Symptoms** In spring and summer, leaves are pierced with longish holes. Some leaves are covered with mould.

▶ **Tree affected** Elm.

▶ **Treatment** There is no cure. To prevent spreading, collect and burn infected leaves.

FIREBLIGHT

▶ **Symptoms** Leaves crumble and look burnt. The bark splits and exudes a whitish ooze, with the inside tissue turning red. Contamination of neighbouring trees is swift.

► Shrubs and trees affected

All members of the *Rosaceae* family, such as hawthorn, cotoneaster, pyracantha.
► **Treatment** Prune out infected growth to healthy wood and spray with a copper-based fungicide. Disinfect tools after use.

FROGHOPPER Light yellow or white mottling on leaves is caused by the bites of this insect. See page 98.

FRUIT FLY These flies can affect many species, including beech, gleditsia, hawthorn, holly, willow. See page 254.

GALL MITE

► **Symptoms** The underside of infected leaves are covered in white spots that turn brown. The leaves blister and become covered in red galls.
► **Shrubs and trees affected** Birch, maple, beech, walnut, elm, lime.
► **Treatment** Cut off and burn the affected leaves.

GALL WASP

► **Symptoms** The undersides of leaves display small, flat reddish galls that contain larvae. Acorns carry a wrinkled gall on the side of the cup. The affected buds turn pinkish and then drop off.
► **Tree affected** Chiefly oak.
► **Treatment** No treatment is necessary as this insect does not harm the tree. The galls protect the larvae, making them difficult to reach.

HAWK MOTH

► **Symptoms** Leaf edges are chewed, especially in summer.
► **Shrubs and trees affected** Many ornamental species.
► **Treatment** Remove the large caterpillars by hand.

LEAF BEETLES

► **Symptoms** In spring and summer, leaves are pierced with holes, although the veins are unaffected. Leaf tops may also be cut off and look shrivelled.
► **Shrubs and trees affected** Elder, lavender, poplar, willow.
► **Treatment** Where practical, pick off adult beetles.

LEAF BLOTCH

► **Symptoms** Grey swellings with brown edges appear on infected leaves. The marks grow larger with the centres turning red and drying up.
► **Shrubs and trees affected** Chestnut, vine.
► **Treatment** There is no cure for this disease. Collect and burn infected leaves and prunings. Improve the drainage around affected plants and feed regularly to aid recovery.

LEAF-CUTTING BEE

► **Symptoms** The margins of leaves are cut out in circular shapes with regular contours.
► **Shrub affected** Rose.
► **Treatment** The damage is more unsightly than harmful to the plant. Treatment is not necessary, especially since the leaf-cutting bee is a pollinator.

LEAF GALL

► **Symptoms** Tumours appear on leafy stems, often around the veins. These roundish swellings have a white covering that turns brown and shrivels.
► **Shrubs affected** Azalea, rhododendron.
► **Treatment** Cut off and burn affected parts. Spray with a copper-based fungicide.

LEAF MOSAIC VIRUS

► **Symptoms** The leaves display cream or yellow spots like a mosaic. Serious infection can cause the foliage to deform and the plant to wither.
► **Shrubs affected** Roses and other ornamental species.
► **Treatment** None available. If the attack is not serious, it is enough to prune the affected parts. Otherwise, dig up and burn the shrub.

LEAF WEEVILS

► **Symptoms** Leaves at the tips of shoots are pierced with minuscule holes; eggs can be seen along the principal vein. These hatch into larvae that hollow a gallery in the leaf, leaving a brownish track. The adult insect sometimes eats the edge of the leaf.
► **Shrubs and trees affected** Beech, buddleja, hazelnut, pines and others.
► **Treatment** Spray with bifenthrin if the weevils are sufficient to cause problems.

OAK PROCESSIONARY CATERPILLAR

► **Symptoms** The leaves are devoured. Large cocoons can be seen on the tips of branches.
► **Tree affected** Oak.
► **Treatment** Prune out the cocoons before the caterpillars emerge. If they become active, spray with *Bacillus thuringiensis* or an appropriate approved insecticide.

PEACH LEAF CURL Typically, peach leaf curl attacks peach trees as well as ornamental plants, such as camellias and poplars. See page 252.

PLANT SUCKERS *Psylloidea* are sap-sucking insects found on ornamental species, most commonly apple and pear trees. See page 252.

POWDERY MILDEW Roses and dahlias are prone to this disease, which is characterised by a white coating on the leaves. See page 253.

RED SPIDER MITE

▶ **Symptoms** Leaves become dull, turn yellow with blotches, then fall. The undersides are covered in a fine web and eggs.
▶ **Shrubs and trees affected** Most ornamental species.
▶ **Treatment** In a greenhouse, introduce the natural control predator *Phytoseiulus persimilis* as soon as the pest is noticed. In other situations, spray with an approved fatty acid or oil-based treatment.

RHODODENDRON LACEBUG
▶ **Symptoms** The leaves turn a yellow mottled colour. The transparent larvae of the insect can also be seen.
▶ **Shrub affected** Rhododendron.
▶ **Treatment** Avoid planting in warm, sunny places. Spray with a bifenthrin-based insecticide.

ROSE RUST

▶ **Symptoms** Orange-yellow patches develop on the upper leaf surfaces, with pustules on the undersides causing the leaves to fall prematurely.
▶ **Shrub affected** Rose.
▶ **Treatment** At the first sign of attack, spray the leaves with an approved fungicide.

ROSE SLUG SAWFLY
▶ **Symptoms** The leaves are perforated, almost skeletonised, leaving only the principal vein. The remaining foliage withers.
▶ **Shrub affected** Rose.
▶ **Treatment** Spray immediately with an insecticide containing pyrethrin or derris. Repeat several times.

SCALE INSECT
▶ **Symptoms** Numerous black or brown spots are visible on the underside of leaves and on the stalks. If pressed with a fingernail, a hard covering can be felt. Waxy or cottony discharge can also be seen. A significant presence of sooty mould is a characteristic sign.
▶ **Shrubs and trees affected** Many species.
▶ **Treatment** Due to the hard protective coat, regular spraying with a fatty acid or oil-based insecticide may be necessary to control this pest.

SILVER LEAF
▶ **Symptoms** The leaves take on a silvery tinge. As the infection spreads, the tree withers and dies back.

▶ **Shrubs and trees affected** Members of the *Rosaceae* family.
▶ **Treatment** There is not a cure for this disease. Prune back affected growth to healthy white tissue (infected wood has a dark stain) in the summer only. Treat the pruning wounds by applying an approved fungicide.

THRIPS
▶ **Symptoms** This pest leaves whitish specks on leaves, which form a silvery marbling.
▶ **Shrubs and trees affected** Privet, palm, gladiolus, ornamental fruiting species.
▶ **Treatment** In your greenhouse, introduce the predatory mite *Amblyseius*, or hang up sticky boards to trap the thrips. Plant *Nicotiana sylvestris*, whose sticky leaves act as a trap.

VERTICILLIUM WILT This fungal disease attacks catalpa and *Robinia pseudoacacia*, causing the foliage to yellow and wither away. See page 99.

VINE WEEVIL
▶ **Symptoms** Irregular nicks occur around the edges of leaves and excreta can be seen on the leaf. Roots are sometimes devoured by white larvae, leaving deep gashes.
▶ **Shrubs and trees affected** Many plants can be affected, including euonymus, hydrangea, rhododendron, yew, skimmia.
▶ **Treatment** Drench infested soil with the natural control nematode *Heterorhabditis megidis* or an approved insecticide. Ring containers with grease bands to trap adults before they lay eggs in the compost.

WEB-FORMING MOTH
▶ **Symptoms** Variously coloured caterpillars devour the leaves and buds of affected plants and form woven, hanging, silky nests.
▶ **Trees affected** Several plants including hawthorn, euonymus, cotoneaster, juniper.
▶ **Treatment** Carefully prune out and burn the nests containing the caterpillars. If the caterpillars become active, spray with *Bacillus thuringiensis* or an approved insecticide.

WINTER MOTH
▶ **Symptoms** Pale green caterpillars devour the leaves, buds and fruitlets. They leave a trail of silky threads.
▶ **Shrubs and trees affected** Carpinus, rose.
▶ **Treatment** Place grease bands around the trunks of affected plants and spray the caterpillars with *Bacillus thuringiensis* or another approved insecticide.

WOOLLY ADELGIDS

▶ **Symptoms** The needles of affected conifers turn yellow. Those of the pine are covered with white, waxy filaments. On spruce, galls appear at the tips of branches. Fluffy balls hang from the branches of Douglas firs. On larch, the insect is covered with a white wool.
▶ **Trees affected** Conifers.
▶ **Treatment** Adelgids are not easy to control, but conifers are able to support populations without any ill effects.

The vegetable garden

A well-planned vegetable plot

The old-fashioned kitchen garden is a productive food factory. Follow a few traditional planning principles to get your vegetable plot off to a really good start and use age-old gardening wisdom to reap a rich harvest.

Begin with the basics

Choosing a site It is common sense that some sites are just not suitable for growing vegetables. Steep slopes, boggy or flood-prone areas, shady sites and locations too far from your water supply are not worth trying. Instead choose a site in full sun, one that is sheltered or can be sheltered from drying wind and, if possible, is free of weeds and debris. Avoid anything less than 10–20 metres away from large tree roots.

A mixed bed of herbs and vegetables in clumps and rows is an attractive garden feature.

Shaping up Vegetable gardens come in all shapes and sizes, but squares or rectangles are most practical for the production of a range of different vegetables with differing requirements and growing seasons. The size of the vegetable plot depends on the overall size of your garden and your vegetable needs.

Paths are essential If you trample on soil you will compact it, so water won't drain away easily – and although plants need water they certainly don't want to be water-logged. A system of paths between beds is the solution: it makes access and maintenance much simpler.
► You can plant vegetables on either side of a central path, but make sure it is at least 90cm wide, so that you can push a full wheelbarrow between the vegetable beds.
► Put down a thick layer of bark mulch or lay paving slabs to reduce weeds on the path. Pouring boiling salted water from pasta or vegetables over weed seedlings will destroy them.

Should you grow vegetables in beds or rows? Choose the system that suits your space and style of garden.
► **Rectangular beds** Some gardeners divide their vegetable gardens into rectangular beds, each one no more than 1.2 metres wide, and separated by narrow paths about 30cm wide. Beds are clearly marked, and you can reach the centre from the access paths, without stepping on the soil.
► **Straight rows** If you are growing to feed a large family you may prefer to grow vegetables in long, straight rows, grouping them by type. In row gardening it is not so easy to work without stepping on the soil, so lay down planks and walk on these when you need access to your crops.

Edge vegetable beds with willow or hazel hurdles to create a rustic, old-fashioned style.

Soil needs You can grow vegetables in most garden soils. Dig the ground over in autumn – if your soil is compacted you may need a rotavator – and work in plenty of well-rotted compost.
▶ If the soil is sandy, you may need to add bulky organic material to it. Improve the soil over the longer term by growing a 'green manure' (see page 269). These are annuals like phacelia or mustard that are dug into the soil before they set seed and, as they decay, enrich the soil with humus.

Clear the plot in warm weather

Remove any waste material and weeds from the patch, and use a hoe to break down the soil to a depth of several centimetres. Rake the soil, removing any remaining stones and debris.
▶ Do this in mild weather, when the soil is neither too wet nor too dry to work. Then broadcast the seed over the whole area.

Label it It is good practice to label everything you plant. Empty seed packets make excellent row markers – attach them to sticks and sink them firmly into the ground, then cover the packets with a plastic bag or a jam jar to protect them against bad weather.
▶ If you've still got seeds left in the packet, make a separate label. Most garden centres sell a variety of labels and row markers made from aluminium, plastic or slate.

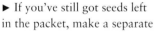

Water on tap A handy source of water is essential for the vegetable garden. Make sure your hose reaches it so you can water thoroughly every day.
▶ If your shed is near the plot, put a water butt in place to collect rainwater from the roof. Keep the butt covered to prevent build-up of algae and other waterborne diseases that might affect young plants.

Tools on hand A garden shed is vital for storing tools, seeds and other garden paraphernalia. Always store your tools there so they are in a convenient place ready for you to use each time you garden. Never leave them outside.
▶ DIY stores sell sheds in flat packs that are simple to erect.

Raised beds end back-breaking work and add height and structure to the vegetable garden.

Display your vegetables Raised beds are useful if you want to avoid bending to work. They look good too: constructed from natural wood, they become an attractive feature, displaying low-growing vegetables as if they were decorative plants in their own right.

Design your plot to suit your needs Don't forget to take into account the time and energy you have at your disposal – allow half a day's work per week for a plot up to 10 square metres, less if you can use a cultivator to break up the soil.
▶ **10 square metres** You can grow a selection of most vegetables, enough to meet the requirements of a single person or a couple.
▶ **50 square metres** You will have the space to grow ample vegetables for two people or a small family.
▶ **100 square metres** Your plot is big enough to support a large family.

Work out the correct spacing for vegetables
If you are sowing two types of vegetable in one small bed, work out the spacing needed between the rows by adding the amount of space required by each crop and dividing the total by two.

Flower borders for old-fashioned charm If you would like to give your vegetable plot the feel of a traditional cottage garden, where practical and decorative plants grow side by side, try putting aromatic flowers and plants around the borders. Culinary herbs such as sage, thyme and summer savory provide a double benefit, as they are attractive in the kitchen garden and useful in cooking. Brightly coloured flowering plants, including sweet william, dwarf dahlias, calendula and phlox, are both colourful and traditional.
▶ If you prefer a more formal look, use a low box hedge instead of flowers to edge the beds or paths. It is slow-growing and has densely packed, small green leaves that can – with regular clipping – be kept in a neat geometric shape.

Planning a plot

Mixed cropping in the vegetable garden

Some gardeners believe that certain vegetables grow better in association with particular neighbours. Here are some traditional 'friends and foes' for mixed or companion planting schemes.

Plant	Good companions	Bad companions
Asparagus	Leeks, parsley, peas, tomatoes	Beetroot
Beetroot	Cabbage, celery, green beans, lettuce, onions	Asparagus, tomatoes
Broad beans	Lettuce, parsnips, potatoes	
Cabbage	Beetroot, celery, cucumber, green beans, lettuce, parsnips, peas, potatoes, tomatoes	Onions, radishes
Carrots	Green beans, leeks, lettuce, onions, parsnips, peas, radishes	
Celery	Beetroot, cabbage, cucumber, fennel, green beans, leeks, peas, potatoes, tomatoes	
Courgettes	Green beans, potatoes, sweetcorn	Cabbage, fennel
Cucumber	Cabbage, celery, green beans, lettuce, peas, sweetcorn	Potatoes, tomatoes
Fennel	Celery, leeks	Cabbage, green beans, tomatoes
Green beans	Cabbage, carrots, celery, courgettes, cucumber, leeks, lettuce, marrows, peas, potatoes, radishes, sweetcorn, tomatoes	Beetroot, fennel, onions
Leeks	Asparagus, carrots, celery, fennel, lettuce, onions, tomatoes	Beetroot, cabbage
Lettuce	Beetroot, broad beans, cabbage, carrots, cucumber, green beans, leeks, onions, peas, radishes, turnips	Parsley
Marrows	Green beans, potatoes, sweetcorn	Cabbage, fennel
Onions	Beetroot, carrots, leeks, lettuce, parsnips, tomatoes	Cabbage, green beans, peas, potatoes
Parsley	Asparagus, tomatoes	Celery, lettuce, peas
Parsnips	Broad beans, cabbage, carrots, onions	
Peas	Asparagus, cabbage, carrots, celery, cucumber, green beans, lettuce, sweetcorn, turnips, potatoes, radishes	Garlic, onions, parsley
Potatoes	Broad beans, cabbage, celery, green beans, peas, tomatoes	Courgettes, cucumber, onions, sweetcorn
Radishes	Broad beans, carrots, cucumbers, green beans, lettuce, parsley, peas, spinach, tomatoes	Cabbage
Spinach	Most vegetables	
Sweetcorn	Courgettes, cucumber, green beans, marrows, peas	Potatoes
Tomatoes	Asparagus, cabbage, celery, green beans, leeks, onions, parsley, potatoes, radishes	Beetroot, cucumber, fennel
Turnips	Lettuce, peas	

'Pioneer' crops When you start a new vegetable garden, you may not have time to dig over the entire area and improve all the soil before planting or sowing your first crops. Dig over what you can in the time available and then use some vegetables as 'pioneers' to help you prepare the soil.

▶ Jerusalem artichokes and potatoes will break up the soil as effectively as any digging. Courgettes, pumpkins and cabbages will cover the soil well, suppressing the growth of weeds. These are surface-rooting crops, as are tomatoes, celery and leeks, so don't need the soil to be well worked to succeed.

▶ It is more difficult to sow small seeds of onions and carrots into rough ground. Carrots need well-dug soil to produce straight, deep-growing roots. French and runner beans and lettuce need well-dug soil that has been allowed to settle, as their roots are prone to attack from insects that can penetrate air pockets.

Manure – a vital ingredient Manure is essential to the fertility of the vegetable garden. It provides the nutrients that plants need and improves the structure and drainage of the soil with the humus that it produces.

▶ If you are starting a vegetable garden from scratch, work in at least 50 kilos per 10 square metres over the entire area. Every year after that, add 30 kilos per 10 square metres to a third of the garden, working on a different third each year, in rotation.

▶ Always use well-rotted manure – never fresh – and dig it into the soil in autumn.

Companion planting You can follow traditional practice and attract beneficial insects that feed on aphids, caterpillars and other garden pests by planting flowers alongside your vegetables in the kitchen garden.

▶ The most attractive flowers and herbs include the orange or yellow-flowered calendula (below), nasturtium, *Limnanthes douglasii* (poached egg plant), dill, coriander, angelica and cosmos.

▶ Plants that develop the same form – for example, leafy vegetables, fruiting vegetables, or bulb and root vegetables – are also usually grown together in the same section of the crop-rotation plan.

The 'spinach' method This is another form of old-fashioned companion planting. Instead of planting rows of associated vegetables, sow 50cm wide rows of spinach, leaving rows between them for other vegetables. The spinach seedlings act as a nurse crop, shading and protecting the interplanted seedlings. The spinach can be harvested to eat or hoed off and left on the soil surface to provide a mulch and, if hoed into the soil, a green manure.

Intercropping
Crops with short growing cycles are ideal for intercropping with those with longer cycles. Plant lettuces (short cycle) between rows of pricked-out cabbages (long cycle) or, in late summer, corn salad or radishes among young strawberry plants.

Extending the rotation If you find that for some vegetables and groups of vegetables, such as potatoes and brassicas, diseases and pests are a persistent problem, it may be necessary to keep them in a longer rotation cycle to get good yields and healthy crops. If this is the case, you will require extra sections in the vegetable garden to carry out the ideal rotation plan.
▶ Strawberries are even more demanding. You need to move the bed every third year and avoid returning to the original section within six or seven years.

Space to grow Even though mixed planting uses every bit of soil, vegetables should never be cramped. You still need to allow space between the rows. Here is a spacing guide for some commonly grown crops.
▶ Trailing marrows – 2 metres.
▶ Tomatoes, aubergines, courgettes, artichokes, cardoons, cucumbers, melons – 1 metre.
▶ Climbing French beans, runner beans, tall peas, New Zealand spinach – 75cm.
▶ Maincrop potatoes – 60cm.
▶ Cabbages (right), strawberries, dwarf French beans, dwarf peas, Jerusalem artichokes – 60cm.
▶ Early potatoes – 50cm.
▶ Chard, beetroot, celery, sweetcorn, parsnips – 50cm.
▶ Endives, chicory, fennel, broad beans, leeks – 40cm.
▶ Garlic, beetroot, carrots, kohlrabi, shallots, spinach, lettuce, onions, dandelions, salsify – 30cm.
▶ Corn salad, turnips, parsley, radishes – 20cm.

Rotating vegetables produces healthier crops without the need for chemicals and pesticides.

Rotating your vegetables

Simple rotation If you grow the same vegetables in the same piece of ground, year after year, the soil becomes overworked. Pests and diseases are likely to become established and, as a result, vigour, health and yields are likely to decrease. So it's best to move the crops around. The simplest way is to have a three or four-year plan and divide your garden into three or four sections, each at a different stage of rotation. Follow a plan like this for each of the sections:
▶ **Year one** Add manure or compost and then grow greedy feeders, such as potatoes, tomatoes, courgettes, pumpkins, celery, leeks and cabbages on the composted area.
▶ **Year two** Plant carrots, beetroot, turnips and onions.
▶ **Year three** Plant green beans and peas.
▶ **Year four** Grow the crops grown in year one or, better still, plant strawberries, artichokes or other perennial vegetables after adding more manure or compost. After two or three years, stop growing these perennials and start a new rotation cycle after adding more organic matter.
▶ There are some crops that you can use to fill any gaps, such as green salad, spinach, radishes and turnips, whatever the stage of rotation.

'Happy families' Crop rotation can be complicated, but if you group plants together, according to their botanical families, their form or their soil and nutrient requirements, you can't go far wrong.
▶ Plants belonging to similar families – for example, *Cruciferae* and *Umbelliferae*, which include Brussels sprouts, cauliflower, broccoli and cabbage – are best grown together.

Dependable brassicas and other tasty greens

Cabbages and leafy 'pot herbs' such as spinach and Swiss chard were among the first vegetables to be cultivated in Europe, as long ago as the Stone Age. The fact that these plants can be very attractive, as well as edible, has meant that they have enjoyed a recent resurgence in popularity, reviving the tradition of growing vegetables among the flowers.

Some cabbages are as attractive as they are productive. Plant them with ornamental flowers among your tomatoes.

Cabbages and sprouts

What to do with a headless cabbage A cabbage 'head' is formed from layers of leaves folded over each other and is, in effect, a large bud. If a cabbage fails to 'heart up' or make a head, don't leave it to become tough and inedible: remove it and use its foliage as spring greens.

Modular trays

Commercial cabbage growers have long used plug plants, and now home growers can raise their seedlings in modular trays as well. The individual plastic cells are ideal for encouraging plants to develop a strong and compact root system so that, when they are transplanted, there is minimum root disturbance and they get off to a good start in the ground. This means that they can often be harvested earlier than nonmodular transplants. Growing your own strong plants from seed will also help avoid bringing diseases into the vegetable garden.

▶ If any seedlings have not formed proper growing points, it is best simply to get rid of them and replace them with healthy, strong-growing seedlings that will heart up successfully.

Using seedbeds or modules Cabbages need to be carefully transplanted or their growth will be checked.
▶ Sow seeds into modular trays, and transplant them only when the seedlings have developed really strong roots, then harden them off before you plant them. Seedlings that have grown in modules will have well-developed roots and should continue to grow well.

Eat up unwanted seedlings Sow cabbage seed into a seedbed, then prick out the seedlings and transplant them into their growing site, where they have more space to develop.
▶ Plant a few extra seedlings so you can remove one or two before they mature and use their leaves as spring greens.

Success with seedlings Plant seedlings to the same depth they were in the seedbed or modular tray. Just before planting, soak the roots of each plant in a mixture of soil and water. When they are growing well, earth them up by drawing soil around the base of each plant. This ensures the stability of young plants as it encourages them to make new roots along their stems.

▶ To deter cabbage root fly, use a physical barrier such as a piece of carpet underlay or cardboard tucked around the stem of each seedling.

Get a double crop Instead of pulling out the stumps left in the ground after harvesting cabbages, use a sharp knife to make a cross on the top of each one. Four or five loosely formed heads will sprout from the cross and you will get a second crop.
▶ Calabrese, or green sprouting broccoli, also yields a double crop. To produce a second harvest from 'Tenderstem Green Inspiration F1', remove its leading shoots or primary head.

Transplanting cabbage seedlings

1 Carefully remove a seedling from its pot or seedbed, use a dibber or trowel to make a hole, and lower the seedling into the planting hole, taking care not to damage the roots.

2 Water the seedling in and use your fingers to firm the soil around the roots. Water well at the base of each plant.

3 Protect young plants from wind and sun by covering with a crate or horticultural fleece. Some gardeners cut back leaves by half to reduce evaporation and water loss.

Preventing club root Club root is a disease triggered when a microscopic fungus that lives in the soil – and can persist there for decades – finds a host plant to live on. Hygiene is vital, so it is imperative that you lift any diseased plants carefully and burn them. Never add plants with club root to the compost heap, or you will simply recycle the disease. You can combat club root with the following cultivational methods.
▶ **Rotation of brassicas** This is the simplest method, depriving the fungus of an appropriate host.
▶ **Raise the pH level of the soil** The fungus thrives in moist, acid soils, so if you achieve a pH level of 7 or 7.5, it will be too high for the club root fungus to survive. Regularly enrich

the soil with lime in the form of powdered chalk, ground limestone or dolomitic limestone. Apply in autumn, so that it acts on the soil before the next growing season begins.
▶ **Improve drainage** Several months before planting brassicas, dig in a barrowload of well-rotted manure per square metre. To lighten heavy soil, add gravel.

Top tips for growing brassicas Ensure your brassicas have the best possible care by following a few basic rules.
▶ **Rotate them** Move brassicas around in a rotation, so that they are never on the same patch in your vegetable garden more than once every three years. If you grow them in the same spot year after year, you are likely to see a build-up of club root and cabbage root fly. Because they are greedy feeders, the soil needs enriching after they have grown there.
▶ **Stake them** Stake individual Brussels sprout plants and rows of broccoli and kale. Support top-heavy ballhead cabbages and cauliflowers to prevent them lying on the ground.
▶ **Protect them** Some plants, including tomatoes, are said to repel cabbage white butterfly, so regularly place the suckers pinched out from your tomato plants, or fresh sprigs of broom or fern, on the cabbage leaves. The butterflies dislike the smell of these plants and, it is said, will avoid your cabbage patch.
▶ **Underplant them** Underplanting cabbages with a green manure may distract insects that would otherwise lay their eggs on the cabbage leaves.

Homespun remedies Cabbage leaves have an age-old reputation as cure-alls for everyday ailments including colds, minor burns and wounds that are slow to heal.
▶ For a compress, choose three to five clean, fresh leaves with a good colour, remove large veins and crush with a rolling pin. Place the leaves on the affected area, and change twice a day. People who use this remedy say it is more effective if you warm the leaves with an iron before applying them.
▶ Cabbage leaves also make an excellent face mask.

Cabbages all year round

NAME	WHEN TO SOW	HARVEST TIME
Ballhead cabbage		
Spring Hero F1	July–August	April–June
Primo II	March–May	July–September
Minicole F1	March–May	September–December
Tundra F1	mid-March–June	October–mid-March
Looseleaf/pointed or spring cabbages (although available all year)		
Greyhound	March–May, August	June–September
Hispi F1	February–August	May–November
Savoy or January King type		
Savoy King F1	February–June	September–February
Marabel F1	April–June	November–March
Ormskirk	April–June	November–March
January King 3	April–June	November–February
Red cabbage		
Primero F1	March–May	July–August
Rodima F1	March–May	October–December

Brassicas and greens

No manure for Brussels sprouts Leafy members of the cabbage family need to be planted in well-manured soil, but not Brussels sprouts since too much nitrogen – one of the main nutrients in manure – will produce open heads, rather than the tightly budded sprouts you are aiming for. If your soil is naturally fertile, you do not need to add any manure to the area where you intend to plant your sprouts. If the soil is infertile, however, add a little well-rotted garden compost.

Removing sprout tops Although Brussels sprouts are tightly packed along the stem, you can twist the buttons off by hand.

If you use a knife to remove them, take care not to damage the smaller sprouts nearby.
▶ When picking a small quantity, take them from the base of the stem and work upwards, as the sprouts higher up the stem will be smaller and mature later than those lower down.
▶ The leaves at the tops of the sprout stems are good to cook and eat as greens. If you remove these green tops, you are also depriving aphids of potential resting and feeding places.

Three cheers for kale! Kale is a leafy, cabbage-like vegetable widely grown in countries throughout northern Europe, but often neglected in British gardens. However, it is worth making space for as it is completely resistant to hard frosts, and although whitefly can be a problem, is relatively unaffected by aphids, caterpillars and other garden pests. Kale is also less prone to club root than cabbages.
▶ Sow kale in April or May. The leaves will be ready to harvest according to your needs after the first frosts, and from then on throughout the winter.

YESTERDAY & TODAY

An earthy touch for flower beds

Cabbages needn't be limited to the vegetable garden. Give flower beds a robust charm by using some of the many plants in the cabbage family to add colour and texture to your borders. In recent years, the tradition of growing vegetables for both decorative and practical purposes has regained popularity in many ordinary kitchen gardens and stately homes alike, harking back to a time when good husbandry demanded that every bit of land was cherished.

Ornamental cabbages are especially suitable, and as temperatures drop in autumn, their colours intensify. 'Black Tuscany', a kale also known as the 'palm cabbage', is a truly spectacular plant with a bouquet of dark, blue-green leaves that can reach a height of up to two metres. Kale is frost-hardy and is especially decorative when its frothy, blue-green or purple leaves are edged with frost.

THE GARDENER'S CHOICE

Know your brassicas ▶

Brassicas include many different types of cabbage, kale, cauliflower, broccoli, kohlrabi and Brussels sprouts.

Savoy cabbage ❶ This ballheaded cabbage has crinkly, textured leaves.

Romanesco ❷ and broccoli ❸ These are two distinctive types of brassica. Though the younger leaves and the stalk can be eaten, they are grown for their flower heads.

Red cabbage ❹ This cabbage has purple-blue outer foliage and dark red, ballheaded centres.

Brussels sprouts ❺ Sprouts are mini cabbages growing at leaf points on the stalk. They are plentiful throughout winter.

Kale ❻ Kale, or borecole, is a nonhearting cabbage with curly, wrinkled leaves.

Cauliflower and broccoli

Cauliflowers are greedy feeders Cauliflowers thrive in deep, fertile soil and need to be watered regularly. If you live near the sea, gather seaweed from the shore and spread it on the ground before digging over. Alternatively, enrich every 10 square metres of soil with 50 kilos of compost; one kilo of fish, blood and bone meal; or another natural manure rich in organic nitrogen. Proprietary fertilisers containing seaweed extracts are also available.

For bright white cauliflowers
If a cauliflower head is overexposed to light and bad weather, it loses its pure white colour. To protect it and preserve its whiteness, bend the largest outer leaves so that the leaf spine cracks, and fold them over and fix them (right) to cover the head.

Romanesco – gaining in popularity For variety, try this delicately flavoured Italian cauliflower. It has an unusual conical shape with pointed, yellow-green florets, but is cultivated like other cauliflowers.

Picking the right moment To get a double crop of broccoli, you need to harvest at exactly the right time – when the flower heads are well formed, but before they open. To harvest the broccoli, cut the heads off at the top of the stalk. Once you cut off the heads, don't pull up the plant. The buds in the axils of the remaining leaves will develop and provide another crop of smaller heads.

Take your pick of greens

Lettuces of every description The word lettuce (*Lactuca sativa*) usually conjures up an image of the lovely, pale green cabbage lettuce. However, lettuces come in all shapes, colours and textures. There are so many different varieties to choose from, you could eat a different one for each day of the week.

▶ **Butterhead types** These are the most familiar British lettuces. They have soft leaves that heart up into crisp centres, and can be all green or have red-tinged leaves.

▶ **Crisphead** The tight, crisp, dense heads of these varieties can be green or red-tinged.

▶ **Cos (or Romaine)** A lettuce with a long conical head, which produces a crisp yellow heart and has deep green outer leaves. Sometimes these are red-tinged.

▶ **Looseleaf** These lettuces include salad bowl and oakleaf types. They can be used as whole heads, or picked by the leaf.

▶ **Mixed salad leaf seed collections** Definitely a good option for the indecisive, these are attractive in the ground as well as in salad bowls.

American and European varieties The American 'Iceberg' lettuce is the descendant of the European Batavia lettuce 'Chou de Naples'. It was introduced into California from Italy in the 1920s. Try 'Great Lakes' or one of the European varieties, such as 'Dickenson' or 'Lollo Rosso', whose seeds are more readily available in Britain. The American Batavia lettuces are resistant to hot weather.

Top tips for growing lettuce To make sure your lettuces are tender and juicy, follow these guidelines.

▶ **Provide moist soil** Grow lettuce in a moisture-retentive soil to prevent the plants from bolting. To increase its water-holding capacity, add compost or manure annually.

▶ **Use available space** If you're short of space, plant lettuces as a catch crop between sowings of cabbages. The lettuces will be ready to harvest before the cabbages take up all the space.

▶ **Water correctly** Water lettuces at the base (left) and not in the heart of the plant. If the heart is soaked it may rot.

▶ **Get rid of weeds** Use a hoe to keep rows weed-free. There's an old saying, 'Hoeing once is the equivalent of watering twice.' This is because hoeing loosens the soil and lowers the rate of evaporation of moisture and, as weeds are competitors for water, getting rid of them gives the lettuces a better chance.

▶ **Pick at the right time** To test whether a hearting lettuce is ready to pick, feel the heart – it should be nice and firm. If it is not, leave the plant in the ground for a few days more.

Vary your salads with red lettuce, oakleaf lettuce and, in the foreground, 'Lollo Bionda', to name but a few.

Lettuces on the level When you prick out lettuces, don't plant them too deeply. The point at which the rosette of leaves joins the stem should be above the surface of the soil. It is hardly necessary to firm them in, just water in lightly.

▶ If you are planting lettuce plugs, plant the top of the plug just level with the surface of the soil.

Growing lettuce under glass Extend the season by growing lettuce in a protected environment. 'Clarion' (butterhead) and 'Challenge' (crisphead) are two lettuces that can be grown successfully in an unheated greenhouse or cold frame.

Producing your own seeds In the past, gardeners often saved seeds from their favourite and strongest growing plants. Lettuce seeds are particularly easy to collect, but don't bother with F1 hybrid seed as they will not come true to type. To harvest seeds, leave one or two plants to go to seed. When the seeds are ripe they look tufty and will start to disperse in the wind. At this stage pull up the plant and hang it upside down in a cool, dry place. Peg large paper bags over the flower heads to catch any seeds that fall from them. Collect the remainder of the seeds by shaking or knocking them into the bag. Clean the seed over the winter, carefully removing any dust, earth or other pieces of debris, and store in a cool, dry place ready for use.

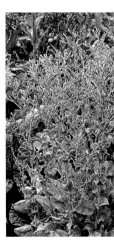

Success with seedlings Sow seeds into trays or modules filled with compost, and water them. Once seedlings appear keep the soil moist.

▶ When seedlings are established and have good root systems, transplant into larger pots if you want to overwinter them in the greenhouse, or plant them directly into the soil in a greenhouse border. Make sure there is good air circulation in the greenhouse to prevent outbreaks of mildew. Several lettuce varieties, including 'Clarion', have good resistance to mildew.

▶ You can sow seed early in the growing season to get an early harvest. As soon as the soil warms up and the weather improves, harden the seedlings off in a cold frame. If it is an overwinter crop, plant them into a cold frame.

Corn salad – an easy salad crop To learn the secret of cultivating corn salad, or lambs' lettuce (variety 'Etampes', below), it is worth knowing its origins. This plant was a weed that grew among crops and was gathered by country folk

working in the fields. The seeds germinated after the harvest, on the hard straw-covered ground. If the lettuce wasn't picked, the rosettes ran to seed in spring and continued their cycle in the next crop or on fallow land.

▶ Although this suggests that corn salad needs little attention, it does best if it is sown into a reasonably fertile soil in an open, sunny site. If you sow in autumn and winter, it will need protection from severe frost and snow. Cover it with horticultural fleece or cloches. Sow it either in the growing position or into modules, and transplant when the seedlings are large enough to handle.

▶ You can use corn salad as a cut-and-come-again salad crop. Water it well during dry periods, and you will be able to harvest it within 4–12 weeks of sowing.

Salad crops throughout the year

SALAD CROPS	SOW IN	HARVEST IN
Chicory 'Zoom F1'	April–May	January
Radicchio 'Augusto' or 'Cesare'	July	February
Corn salad, rocket, land cress	Aug–Sept	February
Radicchio 'Augusto' or 'Cesare', corn salad, rocket, land cress	March–April	March
Dandelion	April–May	March
Winter lettuce 'Winter Density' or 'Marvel of Four Seasons'	August–Sept	April–May
Spring lettuce 'Clarion'	Jan–July	May–Oct
Spring lettuce 'Challenge'	Feb–Sept	May–Dec
Cos types 'Little Gem', corn salad	March–July	May–Oct
Curly endive and endive ('Frisée Fine Curled')	June–July	May-Oct
Summer lettuce 'Lobjoit's Green Kos' or 'Lollo Rossa', purslane	March–July	June–Sept
Endive 'Pain de Sucre', radicchio	June–July	November
'Lollo Rossa', corn salad, land cress, rocket	July–August	December

Quick and easy: cut-and-come-again lettuce Mixed salad leaf seed collections are useful for colour and variety. They take up less space than other lettuce sowings, and you can get three to four cuts from each one of the plants. Grow in a partially shaded site and keep the plants well watered. Sow seeds continuously from March to August and harvest as you require the tender young leaves. Try 'Flamenco', which is an oak-leaf type, 'Lollo Rosso' or 'Lollo Bionda'.

Transplanting lettuce seedlings

1 Use a trowel to lift young seedlings gently from an outdoor seedbed.

2 Hold by the leaves and treat the root carefully. Some gardeners trim leaves to avoid evaporation.

3 Use a dibber to make a hole and lower the seedling into it, so that the leaves are just level with the top of the soil.

4 Use your hands to firm the soil around the plant and water it in.

Endives, radicchio and chicory

Sharp-tasting salad leaves Endives have deeply cut and loose foliage, which can be blanched by covering or tying the leaves up around the heads. Chicory, also known as Belgian chicory or Witloof, is lifted and forced into producing smooth-leaved, tightly packed heads.

▶ Radicchio, or red chicory, has marbled red and white foliage, which is less bitter after forcing.

Preventing bitterness in endives To produce an endive that isn't bitter, you have to prevent the leaves of the heart from turning green by protecting them from the light for about ten days before harvesting. This is called blanching. Make sure the endives are dry, so that the heart doesn't rot, then tie up the head with raffia or rubber ties. Alternatively, place a cloche or dish over the heart of the plant, which will make it stay white.

Chicory is essentially a root

The edible part of chicory is the large bud that develops after forcing. Sow chicory seeds in May, in soil that has been well dug over and broken down. It is not advisable to add manure or compost to the area where you grow chicory, since organic matter, as well as hard lumps of earth, will cause the roots to fork. The aim is to produce regularly formed roots that look like parsnips.

Easy-to-grow chicory 'Pain de

Sucre' (left), named after the shape and size of its head, is an extremely reliable variety of chicory. This variety does not need to be lifted

Forcing chicory

1 Dig up the chicory roots in October–November, using a garden fork and taking care not to damage them.

2 Cut off leaves 2cm above the neck: remove hair roots from the main root. The root should be 15–20cm long.

3 Stand the roots point down in a box part-filled with compost. Fill the spaces between roots with compost.

4 Put the box in a cool, dark place and cover loosely with black plastic. Keep the soil moist.

5 Buds will gradually develop in the dark to form small, tightly packed heads.

6 Once the buds are fully grown, harvest the heads as required.

and blanched. It will heart up in situ and can be harvested and eaten without additional blanching. It produces tender, pale yellow, slightly bitter leaves during autumn and part of winter. The outside leaves will go mushy if temperatures fall below −5°C, but you can remove these by washing them off and the centre will still be edible.

Salad to detoxify the blood Radicchio, cut-and-come-again oakleaf lettuce, corn salad, dandelions, chervil and wild herbs were traditionally made into a salad at the end of winter to purify the blood and balance digestion ready for the coming spring, after the long, sluggish months indoors.

Spinach, cardoons and chard

All you need to know about spinach It is simple to grow spinach, in soil that is lightly dug, but there are a couple of things to bear in mind.

▶ Its worst enemy is damping-off, a disease caused by the parasitic fungus *Pythium debaryanum*. This persists in the soil, lying dormant until damp conditions and the right host – spinach seedlings – are available. Formerly gardeners attempted to prevent this by sprinkling powdered charcoal in the drill when sowing seeds. However, it can be avoided by spacing the seedlings so that there is a good current of air.

▶ Spinach grows best when there are equal amounts of daylight and darkness, so it thrives in spring and autumn. Sow in March, April or September.

Easy to grow New Zealand spinach (*Tetragonia expansa*) has distinctive diamond-shaped leaves. Sow in March, under glass, or outdoors in May, after soaking the seeds for 24 hours. Plant three or four seeds per module or in planting holes in the ground spaced 70cm apart. The plants will spread and produce continuously from July to October. Harvest the leaves carefully without damaging the main stem.

Blanching cardoons The cardoon is a close relative of the artichoke. It has spiky leaves, purple but inedible flowers and a leafstalk that is blanched and cooked like celery.

▶ To blanch cardoons, wrap each plant in a tube of corrugated cardboard (below), held in place with string. This ensures that the stems are tender. In the past, blanching was done with straw matting. To cook, the stalks should be scrubbed and braised in milk and water.

The best way to harvest tender spinach leaves is to pick them carefully, one leaf at a time.

Space invaders Sow cardoons in May, planting three or four seeds in each planting hole. Allow at least a metre between holes in all directions. Two weeks after germination, thin out, leaving one plant per hole. While the plants are small, grow radishes and lettuce as a catch crop between the cardoons, since these vegetables have a short growing cycle and will make use of the available space until the cardoons take over.

Beauty and the beet Chard, which is also called leaf chard or leaf beet, is a large leafy vegetable, as ornamental in the kitchen and flower garden as it is delicious in cooking. There are red-stemmed (right, above) and orange-stemmed (right, centre) varieties, as well as those with green, mixed and rainbow-coloured stems and leaves. The leaves and stalks have a pungent, earthy flavour and are delicious served with a white sauce or butter. The white-stemmed variety, also known as seakale beet, Swiss chard or perpetual spinach (right), has green leaves and white or green stems. A tip for harvesting is to twist the stalk as you pull.

Enrich the soil with nitrogen
Take advantage of spinach's production of nitrogen in its leaves and use any surplus seeds or plants as an alternative green manure. Sow spinach at the end of summer in any uncultivated areas of the vegetable garden. The first frosts will kill the plants. Then simply dig them in just below the surface, and the nitrogen in the spinach leaves will enrich the soil.

Generous legumes, greedy sweetcorn

Beans and peas belong to a large group of vegetables known as legumes, long cultivated by gardeners as useful soil improvers because of the way they absorb nitrogen. They fix it in nodules on their roots and so feed the soil when they rot. Sweetcorn, on the other hand, is a relative newcomer and a greedy feeder.

RHS award-winning runner bean 'Red Rum' is an early-cropping British thoroughbred. Choose a sheltered location to ensure good pollination by insects.

English runner beans, and French beans too

French beans and runner beans Sow seed in soil that has been well manured the previous autumn or winter. These beans need warmth and moisture to germinate, so wait until late spring when the ground has warmed up. Add runner beans, with their colourful flowers, to a flower border.

Earthing up
Old-fashioned gardeners found that earthing up dwarf French beans helps to support the stems, so that the bean plants can establish well. It also maintains moisture around the roots.

Sow French beans in succession French beans are sown from mid-April to July and harvested from June onwards. If you sow them in succession you will have crops at regular intervals, rather than needing to harvest everything at once.
▶ Times between sowing and harvesting vary, depending on the type of bean, but generally allow 7–13 weeks (up to 16 weeks for climbing beans). Using this rough yardstick you can gauge how many sowings you need to make during the growing season.

Runner beans keep on cropping For runner beans, sow from May to July and harvest from July onwards. You don't need to make successional sowings of runner beans, just keep picking the beans regularly to ensure continuous flowering and therefore bean production.
▶ Water runner beans regularly to keep them cropping.

Saving bean seeds Allow the last beans on each plant – those that are too high to harvest – to ripen fully. The pods will turn yellow and begin to look dry and shrivelled. At this point, pick them and remove the beans from the pods. Store them in paper bags in a cool, frost-free, dry place. Label the bags with the name of the bean and the following year you can sow them.

▶ You can also save seed from broad beans and peas, but seed taken from F1 hybrids will not come true to type, so is not worth saving.

Feed runner beans on waste Because they produce their own nitrogen, runner beans are able to digest uncomposted material. In early spring, when you are tidying the garden, fill a trench with the soft greenery and harmless weeds you have just cleared from elsewhere on your plot.
▶ When planting time comes, chop up these cuttings with your spade, cover them with good compost-enriched soil, and either sow runner bean seed or plant young seedlings.

Conserving moisture Although preparing the soil well by digging in uncomposted green waste and well-rotted manure helps to keep the ground damp, take other measures to further reduce the need for watering in dry spells. A mulch of compost or black plastic sheeting will help lock in moisture.

Getting the bird Legume seedlings are very attractive to birds, so you will need to protect them until they have grown into good-sized plants. Horticultural fleece is useful for protecting a whole row of seedlings, and cloches and bird netting are also effective.
▶ Homemade 'humming lines' fashioned from twine strung across the vegetable bed and stretched tightly on canes will deter birds.
▶ Alternatively, giveaway CDs from magazines can be hung around the garden as shiny bird scarers.

Broad bean 'Aquadulce', shown here growing in a string support, can be sown in autumn for crops in May and June.

Tender broad beans

Simple sowing Broad beans are easy to grow in most soil conditions, and sowing couldn't be simpler.
▶ **Early sowing** Make the first outdoor sowing early in March and follow with sowings in late March and April. Place the seeds in a drill at a depth of 3–4cm, at intervals of about 20cm. They will germinate in two or three weeks. Some varieties can be sown later, though many gardeners say that these late-sown beans are more susceptible to blackfly and give a lower yield.
▶ **Autumn sowing** Several varieties, such as 'The Sutton' and 'Aquadulce Claudia', can be sown in late autumn from October through to December, overwintered, and harvested in May or June. Pick as soon as the pods are full and the beans look swollen: the younger the bean, the more tender it will be.

Broad beans need support Tall-growing varieties of broad bean may need support if grown in exposed, windy sites. Tie the plants to individual canes or, to support a whole row of beans, use two stakes with a fork at the top, inserted firmly into the soil at either end of the row. Lay a bamboo cane across from fork to fork and tie it in. Then, at intervals, tie into this horizontal cane some upright canes which will support the beans as they grow.

A bonus crop Thrifty wartime gardeners used to cut broad bean stalks back to 10–15cm after harvesting. Shoots from the base of the stalks would then develop to form bushy stems, and produce a smaller, second crop. While waiting for the second crop you can also grow lettuces as a catch crop.

Sowing French beans outdoors

1 Sow the beans in seed holes, usually three to four beans per hole. Holes should be spaced 30cm apart.

2 Don't sow the beans too deep, no more than 3cm. Hoe or rake over soil to cover the seeds.

3 Water well to settle the soil in the planting holes and moisten the beans.

4 Once the first leaves have appeared, earth up slightly with a hoe and keep the plants well watered.

Pinching out tops

Broad beans are well known for attracting aphids. Some gardeners feel that pinching out the tops, where the youngest and therefore tastiest shoots are found, will rid the plants of the pest. Pinching out will also stop the plants from getting leggy.

Blackfly alert A good tip for pest-free crops is to grow summer savory, a delicious herb, alongside your broad bean rows. While its aroma is said to deter blackfly from the beans, the herb itself is used to flavour cooked bean dishes and, in Germany, is known as beanherb.

Perfect peas

Best time for sowing Peas should be sown in succession according to the following timetable for outdoor sowing. Sugar snap peas are the immature pods, so these can be harvested particularly early, as the peas don't develop fully.
▶ **First earlies** Sow March–June, harvest 11–13 weeks later
▶ **Second earlies** Sow March–June, harvest 13–14 weeks later
▶ **Maincrop** Sow March–June, harvest 14–15 weeks later

Sow peas deep The first two seed leaves develop below ground, which means peas have to be sown at a depth of about 5cm in order to develop a good root system. They also need to be densely planted, so sow seeds close together, no more than 1–2cm apart.

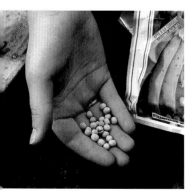

Round peas To produce a quality crop, round garden peas need cool temperatures so they are sown early, between February and April. Try 'Feltham First', 'Oregon Sugar Pod' and 'Meteor', which can also be sown in autumn and overwintered.

Wrinkled peas Wrinkled varieties of peas are sweeter and firmer than the round types when cooked. They are also more resistant to hot weather and can be harvested for a longer period. They are sown between the end of March and May and include varieties such as 'Kelvedon Wonder', 'Little Marvel', 'Hurst Green Shaft' and 'Onward'.

Staking peas with a natural support

1 Support peas with twiggy hazel branches when the tendrils start to develop.

2 Place sticks at intervals of 25–30cm and about 5cm from the plants. Angle them so that they meet above the centre of a double row of plants.

3 Encourage plants towards the sticks. They will begin to use their tendrils to climb up and gain support against windy and rainy weather.

The art of staking peas All types of peas – dwarf, semidwarf and tall – are climbers and need support for their twining tendrils. The most popular kind comes from sticks, known as 'pea sticks', which are twiggy branches often cut from hazel bushes that are coppiced in winter.
▶ It is easier to stake and harvest peas if they are grown in double rows 50–75cm apart, depending on the variety.

Of mice and peas Mice enjoy rearranging your pea seeds under ground, though deep planting may put them off the scent. Old-fashioned gardeners used to dip their pea seeds in paraffin; the strong smell was said to ward off mice. You can also try adding holly leaves to the planting area.
▶ An alternative way to avoid problems with mice is to plant peas in lengths of guttering a metre or so long, filled with soil and kept in the greenhouse or cold frame. When the plants are established, dig a trench, push them out of the guttering along its length and plant them, firming the soil around the roots. You may also need to earth up the plants so the roots are all well covered.

UNDER GLASS

An early start for beans and peas

Under cloches Warm up the soil with cloches two weeks before sowing outdoors. Sow runner beans and French beans in April for a July crop. Sow broad beans in early March for an early June crop. Sow peas in late February for a June crop. Protect sowings and seedlings with cloches until all danger of frost has passed.

In cold frames and greenhouses Sow runner beans in a cold frame in early April, using heat to force germination. Sow French beans in a cold frame in late March and harden off in May. Sow broad beans in a cold frame as early as January and harden off outdoors in March. Sow early wrinkled-seed peas in February (if you can provide temperatures of 7–10°C) and begin to harden off in March.

Harvest time The 'silks' will tell you when it is time to harvest. The cobs develop inside a sheath composed of several leaves known as bracts or spathes, and only the silks – all that remains of the flower styles – are visible from the outside. Initially, the silks are green, but when they have turned dark brown, and look and feel dry, the cob is ripe.

▶ You can check the ripeness of the cob by peeling back the bracts. Before they mature, the kernels are milky and translucent (right). When ripe, the kernels should be plump and tender – test them with your thumbnail – and, depending on variety, bright yellow, pale cream or even black in colour.

A cob of sweetcorn develops below the female flower or 'silk' of the plant.

Succulent sweetcorn

Plant in blocks To produce juicy sweetcorn, it must be wind-pollinated. The plant is adapted for this by having two sets of flowers: male flowers are the long tassels at the top of the plant, and female flowers are the 'silks' below which the cobs develop. Pollen is blown from the long tassels of the male flowers to pollinate the female flowers, so planting in blocks rather than rows favours pollination.

Warm-weather friends Sweetcorn originates in the southern states of North America and in Mexico, so it needs warm weather to get established. Sow it direct once the soil has warmed up, not before early June. Since the carbohydrate-rich kernels are susceptible to attack by fungi, insects and slugs, it

needs the warmth to enable it to germinate quickly.

▶ Sow two or three seeds in holes about 3cm deep and 25–30cm apart. For a greater success rate, sow two or three kernels in a pot, and transplant seedlings out into the garden when all danger of frost has passed.

▶ As plants grow, lateral roots may develop at the soil surface. Leave them in place, as they anchor the plants and provide nourishment for them.

From garden to table There's an old saying in the American South: 'You can walk down to the garden to pick your corn, but you have to run coming back.' What this means is that, to capture its sweetness, you can't keep sweetcorn for long before cooking it. Boil the husked cobs in unsalted water: salt will harden the kernels.

DID YOU KNOW?

Sweetcorn and green beans – a winning combination

Sweetcorn and green beans were both introduced from the Americas where they are widely cultivated. They make excellent companions in a mixed bed, because sweetcorn is a greedy feeder and benefits greatly from the nitrogen fixed in the soil by the beans. The beans, in turn, use the upright-growing sweetcorn as support. The two crops also complement each other nutritionally and are often eaten together.

▶ If you want to grow beans alongside your sweetcorn, wait until the sweetcorn has two or three leaves, then sow a few bean seeds in the spaces between the plants. Choose dwarf or nonvigorous varieties such as 'Hestia' (a dwarf runner bean), 'Maxi' or 'Delinel'.

▶ To grow sweetcorn with pumpkins – another traditional American partnership – sow the sweetcorn when you plant out your pumpkins.

Fruiting vegetables in the summer sun

Tomatoes, marrows and melons swell with the promise of a succulent maturity. Once these rampant growers were confined to the greenhouse, but now improved varieties and techniques mean that most can be grown outdoors too.

Tomatoes – red, ripe and delicious

Seeds need heat Tomato seeds need warmth to germinate. Sow them into seed compost in trays or modules in a heated propagator in January or February for an early start. Transplant into larger pots when they have produced three to four leaves. Harden off outdoor varieties, and plant greenhouse varieties into growbags in the greenhouse.

Planting outdoors Plant out when all danger of frost is past. For extra protection, cover the young plants with a cloche or a layer of horticultural fleece. Old-fashioned gardeners in Mediterranean areas have been known to protect their tomato plants with two terracotta roof tiles propped together.

Staking plants Push stakes firmly into the ground, leaving 60cm between each one, so that the plants have enough room to grow. Make a planting hole about 10cm in front of each stake and place the plants into the holes, angling them slightly towards the stakes. Water the plants in and then gently firm the soil around them, taking care not to damage the stems. As the plants grow, begin to tie them against the stakes to support them. Do this regularly, especially with cordon-type tomatoes.

Water reservoirs Tomatoes need regular and copious watering. To make sure they get enough, sink a small flower pot into the ground near the base of each cane. Pour water into this every day so that it fills up and then slowly drains into the soil near the plants. Another method is to remove the top from the

There is nothing so delicious as home-grown, vine-ripened tomatoes. Pick them regularly as they ripen.

neck of a two-litre plastic bottle, cut the bottle in half and sink the neck into the ground. Fill with water every day.

▶ During the growing season, tomatoes need regular feeding, so use this reservoir for applying water-soluble fertiliser. You can also feed the plants with liquid manure made from nettle or comfrey (see page 269).

Mulching is essential Like many other crops, tomato plants need to be well spaced because of their volume. It is a good idea to cover the soil at their base with a mulch. Use straw, the foliage of comfrey or nettle plants, or ordinary chipped bark, in a layer up to 5cm deep. This suppresses weeds and helps to prevent excessive water evaporation

from the soil surface. Mulch only on damp soil to keep the existing moisture in, otherwise it will prevent the rain reaching the roots and ensure that dry soil simply stays dry.

Stakes and wigwams Cordon tomato plants have a naturally trailing or climbing habit and most need some form of support. Training them upwards not only means they take up less space, but they also escape the adverse effects of damp soil which promotes the development of diseases.

▶ Use hazel poles or canes, at least 1.5 metres long, and push them into the ground near the base of each plant. As the plants grow, use raffia or string to tie the stems to the stakes.

▶ One way to ensure that the stakes are stable is to arrange them in groups of three or four, angled towards the centre,

and tie them firmly at the top to form a wigwam shape for the plants to grow on. This is a good solution if your tomatoes are growing in an ornamental garden.

Bush types Some varieties of tomato, such as the 'Roma', have a bushy habit and don't need staking, However, in a garden, it's a good idea to keep these varieties off the ground to prevent their fruits from rotting. Support them on an upturned crate.

Mixed cropping Tomatoes grow well with asparagus, celery, French beans, onions, parsley, leeks and potatoes.
▶ Tomatoes don't grow well with cucumber, fennel, peas and beetroot.
▶ Plant marigolds (*Calendula*) around them to reduce infestations of whitefly.

The 'copper wire' tip In the past, some gardeners on the Continent have claimed to protect their tomato plants from mildew by piercing the young plants with copper wires at two points along, and at right angles to, the main stem. Though not scientifically proven, it is possible that copper compounds form in the sap and attack the fungi that cause mildew.

Trimming and pinching out Check cordon tomato plants regularly during the crucial stages of their development, and

pinch out all the little shoots that appear in the axils of the leaves. If they are not pinched out the plant will use its energy to become bushy and fruit production will be reduced. Do not pinch out side shoots on bush tomatoes, as they will eventually bear fruit.

A booster shot for tomatoes When your tomatoes begin to bloom, mix two large spoonfuls of Epsom salts in five litres of water and pour onto the soil around the plants. The magnesium and sulphur in the salts encourage healthy fruits.

Hasten ripening In late summer and early autumn, remove any foliage that may be shading the fruit from the ripening effects of the sun.

Basking in reflected light Follow the old-fashioned practice of using backing boards to reflect light onto sun-loving tomatoes. Cover a board with aluminium foil, prop it against

The pick of the tomato crop

Varieties of tomatoes differ in size, shape, flavour, texture, the colour of the fruit, type of skin (smooth or ribbed), picking time and mildew tolerance. So how do you choose between them?
▶ If you like stuffed tomatoes, go for large-fruited varieties.
▶ If you are adventurous and like something a bit different, try growing the lesser-known and more unusually coloured or shaped 'heirloom' varieties.

Black Russian An heirloom variety with a dark skin and a good-flavoured flesh
Big Boy F1 A large, smooth, blemish-free beefsteak-type fruit with thick meaty flesh
Brandywine Another heirloom, a large-fruited, beefsteak-type with good flavour
Crimson Fancy F1 A reliable producer, even for inexperienced growers
Dombito A tasty beefsteak tomato
Gardener's Delight ❶ A late variety with small, very tasty fruits
Green Sausage A bush tomato with yellow stripes and a green flesh which grows well in a container
Ildi A very prolific cherry tomato that produces large trusses of yellow oval or pear-shaped fruit
Marmande and **Super-Marmande** Early heirloom varieties with very large fruits ❷
Polish Linguisa An old heirloom variety dating from the 1800s, which produces unusual-shaped, large, sweet fruits
Roma ❸ An elongated plum tomato, ideal for making tomato sauces and pizzas
Striped Stuffer A tomato best grown under glass, with stripes on its skin. It is good for stuffing.
Super Marzano F1 A giant, disease-resistant pear-shaped fruit
Super Sweet 100 F1 One of the cherry tomatoes that produces red ❹ or yellow, sometimes pear-shaped, fruit ❺

a support and angle it so that it catches the sun's rays and bounces them onto the ripening fruit.

Making the most of suckers You may notice that tomato suckers, like the other green parts of the plant, have a very pungent smell. This is released – at the slightest contact – as a smelly, coloured substance from many tiny glands on the surface of the plant. Some gardeners say that this property can be used to protect other vegetables against garden pests. For example, it is said that if you place tomato suckers on the leaves of cabbages or other brassicas, the smell of the tomato will disorientate cabbage white butterflies and cabbage moths. This prevents them from laying their eggs on the leaves and protects your brassicas from caterpillar damage.

Ripening after picking
In autumn, if tomatoes are slow to ripen outdoors, you may have to pick the crop to avoid frost damage. Bring them into a dry, frost-free room and store them in brown paper bags, newspaper or fruit boxes. You will find that they ripen up in due course. If they don't, use them in green tomato chutneys.

A wide range of colours Many of the old heirloom-type tomatoes taste much better than modern varieties and their varied hues can be used to add interest to the salad bowl. In recent years, yellow, orange, green, pink, purple, black and even striped tomatoes have become increasingly popular.

Producing your own tomato seeds Nothing could be easier than producing your own tomato seeds, provided they come from a traditional variety and not an F1 hybrid. Put the pulp of a ripe tomato into a bowl and add a little water. A whitish bacterial film will soon form on the surface of the liquid. After about 36 hours, add more water and stir the mixture – this fermentation process separates the seeds from the pulp, and the seeds will sink to the bottom. Strain off the liquid through a sieve, rinse the seeds under the tap and leave them to dry on a piece of kitchen paper.

Tomatoes are thirsty growers. Sink a flowerpot up to its rim at the base of each plant. Fill the pot in the early morning or evening, being careful not to wet the fruits or foliage.

Marrows, courgettes, pumpkins and squash

All in the family Vegetable marrows, courgettes, summer and winter squashes, pumpkins and ornamental (nonedible) gourds are all members of the gourd family *Cucurbitaceae*.
► Pumpkins and squash are sometimes referred to as winter fruits. They are harvested late in autumn and can be stored in cool, dry conditions through the winter. The skins of pumpkin and squash, when ripe, develop a tough exterior and are usually orange, stripey or blue-grey. Their flesh is rich in Vitamin C. Pumpkins are less flavoursome than squash, which has a nutty flavour and a finer texture.
► Marrows, courgettes and summer squash are usually harvested earlier in the growing season and do not keep as long as winter squash. Their skins are softer and their flesh has a blander taste.

Easy to grow Sow courgettes, marrows and pumpkins in situ, allowing a metre between plants in all directions and two metres for trailing varieties. Sow to a depth of about 2cm. Don't be tempted to sow until late May or early June, when all danger of frost has passed.

Long-season courgettes
So that you have a plentiful supply of courgettes during the summer, sow them in succession between the months of April and July.
► Sow seeds indoors in April, plant out in late May and harvest from July onwards.
► Sow seeds direct into the ground in June and harvest from late July onwards.

Two's company Courgettes – which are simply young marrows – are extremely prolific, so it's not worth planting out more than two at a time. Remember to create a hollow around the base of young plants for watering. This will hold the water and ensure that it gets to the right spot.

Multicoloured courgettes Courgettes are available in a range of skin colours. The traditional favourite has a dark green skin, but you can also grow courgettes that are light green or yellow in colour. They all taste similar and, if cooked unpeeled, look good when served together.

For an early start use plug plants Buy plug plants, or raise seedlings under glass. Plant out towards the end of June, or sow seeds direct into the ground in late May or early June.

'Tiger Cross' can be harvested when small, as courgettes, or allowed to develop into attractively striped marrows.

Keeping the weeds down If you plant trailing varieties of marrows, pumpkins and squashes, they will soon cover a vast area with their abundant foliage. Plan for this unusual spread and reap the benefit of the foliage keeping the weeds down.

Ladder of success To give them somewhere to trail and keep them out of the way, place an old wooden ladder – one past its best for practical use – against a fence or wall. Plant trailing varieties at its feet, and they will climb up the rungs.

Easy neighbours Courgettes, marrows, squash and pumpkins will grow anywhere, even in poorly prepared soil. If you are starting a new vegetable garden and haven't had time to prepare the ground fully, you can still get a good crop. As long as you can add well-rotted manure to the soil they will thrive almost wherever you plant them.
► All of these vegetable fruits will do best if planted in a sheltered, sunny position.

Sowing on the compost heap Marrows, squashes and pumpkins need plenty of organic matter and thrive if sown or planted directly on the compost heap. Sometimes they even grow without the help of the gardener since the seeds in kitchen waste often germinate unaided. As an added bonus, the foliage of most pumpkin and squash will provide a natural and attractive covering to keep the compost heap shaded and moist. If the seeds are from F1 Hybrids the results may be variable, as the pumpkins won't come true to type.

Top tips for care of pumpkins and squashes Many of these tips will work for tomatoes and cucumbers too.
► **Encourage more fruits** Nip out the growing tips of the main shoots of trailing plants when they are 45cm long, to promote the growth of lateral shoots and female flowers.
► **Help pollination** If the fruits are not setting well, pollinate the plants by hand. Use a small brush to transfer pollen from the male flowers to the female, which you can identify by a swelling just behind the bloom.
► **Remove some leaves** As soon as a small pumpkin develops, remove some of the leaves on the fruit-bearing stem, leaving two or three just above the fruit.
► **Foil pests** If you spread aluminium foil on the soil around the base of the plants, you can prevent viruses transmitted by thrips and aphids. You can deter cutworm by wrapping stems in a sleeve of aluminium foil, making sure the sleeve is buried 2–3cm in the soil. Taping foil behind the plants, on a fence or wall not only increases light but also confuses pests.

A bold splash of colour in the vegetable garden is one of the bonuses of growing pumpkins.

Fruiting vegetables

On the tiles Place a tile, a small board or a flat stone under the fruit (left) to keep it off the damp soil and avoid pests and possible rotting. The tile will absorb heat from the sun and will ripen the fruit more quickly.

When to harvest? Fruiting vegetables will be ready to harvest at different times and in varying quantities.

▶ **Marrows** Harvest as required. Up to 24 fruits can be taken from one plant if they are picked when 30cm long. Leave the last two or three fruits on the plants until October, when they will be fully grown and well ripened.

▶ **Courgettes** Pick courgettes when they are about 15cm long (left). The more you pick the more fruits the plant will produce, and if they are picked at this size they will be very tasty. Any larger and they are half-way to becoming marrows.

The trailing varieties of marrows, squashes and pumpkins will make good use of a wild area of your garden. They can spread for several metres from their planting point.

Eye-catching marrows, squashes and pumpkins ▶

Custard marrow or 'Patty Pan' ❶ The decorative scalloped shape and white or yellow skin of this summer squash conceal tasty flesh that is best when picked small.

Pumpkin The 'Cinderella' type ❷ is an old French favourite, popular because of its deep orange skin and heavy ribbing, although it is also good to eat. However, the sweet sugar-type pumpkin ❺ is the classic cooking pumpkin, good for soups, pies and casseroles.

Turk's Turban ❸ This colourful and shapely squash has a tasty flesh, but it is normally grown for its unusual appearance.

Onion squash ❹ With its well-textured flesh, the onion squash is particularly flavourful.

Hubbard squash ❻ When roasted, this great-tasting squash has a superb nutty flavour. It keeps well.

▶ **Pumpkins and squash** Fruits are ready to pick when they have coloured well and developed a hard skin. Give them a tap and, if they sound hollow, they are ready to pick. Another indicator of ripeness is that the foliage begins to turn brown.

Storing marrows Harvest and store marrows for up to three months in an airy, frost-free place. Many old-fashioned gardeners stored their prize marrows singly in nets hung up in sheds, to keep them from coming into contact with other fruits over the winter storage period.

Curing pumpkins and squash After picking, keep the harvested fruit in a sunny place, or indoors in a conservatory or greenhouse, for about ten days so that their skins harden off well. If you are curing them outdoors bring them indoors if frost is forecast.

Storing pumpkins Blemish-free pumpkins will keep for up to three months in a frost-free environment. For maximum protection, store them on relatively warm surfaces, such as wood, cardboard or several layers of newspaper rather than cold surfaces such as stone or cement.

Living Jack-o'-lanterns You can add some fun to the business of growing pumpkins – and delight the children too – if you make a carving on the skin of a baby pumpkin and watch it grow with the fruit. Mark out a pattern or a face on a young fruit – a large nail is a good tool for the job – and then be patient for a few months. Don't remove the fruit from the plant as it needs to carry on growing. By autumn, the pattern will have expanded and grown with the pumpkin into a life-size face ready for Hallowe'en.

Cucumbers and melons

Cool as a cucumber

Cucumbers can be grown in a greenhouse or outdoors. Indoor cucumbers crop earlier, need to be trained and produce long, succulent fruits. Greenhouse cultivars such 'Futura F1' or 'Telegraph Improved' can also be grown in frames. There are many outdoor varieties including 'Burpless Tasty Green F1'. These varieties tolerate cooler conditions and produce shorter fruits.

Sowing time Sow indoor cucumbers in March or April, into pots in a frost-free greenhouse. Transplant into frames or the greenhouse border in late spring or early summer. Water the plants well, especially while they are flowering.

Plant training Outdoor cucumbers can be grown up canes or along the ground. Remove growing points of stems regularly to encourage bushy growth and better fruit setting. After planting in a greenhouse, 'pinch out' the growing tip above the first three or four leaves. This will cause two fruit-bearing shoots to appear in the leaf axils. Tie these shoots onto canes.

All female flowers Most new greenhouse hybrids are all female and must be unfertilised to prevent a bitter flavour. However, if these plants are stressed by high temperatures or insufficient moisture, they may produce male flowers, which lack the immature cucumber present behind the petals of female flowers. Remove any male flowers from the plants.

Straight and narrow Victorians Glasshouse cucumbers were a favourite of the 19th-century gentry, whose gardeners grew them in glass sheaths to keep them straight and tender.

Harvest for the best flavour Harvest cucumbers when they have reached a good size but before they turn yellow.

Ridge cucumbers Small outdoor cucumbers are easy to grow and modern varieties are not bitter or as thick skinned as they used to be. Gherkins are the immature fruits of these outdoor ridge cucumbers, usually picked at 8cm or shorter and pickled in vinegar and spices to accompany savoury dishes.

Growing melons under cover

Sweet melons are trailing plants. They come from warm regions and in our climate are tender. They need plenty of well-rotted manure and should be grown under cover in a cold frame or unheated greenhouse. To get a well-structured plant with good fruits you need to train the plant. Pinch out the leading stem above the second leaf, and pinch out the new shoots that arise above the

third leaf. Then, when melons appear, pinch out the stems two leaves above the fruits, and support them with netting (right).

When to sow melons Sow in spring and early summer direct into the greenhouse or cold frame soil, but remember the seeds need a minimum temperature of 16°C to germinate. The plants will thrive if a temperature of 20°C can be guaranteed.

Watering Melons need regular and copious water especially when in flower so that good fruits develop. They need plenty of nutrients so use a tomato fertiliser with added magnesium.

Keep pollinating insects out until it's time As soon as the first melon fruits set, no others will develop, so you need to keep pollinating insects away from the flowers until all of them – or enough for your needs – have fully opened. To keep insects out use cloches or fleece over the plants, then once the flowers are open lift the cloches or fleece and allow the insects access. They will pollinate the flowers and you will have a number of fruits ripening at the same time.

Traditional cloches You may be lucky enough to find traditional glass cloches in secondhand shops or at car-boot sales. Snap them up if you do. In the past, these wonderful objects were used to protect young melon plants at the beginning of the season, and they are still extremely useful today.

Traditional hotbeds This old-fashioned method gives all fruiting vegetables, including marrows and cucumbers, a good start. Before planting, dig out a bed and fill it with organic matter which, as it decomposes, releases heat and helps the plants develop. (In the old days, this would have been fresh manure as it was widely available, but any organic matter will work.) Cover the organic matter with a good layer of soil, and sow or plant into that. The soil cover prevents heat loss from the hotbed and protects the young plants, which might otherwise rot due to the heat and moisture from the heap. For a finishing touch, you could cover each plant with a cloche.

Glossy aubergines and sweet peppers

Aubergines As a native of the tropical regions of Asia, the aubergine requires a great deal of heat to grow well, and so they are best grown here under glass.

▶ If you are tempted to try to grow aubergines outdoors, however, plant them from mid-May onwards on a sunny site, sheltered from the north wind. If necessary, protect young plants with cloches.

▶ 'Moneymaker', 'Black Enorma', 'Violet Pearl' and 'Bonica F1' are among the best varieties.

Restricting growth for an early harvest You need to force aubergines into producing flowers as early as possible. To do this, pinch out the growing point once the plant has produced up to five leaves, taking it out above the fifth leaf. Soon flowers will be produced by the lateral shoots, which you should also pinch out above their fourth leaves. This second pinching-out will force the plant to put all its energy into producing fruit, which you will be able to harvest earlier than if the plant was left to grow its own way.

Pepper pots Peppers need warmth to grow and normally have to be planted in a greenhouse to crop well. However, if you have a warm spot try a pepper in a 30cm pot supported by a cane. Pinch out the growing point when the plant is 15cm tall and water well. If growing in a greenhouse, mist regularly to increase the humidity. Use a foliar feed of dilute seaweed solution and guard against slugs, which love the fruit.

▶ For the largest peppers grow 'Big Bertha', or try 'Californian Wonder' or 'Canape'.

Stars of the pepper family

The capsicum or pepper plant can be divided into two types: the sweet (bell) type and the hot (chilli) type. The larger sweet peppers have a milder taste. Grow all types in a greenhouse, or in milder areas try a few in a pot on a sunny patio. Water them well in hot weather.

Purple Beauty ❶ This is an unusual deep-purple colour and is sweet and juicy straight off the plant.

Minibel A newly developed variety.

Jalapeño ❷ This classic American hot chilli pepper is used on pizzas.

Cherry Pick ❸ This produces small, round fruits, on vigorous, disease-resistant plants.

Habañero A very hot pepper used in curries and other spicy dishes.

Corno di Toro ❹ This is a long pepper which is red or yellow. It is great stuffed, stir-fried or eaten raw.

Aubergines thrive in the border of a greenhouse. You may be able to grow them outdoors in very mild areas. Try 'Mohican F1', which produces white-skinned fruits.

Gardening by the moon

According to old-fashioned gardening wisdom, the intensity of the moon's light at different stages in its cycle could encourage the germination and growth of plants.

▶ When the moon was waxing, or growing larger, gardeners sowed and planted species they wanted to be vigorous. They would also gather medicinal herbs, root vegetables and fruiting vegetables, including tomatoes, marrows, pumpkins and peppers (above).

▶ When the moon was waning, they would sow and plant species whose leaves they wanted to restrict, such as fruiting vegetables, as restricted leaves resulted in larger fruits.

Enjoy perennial vegetables, year after year

Asparagus, Jerusalem artichokes, globe artichokes and rhubarb are all perennial vegetables with an enduring appeal for self-sufficient gardeners. Once starter plants are well settled into the kitchen garden, they will go on producing plentiful crops indefinitely.

Asparagus is harvested just below ground level when the tips are about 7–10cm above the ground.

Planning for the long term

Asparagus grows best on light, sandy soil Create the ideal environment for an asparagus bed by lightening the soil with nonacidic river sand, available from garden centres.
► To plant asparagus in spring, prepare the ground in autumn by digging over and adding compost or well-rotted manure (about 50kg per 10 square metres) and a complete organic fertiliser (30–40g per square metre). Remove all weeds as asparagus plants must not have competition, but do not hoe around them or they will not thrive.
► After harvesting, spread compost or manure on the asparagus bed and cut back old stems to soil level once they have turned yellow or brown.

Choosing the sex of your asparagus Asparagus is a 'dioecious perennial'. That is, plants have either male or female flowers. Male plants produce more vigorous shoots, but you'll have to trust your supplier, since the only way to distinguish female plants is by their red berries in summer.

Don't buy dry roots Asparagus roots must be fresh before planting. If you can't plant the roots immediately, cover them with a damp cloth, sacking or sand.

Harvesting asparagus The knack to harvesting asparagus is to cut it off at an angle with a sharp knife, just below ground level. Asparagus is ready to harvest in April and May when the tips of the young, green shoots are 10–15cm long.
► Asparagus is best harvested after its second or third year, when the roots of the plant have become well established in the soil. If you start harvesting shoots too soon, you'll weaken the plant and possibly affect the next year's harvest.

Asparagus loves plaster
If you get a chance to lay your hands on some plaster from renovation or demolition work, give your asparagus plants a treat. Asparagus loves sulphur and calcium, two of the basic chemical elements used to make plaster. Spread the pieces of plaster on your asparagus bed in autumn (2kg per 10 square metres). They'll be broken down by frost and incorporated into the soil when you earth up.

Planting asparagus

1 Dig a trench and position a stick every 50cm to mark the position of each plant. Heap soil around each stick.

2 Place an asparagus root on each mound of soil, making sure it is well spread out over the mound.

3 Fill in the trench with good-quality soil and compost or manure, and earth it up slightly, retaining the sticks to mark the position of the roots.

Start out with globe artichoke offshoots Nurseries and garden centres sell young artichokes in pots. However, you may be able to find a gardener who grows artichokes and ask for some offshoots in April or May. To remove these from the clump, simply separate some strong-looking shoots from the main plant with a garden spade. It is essential that the shoots have rootlets at the base. Cut back the leaves to half their length and plant immediately, leaving 80cm between plants.

Bigger artichokes

Old-fashioned gardeners suggest that, as soon as young artichokes form, you should pierce the stem, just below the flower head, with a piece of wood sharpened to a point. No one knows the science of this tip, but the fact remains that the artichokes grow bigger as a result.

▶ As they develop, leave only four to six flower heads per plant. By limiting the number of artichokes, you are already thinking ahead to the following season by preventing the plant from exhausting its reserves.

▶ For tender artichokes, the bud must grow rapidly. Water regularly, especially in dry weather, mulch with compost or bark and add manure.

Forever faithful – Jerusalem artichokes Once planted, Jerusalem artichokes are in the garden for ever. When you harvest them, it is impossible to remove all the tubers, and so some remain in the ground, ready to be next year's crop. Jerusalem artichoke plants are relatively tall, growing to three metres, so it is best to place them where you have space for a permanent stand. You can make the most of their height and get double value from the plants by using them as a sheltering windbreak in the vegetable garden.

Dependable performers Jerusalem artichokes grow well on most soils in sun or shade. Plant tubers in spring to a depth of 10–15cm, about 30cm apart, and harvest from late autumn through winter.

▶ Jerusalem artichoke 'Fuseau' has long, white tubers that resemble some potato varieties. 'Dwarf Sunray' produces tubers that don't need to be peeled. You can grow tubers bought from the greengrocer or saved from your own stock if you have grown them previously.

Instant rhubarb If you want to be able to harvest rhubarb soon after planting, don't buy plants sold in pots at garden centres and nurseries – they will take years to mature. Instead,

Artichokes are sensitive to the cold

Artichokes are Mediterranean plants. In their native climate and in milder coastal regions, they keep their leaves throughout the year and produce flowers – the edible part of the plant – in April and May. In regions with colder winters, frosts as cold as –5°C are enough to destroy the leaves, while more severe frosts will destroy the whole plant. If they are cut back by frost the artichoke begins to grow back in spring and flowers from June or July until autumn. It is possible to protect the roots in winter by earthing up, covering them with dried leaves or wrapping them in hessian or bracken leaves.

in March, ask a gardening friend who already has an established patch of good-quality rhubarb for some healthy pieces of root with one or two buds for propagation. Dividing the roots of old clumps of rhubarb revives and reinvigorates them, so this will keep everyone happy.

Keep them cool Rhubarb grows well under average conditions. All it needs is a cool – even damp – place in the sun or semishade. It is hardy so doesn't need protection against frost in winter, even in the coldest regions, since rhubarb is actually a native of Siberia.

Harvesting rhubarb To harvest rhubarb without breaking the stems, simply twist slightly and pull gently.

▶ If you harvest rhubarb regularly it won't flower. The flowers are not unattractive, but the plant puts its energy into producing them rather than the leaf stalks. If you see a flower stem developing, cut it out.

Never eat rhubarb leaves Rhubarb leaves are poisonous; don't be tempted to eat them.

Satisfying root vegetables

The provident gardener was once judged on the richness of his winter reserves. So it's hardly surprising that easy-to-store beetroot, carrots and turnips were, and still are, mainstays of the kitchen garden.

The winter-hardy beetroot

Round or long? The two main varieties of beetroot are the globe and the long-rooted.

▶ **The globe beetroot** The familiar round beetroot is less prone to bolting than other varieties and can be sown several weeks earlier, to provide roots from June. 'Avonearly', 'Boltardy' and 'Early Bunch' are recommended. For later sowings to provide roots for autumn and early winter use, sow the small-rooted, quick-growing 'Little Ball'.

▶ **The long-rooted types** This variety is still frequently used for a main crop that is allowed to mature in the ground before being harvested and stored in early winter. 'Cheltenham Green Top' is a good variety. 'Cylindra' is another long-rooted variety, which is easy to prepare for cooking.

Long rooted beetroots, such as 'Cylindra' and 'Forono', are easy to slice, producing uniform slices with little wastage.

Traditional cultivation Beetroots thrive on light soil, but will grow successfully on most fertile, well-cultivated vegetable patches. Sow seed thinly in rows 30cm apart. Barely cover with soil and water in well. Thin out as seedlings develop to a spacing of 15cm between plants.

A harvest you can leave in the ground Beetroot is grown for harvest any time from June into early winter, depending on the variety.

▶ As soon as they are large enough to cook, you can pull early globes whenever you need them.

▶ Main crops for winter use can be left in the ground until required if they are covered with straw or bracken to protect them from frost. Alternatively, lift them in November and store in boxes of sand in a frost-proof shed, or outdoors in a clamp. Cut the tops off the roots for storing, being careful not to cut too close to the crown or the root will bleed.

A visual feast If you like decorative dishes and a touch of originality, grow yellow beetroot, such as 'Golden', or even two-tone beetroot with concentric circles of red and white, such as 'Pink Chioggia' (right). You'll be able to buy the seeds from most good vegetable seed catalogues.

Carrots for all seasons

A fine tilth For best results grow carrots in light or sandy soils. The ground needs careful preparation before you can sow them. Fork the soil over and rake out all stones and debris. Also remove perennial weeds.

▶ Carrots can develop long taproots, depending on variety, and need to be able to grow straight down into the soil. If you don't prepare the soil well, the result will be carrots that are forked or otherwise misshapen.

Growing in heavy soil You can get round this problem by growing short or intermediate varieties in raised beds. Break down the soil with the back of a rake, then build up long ridges about 10cm deep and 30–40cm wide. Sow the carrot seeds, preferably coated as they are so small (see page 187), into their ridges. You may also need to install a leaky hose system for economical watering as these ridged beds dry out very quickly.

Carrots thrive in a friable soil with a fine, uniform texture and no stones or hard lumps.

Carrot shapes There are short-rooted, almost round carrots for growing in the smallest spaces (left, top), intermediate carrots (left, centre) and long-rooted carrots (left, below) with tapering roots. Short-rooted carrots are harvested relatively early. They are tender but less productive than the other types.

▶ Short-rooted carrots, harvested in early summer, include 'Parmex' and 'Parabel'.

▶ Intermediate-rooted 'earlies', harvested in summer or autumn, include 'Early Nantes', 'Early Scarlet Horn' and 'Amsterdam Forcing III'.

▶ Intermediate-rooted 'lates', harvested in late autumn, include 'Flyaway F1' and 'Royal Chantenay 2', which are shorter and well suited to heavy, shallow soils.

▶ Long-rooted carrots, harvested in late autumn, include 'St Valery', 'Kingston F1' and 'Autumn King 2', which are suitable for light soils and have a high yield.

Trick those weeds Carrots are slow to germinate and weeds can soon take over the bed. This is why carrots have a reputation for being a 'messy' crop. It can be tricky trying to pull up weeds without uprooting the carrots.

▶ There is a partial solution to the problem – mock sowings. Prepare the soil as if you were going to sow your carrot seeds, but don't actually sow them. Wait for it to rain and for the weeds to come through. As soon as the soil dries out, uproot the young weeds with a rake. Repeat the process a few days later, when the soil is dry, then sow your carrot seeds for real.

Pre-germination
Cover carrot seeds with warm water and leave them to soak overnight. If you have a sprouting jar for mung beans, use it to 'pre-germinate' the seeds for 48 hours and then sow immediately – don't let them dry out.

Sowing sparsely According to an old saying, if you sow seeds thickly you'll have a sparse harvest. This is particularly true of carrots, whose fine seeds are difficult to sow evenly in the drill. The ideal spacing would be one seed every 5cm, but you need to sow more to allow for those that don't germinate.
▶ To sow sparsely, hold the seed packet fairly high above the drill, which should be about 8cm wide. As you move slowly along the drill, tap the packet to release the seeds. Don't do this if it's windy or the seeds will blow all over the garden.

▶ So that you're not too heavy-handed when sowing carrot seeds, mix the quantity of seeds required (4g per 10 square metres) with dried coffee grounds. It's easier to scatter this relatively bulky and clearly visible mixture in the drill. It is also said to protect the crops from carrot rust fly and other insects.
▶ Alternatively, mix the seed with sand and you will also be able to sow the seed more evenly. You will still have to thin the seedlings to give the plants enough space.

Sow carrots with onions and leeks These plants are all attacked by specific flies or moths that are attracted to their host plants by smell. Planting alternate rows of carrots and onions, or leeks, disorientates and discourages these pests.

An off-putting smell Some gardeners believe that a strong-smelling substance such as soot or powdered seaweed applied on the soil will deter carrot fly.

Mix carrot and radish seeds
Sow these crops together and, because radishes germinate much more quickly than carrots, they will mark out the rows and enable you to see where to hoe. You'll have harvested the radishes before the carrots need the space.
▶ You can also mix carrots with aromatic herbs, especially coriander, dill and rosemary. These have the advantage of providing a certain degree of protection against carrot root fly.

Carrot fly barrier
The carrot fly, whose maggots do so much damage by burrowing into the roots, finds its host plant by flying just above the surface of the soil. Protect your carrots by erecting a barrier of fine netting

Thinning out carrots

1 Wait until the seedlings have two or three true leaves, apart from the cotyledons, before thinning them out.

2 Leave one plant every 5cm. Save time and energy by pulling up weeds as you thin out the carrots.

or horticultural fleece attached to a frame around one or two rows at a time. The frame should be higher than the plants and can be kept in place with canes.
▶ Remove and destroy any infested plants immediately.
▶ As the carrot fly lays its eggs in late May, sow plants from mid-June to early July to avoid infestation.

Precision weeding
Removing weeds from a row of carrots is an extremely delicate operation. Old-fashioned gardeners suggest that it is best done with a knitting needle.

Forked roots Carrots can be deceptive. Large necks, full of promise, may emerge above the soil but, when it's time to lift them, the carrots revealed by your garden fork are often a disappointment – the root has stopped short after a few centimetres and given rise to new taproots. These are known as forked roots.
▶ The fault lies in the soil. Forked roots are caused by a deeper, compacted layer of soil (the result of working the soil to the same depth each year), by poorly structured soil with hard lumps, or by the presence of partially rotted manure. They can also be caused by insects and other disease-causing parasites. Dig the soil deeper and more thoroughly next year.

Goodbye, Peter Rabbit Some gardeners have had success in deterring rabbits with the old-fashioned practice of poking matchsticks, head down, into the soil near each carrot.

Harvesting carrots Usually, if you try to pull a carrot by the foliage, you'll end up with the leaves in your hand and the root still firmly in the ground. Before pulling, push the carrot gently into the soil – this enlarges the hole, breaks the rootlets that anchor the root in the soil and makes it easier to pull up.

An old-fashioned clamp In the past, carrots, potatoes, turnips, parsnips and beetroot were stored over winter in an outdoor 'clamp' to protect them from the weather. Vegetables had to be retrieved for eating with care and any gaps closed to avoid unbalancing the heap. It was also recommended that the heap was opened only at noon so that the sun's rays would prevent that part of the heap from being frozen.

▶ Alfred Smith, a market gardener in the 19th century, wrote about the traditional construction of a clamp, which was placed in a high but sheltered place where the ground was well drained. A shallow pit 30cm deep and 1.5 metres square was dug in the soil and covered with a thick layer of straw. The vegetables were then arranged on the bed in a ridged heap 90–120cm high. Another layer of straw was placed over the vegetables, at least 30cm thick, followed by a 30cm layer of the soil dug from the pit. Funnels of straw were then made in the sides or at the top for ventilation, to prevent rotting.

▶ Carrots were piled up to form a cone shape, their top ends facing outwards, and covered in sand only, not straw or earth. Potatoes were piled this way too.

Drying out is essential Once you've pulled or lifted your carrots, leave them on the surface of the soil for a day or two

DID YOU KNOW?

To fertilise or not to fertilise?

Before you plant out or sow vegetables, the ground needs to be well prepared and well-rotted organic material added. It is preferable to do this soil preparation in autumn, so that the organic matter is broken down in the soil and the nutrients are released, ready for the plants to use next spring. If the soil is well prepared in this way, it is unlikely that you will need to add fertilisers during the growing period.

Root crops don't have the same nutritional needs as salad greens or tomatoes. Although they need nitrogen to promote a good yield and early cropping, too much nitrogen will produce watery roots that don't store well. In addition, they need phosphorous and potassium to promote the build-up of reserves in the root and produce good-quality vegetables, as well as the magnesium and trace elements essential for human health.

If you haven't been able to prepare the soil in advance, all these elements are available in commercial organic fertilisers made from natural products. Fertilisers for root vegetables should contain less phosphorous than nitrogen and a lot more potassium – check the NPK (nitrogen, phosphorous, potassium) formula on the packaging. Also check that they contain reasonable quantities of magnesium.

to ensure that they keep well. This process, known as 'drying out', firms up the skins and is essential before they are stored in a clamp or in a cool cellar over the winter. When carrots have been lifted, cut off the foliage just above the neck, the point where it joins the root.

Storing carrots in the ground The best way to store main-crop carrots is to leave them in the ground over winter. But if the temperature drops below –5°C, they may be damaged by frost. A 5cm layer of dead leaves or straw, held in place with horticultural fleece, offers a degree of protection.

Storing root vegetables in a crate

1 Store root vegetables in a cool, damp, frost-free place. A wooden crate is an ideal container.

2 Cover the base with a layer of sand or sawdust and place unwashed but dried out root vegetables on it.

3 Cover with a layer of sand or sawdust and make more layers. When the crate is full, cover it with an airtight lid.

Using crates Line a wooden fruit crate with hessian. Remove excess soil from the carrots, taking care not to damage the roots, but do not wash them. Place a layer of carrots into the box, on a generous layer of insulating material: compost, sand, sawdust or leaf-mould. Cover with the insulating material and layer again. Store the crate where the temperature will be a constant 0–4°C.

Nice and spicy radishes

Choose radishes for a quick crop The radish, with its colourful skin and white flesh, is one of the spiciest roots in the kitchen garden. Radish seeds can be sown in succession from February to September to produce a regular harvest of roots. Seeds take only 20–30 days to mature. Sow a little and often – into short rows every 14 days – and you will have radishes all summer long.

▶ Radishes are often used as a 'starter plant' for children, who like to see quick results. They also grow well in containers.

Radishes are round or cylindrical in shape Depending on variety, radishes have white ('Long White Icicle'), red ('Giant of Sicily') and red with white tipped skins ('French Breakfast'). Radishes are a rich source of calcium, iron and vitamin C.

Right shape, right depth Radishes can be divided into two categories: summer and winter types. Summer radishes are mainly the globe or round red roots, although some

Fast-growing radishes make an ideal 'catch crop' for planting between main crops of slower vegetables.

summer radishes are more elongated and are known as intermediate radishes. Winter radishes are long and cylindrical in shape.

▶ Sow globe or round radishes to a depth of 1cm, intermediates and winter radishes to a depth of 1–2cm. It is important to sow them evenly. If sowing is uneven it results in erratic germination, and early developing seedlings will overshadow later ones.

Protect early sowings Radishes dislike root disturbance and need to be sown in situ. Those sown early, from February through to late spring, will need protection. Use horticultural fleece or a plastic cloche to protect the seedlings from frost.

Sun or shade? Full sun for early and late sowings will mean your radishes do well, but a little shade is needed for those sown in midsummer. Radishes prefer well-drained, light soil, but should be well watered to grow succulent and tasty roots.

Getting the best out of radishes For juicy well-shaped radishes, sow them into moist soil and water the growing plants well once the seedlings are established. Thin seedlings to 2cm to avoid the overcrowding that results in lanky plants.

Intercropping and catch cropping As radishes mature so quickly, they are particularly useful for intercropping: sowing between other crops while they establish themselves. They are also useful as catch crops in between plantings of main crops. In midsummer, sow radishes as a catch crop or intercrop – they will benefit from being shaded by the other crops, preventing them from bolting in excessive heat.

THE GARDENER'S CHOICE

The long and short of radishes

Grow summer radishes and use them raw to add colour and bite to salad dishes. In winter, radishes can be cooked to enliven seasonal fare such as soups and stews.

SUMMER RADISHES

Globe or round 'Sparkler 3', with a white tip ❶, 'Scarlet Globe' ❷, 'Cherry Belle' and 'Juliette F1' are reliable, heavy croppers, suitable for adding a little decorative zest to summer salads.

Intermediate 'Flamboyant Sabina' and 'Fluo F1' ❸ are dependable intermediate varieties. If you want a pure white-skinned radish, grow the intermediate 'White Icicle'.

WINTER RADISHES

Round Winter radishes are usually long, but the Asian radish 'Mantanghong F1', with its magenta flesh and 'Black Spanish Round', which has black skin ❹ are round in shape. 'Mino Early', has long white succulent roots that can be sliced to make a tasty addition to winter salads, soups and stews. Sow all these varieties in summer for a winter harvest.

Long For strong flavour in a long variety, try 'Rosa 2'. For length and flavour, grow the Japanese radish 'April Cross F1'. It has a crunchy texture and mild flavour and can be left in the ground until you are ready to harvest. It is also known as mooli radish.

Old-fashioned salsify, scorzonera and horseradish

Salsify, the oyster plant Salsify is a biennial root vegetable that produces attractive mauve flowers, which are also edible. The roots are long and brownish, with wrinkled skin and a delicate flavour, often compared to oysters or asparagus. It needs an open site and does best on light soils. On heavy clay, it is best to sow into a trench filled with compost or loam. Don't apply manure just before sowing, rather sow into a soil that was manured for a previous crop, as salsify doesn't do well in ground that has been freshly manured.

▶ Sow seed in situ in spring for an autumn to winter harvest. The roots keep in the ground, but once harvested they should be eaten promptly, as they tend to shrivel quickly.

Scorzonera, a dramatic root Scorzonera is a hardy perennial. It produces smooth, black-skinned roots, which can be left in the soil to grow to a larger size for a second season. Sow seed into open sites in sandy soil. If soil is heavy, trench as you would for salsify. Sow to a depth of 1cm and thin seedlings to 10cm.

▶ When you harvest the roots, take care not to damage them as they tend to bleed if the skin is broken.

▶ Scorzonera is said to deter carrot fly, so it is a good crop to plant near your carrots.

Scorzonera, although similar to salsify, is fleshier and has a more delicate flavour.

Don't waste any part of your radishes It's a shame to discard the leaves of freshly picked young radishes. Chopped up, they make a delicious garnish or salad ingredient. There is even a variety of radish called 'Rat's Tail', which is grown especially for its hot seed pods.

Horseradish, an English classic

The hardy horseradish is grown for its long taproots, which have a pungent, peppery flavour.

▶ Dig and manure the bed in winter. In February, purchase roots, known as thongs, about 25cm long and finger-thick. Plant them vertically so that their tops are 5cm below the surface.

▶ Lift the roots as required during summer; in winter, lift and store. To save on storage space, borrow a technique from old-time gardeners and lift a root from the winter garden, cut off a piece to use, then replace the root in the soil for another day.

▶ The long roots are difficult to eradicate, so horseradish should be grown as a perennial in a corner where it can be left undisturbed, or dug up each year and replanted in spring.

▶ A traditional way of controlling invasive horseradish plants and coaxing them into putting down long, straight roots is to plant them in galvanised drainage pipes. Sink the pipe up to the rim in a deep hole. Fill with compost-rich soil, insert the horseradish and firm down.

Easy sowing with treated seed

The seedlings of root vegetables usually need to be thinned out so that they have enough room to produce good crops. To avoid this painstaking chore, you need to sow the correct amount and density of seed. But this is not always easy to do, especially with tiny seeds. Fortunately there are now some specially treated seeds available that make accurate sowing much easier. The only drawback is that seed treated in this way is expensive, and there is a limited choice of varieties available.

Seed tapes Seeds are embedded into tapes (left) at even intervals suitable to the variety for regular sowing. The tapes are biodegradable, so they break down over time when the sowings are watered. All you have to do is make the drill, lay the strip along it and cover it with soil. The days of thinning out will be over for ever.

Coated seed Coated or pelleted seeds are surrounded by a protective material that makes them ball-shaped and therefore much easier to handle. This in turn makes it simple to sow them at the correct spacing.

Turnips, swedes and parsnips – the old standbys

A traditional winter crop Turnips were once grown only as winter vegetables, but you can sow fast-maturing types such as 'Purple Top Milan' and 'Snowball' to eat as soon as they reach a suitable size, normally in around 50 days.
▶ Later-maturing types such as 'Green Globe' can be stored to eat over winter. Crops can be harvested most of the year.

Tempting turnips The swollen, fleshy roots, usually white, have a delicate mustard flavour. The tender leaves are also used as a winter green vegetable, and the young shoots may be blanched and eaten. These vegetables should be grown quickly and, except for winter-cropping varieties, may be used as a catch crop.

Choose your varieties There are globular, flattened and long-rooted types of turnip.
▶ 'Aramis' and 'Model White' are flat-rooted varieties suitable for an early crop.
▶ For summer crops, the globular 'Tokyo Cross' or 'Snowball' are recommended.
▶ 'White Globe' (left, above) is a white, ball-shaped turnip with a deep rim of red at the top.
▶ For a winter crop, choose the globular 'Golden Ball' (left, below), which has sweet-tasting yellow flesh and particularly hard roots that store well.

Sow under glass or outdoors
Sow early turnips in spring under cover of cloches or in a cool greenhouse. Sow seeds to a depth of 2cm into shallow drills spaced about 25cm apart, then thin to 10cm apart. For a main crop sow outdoors.
▶ For those to be stored from late autumn through to winter, sow well-spaced in rows 30cm apart, later thinning them to 15cm. Choose varieties suitable to the season and sow in succession every 21 days.
▶ Turnips grow well in open sites in light, fertile soils that have been well manured. Be careful to bury the manure deeply or the roots may fork and have an earthy flavour.

Turnips need water Turnips need regular water throughout their growing season or their centres become woody. Spring

rainfall usually helps the gardener, but in dry seasons remember to water them well. Lack of moisture later in the season, especially for midsummer-sown turnips, can result in stunted, woody plants, bolting and susceptibility to pests.

The swede, a chunky vegetable Swede is a winter-hardy crop grown for its sweet-tasting yellow flesh. It stores well over winter in a vegetable clamp. Sow seed in spring to a depth of 2cm and thin out to 25cm.
▶ An open, sunny site in light, well-drained, fertile soil suits this root crop well. It needs regular watering. 'Best of All' and 'Marian' are two reliable varieties.
▶ The swede has a bad reputation that is totally unjustified, probably a legacy of its overuse in rationing during the Second World War. This hardy vegetable, which matures in three to four months and is exceptionally trouble-free to grow, deserves its place in our kitchens and vegetable gardens.

Parsnips in the wild In its natural state, the parsnip is part of the indigenous flora of Europe. Before carrots and potatoes took over our vegetable gardens in the 19th century, the parsnip was the predominant root vegetable and was mainly used in soups. Its long ivory-coloured roots are tender and full of flavour.
▶ There are several good varieties to grow that are canker-resistant. Tried and tested favourites include 'Gladiator' (right), 'Tender and True' and 'Cobham Improved Marrow'.

Top tips for growing parsnips Parsnips do best in sunny, open sites and, although light soil is best for root formation, they will grow on heavy soil too. Prepare the soil the previous autumn.
▶ **Sow thinly** Sow parsnips in spring in groups of two to four seeds to a depth of 2cm. They are slow to germinate, but when necessary, thin out the seedlings leaving 15–20cm between plants, depending on size of roots required.
▶ **Avoid drought** During the growing season keep weeds under control and water in dry periods or the roots will split.
▶ **Harvest after the first frost** Though it is possible to harvest parsnips from the end of summer onwards as you need them, wait if you can until the leaves have been damaged by the first frosts, as this improves their flavour.
▶ **Leave in the ground** Parsnips can be left in the ground whatever the weather, since it is where they'll keep best. Alternatively, store them in crates filled with sand.

Kohlrabi – not exactly a turnip The kohlrabi, or turnip cabbage, is a member of the cabbage family and produces a swollen, edible stem. Although it is not a root vegetable, it has a similar taste and use to the turnip, but is easier to grow. It is also drought-tolerant. So long as the soil is well manured, with a high pH level to lessen the likelihood of club root, kohlrabi will grow equally well in either sandy or heavy soil.

THE GARDENER'S CHOICE

Kohlrabi

One of the lesser known vegetables, kohlrabi comes in a wide range of varieties, both classic and new. If you come across seeds for 'Superschmelz', don't miss the opportunity to grow some truly phenomenal vegetables. This variety has particularly large globes, some supposedly weighing as much as 20kg.

Lanro This is a new strain of the classic 'White Vienna' ❶, and as such is still one of the most reliable varieties of kohlrabi.

Purple Vienna ❷ Another reliable classic, this has been improved as the variety 'Blaro'.

An early developer Sow kohlrabi in pots or a nursery bed in late May or early June. Wait for the soil to warm up before sowing – if you sow when temperatures are below 10°C, the plants will bolt. The roots are ideal for autumn soups and stews, so don't grow kohlrabi too early in the season or it will develop too rapidly.
► Sow heavily and thin plants out rather than transplanting them, as this avoids root damage. Prick them out in their growing positions when the plants have a few leaves, spacing them at 25cm between each plant.
► Harvest as soon as the globes are well formed so that you can enjoy them while they are tender. If left, they become hollow and fibrous, and split open.
► A useful tip: earthing up slightly as the globes begin to form will keep them tender.

A rooty parsley Hamburg parsley has roots that look and taste similar to parsnips. They are smaller than parsnip roots, however, but their foliage stays on the plant throughout winter and can be used as a parsley substitute.
► Hamburg parsley grows well in full sun in light or heavy soils. Sow seed in spring and summer to a depth of 2cm and thin plants to 15–20cm.
► Harvest the roots from the end of summer as and when you need them, and store them over winter either in the ground or in crates of sand.

Celery-flavoured celeriac

Celeriac needs an introduction Celeriac has long been popular on the Continent, but is increasingly grown in Britain, where it contributes admirably to the traditional self-sufficiency of the winter kitchen garden. Celeriac is cultivated for its thick roots which are used as an autumn or winter vegetable. The plant resembles celery, but at ground level it develops a swollen root similar to a turnip. Apart from the edible roots, which have a celery flavour, the leaves can also be used fresh for flavouring.

Celeriac prefers an open sunny site Plant seedlings in fertile soil and water copiously during the growing season. You can leave mature plants in the ground to harvest as you need them, but if temperatures are set to drop to below –10°C, you will need to cover them with a straw mulch or horticultural fleece.

Looking after celeriac
For big celeriac with a good shape, give the plants plenty of room, with rows spaced 45cm apart and plants spaced at 30cm. Remove any faded lower leaves to expose the top of the stem (right), and use a knife to cut off any rootlets that develop above the surface of the soil (right, below). A good variety to choose is 'Snow White'.

Disease-resistant varieties
Celeriac is affected by similar diseases and pests to celery. The best solution is to grow disease and pest-resistant varieties such as 'Monarch' or 'President'.

UNDER GLASS
A long growing season for celeriac
Expect celeriac to have a growing season of at least 26 weeks from sowing, in order to produce good-sized roots. This means it should ideally be started out under glass. Germination can be slow and erratic, so keep an eye on seed trays. You can either sow into a heated propagator in late winter or early spring, or into a cool greenhouse or cloches in mid spring. When seedlings are large enough to prick out, move them on into 7.5cm pots. Harden them off when all danger of frost is past and weather is uniformly warm. Sudden drops in temperature cause the plants to bolt. Plant out in June or July.

Easy-growing bulbs, stalks and tubers

When the humble potato was first introduced from the New World, it was thought so exotic that it was presented as a curiosity at court. Today, along with onions and other flavoursome bulbs and stalks, they are still valued highly as staples of the kitchen garden and the winter larder.

Aromatic onions, shallots and garlic

For best results Onion, shallot and garlic bulbs are fairly easy to grow, and you can produce good yields from year to year if you follow a good rotation system. Allow a gap of two to three years before you grow any other member of the onion family on the same piece of ground. Rotation lessens the likelihood of build-up in the soil of pests and diseases that affect onions, which means that the plants will be healthy and your harvest from them successful.

Prepare soil well in advance If you add manure to soil destined for onions too close to planting time, the bulbs are likely to rot off in the ground. And if they do grow, they probably won't be good for keeping. Avoid planting in soil that is high in nitrogen, which promotes leaf growth at the expense of the bulb.

The secret of successful planting
Onions, shallots and garlic are all planted in the same way. Hold the bulb between your thumb and first two fingers and push it into soil that has been well broken down, so that the point is uppermost and slightly lower than soil level. This will protect the bulbs from birds that might pull them out.
▶ Sometimes the bulbs are pushed out of the soil by the developing roots a few days after planting. Prevent this by planting each bulb in a narrow but fairly deep hole made with your finger or a dibber.

After lifting onions, leave them to dry on the ground for a few days before bringing them in for storage. The drying process firms the outer skins.

If bulbs are pushed out of place, they will need to be repositioned, otherwise the roots will grow sideways rather than downwards.
▶ If you buy onion, shallot and garlic sets for planting from a garden centre, choose plump, healthy sets.

Tasty varieties of onions and garlic
Onions 'Red Barron' is a red globe-shaped onion, 'Sherpa F1' is a golden globe-shaped onion and 'Albion F1' is a white globe-shaped onion.

Spring onions 'Ishikura' is a Japanese-type bunching onion, 'White Lisbon' is an old favourite with pearly white to green stems, while 'Deep Purple' and 'North Holland Blood Red' both have red stems.

Pickling onions 'SY300' has small brown-skinned round onions, and 'Pompei' is similar, with silver skins. Both varieties are grown for pickling, but can be used as spring onions before they bulb up.

Shallots 'Golden Gourmet' is a yellow-skinned shallot, 'Longor' is cylindrical in shape and has a good flavour and 'Red Sun' has a reddish skin on a round bulb and stores well in winter.

Garlic 'Elephant Garlic' is the biggest bulb of them all, up to 10cm across, and produces juicy cloves with a mild sweet flavour. 'Giant Wight' has a strong flavour. 'Sultop' has rosy red skins. 'Cristo', a classic French variety, has pink cloves.

Know your onions Choose onions to suit your requirements.
▶ Spring onions are sown in summer to be harvested and used fresh up to the following spring. They are left in the ground and picked as needed for use in salads.
▶ Globe onions are harvested in late summer and stored in a dry place to keep through winter.
▶ To grow small white onions for pickling, sow 'Pompei' and 'Paris Silverskin' densely from February to May. They will be ready to harvest and pickle in summer.

Planting onions For an early start, sow onion seed in January in the greenhouse. Or plant onion sets – small onion bulbs, normally heat-treated – in the ground in early spring once the soil has warmed up. Heat-treated onion sets are less likely to bolt and run to seed in hot dry conditions.
▶ For large onions, either sow them early or buy onion sets in February or March. Planted at a depth of 3cm and at intervals of 10–15cm, these onion sets will be ready to harvest several weeks earlier than onion seeds sown at the same time, and the bulbs will be much bigger.

When the leaves collapse, onions continue to swell

As onions reach the end of their growing cycle, the necks appear to collapse and fold over the bulb, sideways. They also begin to turn yellow and dry off. They should all do this at the same time, for uniform harvesting. If they are late collapsing, you can give nature a helping hand by gently drawing a rake – prongs upwards – across the onion bed, or fold the necks sideways by hand. Leave the onions in the soil to mature.

When to harvest Harvest onions, shallots and garlic when the foliage has all turned yellow, and when the weather is dry and sunny. Don't remove the foliage: when it has dried out completely, the bulbs can be stored in crates in a cool, dry place. Alternatively, plait the dead foliage to make a string, or store bulbs in clean old stockings or tights, knotted between each bulb to prevent contact. Hang for the winter.
▶ Before harvesting garlic, some gardeners suggest that you tie a knot in the green stems. Deprived of sap, the leaves will dry out more quickly and force the bulbs to swell. If you do this take care not to break the stems.

Secrets of shallots You can sow shallot seed in a greenhouse from March to April, but it is more usual to grow shallots from sets. Plant shallot sets outdoors in early spring when all danger of frost has passed.

Grow your own garlic In autumn or early spring, plant cloves of garlic in the ground, spaced about 10cm apart.

▶ When planting garlic, use the largest cloves on the outside of the head. Those on the inside tend to be less successful.
▶ If you leave two or three heads of garlic in the ground when harvesting, you can use these cloves for your new crop. Plant them individually when they begin to produce little green shoots. As they already have roots, they will grow quickly.

Garlic varieties 'Thermidrome', a white garlic (right, top) is planted in autumn or early winter for summer harvest. If you plant in autumn you will get higher yields. 'Sultop' is a rosy red variety (right, centre) for spring planting, to harvest from midsummer. 'Elephant', the biggest garlic of them all (right, below) is planted in spring.

Preventing rot Garlic is prone to rot in damp soil. Avoid this by planting in spring into light, sandy soil. Some traditional gardeners used to space the rows widely to 30–40 cm. In spring, once the cloves start to shoot, use a hoe to clear some of the soil from around the bulbs.

Plaiting garlic for storage

1 The foliage and heads must be completely dry. Start with three heads and plait their foliage together.

2 Introduce new heads as the plait lengthens, so that the new foliage continues where the previous foliage finishes.

3 Continue to plait until you reach the required length. Tidy up any loose ends.

4 Hang your garlic plait in a cool, dry place. It will keep you supplied with garlic for an entire season.

Leeks, fennel and celery – vegetables for blanching

Enjoy leeks through the year The varieties of leeks have different harvest times. The hardiest of them will overwinter well in the ground. They are usually sown at the same time, but take longer to mature.

▶ **Early varieties** These small to medium-sized leeks are not particularly hardy. They usually take five months to mature from sowing to harvest and are ready for use from September to November. Try 'Armor' and 'Swiss Giant-Zermatt'.

▶ **Midseason varieties** These are not particularly frost-resistant and are relatively slow to mature, taking seven months from sowing to harvest in November to January, but they are larger than the earlies. Try 'Lyon 2-Prizetaker'.

▶ **Late varieties** These are even slower to mature, taking eight months from sowing to harvest, but are productive and frost-resistant. Try 'Giant Winter 3 – Vernal' or 'Musselburgh'.

A touch of whimsy Some gardeners protect their leeks against stem and bulb eelworm by using eggshells turned upside down on sticks inserted along the rows. Whether the eelworm moth is disorientated by these strange objects is difficult to say – but they do seem to work.

For snowy white leeks Plant leeks deeply if you want them to be really white. Use a hoe to make a furrow 5cm deep in a 30cm-deep trench that has been prepared with well-rotted manure. Then plant young leeks using a dibber pushed into the soil as far as possible. About a month after planting, draw 3–5cm of soil back into the trench around the stems.

▶ Repeat this process each month until there is a ridge of soil on either side of the stems reaching just below the base of the leaves. Tie corrugated cardboard collars around the stems before earthing up, to keep grit off the leeks.

▶ When you hoe off weeds, leave the dead weeds in the furrow to cover the leek stems. They will rot down when covered by the soil in the ridge as it is built up, and help to 'blanch' the leeks as they grow.

Leeks are a useful crop that earn their place in any vegetable garden. By growing different varieties, you can harvest them all year round for use in the kitchen.

Get baby leeks from a late sowing Leeks take a long time to mature. But if you have forgotten to sow them in seed beds in March, you can still sow short-season but hardy leeks such as 'Swiss Giant-Zermatt' as late as July and they will overwinter for harvest in spring. However, these late-sown leeks will not be as large as those sown at the right time.

▶ Because they grow in winter, you can plant leeks where early peas and salad crops have been harvested.

Planting out young leeks

1 Leeks are ready to plant out when they have reached the size of a pencil. Cut roots back to 1cm and snip off part of the green foliage, reducing the plant to about 20cm long.

2 Make a hole with a dibber and plant the leeks so that 10cm – about half their length – is in the ground.

3 Water into the planting hole formed by the dibber. Leave the leeks to find their own level. Check daily while they establish, and replant any that the birds pull out.

Beneficial associations Old gardeners knew, from trial and error, that there are good and bad companions in the vegetable patch. Carrots, celery, fennel, corn salad, onions and tomatoes can all be grown with leeks – an association that appears to be mutually beneficial. These pairings seem to work because the plants need the same nutrients and, occasionally, protect each other against predators.

Faithful standby Leeks are hardy and sit steadfastly in the ground throughout autumn and winter, hardly growing but not deteriorating as long as the temperature stays cold. Leave them in the ground and lift as required.

Florence fennel needs the sun Sow the annual Florence or globe fennel in early summer into a sunny, well-drained soil. Thin seedlings out so that they are spaced 30cm apart. Fennel needs regular watering during its growing period, and if you earth up the soil as the plants begin to fatten up, the resulting bulbs will be whiter and more tender. ▶ Choose annual fennel for its squat, bulbous edible stems and sweet, tender leaves, rather than the tall perennial kind, which is often found in the herb garden.

A difficult neighbour Probably due to its powerful aroma, fennel is particularly aggressive when grown next to a number of other vegetables. Apparently, only leeks and celery are able to live in the same vicinity.

Fit for the harvest Fennel will be ready to harvest in early to late autumn. Cut the bulb off the stem at ground level, and if you are lucky some flavoursome shoots may regrow from the stump. If you notice that the bulb is beginning to elongate, harvest it at once. This is a sign of bolting, which means that the plants will go to seed and the edible parts will become too tough to eat. There are a number of bolt-resistant varieties including 'Argo', 'Amigo F1' and 'Zefa Fino'. If you use these varieties you can sow fennel seed earlier, in the late spring.

Easy-to-grow celery Celery is a delicious stem that needs blanching, though you can also find self-blanching or green celery. It needs a sunny site and a well-prepared loam soil. For an early start sow into modules in a propagator in a

Improve celery's taste and tenderness by blanching it. Wrap stems in newspaper or cardboard then earth up around them.

YESTERDAY & TODAY

An immigrant with a distinguished past

Fennel is a native of the Mediterranean world and was brought to Britain by the Romans. It is mentioned in early Anglo-Saxon herbals and was regarded as one of the nine sacred herbs, said to guard against unseen evil and to restore the eyesight. Chaucer refers to fennel; as does Shakespeare, and fennel grows in his birthplace garden.

Henry Longfellow, the 19th century poet, describes the tall, perennial fennel in 'The Goblet of Life':

Above the lowly plants it towers,
The fennel, with its yellow flowers,
And in an earlier age than ours
Was gifted with the wondrous powers,
Lost vision to restore.

greenhouse. Transplant seedlings sown in the propagator in spring and early summer. If you have sown self-blanching celery, space it 25cm apart. Otherwise trenching varieties need 20–25cm spacing between the plants.

Blanching celery Once the stems are growing well you need to earth the plants up, or enclose each plant with a tube of cardboard. This keeps the stems clean and blanches them. ▶ Self-blanching varieties include 'Lathom Self-Blanching', 'Greensleeves' and 'Golden Self-Blanching'. They are all ready for harvest from late summer to autumn. Sow them under cover in early February and transplant them in the garden from May onwards.

Why bother to blanch? The purpose of blanching is to tenderise and sweeten a plant's edible parts. Plants that are naturally bitter when grown in full light are usually more palatable when light is restricted. Though some modern varieties are 'self-blanching', traditionalists claim they don't have anything like the flavour and texture of the earlier kinds.

Potatoes for storing and eating throughout the year

Potatoes for planting You can always replant small potatoes from last year's crop, but there's no guarantee they'll be disease-free – they may have been contaminated by a virus or be carrying blight spores. A more reliable option is to buy seed potatoes that are certified as disease-free – look for this on the label of the net in which they are sold. You can also buy seed potatoes in larger quantities.

Growing early potatoes Plant earlies into trenches in full sun in well-drained, well-manured soil in early spring. They will be ready for harvest in late June, but you will need to protect them with a cloche or a layer of horticultural fleece. In the north of England plant them in late spring.
▶ Plant your potatoes to a full spade's depth: at least 30cm.

Potatoes and runner beans grow well together, having similar requirements for soil conditions and positioning in the vegetable garden.

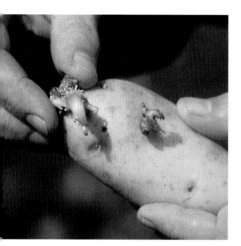

Chitting the potatoes
Potatoes naturally produce sprouts or 'chits', for these are what produce the new plants. After you purchase your seed potatoes, place them in a box or tray in a light and frost-free room to chit them. The sprouts should be short and firm. Several sprouts may develop on each tuber, though some gardeners suggest you remove all but three.
▶ Try sprouting your seed potatoes in an old egg carton. Set them fattest end up, as this end produces the best sprouts.

Beware of late frosts Young potatoes can still be destroyed by late frosts up until May, especially on clear nights. Hoe and earth up potatoes in their trench if there is any danger of frost. If they are in leaf, you will need to cover the leaves with the soil as well. You may also need additional cover such as horticultural fleece.

Natural die-back of foliage Potatoes will come into flower as the tubers ripen. Soon after, you will notice that the foliage begins to turn yellow and starts to fall onto the soil. This is natural, and you should leave it until you are ready to harvest the tubers from the ground. You will probably harvest earlies well before the leaves have turned brown.

A nourishing mulch
Generations of seaside gardeners have valued seaweed as a mulch and feed for potatoes. For a trouble-free potato patch, fill your trench with seaweed, plant up and cover with another 15–20cm of seaweed. You can then forget about your crop until it's time for the harvest.

Earthing up potatoes

1 Plant potatoes to a spade's depth of 30cm, leaving 50cm between plants in all directions. Cover the tubers.

2 When the foliage appears, heap the earth around the base of the plant so that it hides the stems and forms a mound from which the leaves emerge.

3 Continue to 'earth up' along the entire row. This enables the tubers to form in a compact cluster and protects them from early-season frosts.

The potato harvest Lift maincrop potatoes in fine weather and leave on top of the soil for 24 hours to harden the skins. If you have to harvest in rainy conditions keep them in a dark but warm, well-ventilated place and leave them for a few days. This will enable them to dry out properly and lose some of their water content. Avoid storing any that are damaged or blemished in any way.

The best tool for the job

The potato hook or Canterbury hoe, with two long, slightly curved prongs, is much better suited to lifting potatoes than the garden fork. If you stand at right angles to the row, you can sink the prongs beneath each plant with a single blow. Then all you have to do is pull on the handle of the hoe and any stems above the surface of the soil.

Safe storage You can transfer your potato harvest to the basement, shed or storeroom, if it is frost-free and dark. A root cellar was a popular old-fashioned place for storing root crops, potatoes and apples.

▶ Potatoes must not be exposed to light. If they are, they will turn green and build up a bitter and toxic alkaloid known as solanine. Store them in wooden crates or sacks, provided no light gets into the storage container. Avoid storing potatoes in plastic, which will make them sweat and rot.

Top tips for combating the Colorado beetle The Colorado potato beetle was imported into Europe in the early 20th century. It devours the leaves of potatoes and can soon wipe out an entire crop. It is regarded as such a serious pest that the authorities have to be notified if you find it.

▶ **Spray it** If you find Colorado beetle on your potatoes, you can destroy it with an organic insecticide containing rotenone in spray or powder form. Apply it to the top and underside of the leaves and repeat one week later, though it may be easier to pick the larvae and eggs off the leaves by hand.

▶ **Outsmart it** Never plant potatoes in the same piece of land two years running. The beetles overwinter in the soil and will attack the next year's crop. You can safely plant the tubers in a bottomless half-barrel filled with fresh soil.

▶ **Deter it** A traditional method for keeping the Colorado beetle away is to plant onions or garlic around potato plants.

Tasty potato bait for wireworms The larvae of the click beetle, wireworms feed hungrily on all kinds of root vegetable including carrots, potatoes, turnips and beetroot. Cut a potato into pieces and pierce with a stick. Then bury the sticks around your plants, a few centimetres in the soil but with the sticks protruding. Every week or so, pull up the sticks and destroy the infested pieces. Rebait the sticks as needed.

Early or maincrop, waxy or floury?

It is useful to know if a potato variety is 'first early' (three months from planting to harvest), 'maincrop' (four months) or 'second early' (between the two). Culinary characteristics help to determine the gardener's choice of variety. Firm or waxy potatoes (A) are boiled in their jackets, sliced in salads and sautéed. Tender and floury potatoes (B) are ideal for baking, puréeing, mashing and adding to soups and stews. You can make good chips with any type of potato.

Consider how disease-resistant your chosen variety is, and how you will treat your crop if it needs protection.

* Poor   ** Average   *** Fairly good

Varieties	Early/Maincrop	Culinary group	Disease-resistance
'Amandine'	First Early	A, B	***
'Amour'	Maincrop	A, B	***
'Arran Pilot'	First early	A, B	***
'Belle de Fontenay'	First early	A	*
'British Queen'	Second early	B	**
'Désirée' ❶	Maincrop	A, B	**
'Pink Fir Apple' ❷	Maincrop	A	**
'International Kidney'	Maincrop	A	**
'Kestrel'	Second early	B	***
'King Edward'	Maincrop	A, B	**
'Nadine'	Second early	A, B	***
'Pentland Javelin' ❸	First early	A	***
'Ratte'	Second early	A	*
'Roseval'	Maincrop	A	*
'Vilja'	Second early	A, B	***
'Winston'	First early	A, B	***

Preventing potato blight There is no miracle cure for potato blight which, if the season is wet, can ruin the whole crop.

▶ If you garden in a region with wet summers, choose a variety that is blight-resistant.

▶ Use only well-rotted manure on potato beds as new manure will encourage disease.

▶ Spray plants with Bordeaux mixture or a copper oxychloride base in an organic culture. Carry out the first treatment when plants reach a height of 30cm and then spray every two to three weeks, or every ten days in wet weather.

▶ If symptoms appear, remove badly affected foliage to prevent contamination of the tubers. Dispose of the affected foliage, but do not put it on the compost heap.

Protecting your vegetable crops

The main enemies of vegetables are winter frosts, cold spring temperatures and summer drought. Over the centuries, gardeners have learned to deal with these threats by protecting the soil and their crops from inclement weather.

Dried grass cuttings make an economic and effective mulch, so long as there are no weed seeds lurking there.

Covering the soil

A traditional mulch In the past, gardeners used a mulch consisting of partially rotted manure. It is easy to break down and ideal for covering – or mulching – the soil. A thin layer of mulch spread over a seedbed promotes germination by helping the soil to retain its moisture. A relatively thick layer enables recently planted cabbages, leeks, celery, courgettes and strawberries to get established.

Top tips for effective mulches Anything that covers the soil and protects it from light and heat can be used as a mulch. There are lots of materials that make ideal mulches and are absolutely free. They all reduce the evaporation of moisture and keep the weeds down.

▶ **Grass cuttings** These can be spread on the ground once they have dried out. Always spread thinly, even if it means renewing regularly – you should still be able to see the soil. If the layer is too thick, the grass mulch tends to form compact lumps that will eventually go mouldy and attract slugs.

▶ **Flat stones** These make a great mulch while allowing gardeners to walk on them freely. They can be used to cover the soil between rows of crops, and around trailing vegetables such as marrows, which are extremely prone to rotting on cool, damp soil.

▶ **Paper and cardboard** Newspaper, folded in half or in quarters, and corrugated cardboard, with sticky tape and staples removed, make a practical mulch for widely spaced vegetables. Cover with a scattering of dried grass for a more pleasing aesthetic effect.

▶ **Spent hops** Available from local breweries, these make a practical, attractive and natural mulch.

▶ **Forest bark** Bark is a popular mulch in the ornamental garden, but is not really suitable for a vegetable garden, except for pathways and strawberry beds, as strawberries like its acidity and the drainage it provides. If you do use bark as a mulch, don't dig it in afterwards as you'll create an imbalance in the soil structure. Add fertiliser to the soil when you dig it over for another crop and it will improve the structure.

Retaining moisture Mulching helps to prevent the moisture in the soil from evaporating. The best time to mulch is in spring, when the soil is warm but still moist, and any time after it rains. However, don't mulch when the soil is dry, as this will prevent the rain getting through and just keep the ground dry.

Weather protection

Cloches to keep out frosts and cold wind These transparent covers protect seeds sown in situ, cuttings and young plants by providing protection from rain, cold snaps and frost. They also maintain moisture in dry spells. Place them in position about a week before sowing and planting to warm up the soil, and use them to overwinter hardy crops, such as lettuces and carrots.

Old-fashioned glass bell cloches Although there's nothing more attractive than a real glass cloche, like the ones used in the past in their hundreds (right), they are expensive – and very fragile. They can also be awkward to use, as they have to be propped open and then closed again depending on weather conditions.

▶ Plastic carbonate cloches, which look like the old-fashioned ones but are easier to use, are much less expensive and less fragile. As they are light, they must be anchored down or they will fly away in a high wind.
▶ Plastic cloches that look like rigid boxes or tents are available in standard lengths and will fit, or can be adapted to fit, most lengths of vegetable rows.

Practical polytunnels If you don't want to be on permanent 'cloche duty', a polytunnel – like the ones used by commercial

growers – will protect seeds sown in situ and early seedlings from the last frosts. These tunnels consist of a piece of plastic sheeting stretched over a framework of metal hoops. The ambient temperature is more moderate and easier to regulate than in cloches.

▶ A polytunnel can also be used to hasten the ripening of strawberries. Remove it as soon as external temperatures are high enough or your crops are well established.

Cold frames for small-scale greenhouse gardening
A cold frame was an indispensable item in our grandfathers' gardens. It consists of a wooden frame that covers a piece of ground, and is lower at the front than the back, plus a glass cover. It is ideal for germinating seedlings such as cabbages and lettuces, which will then be pricked out into their final positions. A cold frame is also a good home for young plants pricked out for the first time.

Save room in your greenhouse A cold frame can be used to raise early crops of low-growing vegetables such as lettuces, radishes and spring onions, so leaving room in the greenhouse for tomatoes, climbing French beans and other tall plants to make use of the extra height.

Keep your vegetables from drying out Newly pricked-out plants such as cabbages, lettuces, tomatoes, beetroot and artichokes are particularly susceptible to being dried out by the sun and cold winds in spring. Protect them by floating over a layer of horticultural fleece, which acts as a barrier against adverse weather conditions.

Making a cold frame from an old window

1 Remove the parts you don't need – bolts, handles, weatherboard, hinges – and give the frame a coat of paint.

2 Fix metal handles to an outside edge for opening and closing the lid.

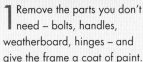

3 Make a bottomless rectangular frame, lower at the front than the back, and the same size as the window.

4 Give the frame a coat of Bordeaux mixture to prevent the wood from rotting, and then paint it.

5 Attach the window to the frame, ideally using hinges as this will make the structure more solid.

6 Place your cold frame in a south-facing position so that the sun can warm up the plants inside.

Fresh herbs at your fingertips

Imagine an old-fashioned garden and you will probably picture a sunny bed of herbs. Growing these aromatic plants – highly prized for their culinary and medicinal qualities – has a long and ancient tradition we still value today. Fortunately, herbs are very easy to grow and positively thrive on poor, dry soils.

Herbs to sow annually

Dill and carrots make good partners Dill is an aromatic annual that is ideal for sowing among carrots (one or two seeds per metre along a row) as it is said to act as a deterrent to that well-known pest, the carrot fly.
▶ Its aromatic summer leaves flavour omelettes and fish dishes, especially salmon.

Basil comes in unusual varieties Basil is a highly aromatic herb. It is grown as a half-hardy annual in cool temperate climates. Most people know the large, floppy foliage of 'lettuce-leaf' basil but there are many other varieties to choose from, such as 'Dark Opal' with purple leaves. Basil is useful in salads as well as in cooked dishes.
▶ If you get the chance, try planting bush basil, with masses of tiny leaves, 'cinnamon' basil, 'anise' basil, and lemon basil.

The traditional English herb garden has a good mix of plants for culinary, household and medicinal uses.

▶ Cut out the growing tip of the basil shoot to encourage the plant to bush out.

Sowing basil in a greenhouse Basil is best sown into seed trays or modules in a greenhouse and then hardened off and transplanted when all danger of frost is past. Seeds need a minimum temperature of 20°C. Water sparingly by standing the seed tray in a bath of water so it will draw moisture in, rather than watering from overhead. When the seedlings are growing well, prick them out into larger pots and grow on until it is safe to plant them outside. In warmer climates where night temperatures do not fall below 13°C you can sow direct into the soil. Again, water plants from the base.

Aniseed for flavouring cakes Aniseed is a half-hardy annual. Sow the plants directly into the soil when all danger of frost is past. Aniseed needs full sun, some shelter and well-drained soil to thrive. By late summer the seeds are ready to harvest and use in the kitchen.
▶ The ripe seed is ideal for flavouring cakes and pastries, and the feathery foliage, which you can cut all through the growing season, is also delicious in salads.

Borage adds a touch of blue

The star-shaped flowers of borage are sky-blue, and are highly ornamental in the garden and at the table. The grey-green leaves are thick and hairy. However, borage is best known as a medicinal plant and will also attract bees for honey production.
► Once you've introduced it into your garden, it will be there for ever, as it self-seeds copiously. If it appears where you don't want it, treat it as a weed and pull it up.

Perennial onions to sow

Welsh onions are useful all year round. A small clump will bulk up over time to form a large one. Lift and divide the clumps in spring to make more plants or, if you leave a few flower heads to set seed, the seeds are easy to gather and sow to make more plants.

The subtle taste of chervil Chervil has aniseed-flavoured feathery foliage. It is a hardy biennial, although it is usually treated as an annual. Sow seed in trays or pots in a cool greenhouse in early spring or outdoors in late spring. Where it is sown directly into the ground, thin seedlings to 25cm. Chervil seedlings are delicate and need careful handling when planting.
► Grow them in partial shade as otherwise the plants will bolt and run to seed.

Chives for the border Chives are hardy perennials, but they die down in winter so are often sown annually. Sow seed early in trays of modular cells in a greenhouse in spring. Harden off and plant out in late spring or early summer, in well-drained soil in full sun. Alternatively, you can buy small plants from garden centres or herb specialists. Their pink flowers make them attractive in the front of a border.
► In mild winters the new shoots may develop early. If this happens, cover them with a cloche or horticultural fleece to

protect them and encourage the shoots over winter.
► To ensure the plants are vigorous and healthy, divide the clump into smaller sections every two to three years, in early spring. Plant the smaller sections 25–30cm apart in rows. You can divide chives in summer; if you do, cut them back to 5cm above ground level and they will grow well.

Coriander – leaves or seeds? For best results sow coriander direct into its growing site when all danger of frost is past. If you are growing it primarily for seed, give the plants adequate space and plant them early, in May or June. If the aromatic foliage is of more interest, sow seed later, in July. There are also some varieties that are specially developed for their foliage. Grow coriander in partial shade for better leaf production.

Tasty cumin and caraway seeds Cumin and caraway produce masses of seeds that lend a distinctive taste to spicy and fragrant dishes.
► Cumin is a tender annual. Sow it in a heated propagator in a greenhouse in spring. Transplant into well-drained soil in a sheltered, sunny site.
► Caraway is a hardy biennial. Sow seed into rich loamy soil in spring. It grows well in full sun. You can also sow it in early autumn to overwinter.

Tarragon for a delicate flavour

Tarragon thrives in well-drained, frost-free and sunny sites. It needs protection at its crown from excessive winter wet. Plant it out into the ground in spring when all danger of frost is past, or grow it in a large container. Although it has small yellow flowers, they rarely appear, nor does it set seed in cool climates. It is best to propagate by taking cuttings in spring or early summer.

Ever-useful winter and summer savory

Summer savory is an annual that is often grown with broad beans. The beans are delicious cooked with summer savory and the plant is said to deter aphids from attacking the bean plants. Winter savory can be used in a similar way. It is a hardy perennial and provides good flavour in winter.

Use sorrel like spinach

Sorrel is a hardy perennial whose large leaves can be lightly cooked and used in the same way as spinach. The lemony young leaves can also be added raw to salads or as a tasty addition to savoury white sauces. Common sorrel *Rumex acetosa* may be too invasive so you may prefer to grow the ground-covering buckler leaf sorrel (*R. scutatus*), with silvery green shield-shaped leaves. Sorrel grows well in partial shade in well-drained soil.

Popular parsley

Iron-rich parsley is a must in any vegetable garden. There are many varieties of curly and flat-leaf parsley.
▶ Flat-leaf parsley has the most flavour. A good one to try is the variety 'Giant Italian'.
▶ Curly-leaf parsley, such as 'Moss Curled', is less aromatic than flat-leaf parsley but very tasty, with a crunchy texture.
▶ Sow seed into trays in the greenhouse in spring or in the ground when the soil has warmed up. It takes a while to germinate, but germination is not difficult.

Keeping parsley to use later

Parsley stores and freezes well. To keep it for a few days without freezing, wash and place in the refrigerator in an airtight box. To freeze parsley, wash it, pat dry with kitchen towel and put it whole in plastic bags in the freezer. When you use frozen parsley, simply crumble it into the dish or pot before it thaws out.

Running to seed Parsley is a biennial, and in its second year it sends up flowering stems and produces seed. To make sure you have parsley for cutting, sow successively every year. When the plants go to seed, it is best to dig them up and use the space for other plants.

Shade-happy herbs

Sweet cicely A relatively large plant with feathery, fern-like foliage, this stately herb grows to a height of over a metre. It is hardy and, once established, will thrive in most conditions. Its freshly picked leaves with their lovely aniseed aroma and slightly sweet taste are ideal for flavouring and sweetening desserts. The seeds are also tasty and were once used to freshen and sweeten breath. They were also used as sweets in Tudor times, hence the name, sweet cicely.

Scented lemon balm Although it smells of lemon, lemon balm is botanically close to mint and its leaves have a soothing effect when rubbed on insect bites or nettle stings. It is also used to flavour sauces for chicken and fish and in herbal teas.
▶ Lemon balm is a perennial that makes a strong clump in cool, damp soil and can be invasive. Plant a root fragment or a small pot plant. It will seed itself readily.
▶ If you have planted the variegated form and then allowed it to seed, only green-leaved plants will appear, as it does not come true from seed.

THE GARDENER'S CHOICE

Aromatic and decorative ▶

Growing a selection of herbs will add colour to your vegetable garden, and bring traditional tastes to your table.

Sage (*Salvia officinalis* 'Tricolor') ❶ Sage needs warm sun to develop the oils that provide its distinctive flavour.

Lemon verbena (*Aloysia triphylla*) ❷ Their scented leaves and tiny flowers make these old-fashioned shrubs a real delight.

Borage (*Borago officinalis*) ❸ Bees love the blue flowers of borage, whose young leaves emit a cucumber fragrance.

Camomile (*Chamaemelum nobile*) ❹ You can make tea with the lovely flowers of this mat-forming evergreen perennial.

Peppermint (*Mentha piperita*) ❺ No garden should be without mint, and this variety has a particularly good flavour.

Purple basil (*Ocimum basilicum* 'Rubin') ❻ Grown as a half-hardy annual, basil is the quintessential Mediterranean herb.

Herbs

Flavoursome lovage This unusual hardy perennial has a strong flavour, similar to celery. Lovage grows best in partial shade or sun in well-drained soil and spreads to form large clumps. Top-dress with well-rotted compost in autumn.

Architectural angelica This giant herb is a biennial and grows to several metres. The stems of second-year plants are used in confectionery and baking. Macerate a few pieces of angelica in white wine to make a delicious aromatic wine cup, or use it to flavour cakes and cooked fruit. Angelica produces huge amounts of seed, which will self-seed copiously if you leave it all on the plant.
▶ Once angelica has set seed, the plant dies and you need to remove old plants. You can hoe off any unwanted plants in spring, leaving a few to develop.

Horseradish – strong sensations guaranteed Horseradish is a perennial plant that produces large, elongated leaves and a head of white flowers in summer. The plant is grown for its white roots, high in vitamin C, calcium and magnesium.
▶ The variegated form of horseradish is particularly decorative. Horseradish spreads from root cuttings, so when you dig it out, take care not to leave behind pieces of root.

Old-fashioned horseradish fungicide Gardeners used to steep chopped horseradish leaves in water, then filter the liquid and use it to spray fruit trees for the brown rot that attacks them. It was thought that if it was caught early enough, this spray would help to combat the fungus.

Top tips for mint There are many species and varieties of mint. Low-growing types, such as Corsican mint, are best grown as ground cover rather than for culinary uses. Here are a few of the most popular and best-known varieties.
▶ **Spearmint** A mild flavoured mint, this is used to flavour cucumber, yoghurt and tabbouleh, and to make mint tea.
▶ **Peppermint or black peppermint** More strongly flavoured than other varieties, peppermint is used to make infusions.
▶ **Eau-de-cologne mint** A mint with green, purple-veined foliage, it is highly prized for culinary use.
▶ **Pennyroyal mint** This strongly scented wild mint has medicinal properties.
▶ **Bowles mint** This is the best mint for making a strong-flavoured mint sauce.

Angelica grows to a height of two metres so needs careful positioning to avoid overwhelming other plants.

Keep mint in check Mint is well known for its vigorous, invasive habit, spreading by means of creeping underground stems. To prevent it from taking over completely, plant it in a large pot with drainage holes – if the pot does not have drainage holes the mint will become waterlogged and rot. Sink the pot into the ground so that its rim is just above the surface of the soil. Check the rim of the pot from time to time and cut off any escaping runners.

Keep flies out A sprig or two of mint in a glass of water is said to be a good way to keep flies out of a room. You will find that the mint roots very quickly in water and in no time you will have extra plants to give to your friends.

Sun-loving perennials

True and false camomile Camomile is an evergreen perennial herb. Apart from the common or Roman camomile used as sweet-smelling lawns, there is German camomile, which has medicinal properties. Feverfew is also regarded as a camomile, and it is said to be effective in treating migraines and headaches. It has pale green, sometimes golden, foliage and lots of tiny white flower heads with yellow centres. It also has a strongly aromatic foliage and its flowers are thought to be beneficial in deterring insect pests from invading other garden plants.

Forever fennel The common fennel is another one of those plants that, once established in your garden, will stay there for ever. Although it is a short-lived perennial, fennel produces so much seed that it ensures its survival in most garden conditions. It thrives in full sun, in well-drained soil, and reaches 1.5 metres or more. For variety, grow the bronze-leaf form in the ornamental flower garden.

▶ Fennel can be used cooked or raw: its aniseed flavour is a welcome addition to fish dishes. Both the leaves and the crunchy-textured bulb are useful in the kitchen.

▶ As fennel comes from the Mediterranean region, a cold British summer may cause it to run to seed before the bulb has developed properly. To avoid this, grow a bolt-resistant variety, such as 'Zefo Fino'.

Marjoram or oregano? Marjoram is a hardy perennial grown for its aromatic foliage, while sweet marjoram, also known as oregano, is a half-hardy perennial shrub.

▶ Marjoram thrives in full sun and well-drained soil. To encourage new leaf growth, cut back the stems after flowering. Divide established plants in autumn or spring.

▶ Sweet marjoram is usually grown in cool temperate climates as an annual. Sow seed in a heated propagator in spring and transplant into the garden in early summer. It grows best in well-drained soil with added grit.

Growing bay A tree prized for the flavour of its evergreen leaves, bay laurel grows well in the ground and in containers and is often clipped into topiary shapes. Although it is fairly slow-growing, in the ground

it can grow to be a large tree of up to 15 metres. If you don't have space for such a large plant, cut it back, but wait until all danger of frost is past.

▶ Move bay grown in tubs into larger pots annually. Protect the pot against frost, which damages the roots.

▶ The golden form (*Laurus nobilis* 'Aurea') looks good grown in combination with the green form.

WATCH OUT

Bay watch! Although the leaves of sweet bay or bay laurel (*Laurus nobilis*) are used in cooking, never eat the berries as they are poisonous. There are a number of plants with leaves that can be mistaken for sweet bay. However, they are not safe to eat. Watch out for the following.

▶ Cherry laurel or common laurel (*Prunus laurocerasus*) is an ornamental – and poisonous – laurel, with large, thick, glossy leaves. It is widely used for hedges.

▶ Oleander (*Nerium oleander*) is an attractive – and poisonous – shrub with very elongated leaves and pink flowers. It is usually grown as an ornamental pot plant.

Satisfying sage Forming a shrubby plant in the garden, sage is one of the best-known culinary herbs. There are several varieties with different shaped, coloured and aromatic evergreen foliage.

▶ Purple sage (*Salvia officinalis* Purpurascens Group) looks particularly attractive in the flower border.

▶ Narrow-leaf sage (*S. lavandulifolia*) has attractive narrow leaves and strong blue flowers.

▶ Harvest the leaves for cooking just before the plant flowers (above), when they are at their most fragrant.

▶ Although sage is usually grown for its foliage, its flowers are very attractive and can be used to perfume drawers. Cut back sage plants after flowering to encourage a compact shape.

Propagating sage Although you can increase your stock of sage plants by taking cuttings in the usual way, you can also use a traditional layering technique. In April, fix a trailing stem into the soil and cover it with soil. Wait until late summer for the new plant to root and then cut it free.

Gathering and drying marjoram

1 Harvest marjoram early in the day, when the dew has dried. Use secateurs to cut through the twiggy stems.

2 Arrange the stems in small bunches and tie them securely with string.

3 Use the ends of the string to make a loop for hanging the bunches.

4 Hang on a line in a dry, well-ventilated room such as an attic or hang in an airing cupboard.

Herbs

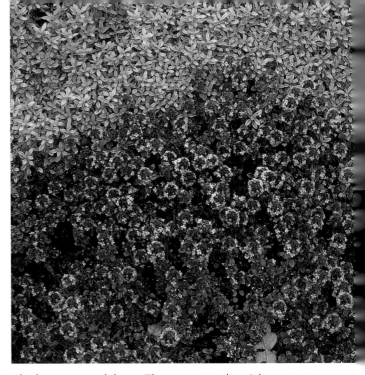

Thyme to choose This native of the Mediterranean scrubland is one of the most versatile herbs in both the garden and the kitchen. Most thymes are hardy perennials, but thrive in full sun in light, well-drained soil.

▶ There are many different thymes to choose from, boasting different leaf and flower colours and aromas. Some grow as woody small shrubs, such as the lemon-scented thyme (*Thymus* x *citriodorus* 'Silver Queen'), caraway-scented (*T. herba-barona*) and common thyme (*T. vulgaris*). Other thymes are spreading, mat-forming plants that flower at ground level, such as *T. serpyllum*, with small pinky-mauve flowers, and *T. var. coccineus*.

▶ Use upright varieties, such as *T.* x *citriodorus*, as small edging plants for formal borders or a herb garden. For a decorative effect, plant mat-forming varieties in cracks in paving and paths, or to tumble over rockeries.

▶ Give shrubby thymes a light trim after flowering, to encourage a bushy, compact shape.

▶ As well as pleasantly scenting the garden, thyme can be used throughout the year in salads and in savoury cooked dishes.

The lemon-scented thyme (Thymus x citriodorus) *has attractive light green foliage and combines well with the flowers of common thyme,* T. vulgaris.

Easy thyme cuttings Simply cut a sprig or two from the mature plant, remove the lower leaves from each stem, and plant so that two-thirds of the stem is in the soil. Water well and the cutting should root in three to four weeks.

Hyssop, an underrated herb Hyssop was highly prized by our ancestors and is mentioned in the Bible. In the 17th century, it was used to dress wounds. Today, it tends to be widely – and unjustly – ignored. Its flowers attract bees and butterflies to the garden and the bitter, minty taste of its leaves is ideal for making infusions and flavouring dishes.

▶ Hyssop is a hardy herbaceous perennial native to the Mediterranean mountains, where it thrives in arid, stony soil. It is fully hardy in this country, as long as it is kept in full sun on well-drained soil. Its needs are similar to those of lavender, catmint and rosemary, and it grows well with them.

▶ Grow hyssop from seed sown in autumn or from softwood cuttings in summer and cut it back annually to prevent it becoming too woody.

Rosemary shapes up Rosemary is an evergreen shrub native to Mediterranean scrubland. It responds well to shaping into pyramids, cones, balls and spirals. Trim often and cut it back in spring, removing any damaged or dead branches. Do not let the plants get leggy.

▶ Rosemary grows best in full sun, in very well-drained soil, producing small flowers in spring and summer. It needs shelter from harsh winds and does not tolerate winter wet at its roots. 'Miss Jessopp's Upright' is an old favourite with pretty blue flowers in late spring and autumn. It is useful for hedging.

Protect your lemon verbena Lemon verbena needs winter protection in cool temperate climates, so if you grow it in containers, bring it into a frost-free greenhouse in winter. Water well during the summer and cut back stems just as the plant begins to flower. Before you bring it indoors in autumn, cut it back again. Water it sparingly in winter.

▶ If you want to grow lemon verbena outside, plant it against a south or west-facing wall or grow it from softwood cuttings, taken each summer.

▶ Lemon verbena can be dried for use in pot pourri and as a flavouring in herbal teas.

Taking rosemary cuttings

1 In Spring, cut young shoots about 15–20 cm long. Remove the lower leaves.

2 Plant the shoots in trays filled with a multi-purpose compost with added grit.

3 Water sparingly. After four to six weeks check if roots have developed. Plant out in situ the following spring.

Pests and diseases of vegetables

Traditional organic growing techniques produce strong, healthy crops, resistant to pests and diseases. But if your crops do get infected, use natural remedies where possible.

Leafy vegetables

BLACKFLY AND GREENFLY

These aphids collect in colonies on stems and flower heads of artichokes and most other leafy vegetables. Companion planting can help combat these pests: chervil, marigolds, nasturtiums and savory are all reckoned to be effective deterrents. See page 97, and pages 251 and 252.

CABBAGE MOTH

▶ **Symptoms** The leaves of infested plants are covered with varying-sized holes made by yellowish brown or green caterpillars. On cabbages, these caterpillars bore into the heart and ruin the edible parts with their excrement.
▶ **Plants affected** Brassicas, swedes, turnips.
▶ **Treatment** Check brassicas regularly and remove the eggs, which are laid in groups of 20–100 on the undersides of the leaves, and caterpillars. If the larvae are numerous, before they burrow into the heart leaves, spray with *Bacillus thuringiensis*, a bacterium which will kill the caterpillars within a few days, or an approved insecticide.

CABBAGE ROOT FLY

▶ **Symptoms** The maggots of the cabbage root fly (*Phorbia brassicae*) tunnel into the roots, which become riddled with holes and discoloured. The plant is weakened and its growth retarded, while the leaves wilt in hot weather. Serious attacks can cause plants to die. It is mainly the first generation of maggots that tunnel into the roots, while subsequent generations attack the aerial parts of the plant.
▶ **Plants affected** Brassicas.
▶ **Treatment** Destroy the overwintering larvae by practising crop rotation, and use companion crops such as onions to prevent infestation. As the fly lays its eggs at soil level, placing collars around the stems where they meet the soil can help to prevent the larvae getting to the roots. Feed the plants with liquid nettle manure (see page 255) to strengthen their natural resistance to all types of pests and diseases.

CABBAGE WHITE BUTTERFLY

▶ **Symptoms** The leaves are ragged and full of holes, and the heart is riddled with tunnels. Inside are the blue-green or greenish yellow caterpillars (*Pieris brassicae*), responsible for the damage. If you do not act quickly, only the veins of the leaves remain. Cabbage white caterpillars often live in colonies and are easily recognised by their colour, longitudinal stripes and black markings.
▶ **Plants affected** All members of the cabbage family, including broccoli, sprouts.
▶ **Treatment** Take action at the first sign of attack, before the caterpillars burrow into the heads of the plants. Use an insecticide containing rotenone (derris), natural pyrethrins or *Bacillus thuringiensis*. Remove and crush any eggs that have been laid.

CELERY FLY

▶ **Symptoms** White maggots of the celery fly or leaf miner (*Eulia heraclei*) tunnel within the leaves, causing brown spots to appear. These maggots later become brown pupae. The leaves shrivel and dry up and, if harvested, the stalks have a bitter, burnt taste.
▶ **Plant affected** Celery.
▶ **Treatment** Pick off affected leaves and destroy. Spray the foliage with an approved insecticide such as derris or pyrethrins. Liquid feed the crop with nettle manure (see page 255) to strengthen growth.

CHICORY FLY

▶ **Symptoms** Small white maggots tunnel within the leaves, and sometimes the leaf stalks, which eventually shrivel and dry up. Damage is caused by the maggots of the chicory fly (*Ophiomyia pinguis*).
▶ **Plant affected** Chicory.
▶ **Treatment** Pick off affected leaves and destroy them. Spray the foliage with an approved insecticide.

CLUB ROOT

▶ **Symptoms** Swollen and deformed roots are caused by a soil-borne fungus (*Plasmodiophora brassicae*), which penetrates the plant and forms swellings. The leaves turn yellow and wilt in sunny weather. Symptoms are similar to those of the gall weevil. The spores that are released by the swellings can remain in the soil for up to ten years before becoming active.
▶ **Plants affected** All members of the cabbage family.
▶ **Treatment** Crop rotation is essential to prevent the disease recurring year after year. Treat young plants with an approved club root treatment before planting out. Lift and burn any affected plants. Make sure that the land is limed and well drained as this fungus flourishes on very acid soils. Before planting, check that the roots of bought brassicas and related plants are healthy. Improve drainage by deep digging and incorporating plenty of humus into the soil.

Pests and diseases

CUTWORM
► **Symptoms** The roots are eaten away, severed or riddled with holes. The leaves turn pale and acquire a papery texture. Then perforations appear, revealing the presence of green or yellowish brown caterpillars. These are the larvae of a number of moths including the turnip moth, the heart and dart moth and the yellow underwing, which you may see fluttering against windowpanes in summer. They live in the ground, where they feed on roots, but also come to the surface at night to devastate the lower leaves and sever plants at ground level. Plants weaken, wither and soon die.

► **Plants affected** Artichoke, cabbage, lettuce.

► **Treatment** Weeds provide a favourable environment for these pests, so weed borders and beds regularly. *Bacillus thuringiensis* is a very effective biological solution, destroying the larvae by stopping them eating. Alternatively, pick off the larvae by hand at night when they are at their most active. Maintaining humidity levels in very dry weather also hinders their development. When the pest is active, spray with an approved insecticide. Hoe soil around plants during the danger months of spring and early summer, picking up and destroying any caterpillars that you see.

DOWNY MILDEW
► **Symptoms** A pale grey fungus appears on leaves, flowers and young shoots and the plant beneath the mildew yellows. The symptoms worsen under cool, damp conditions.

► **Plants affected** Artichoke, brassicas, celery, leek, onion, spinach, salad greens.

► **Treatment** Remove and burn all affected parts, then spray with Bordeaux mixture. Practise crop rotation, avoid overcrowding when planting and limit humid conditions: in a greenhouse ensure good air circulation and avoid splashing leaves when watering. Getting rid of plant debris and damaged plants helps to reduce the conditions under which this fungal disease can thrive.

GALL WEEVIL
► **Symptoms** Hollow swellings (or galls) can be found on the roots. These are the plant's reaction to being attacked by 4mm-long white maggots that can be found in the galls. These are the larvae of the adult weevil (*Ceuthorrhynchus pleurostigma*), which is active from late spring to summer.

► **Plants affected** All members of the cabbage family.

► **Treatment** Gall weevils are not a damaging pest on established brassicas. The galls do not interfere with root action and growth remains unaffected. However, seedlings are more susceptible. Treat infected crops with a plant-based insecticide containing rotenone (derris).

LEAF MOSAIC VIRUS
► **Symptoms** Infected leaves become discoloured with yellow or pale green mottling. The plant becomes stunted and deformed and eventually dies. This virus is spread from infected plants by several species of aphid.

► **Plants affected** Lettuce. Also beans, cucumber and peas.

► **Treatment** Lift and burn affected plants to prevent the virus spreading. Spray crops with an approved insecticide to control aphids: the carrier of this disease.

LEEK MOTH

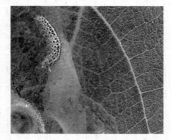

► **Symptoms** Light brown patches appear on the foliage, which is subsequently pierced by numerous tiny holes. The adult moth (*Acrolepiopsis assectella*) has brown wings marked with white and is active between spring and autumn. This moth is mainly a problem in coastal southern and eastern England.

► **Plants affected** Chive, leek, onion.

► **Treatment** Plant carrots and celery near leeks to limit an infestation. In the event of an attack, spray with an organic insecticide containing rotenone (liquid derris) or pyrethrins. Search for the pupae in their net-like cocoons on the leaves and crush them.

MEALY APHID

► **Symptoms** Attacks by a waxy, greyish greenfly are characterised initially by discoloured leaves. The plant is weakened and dies.

► **Plants affected** Apple, cabbage, chervil, plum, radish, turnip.

► **Treatment** Ladybirds are the ideal predators for this parasite but, in the event of serious attack, spray with an insecticide containing pyrethrins or rotenone. Dig up and destroy old brassica stalks to prevent the infection from spreading.

ONION FLY
► **Symptoms** Onion bulbs are riddled with tunnels. This weakens and often kills the plant. The pest is a fly, *Hylemya antiqua*, which looks like the common housefly. Its maggots burrow into the bulbs, moving from plant to plant and often attacking an entire crop.

► **Plants affected** Onion, shallot.

► **Treatment** Practise crop rotation. In the event of an attack, treat with an organic insecticide containing rotenone (derris) or pyrethrins. Lift and burn badly affected plants. Dig over infected land in winter to destroy the maggots. Grow seedlings under fine netting or fleece to prevent the flies from laying their eggs.

RUST Characterised by orange blotches on the leaves, this disease affects chicory, spinach and also leeks. Cabbages are affected by white rust (or white blister), which takes the form of white fungal masses on the leaves. See page 153.

SLUG This gastropod attacks most vegetables in the garden, especially young plants with tender leaves. Do not throw slugs onto your compost heap to get rid of them, instead, place them into polythene bags, tie the top and place in your waste bin. See page 99.

THRIPS Tiny winged insects that attack mainly leeks, causing silvery mottling on the upper surface of the leaves, while the undersides appear dirty. Use sticky traps to eradicate these pests from the greenhouse. Frequent watering may also help as thrips prefer dry conditions. See page 153.

Root vegetables

ALTERNARIA LEAF SPOT
▶ **Symptoms** The fungus *Alternaria* causes grey or brown circular patches of more or less dead tissue to appear on leaves. The leaves dry up and, in some cases, fungus forms.
▶ **Plants affected** Carrot, chicory, potato.
▶ **Treatment** Limit the spread of the disease by removing and burning affected leaves as soon as possible. Spray infected plants with a fungicide containing mancozeb.

ASPARAGUS BEETLE
▶ **Symptoms** The plants lose their foliage as the adult beetles and their larvae eat the leaves and outer bark from the stems. This damage causes the stems to dry up and turn yellowish brown. The adult beetles are black with six yellow blotches on their wing cases.
▶ **Plant affected** Asparagus.
▶ **Treatment** At the first sign of an attack, spray both the plants and soil with an approved insecticide and repeat as directed.

BEET LEAF MINER
▶ **Symptoms** The leaves become marked with fairly large brown spots. The tiny white grubs of the mangold fly (*Pegomya hyoscyami*) burrow inside the leaves and can cause considerable damage.
▶ **Plants affected** Beetroot, spinach.
▶ **Treatment** Pick off and destroy affected leaves or

squash the larvae in their mines. Spray the foliage with an approved insecticide at regular intervals until the pest is cleared.

CARROT FLY

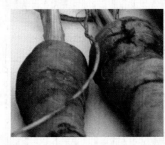

▶ **Symptoms** The roots are riddled with narrow tunnels, while rusty brown lines appear on the skin. The plant is weakened and, in some cases, dies. This destruction is caused by the creamy yellow grubs of the carrot root fly (*Psila rosae*). The grubs are about 7mm long, and the adults are shiny black flies with transparent wings and reddish yellow legs.
▶ **Plants affected** Carrot, celeriac, chicory, parsnips.
▶ **Treatment** To prevent infestation, choose resistant varieties and sow carrots in early spring or midsummer. Protect plants with fine netting or fleece and lift and destroy infected plants immediately.

COLORADO BEETLE

▶ **Symptoms** The leaves are riddled with holes and, in severe cases of infestation, are completely eaten away. The beetle is about 1cm long and lays its eggs on the underside of the leaves. The beetle has

distinctive black and yellow markings, and the larvae are pink with black markings. Both adults and larvae do a huge amount of damage.
▶ **Plant affected** Potato.
▶ **Treatment** You are legally obliged to destroy these pests, which can devastate an entire crop if you do not act quickly. This is a notifiable pest; an outbreak must be reported to DEFRA (the Department for the Environment, Food and Rural Affairs), and the crop must be completely destroyed.

EELWORM
▶ **Symptoms** The main roots bear either tiny white cysts (potato cyst eelworm) or large yellow or brown swellings (root knot eelworm). The lower leaves turn yellow and wither. The plants are often killed before the end of the summer and, consequently, the tubers may be particularly small.
▶ **Plants affected** Onion, potato, tomato.
▶ **Treatment** Lift and burn affected plants and tubers, and practise crop rotation. African or French marigolds (*Tagetes*) planted near your susceptible crops will help to keep this parasite at bay. Do not grow potatoes, tomatoes or onions in infected soil for at least six years. With potatoes, try growing resistant varieties, such as 'Pentland Javelin' and 'Maris Piper'.

FLEA BEETLE These beetles are found on seedlings of beetroot, brassicas, radishes, swedes and turnips. They pierce small holes in the leaves, which turn yellow. See page 98.

FOOT ROT
▶ **Symptoms** The leaves turn yellow, wilt and dry up partially or completely. The

base of the stem becomes darker in colour and softens. The roots may also rot. This bacterial disease starts at the base of the stem and works its way upwards. Plants that are growing in greenhouses are particularly susceptible.
▶ **Plants affected** Beetroot, celeriac, cucumber, melon, tomato.
▶ **Treatment** Prevent the disease from spreading by destroying infected plants. Replace the surrounding compost and make sure that you use hygienic cultivation techniques. Use only mains water on young seedlings.

GANGRENE
▶ **Symptoms** Brown patches appear on the skin and flesh at the ends of potato tubers and around the eyes and lenticels (small openings). The diseased area then enlarges until most of the tuber is decayed and shrunken. The responsible bacterium, *Phoma exigua* var. *foveata*, mainly attacks the blemishes caused by forks when lifting potatoes.
▶ **Plant affected** Potato.
▶ **Treatment** Plant only undamaged, certified seed tubers. Take care when lifting potatoes and remove any damaged tubers. Store only healthy tubers in an airy, frost-free place and discard any that appear to be infected.

RED SPIDER MITE *Tetranychus urticae* is a parasitic mite that attacks celeriac, causing mottling of the leaves, which subsequently turn yellow, wither and die. It also attacks courgettes, cucumbers, French and runner beans, marrows, peas and tomatoes. Spraying leaves with water will help as the mites thrive in dry conditions. See page 153.

SCAB

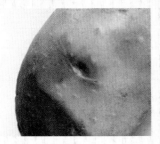

▶ **Symptoms** Flat, raised or concave patches appear on the surface of roots or tubers. Common scab is brown, while powdery scab has corky patches that release a brown powder. Scab is caused by bacteria of the genus *Streptomyces*, which thrive in light, sandy or very chalky soil.
▶ **Plant affected** Potato.
▶ **Treatment** Use prevention rather than cure. Dig in compost but do not lime the ground before planting potatoes. Practise crop rotation, increase the acidity of chalky soils and grow scab-resistant varieties. Do not grow 'Desirée' as it is susceptible to powdery scab. Make sure you plant only healthy seed.

WHITE BLISTER

▶ **Symptoms** Raised white spots with opaque blisters, arranged in concentric circles, appear on the lower leaf surfaces. The affected leaves become puckered, with sunken, slightly yellow pits. White blister usually attacks crops between early summer and late autumn.
▶ **Plants affected** Members of the cabbage family, radish, turnip.
▶ **Treatment** As there is no effective treatment, if the problem is still fairly contained, simply remove the affected leaves. If plants are severely affected, pull them up and dispose of them. Grow resistant varieties.

WIREWORM

▶ **Symptoms** Roots and tubers are riddled with narrow tunnels bored by a thin yellow grub about 2–3cm long. The grubs are the larvae of the click beetle (*Agriotes*, family *Elateridae*), which can live for up to five years before turning into an adult. A major infestation can destroy an entire crop.
▶ **Plants affected** Asparagus, beetroot, carrot, potato and many other vegetables.
▶ **Treatment** It is quite easy to pick up the larvae by hand when digging over the soil. Keep land well cultivated to expose any wireworms to the birds. Traps are also effective. Place small pieces of carrot or potato on spikes and bury them in the soil at a depth of about 5cm to lure the grubs. Inspect and replace the traps regularly. Lift your potatoes as soon as they are mature to prevent attack. Wireworms tend to be more of a problem on old pasture land.

Fruiting vegetables

BLACK BEAN APHID (BLACKFLY) Black bean aphid
is found on the leaves and stems of beetroot, broad beans in spring, and French and runner beans during July and August. Large colonies of these aphids stunt the growth of the host plant. See page 97.

COLORADO BEETLE This striped yellow beetle is usually found on potatoes, but also attacks aubergines, peppers and tomatoes. See page 207.

CUTWORM

▶ **Symptoms** Stems on small plants are severed by earth-coloured caterpillars that gnaw away the outer membranes at soil level.
▶ **Plants affected** ,Carrot, lettuce, potato.
▶ **Treatment** At night, remove the large caterpillars by hand. Rake through the soil to bring the culprits to the surface for the birds to eat. Good cultivation in weed-free plots helps to limit cutworms. Apply the natural-control nematode *Steinernema carpocapsae* onto the soil around the plants to parasitise the caterpillars and quickly destroy them.

DIDYMELLA STEM ROT
▶ **Symptoms** This disease primarily affects the leaves, but can also attack the stems and fruit of members of the squash and marrow family. Slimy brown patches appear along the edge of the leaves, which turn yellow. Stem tissue dies and the end of the fruit shrivels as it rots from the inside. Didymella stem rot is caused by a fungus that also attacks certain ornamental plants such as chrysanthemums, fruit bushes and raspberries.
▶ **Plants affected** Cucumber, marrow, melon, squash, tomato.

▶ **Treatment** Feed the crop with liquid nettle manure to strengthen growth. Dig up and burn badly affected plants. Do not throw plant remains onto the compost heap. Clear up all crop debris at the end of the season and grow crops on a fresh site each year.

GUMMOSIS
▶ **Symptoms** Dark grey, sunken spots covered with an olive green mould appear on the fruit. The fruit splits and gum oozes from the cracks. Mould develops on the surface of the gum. As the blemishes heal, corky tissue forms around the edges. The damage is caused by the fungal pest *Cladosporium cucumerinum*, which becomes active when daytime temperatures reach 18°C after a cool night.
▶ **Plants affected** Courgettes, cucumber, marrow, squash, tomato.
▶ **Treatment** Destroy all diseased fruit, then raise the temperature and reduce humidity if plants are grown in a greenhouse. Grow resistant cultivars. Spray a copper-based treatment to help to prevent the spread of the disease.

LEAF MOSAIC VIRUS

Cucumbers, marrows and tomatoes are particularly susceptible to the mosaic virus. Mosaic-like or mottled patches appear on the leaves, which become deformed and reduced in size. Young shoots become curled, and the whole plant may be stunted and die early. On some plants, flower colour is affected. See page 152.

PEA AND BEAN WEEVIL

▶ **Symptoms** Seeds bear small round holes, while the larvae can be seen on the surface of the soil, feeding on the first leaves. Light brown patches may appear on the seed coat. These weevils belong to the genera *Acanthoscelides* and *Bruchus,* whose larvae bore into the pods, then the seeds. They are active while the plant is growing, but they also wreak havoc among stored vegetables.
▶ **Plants affected** Broad bean, French and runner bean, pea.
▶ **Treatment** Established plants can usually tolerate weevil damage. Only act if the weevils are eating young plants: either use an approved insecticide or cover with fleece to prevent the pest from getting to them.

ROOT ROT

▶ **Symptoms** The roots show signs of rot, the base of the stem changes colour and shrivels, and the plant dies fairly rapidly.
▶ **Plants affected** Aubergine, beans (broad, French and runner), courgette, cucumber, marrow, pea, squash, sweet pepper, tomato.
▶ **Treatment** Dig up and discard infected plants and remove the surrounding soil to prevent the spread of infection. Maintain good hygiene and use only sterilised compost to prevent root rot.

SCLEROTINIA ROT (BROWN ROT)

This disease affects a wide range of vegetables, such as aubergines, broad beans courgettes, cucumbers, French and runner beans, Jerusalem artichokes, marrows, peas, and sweet peppers. It is characterised by a white cottony mould on the leaves and fruit, which becomes discoloured, turns brown and rots. The stems of affected plants become discoloured and are covered in dense fungal growth. Large black sclerotia (fungal resting bodies) are embedded in the fungal growth. See page 254.

THRIPS Tiny winged insects that cause silvery mottling on the leaves of aubergines, courgettes, cucumbers, marrows, peppers, and tomatoes. See page 153.

WHITEFLY Members of the insect family *Aleyrodidae,* whiteflies frequently attack fruiting vegetables, weakening the plants by sucking their sap. See page 99.

Pods and cobs

ANTHRACNOSE A fungal disease, anthracnose attacks peas, and French and runner beans in wet weather. Dark brown cankers form on stems, leaf ribs turn pinky brown and sunken brown spots appear on the pods. See page 254.

BLACK BEAN APHID (BLACKFLY) These aphids are particularly attracted to broad and runner beans, so much so that some gardeners grow a few bean plants in their ornamental borders to keep flowers and shrubs free of blackfly. See page 97.

HALO BLIGHT

▶ **Symptoms** Greasy, water-soaked spots appear on the leaves and pods. Those on the leaves become surrounded by a greenish yellow 'halo', while those on the pods exude a pale cream or silvery bacterial ooze. Infected pods become discoloured and shrivelled, and the seeds are contaminated. This blight is caused by the bacterium *Pseudomonas phaseolicola*, which becomes active in wet, windy conditions that turn dry and hot in the flowering season.
▶ **Plants affected** French and runner bean, broad bean.
▶ **Treatment** Spraying with copper may protect plants from the disease. Lift and destroy diseased plants, practise crop rotation and do not soak seeds before planting.

PEA MOTH

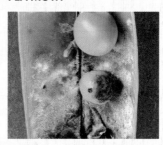

▶ **Symptoms** Inside the pods, the greenish yellow, black-headed caterpillars burrow into the seeds. They are about 1–2cm long and are easily detected by their excrement, which remains attached to a silken thread. The pea moth (*Laspeyresia nigricana*) has a wingspan of about 3cm. It is particularly active in hot, dry weather and during summer.
▶ **Plant affected** Pea.
▶ **Treatment** Treat affected plants with an organic insecticide containing rotenone (derris) or natural pyrethrins, spraying about seven days after

the onset of flowering. Kill the adult moths by using a pheromone trap.

RUNNER BEAN RUST

▶ **Symptoms** Yellow pustules cover the upper surfaces of the leaves, while yellow blisters distort the underside and eventually affect the pods. These blemishes turn brown, then black. This strain of rust is caused by the *Uromyces appendiculatus* fungus, which develops during hot, wet summers.
▶ **Plants affected** French and runner beans.
▶ **Treatment** Grow beans in well-manured ground and feed regularly with liquid nettle or comfrey manure (see page 255). At the first sign of attack, spray with an approved sulphur-based fungicide.

SMUT

▶ **Symptoms** Sweetcorn seeds turn black and release a black powder when opened. Brown patches appear on the leaves of leeks. Different genera of fungus are responsible for this disease – *Entyloma, Sphacelotheca, Ustilago, Uroscystis* – and are spread by rain splash or watering.
▶ **Plants affected** Sweetcorn, leeks, onions.
▶ **Treatment** Lift and burn plants at the first sign of attack. Do not plant the same crop in a place where the previous crop was infected. Fungicides have no effect on smut.

Fruit from the garden

The strawberry, queen of the garden

Steeped in tradition, strawberries are an essential part of the English summer. The juicy red fruits can be raised in pots and hanging baskets, as well as the traditional strawberry patch.

Give strawberries their heart's desire

How big a patch do you need? It really depends on how many strawberries you want. A single six-metre row will keep a family fed through the season, or if you're on your own, plant up a strawberry pot.

Plant early in the season A stem from an axillary bud that grows on the surface and forms roots to produce a new plant is called a stolon. Replant these from your strawberry patch from July onwards until the end of August.
▶ If you can propagate from an existing plant, you will have an advantage over those who have to buy young plants, since they are only available in garden centres in September and

When picking strawberries, leave some of the stalk attached, or the berries will lose their freshness.

October. Strawberry plants develop roots and accumulate food reserves between the time of planting and the winter, so if they are planted late, or worse still in spring, they will not be productive in their first year.

The right depth Strawberry plants should not be planted deep in the ground. Ensure that the crown – the boundary between the roots and the head of leaves – is just above the soil surface. Dig a fairly wide hole, and spread out the roots before covering them with soil and packing it down. No matter how many you have to plant, don't be tempted to use a dibber as the holes will be too narrow.

Rediscover the old flavours Study specialist catalogues to track down those old-fashioned strawberry varieties that were created above all else to please the palate. Their tender fruit is best savoured fresh from the garden.
▶ Old varieties of strawberry include 'Royal Sovereign' (early), 'Redgauntlet' (midseason) and 'Talisman' (late).

Modern varieties More recent varieties have been bred to grow vigorously, resist disease and improve fruit appearance, but often at the expense of the flavour. New varieties that are readily available include 'Calypso', 'Gorella' and 'Elvira'.

Some of the tastiest strawberries

Cambridge Favourite ❶ An early strawberry producing large, firm fruit for a long period in midsummer; a vigorous and reliable plant.

Elsanta An early cropper whose fruits are often sold commercially, but taste better when eaten straight from the plant. Fruits are ready for picking from late spring to midsummer.

Aromel ❷ A double-cropper with fruits in June–July and August–September.

Symphony A late variety, perfect if you like to have strawberries beyond the Wimbledon season. Not a fussy plant, so a great option for less than ideal growing conditions. It has an outstanding flavour.

Delicate seedlings When up-rooted from the ground, young strawberry plants are quick to dry out. Do not leave them lying around in the sun. Instead, put their roots straight into a mixture of potting compost and water, and plant them again as soon as possible.

Plant your strawberries on a ridge If the soil in your garden is heavy and wet, it is not the ideal situation for growing strawberries. So when you prepare your strawberry patch, make sure you

provide well-drained soil for the roots. For a double line of plants, build up a flat-topped ridge of soil about 20cm high and one metre wide, and set the plants in that.

Strawberries on the patio All is not lost if you love strawberries but have only a balcony or a patio. You can grow them in special strawberry pots with honeycomb cavities, in a graduated stack of terracotta pots, or in large tubs or barrels filled with a mixture of well-decomposed compost and sand,

or rich but light earth. Place them in a fairly shady spot, make sure that they never lack water, and regularly remove the stolons so that the plants do not become exhausted. Enjoy the crop – but don't expect to have enough to make jam.

The truth about double-cropping strawberry plants
Don't be deceived by the term 'double-cropping', which is used to describe some varieties of strawberry plant. It is, in fact, rare for strawberries to produce two harvests worthy of the name. Sacrifice the first flowers, which are supposed to provide a spring crop, in order to improve the second crop, and consider the double-cropping strawberry plant simply as a single-cropping one that bears fruit later than the actual single-cropping varieties.

At home in the woods Originally the strawberry grew in forest clearings, which is why it particularly likes the rather acidic qualities of tree humus.
▶ Fertilise your strawberry patch by spreading a generous layer of leaf-mould over it.
▶ A reliable old-fashioned tip is to cover the soil between the stalks of the plants with conifer needles, ferns and ground pine bark or, failing that, a good layer of straw. This porous carpet has the added advantages of discouraging weeds and purifying the surface of the soil so that your strawberry plants will be less vulnerable to grey mould and slugs.

Take off leaves The leaf diseases that strike strawberry plants occur in late autumn. So, as soon as possible after the harvest, clip off their leaves, taking care to cut high enough not to touch the heart of the plants. Your plants will soon start to grow healthy new leaves.

Susceptibility to weeds One of the big problems with growing strawberry plants is their vulnerability to vigorous weeds such as convolvulus, couch grass and buttercups. The plants are suffocated by the weeds, their fruit is deprived of sunlight and their soil loses its richness. If weeds start to become a problem in your strawberry patch you may have to move it to a new, weed-free site.

Combination planting Use the soft, loose soil between two rows of strawberry plants for a line of spinach, white onions or lettuces: crops that are not greedy and will not rob the strawberry plants of nutrients.

Keep their hats on Never hull strawberries before washing them. If you do, the berries soak up water, which spoils their delicious flavour.

Propagating strawberries

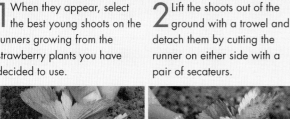

1 When they appear, select the best young shoots on the runners growing from the strawberry plants you have decided to use.

2 Lift the shoots out of the ground with a trowel and detach them by cutting the runner on either side with a pair of secateurs.

3 Keeping as much earth as possible around their roots, move the shoots to where they are to be planted, and replant them immediately.

4 When replanting, ensure that the crown is not buried, and then water the shoots generously.

Tempting berries from the bush

Filling a basket with raspberries, blueberries, currants, gooseberries and blackberries is a joyful reminder of simpler times. You don't need a large garden to enjoy these fruits, and once you've grown a few you'll be hooked.

Raspberries and blueberries

Mulch the soil for a good crop The raspberry is a woodland plant that appreciates a mulch of partially composted dead leaves, twigs, straw, tree bark, wood shavings, pine needles or any other woody debris. Added on a regular basis, these materials will decompose and create the acidity that the plant needs to grow. Mulching also provides protection against diseases such as spur blight – a common problem in cooler parts of the country – and helps to keep weed growth down.

Raspberries need support Raspberry stems, or canes, are extremely supple and are liable to be flattened by wind, rain and the weight of the fruit. It is essential to provide some kind of support; for example, a post-and-wire system.

▶ Sink two posts into the ground at either end of the row of canes, reinforcing each one with an angled strut.
▶ Stretch galvanised wire between the posts, at a height of about 1.7 metres. Tighten one end with a straining bolt.
▶ Tie each cane to the wire with a plastic tie, a piece of garden twine or a length of raffia.

Pick blueberries by hand – use a large, shallow basket or container so that they do not get crushed.

Easy-growing raspberries

SUMMER-FRUITING VARIETIES – EARLY JULY
Glen Clova ❶ An old favourite with high yields of fruit; the fruits are small, so ideal for freezing.
Glen Moy A popular choice as it is spine-free, has large berries and produces plenty of fruit.

SUMMER-FRUITING VARIETIES – LATE JULY
Leo Tangy but tasty orange-red fruits; aphid resistant.
Malling Admiral A good all-rounder; doesn't do well in wet soil but is resistant to spur blight.

AUTUMN-FRUITING VARIETIES
Autumn Bliss A self-supporting variety with good flavour; fruits ripen from August onwards.
Fallgold A late variety with yellow fruit.
Heritage ❷ A high-yield variety with average flavour; second harvest from late August until the first frosts.
September An aromatic fruit with a slightly sharp taste; second harvest in September–October.
Zeva A well-known, large-fruited variety; second harvest in September–October.

Pruning raspberries Regular pruning ensures a succession of healthy new canes and good fruit production. When and how you prune depends on the variety of raspberry.

▶ **Summer-fruiting varieties** Once fruiting is over, cut the canes that have just fruited down to ground level. Tie in canes that have grown during the current season. The following spring, cut back the tips on the new canes to a healthy bud.

▶ **Autumn-fruiting varieties** Prune in February, cutting all the canes down to ground level.

Combating raspberry beetle This pest is often spotted when you are picking the ripe fruit. Keep an eye out for the adult beetles, which lay their eggs on the flowers, and for the brown grubs, which burrow into the centre of the fruit.

▶ A traditional way to prevent the problem is to plant forget-me-nots (*Myosotis*) next to your raspberries. They self-seed readily and will act as a deterrent.

▶ Inspect your raspberries regularly during the summer. Make your way along the row, tapping the foliage and collecting any beetles in a bowl held beneath the leaves. Then all you have to do is take away the insects and destroy them.

Blueberry history The American blueberry (*Vaccinum corymbosum*) is a modern variety, and is much more productive than the small European species (*Vaccinum myrtillus*), although some say it has less flavour. The European blueberry, or bilberry, grows wild in many European countries, including Britain. It is extremely difficult to grow outside its natural habitat, so in a garden the American blueberry may be a better choice.

▶ The American blueberry reaches one to two metres high and produces 1–3kg (and sometimes as much as 10kg) of fruit per bush. It is very decorative when its leaves turn red in autumn.

▶ Unlike the European blueberry, which grows happily in woodland, the American variety only fruits well in full sun, so choose its position carefully.

Blueberries need acid soil Like its wild counterpart, which grows on peaty heaths, the cultivated blueberry needs an acid soil.

▶ You'll be able to identify your soil type by looking at the local flora. Bracken, gorse, broom and foxgloves are all acid-loving plants.

▶ If you don't have the right soil, blueberries can be grown in a large container of ericaceous compost.

▶ When planting blueberry bushes, dig a hole 50cm across and fill it with a

Autumn and summer-fruiting raspberries

The raspberry is a perennial that sends up new shoots from its underground roots at different times of the year, depending on whether the variety is summer or autumn-fruiting.

▶ **Summer-fruiting varieties** These fruit once a year, in summer. As some of the shoots bear fruit, others are growing and developing. The new shoots will bear fruit the following year, while the current fruit-bearing shoots will die off.

▶ **Autumn-fruiting varieties** The fruit on these varieties appears from September until the first frosts, on canes that have developed in the current year.

mixture of equal parts ericaceous compost, leaf or pine-needle mould and well-rotted garden compost. Leave 1.5 metres between plants.

▶ Give the plants an annual top-dressing of moss peat or acid leaf-mould to enrich the soil. Alternatively, feed them with an ericaceous plant food.

Always pick blueberries by hand Don't be tempted to use any of the contraptions which are available for gathering wild fruit. Apart from the fact that they gather as many leaves as berries, they will damage berries of the large-fruited cultivated varieties. There's only one solution – lots of patience and picking by hand.

Blueberry pairing Cultivated blueberries require a pollinating partner to ensure a good crop of fruits. Therefore, you need to plant two different varieties, making sure they will flower at the same time to ensure cross-pollination. Choose between early varieties, such as 'Bluetta', 'Duke', 'Patriot' and 'Bluecrop', whose fruit ripens in July, and later varieties, such as 'Nelson' and 'Brigitta', which ripen in August and September.

Planting raspberry canes

1 Plant raspberry canes in autumn. Add well-rotted manure to the base of the planting hole and, if your soil is dry or chalky, mix in a quantity of ericaceous compost.

2 Plant only about 10cm deep and spread the roots out. Planting too deep inhibits the development of beneficial suckers. Firm the soil around the base of the canes.

3 Leave a hollow around the base of each plant, and water well. Once the plant has settled in, cut down the canes to 25cm above the ground, cutting at an angle above a bud.

Currants and gooseberries

Planted to perfection Plant young redcurrant or blackcurrant bushes deeply. If the neck of the plant – where the roots join the branches – is 5–10cm below the surface of the soil, it will produce a number of suckers which will later become the important framework branches.
▶ Twelve is the ideal number of branches for a blackcurrant or redcurrant bush to encourage maximum fruiting.

Plant cuttings in situ If a friend has a currant bush you've always admired, why not ask for a cutting? In early spring, clear and break down the soil in the spot chosen for the new bush and push two 25–30cm long cuttings or sections of branches, taken from the previous year's growth, into the ground. These cuttings should be pushed in at an angle, about 10cm apart, with only one bud showing.
▶ Planting cuttings directly in their growing positions will encourage the plants to put out deep roots. This will make the young bushes less susceptible to drought than if they are transplanted as baby bushes.

Turning a cutting into a fruiting bush When growing a new bush from a cutting, cut it back every winter for three years before allowing it to fruit.
▶ **The first winter** After planting, cut back any new shoots that have developed to two buds.
▶ **The second winter** Cut back any new shoots to three buds, and any suckers to 15cm above ground level.
▶ **The third winter** Cut back shoots to four buds above their base and suckers to 15cm above ground level. The following year, your currant bush will be ready to produce fruit.

For healthy redcurrants The caterpillars of the currant clearwing moth tunnel into the pith of the shoots of currant bushes. In autumn, cut out and burn any dry, brittle twigs to destroy the larvae and prevent a recurrence. Don't put the debris on the compost heap or the problem will spread.

Watch out, birds about It won't take long for the local bird population to spot your new fruit bushes. They can quickly rob the plant of its fruit or strip the buds from the branches, leaving bare unproductive wood.

▶ There are deterrents such as vibrating tape, which is effective, but only for a few days. It has to be changed regularly or the birds simply get used to it.
▶ If you are growing a number of fruit bushes, it is worth building a fruit frame and covering it with netting (left) to keep the birds away.

Outwitting the birds
Blackbirds and starlings love soft, red fruit. You can outwit them by choosing white and pink varieties of currant such as 'White Versailles' (right) and 'White Dutch'.

Aromatic blackcurrants The blackcurrant is the king of aromatic fruits. It is at its best and produces the sweetest aroma in rich alkaline soil, but if your soil isn't limy, add some crushed limestone to the soil used to fill the planting hole.
▶ France is famed for cassis, a heady blackcurrant liqueur, and a traditional French tip for stimulating the aroma of blackcurrants is to spread pieces of old plaster around the base of the bushes in winter. As the plaster is broken down by the winter frosts, the calcium sulphate from which it is made will easily be absorbed by the roots.

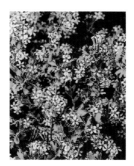

An ornamental currant Currants aren't grown just for their fruits: many have valuable decorative qualities. *Ribes odoratum* (left) has wonderful yellow flowers in spring, followed by inedible purple fruits and a later show of autumn colour. *Ribes sanguineum* is often planted as part of an informal mixed hedge for its red-pink, late spring flowers.

Failure to fruit Modern varieties of blackcurrant are fairly reliable. However, if there is a year when fruit is sparse, it may be because pollen has been washed off plants by rain, winds or frost. Don't give up, hope for dry weather next year.

Mouth-watering currants and berries ▶

Johkheer van Tets ❶ One of the first redcurrants to ripen in early July, with large crops of succulent fruit.

Bluecrop ❷ A heavy-cropping blueberry that has large, pale blue berries. It is fast-growing and vigorous.

Black Satin ❸ For dessert fruits, grow this thornless blackberry with large, black shiny berries that are quite acidic.

Zeva ❹ Generous crops of large raspberries grow on self-supporting canes. Fruits ripen in September–October.

Invicta ❺ An easy-to-grow gooseberry with almost hairless, pale green fruits. It has some resistance to gooseberry mildew.

Ben Lomond ❻ A late-fruiting blackcurrant. The original of the 'Ben' varieties, it is the parent of other 'Ben' blackcurrants.

Fruiting bushes

New varieties of blackcurrant Many of the very old varieties of blackcurrant have been overtaken by new introductions. Most older varieties flowered and produced fruitlets as early as April. As a result, they were often damaged by frost and their yield was variable.

To solve this problem, plant breeders introduced the 'Ben' group, which flowers much later and is less prone to frost damage. These newer varieties, such as 'Ben More' (left), have made growing blackcurrants far easier. This variety has large black shiny fruits with a sweet acid flavour, high in vitamin C, and has resistance to mildew and leaf-curling midge.

Plan for fruits all summer Traditionally, redcurrants ripen from mid-June to the end of July, depending on the variety. To have fruit all summer long plant a selection of different varieties. The following are in order of ripening, from the earliest to the latest: 'Jonkheer van Tets', 'Junifer', 'Laxton's Number One', 'Red Lake', 'White Versailles' and 'Rondom'. However, there are also August-fruiting varieties such as 'Redstart' and 'Rovada', which will extend your crop further.

A standard currant If you'd like a currant that can be picked standing up, doesn't take up a lot of space and is easy to weed around the base, turn your cutting into a standard bush.
▶ Remove all the buds from the lower half of the cutting, so that shoots do not develop below ground level. Push the cutting vertically into the ground at the chosen position.
▶ Once it has rooted and new shoots have developed, tie the strongest shoot to a bamboo cane and remove the rest.
▶ Allow the stem to grow to about one metre, then prune the tip. Side shoots will grow from the top three or four buds.

Rejuvenating currant bushes The simplest way to give new vigour to an old currant bush is to cut all the branches back to ground level in winter. The following spring, a number of suckers or shoots will emerge from the soil and develop during the summer. They should begin to bear fruit the following year.

Growing gooseberries Gooseberries are synonymous with an old-fashioned British summer, and fortunately they are very easy to grow in any type of well-drained but moisture-retaining soil. They thrive in full sun or partial shade, but do not plant them in frost pockets – they flower in early March and may be damaged by a severe late frost.

Pruning gooseberries the simple way You will need to wear leather gloves when pruning all but the thornless gooseberries. You should prune during autumn or winter, but if birds are likely to damage buds, delay pruning until bud-burst so they do not strip the few remaining buds.

Standard redcurrants are a space-conscious option. They are easy to weed around and less back-breaking to pick.

▶ Cut out dead wood and any crossing branches, and cut back by half any new growth shooting from the main branches.
▶ In late June cut back all newly produced side shoots to four or five leaves from the base.
▶ Aim to create a plant with a good goblet shape, to make picking easier, and with space in the centre of the bush so that air can circulate around the fruit, helping to prevent disease.

Gooseberries without thorns To make picking less painful, it is worth looking for thornless varieties of gooseberries such as 'Captivator'. This variety is also resistant to powdery mildew, a disease that often affects gooseberries.

For cooking or for eating? There are two types of gooseberry – culinary and dessert. Culinary varieties are ideal for cooking but have too sharp a taste to eat straight from the bush. Dessert gooseberries are sweeter and can be eaten fresh. If you don't have much room, choose a dessert type as younger fruits can be used for cooking and ripe fruits for eating fresh.

Strange fruit An inquisitive nurseryman hybridised the blackcurrant and the gooseberry, which produced the Worcesterberry, *Ribes divaricatum*, a small black 'gooseberry' that tastes of blackcurrant.

DID YOU KNOW?
A treat for all soft fruit
Gooseberries, currants, raspberries and blackberries all benefit from added compost, as a source of humus. Add a couple of shovelfuls of this precious enriching organic material around the roots of each bush or plant in autumn and the earthworms will drag it into the soil.

Blackberries

Pain-free brambles The thornless blackberry is a cultivar, or cultivated variety, of the familiar wild blackberry. It is the product of genetics and pure chance, since the 'thornless' gene does in fact exist in several species of wild American blackberries. By hybridising various combinations of these species, breeders produced thornless varieties. The fruit of the cultivar doesn't taste as sweet as that of the wild bramble, but it is larger and easier to pick, and there are now several varieties to choose from (see box, right).

As nature intended In the old days, gardeners would have avoided growing the rampant blackberry and simply collected fruits from the hedgerows. Now that there are more compact hybrids available they deserve a place in our gardens.
▶ When planting a mixed informal hedge in a cottage garden, or even the vegetable garden, add a few blackberries and enjoy picking them the traditional way – from the hedgerow.

They're not fussy Blackberries can be grown in most conditions. If you have had trouble growing berried fruit in

Don't pick blackberries as soon as they turn black. Leave them for a few days and they'll taste sweeter.

Blackberries without thorns

Blackberries are extremely tolerant of site and soil conditions, although thornless varieties are fussier than their prickly cousins. Give them the best possible start by planting in moist, well-drained soil in a sunny spot.

Black Satin Vigorous, productive and hardy with large, black, conical fruits of exceptional quality. Harvest from early August for 4–6 weeks.

Merton Thornless ❶ An ideal variety for a small garden as it has short canes. The fruits are of a good flavour but it's not a heavy cropper. Fruit will be ripe for picking in August and September.

Oregon Thornless ❷ A very popular variety, decorative enough to grow over a trellis, thanks to its coloured autumn leaves. The small to medium-sized fruits have a mild, sweet flavour and are ready to harvest from late August to the end of September.

the past then this is one to try, especially as they are hardy and will even put up with a bit of shade, making them ideal for gardeners who are surrounded by overhanging trees. They would thrive in a woodland setting alongside bluebells and cranesbill, where the free-draining, moist acid soil suits them.
▶ As blackberries do not flower until June, they can even be planted in a frost hollow.

One for the birds Normally, gardeners would jealously guard their fruit bushes from the marauding birds that love them so much. But blackberries are such prolific producers that you can afford to share them – there is no need for bird-scarers or fruit cages. In fact, blackberries are a good way to attract birds, bees and butterflies to a wildlife garden.
▶ Because blackberries are so rampant, you will need to cut them back from time to time. But make sure you don't disturb any nesting birds in the process.

A natural rooting hormone Like their wild counterparts, blackberry cultivars produce roots at the point where their stems touch the ground, from which new plants will grow. This is known as propagation by natural layering, and the new roots contain a hormone that makes them very vigorous.
▶ Use this organic boost when you are propagating any new plants from cuttings. Cut off some of these small white roots, chop them finely and leave them to macerate in the water in which you are soaking your cuttings. After 24 hours, you can plant your cuttings with every chance of success, thanks to the hormones in the young blackberry roots.

Fruiting bushes

The growing cycle – the key to pruning During the first year of a blackberry's development, the root stock produces shoots that emerge from the soil and put on several metres' growth. The following year, lateral shoots appear on the long climbing stems. These shoots will flower and produce fruit during the summer and then die off in the winter. During this time, other vigorous shoots will develop from the root stock and produce fruit the following year, and so on.

▶ When pruning, cut out dry, dead stems at the base. Leave all visible new shoots as they will produce the following summer's fruit. See below for how to prune, step by step.

Support required Even a modern compact variety of blackberry can put on several metres' growth in a single season. It is essential to provide its supple climbing stems with support so that they don't sprawl all over the ground. You can, however, wait for a year after planting before putting a support system in place.

▶ Sink wood or metal stakes at least two metres long into the ground at five-metre intervals and, if possible, support each one with an angled strut. Then stretch three lengths of thick, galvanised wire horizontally between the stakes at a height of 1 metre, 1.3 metres and 1.6 metres above the

ground. Tighten each wire at one end with a straining bolt. Finally, plant blackberries along the support system at intervals of 2.5 metres.

▶ As the shoots grow, tie them to the wires at an angle (above) using soft, pliable ties that won't damage the young stems. You can buy practical, reusable ties from garden centres or, alternatively, use strips of fabric or old nylon tights.

In cold regions Here's a technique that has been used for many years and still works well today. In regions where winter frosts could prove fatal for young blackberry shoots, bend the stems, lay them flat along the row in autumn and protect with a layer of straw, dead leaves or bracken.

Keep out of the sun Once blackberries are picked, they tend to turn red and hard if left in the sun. Cover your crop with a tea towel while you are picking, and keep them in the refrigerator until you use them.

A rose by any other name Blackberry blossom is large and lasts for several weeks – many old fashioned cottage gardens had a trellis covered in blackberries for the beauty of the blossom as well as for the bounty of the fruit.

Loganberries In 1881, James Logan of Santa Cruz, California, a judge and an occasional plant breeder, created a new plant with conical, red berries while attempting to hybridise two varieties of blackberry. One of the parent plants was in fact a nearby raspberry whose pollen had accidentally fertilised one of the blackberry flowers. Varieties such as 'Thornless Loganberry' are cultivated in the same way as the blackberry. It is not frost-hardy and its fruit, which is harvested at the end of July, tends to be rather hard and tart. This makes it more suitable for making jam than eating raw, although it also freezes well.

Pruning blackberries

1 Prune in early spring. Start by cutting out two-year-old stems at the base. Then remove spindly growth from the end of new canes.

2 If you have few new canes, leave some old canes in place to fruit again. Cut back any damage on these old canes to a healthy bud.

3 Remove damaged and diseased wood and any canes that you feel will obstruct paths.

4 Carefully tie in the new year-old stems as these will produce the most fruit. They'll be cut off at the base the following year.

Fruits of the vine

Vines have been cultivated in Britain for centuries. In greenhouses or sheltered gardens, grapes and some more exotic newcomers are easy to grow, and produce excellent crops of fruit.

Sweet, succulent grapes

Grow a vine in a pot Fill a large pot 35–40cm in diameter with a mixture of 50 per cent garden soil, 25 per cent soil-based compost and 25 per cent coarse sand. Plant a young vine whose climbing stems can be trained up a pergola or trellis. It will do well on your patio in a sunny position. At the end of the summer you will be able to pick a few bunches of delicious table grapes.
▶ Repot the vine every two years if possible or replace the first few centimetres of soil with fresh compost mixture.

Do you live in a vine-growing region? Like all cultivated plants, the vine has climatic requirements, especially when it comes to summer temperatures. While it can withstand extremely cold winters, it does not like late spring frosts,

Given a sheltered spot, plenty of sun and good support, an outdoor vine will happily live in a large trough.

which destroy the buds, and it needs warmth and baking sun during the summer months to ripen the fruits. Vines planted in the south have a greater chance of success than those grown in the north. Plant them against a south-facing wall where they will have both shelter and full sun.

Vines for wine Grapes have been grown for hundreds and hundreds of years in Britain. They do need plenty of attention, so often become a specialist hobby for gardeners, especially those who fancy making their own wine. A well-loved vine will produce grapes for decades but can take up to four years to give you a substantial crop.
▶ Many large estate gardens of the past had glasshouses dedicated to grape vines, and by paying great attention to the temperature requirements of each vine they would have been able to produce grapes nearly all year round.

The best time to plant vines Plant vines in November and December. Whether the plant has a rootball or is bare-rooted, make sure the point where it has been grafted onto the rootstock is about 4cm above the level of the soil.
▶ If you experience very cold winters, or live in a frost pocket, protect the upper part of the plant by earthing up sand or light soil to cover the graft – or the lower buds where there is no graft. Remove in spring, after the risk of frost has passed.

The best time to prune Prune a trellised vine when it starts to produce leaves in March. In cooler northern regions this will prevent damage by late April frosts. It will also preserve the buds at the base, which will go on to develop later.

Vines for protected positions

VINES UNDER GLASS
Muscat Hamburgh ❶ A classic Muscat variety which has large, dark red fruits.

Muscat of Alexandria ❷ Large fruits that are ready for picking late in the season.

Buckland Sweetwater ❸ Round, pale green fruits which ripen to amber. They have a sweet flavour and grow in short, broad bunches. A heavy cropper.

OUTDOOR VINES
Brant Sold by many nurseries and garden centres. Its heavy crop of sweet fruit makes this dessert grape very popular. The vine will cover a wall but must get as much sun as possible.

Cascade A winner due to its resistance to mildew; a wine-making grape with small dark fruits. Sometimes listed as 'Seibel'.

Fruiting vines

Rejuvenating an old vine Once a vine reaches 20–25 years old it becomes less productive. Hard pruning will promote new vigour, but should be carried out over two years so that it is less traumatic for the vine.

▶ During the first summer, deal with the vine's leaf and grape-bearing shoots that originate near the base of the vine – these are the ones you will keep. Train them in the best direction by staking and trellising.

▶ In winter, cut out some of the vine shoots, leaving those produced by the branches you have decided to keep.

▶ The following winter, use a saw to cut the vine stock, or trunk, just above the shoots to be retained. Smooth off the cut with a well-sharpened knife or pruning knife and seal with candle wax to prevent infection from pests and diseases.

Protect grapes
Here's an old-fashioned tip that can improve the quality and quantity of your crop. Before your grapes ripen, protect them from wasps and birds by wrapping them in paper bags pierced with holes.

Pruning a vine in March

1 Cutting cleanly and at an angle, remove all the branches that bore fruit the previous year.

2 Cut back the spurs you are keeping to the second bud. The upper bud will produce this year's fruit.

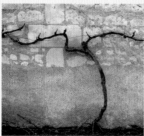

3 Cut back a long lateral shoot to 20cm and tie it carefully to the training wires. This will extend the vine.

4 De-bud the vine later in the year by removing surplus shoots in summer.

By growing vines in a conservatory, you'll ensure sweeter grapes and provide welcome shade in the heat of summer.

Top tips for a good grape harvest To get plump, perfectly shaped dessert grapes, thin the bunches when the fruit first appears by removing damaged, diseased or misshapen grapes using nail scissors. Don't thin grapes being grown for wine – any shape or size will do for this purpose.

▶ **Let the sun in** As the fruit ripens, tie back, or remove some of the foliage so that the sun can reach the fruit.

▶ **Pick on time** When the stem that attaches the bunch to the vine starts to go brown, the fruit is ready for picking.

▶ **Cut a branch** Take the whole bunch, not individual grapes: they are easier to store and should last longer.

▶ **Store well** Put in a box with a soft lining and store in a cool, shaded place for up to one month.

Grapes until Christmas In the past, gardeners on country estates kept grapes well into winter. To do this they cut individual bunches from the vine with a 30cm section of stem on either side. One end of the stem was placed in water in a specially designed bottle, so the grapes were supported at the neck; the other end of the stem was sealed with sealing wax. The bottles and grapes were stored on shelves in a cool, dry, well-ventilated room.

▶ To do the same, cut the grapes from the vine in a similar way. Place one end of the stem in water in a large champagne bottle and seal the other end using grafting mastic or candle wax. Drop a piece of charcoal in the water to purify it.

Indoor vines If you are intending to grow grapes in a greenhouse, it must face south or south-west. If your greenhouse is unheated, choose varieties that do not require extra heating, such as 'Chasselas d'Or', and maintain frost-free conditions. Allow space above head height for training and plenty of ventilation.

Exotic climbers

Add a bit of sunshine Kiwi fruit (*Actinidia*) is not widely grown in Europe. It was only introduced for fruit production in the 1960s. However, this Asiatic climber is well worth growing if you're in the south of England and have a sheltered spot. You'll also need plenty of sunshine to ripen the fruits. Don't be tempted to grow kiwi fruit under glass unless you have a very big greenhouse, as the annual growth can exceed nine metres. It isn't vulnerable to insects or disease, which makes it an ideal plant for the organic gardener.

▶ Kiwis flower in June, long after the last frosts. You may have to wait up to seven years for a good crop, but the fruit will be ready to pick in October, before winter sets in.

Kiwi and edible passion fruit

KIWI FRUIT
Bare-rooted plants are hard to come by but they do establish better than plants sold in pots.

Bruno A productive variety with large, elongated fruit.

Hayward ❶ This is a hardy plant with large fruits; it flowers late, which means fruit doesn't always have time to ripen in cooler regions.

PASSION FRUIT
This evergreen climber should be planted in spring, ideally in a greenhouse border.

Purple Granadilla ❷ A self-fertile variety, with deep purple fruit.

Sweet Granadilla A specialist plant with deep yellow fruit. It requires a controlled high temperature and humidity to grow well.

The flower of the passion fruit is remarkably ornamental, such as this flower of Passiflora edulis.

Beware of cats Once you've planted your kiwi fruit, you may notice local cats rolling near the base of the plant – cats are wild about the aroma released by the roots. They're only a serious threat to your plants if they sharpen their claws on the trunks, so it might be worth using protective sleeves.

Heavy stuff Kiwi fruit is surprisingly vigorous, a fact that you should bear in mind when building a pergola to support this fruiting climber.

▶ Make sure the structure is solid. The shoots can grow several metres a year, which not only means there is a lot of foliage to catch the wind, but also that the plant is extremely heavy.
▶ The ideal height for a pergola is 2.5 metres. Plant a kiwi at the base of just one of the uprights: one plant per pergola is heavy enough.

Passion flower, a South American beauty Only two members of the *Passifloraceae* family from Brazil and Peru produce edible fruits in Europe, the passion flower (*Passiflora caerulea*) and the passion fruit (*Passiflora edulis*). The first can be grown outdoors in warmer, southern regions, while the second is one for the greenhouse. The plant gets its name from the way it evokes Christ's Passion – the threadlike appendages recall the crown of thorns; the stamens, the sponge steeped in vinegar; and the stigmas, the nails of the cross.

Hothouse fruits Plant passion fruit in an internal greenhouse border, where the climbing stems can attain a length of six metres when trained along wires. Keep soil moist in winter and mulch in March. In summer, water freely, give light shading, and ventilate when the temperature exceeds 21°C. Syringe flowers with water to encourage fruits to set. Do all this and the egg-shaped purple or yellow fruits will ripen in August and September.

The fruit garden of your dreams

Few gardens now have the luxury of space for an orchard devoted exclusively to fruit trees, with fruit bushes and climbers planted elsewhere. But even if you don't have much room you can still, with careful planning, have a fruit garden that will take you through the seasons.

Using space wisely

The best position for a fruit garden In today's smaller gardens, all fruit plants – trees, bushes and climbers alike – are often planted together. Fruit gardens and orchards should, as far as possible, occupy an open space that is neither too wet nor susceptible to spring frosts.

▶ The best positions are on a south or west-facing slope, just below a sheltering wall or hedge.

▶ The worst positions are in a frost pocket or on waterlogged or frequently flooded ground – for example, on a slope just above a high wall, a tall hedge or a wood.

▶ Avoid the area to the south of your vegetable garden, as the tall fruit trees will cast shadows over your crops.

▶ If possible, don't choose a site that is isolated from other gardens. If you do, you are likely to suffer from more than your fair share of fruit-plundering birds, and your trees won't be pollinated by other fruit trees in the neighbourhood.

You don't need a huge garden to grow fruit – choose wisely and you can grow trees and soft fruit among your vegetables.

What to plant where Plant fruit trees in a lawn or meadow, but remember to leave enough space to mow the grass between the trees. Don't forget height either – some standards, especially cherries, can grow to 15 metres, whereas dwarf fruit trees may be so low that you have to duck when mowing, making it a better option to plant them in a border on their own.

▶ Plant espalier vines and trained soft fruit bushes against a sheltered, sunny wall.

▶ Plant cordon and fan gooseberries, blackcurrants and raspberries around the edge of the vegetable garden or in a fruit frame. Strawberries also go well in the vegetable garden.

Three old-fashioned tips for planting fruit trees

1 A large stone in the bottom of the hole will keep the tree from sinking when the soil is firmed down (see opposite).

2 A handful of cereal grain will germinate in the soil and give off hormones that promote the tree's root growth.

3 One or two crushed food tins in the hole form iron oxides and sulphates that will prevent the roots from rotting.

Check height and spread
A tree is a long-term commitment, so try not to plant one that will take up a lot of space in a small garden. You, or your successor, will be forced to cut it down prematurely as it outgrows its space. This is particularly true of walnut and cherry trees, both of which can eventually grow to at least 15 metres tall and spread to between 10 and 18 metres wide.

Ask the neighbours There's nothing better than taking a good look around the neighbourhood when you are planning a small orchard or fruit garden. To find out which species and cultivars thrive in your area, ask neighbouring gardeners for their recommendations as well as their advice on what should be avoided. Local farmers' markets also reflect what grows well in a region and may help you to choose trees and fruit bushes that will be happy and that are sure to produce fruit in abundance. But that doesn't stop you experimenting, trying some old varieties and using a bit of imagination.

Terms for trees Fruit trees have different forms, depending on their vigour and habit, and the size and structure required.
▶ **Standard** A tree growing freely on a trunk that is 1.8 metres to 2 metres tall.
▶ **Half standard** The same as a standard, with a trunk 1.2 metres to 1.6 metres tall.
▶ **Small standard or bush** A standard with a very short trunk. The vigour of the tree depends on the rootstock, which produces either a dwarf bush or one that develops much more freely.
▶ **Cordon** A single-stemmed tree with no framework branches, the fruit-bearing branches being arranged along the central leader. There are vertical cordons, those that are planted at a 45° angle and horizontal cordons, which are known as 'step-overs' as they can literally be stepped over.
▶ **Fan** A tree that has been trained to grow flat in a fan shape, either against a wall with wires or on a free-standing network of wires. A fan tree is a good, space-saving way to grow both cherries and plums.
▶ **Espalier** A tree trained flat against a wall on a framework of wires, with pairs of branches stretched out horizontally every 40cm or so like a ladder. This is a very formal way of training.

The ultimate size of a tree Before planting a group of fruit trees make a note of their eventual spread. When mature they will suffer if they are planted too close together. Fruit trees do, however, appreciate a pollinating partner nearby so that bees can dance from one tree to the next. You will get far more fruit if trees are in groups.

Planting a fruit tree

Buy your trees in autumn The current fashion is for container-grown trees that can be bought all year round. However, at certain times of year nurseries offer a wide choice of bare-rooted trees, which is a more traditional way to buy fruit trees. Although they are available throughout the period when the trees are dormant, they are best bought and planted in late autumn. They will then have the entire winter to put down the new roots they'll need to get away in spring.
▶ If possible, visit the nursery and choose the trees yourself. Select only those with shiny bark, a good root system and well-balanced branches in good condition.

Long-lasting stakes Stakes are vital if you do not want your young standards and half standards to blow over in the first gust of wind. Choose a stake that is as thick as your arm and long enough to sit just below the crown of the tree once it is hammered into the ground. Char the part that will be buried to prevent rotting (right).

A choice of trees to suit your garden		
Species	**The best type**	**Spacing**
Apple/pear	Standard or half standard	8m
Apple/pear	Bush, fan, espalier	3–4m
Apple/pear	Cordon	2.5m
Apricot	Half standard	5–6m
Cherry	Half standard or standard	5–6m
Fig	Small standard/bush	3–5m
Peach	Half standard	5–6m
Plum	Standard or half standard	5–6m
Quince	Half standard	5m
Walnut	Standard	15m

A precious stone Before you plant your tree, place a large stone in the bottom of the planting hole. It will serve as a wedge that prevents the tree sinking when the hole is filled in and the soil firmed down. It is bad for the roots to be planted too deeply – the uppermost roots should be almost level with the surface of the soil.

Planning a fruit garden

In wet soil, plant on a mound There's nothing worse for the roots of fruit trees than to be in permanently wet soil. You can create good drainage in heavy, waterlogged soil by building up a mound of soil to which you have added well-rotted compost. Then plant the tree in the mound so that its neck is 10–20cm above the surrounding ground level.

Recycle old tights In a fruit garden, you always need ties for securing a young trunk to a stake, or for training or supporting a branch. A perfect and inexpensive solution is to use old nylon stockings or tights. They form a wide, soft tie, and will not cause damage to the growing trunk.

Great expectations In some years, spring frosts and rain can result in a poor yield, especially for stone fruit trees.
▶ Standard apple trees tend to alternate naturally, producing fruit one year and not the next.
▶ Strong winds in spring and summer can impede the movement of pollinating insects and damage young fruits and shoots, reducing the yield. Improve shelter on exposed sites.

How much fruit will you get?

The amount of fruit produced by a tree will vary depending on its planting position and variety.

Species	Production per tree/bush/plant
Apple (tall)	Irregular: from nothing to over 100kg
Apricot	Irregular: from nothing to several dozen kilos
Blackberry	Regular: several kilos
Blackcurrant	Regular: 1–2kg
Cherry	Irregular: from several kilos to several dozen kilos
Hazelnut	Irregular: from nothing to several kilos
Kiwi	Regular: several kilos
Peach	Irregular: from nothing to over 10kg
Pear (small or medium)	Irregular: from several kilos to several dozen kilos
Pear (tall)	Regular: several dozen kilos
Plum	Irregular: from nothing to several dozen kilos
Quince	Irregular: from several kilos to several dozen kilos
Raspberry	Regular: several kilos per 10 square metres of canes
Redcurrant	Regular: 1–2 kilos
Vine	Regular: several kilos
Walnut	Irregular: from nothing to over 100kg

Increase fruit production and fill your fruit garden with a gentle hum by keeping a few beehives in the orchard.

To grass or not to grass Grass is a practical way to cover the ground in an orchard, since it provides a secure footing, even when it has rained, and offers a soft landing for any falling fruit. Grass also enriches the soil by continually manufacturing humus. Finally, it does away with the chore of weeding. All you have to do is cut it regularly – less often than an ornamental lawn – and you can even leave the grass cuttings on the ground. However, don't grass right up to the trunk or you may damage it with your mower or strimmer.

▶ There is a downside to grassing your orchard. The covering of meadow grass competes with the trees by absorbing some of the moisture from the soil, so it is best to grass between the rows and leave an area of bare soil around the base of the trees. In dry areas, you can cover the soil with a mulch of leaf-mould, bark or gravel to limit evaporation.

Protect the bark of young trees and bushes The bark of newly planted trees and bushes is susceptible to frost, and especially to thaws. If you live in a frost pocket, use this old-fashioned method of protection. Wrap trunks with straw, or paint them with a mixture of water and earth that has the consistency of a batter mixture. Adding milk to the mixture helps it stick to the trunk.

An ecologically friendly fruit garden

Working with nature You can improve the health and productivity of your fruit garden naturally, by planting shrubs, colourful flowers and herbs amongst the fruit to attract beneficial insects, birds and bees.

A fruitful hedge Recent scientific research has shown that certain trees and shrubs have a favourable effect on nearby orchards by providing a habitat for beneficial insects and birds that help to keep pests under control – something our forefathers knew all along.
▶ If you would like to enclose your orchard with an attractive flowering and fruiting hedge, choose several different species from this list: viburnum (*Viburnum tinus*), blackthorn (*Prunus spinosa*), crab apple (*Malus sylvestris* or *M. pumila*), quince (*Cydonia oblonga*), Judas tree (*Cercis siliquastrum*), alder (*Alnus*), bay laurel (*Laurus nobilis*), hawthorn (*Crataegus*), berberis, *Pyracantha coccinea*, hazelnut (*Corylus avellana*) and elderberry (*Sambucus nigra*).

Keeping bees Because they play an essential role in pollination, bees have been a feature of the orchard for centuries. In days gone by, it was the lucky orchard owner who had a hive under his trees. Beekeeping is a specialist hobby, but if you do want to take it up it will benefit your fruit trees and give you delicious honey.

Attractive plants Include buddlejas and lavender to attract pollinating bees; colourful, open-centred flowers for ladybirds; and marigolds (*Calendula*) and French marigolds (*Tagetes patula*) to attract lacewings and hoverflies.

Winter shelter for good friends Green lacewings, with their iridescent wings, can sometimes be seen on window panes in winter. They and their larvae are formidable predators when it comes to aphids, caterpillars and other orchard pests. Keep them in the garden to continue their good work by providing shelter, especially in winter.
▶ Fill a flowerpot with straw and hang in a tree to provide a winter retreat for lacewings.
▶ Some shrubs, such as mallow (*Lavatera olbia*), provide a good habitat for ladybirds to overwinter.
▶ Encourage hedgehogs – who keep slugs under control – by piling up a few logs in a quiet corner of the garden so they can hibernate. Make sure there is a cavity lined with dry leaves.

Four-legged lawnmowers Few of us have a large enough orchard or fruit garden for keeping sheep, but years ago they used to graze the grass under trees. One or two would happily keep an orchard trim, but make sure the boundary around your property is secure.

Planting a fruit tree

1 Dress the roots by soaking the entire root system in a mixture of well-rotted garden compost and water for an hour or so.

2 Cut out a circle of turf about 1m across and remove the topsoil.

3 Dig out a 50cm deep hole and arrange the lumps of turf upside down in the bottom. Trim any damaged roots from the tree.

4 Position the tree with the neck just above soil level. If necessary, put some topsoil back in the bottom of the hole to raise it a little.

5 Shovel some soil over the roots, gently shaking the tree so that it settles. Hammer in a stake between the roots, near the trunk.

6 Attach the tree to the stake, wedging a handful of straw between tree and stake where they touch. Fill in the hole and water well.

Three English beauties – apples, pears and quinces

If you were lucky enough to grow up with an apple or pear tree in your garden, you will probably want to continue the tradition. There is a shape to suit even the smallest space, and today's disease-resistant varieties make growing such fruit easier than ever before.

In a fruit garden, you can grow all kinds of tree types: a half standard apple is easy to pick from.

Getting the right shape

Trained trees for small gardens Trained flat against a wall or trellis, fruit trees take up relatively little space. Stretching the branches out horizontally produces an espalier tree, while fanning them out from the main branch produces the fan (see page 225). The 'step-over' – a form of cordon, or single-stemmed tree – is ideal along paths in the vegetable garden.
▶ You will need to prune most trees each year or they will lose their structured shape.

Save time on pruning If you don't want to prune every year and only have a small space to grow a fruit tree, plant trees grown on dwarfing rootstocks. Trees on an M27 rootstock will only reach 1.8 metres and M9 will reach 2.4 metres.
▶ If you have a large lawn or meadow, buy a half standard or standard tree with a long trunk (1.2–1.5 metres). You can let them grow relatively freely and prune lightly but regularly in winter every two or three years. This is the only suitable method for quinces, which need only occasional light pruning.

The art of hard pruning This kind of pruning removes quite a lot of wood. It is also known as three-budded pruning since it involves cutting apple and pear trees back to the third bud on fruit-bearing branches, and is recommended for artificially structured apple and pear trees such as cordons and fans.
▶ You need to take account of how vigorous the tree is before you prune it. If last year's growth was less than 50cm, then it is not particularly vigorous and will benefit from hard pruning. Prune in winter when the tree is dormant and cut back to three buds on each spur bearer, a lateral branch that grows on a framework or primary branch.

▶ If last year's growth was more than 50cm, then you are dealing with a vigorous tree that will be difficult to control with hard pruning. Bend the rules of three-budded pruning and don't cut back as hard, leaving four, five or six buds on each spur bearer.
▶ If trees have been neglected, the spur bearers are often multiple and complicated. Don't have any qualms about simplifying them by keeping only those closest to the framework branches.

Natural pruning Today, most commercial fruit growers don't use the hard-pruning method. They prefer to manage their trees more naturally, an example you could easily follow.
▶ Allow the fruit-bearing branches to produce fruit naturally and then prune a few each year by cutting back to just above a young lateral branch that will replace them. This is known as renewal pruning.
▶ If the spur bearers have a lot of fruit buds, you can also prune to limit the amount of fruit produced.

The quince revival
Favoured by the Victorians, the quince is a beautiful, modest tree, which is often used as a rootstock for pears. It provides light shade and produces magnificent flowers and aromatic, apple-like fruits used in making preserves.

An espalier pear is an ancient, formal shape.

A cordon apple is suitable for growing in the smallest of gardens.

A fan-shaped apple tree is perfect for a sunny wall.

Beautiful flowers mean bountiful fruit

Where have the flowers gone? The most common reason for a tree failing to flower is overpruning. If you want your trees to flower and produce fruit, put away your secateurs. At the very most, prune lightly, leaving at least six buds on each young branch. Because they are pruned only occasionally, quinces don't tend to suffer from this problem.

▶ There is another, natural, reason for a tree not producing blossom – it may be too young. It sometimes takes up to ten years for standard or half standard fruit trees to produce fruit, but only two to three years for smaller standards.

Don't forget about pollination Unlike the self-fertile quince, many apple and pear trees need pollinating. To produce fruit, the blossom on these trees must be fertilised by other very specific species whose pollen is transferred by bees and other pollinating insects such as butterflies.

▶ Ensure that the surrounding hedges contain bushes that will attract bees.

▶ Attract pollinating butterflies to your garden by providing a saucer of water and a bit of sugar or jam to feed on during the flowering period.

Pollinating companions When planning your orchard, make sure you have varieties that flower at the same time and that one is a good pollinator. 'Conference', 'Doyenne du Comice' and 'Beurré Hardy' are all good pollinating varieties of pear. 'Reine des Reinettes', 'Golden Delicious', 'James Grieve' and

'Cox's Orange Pippin' are pollinating apples. 'Evereste' is a pollinating crab apple. Crab apples have small fruit, which is used only for making jam or jelly.

▶ If there are lots of apple and pear trees growing nearby there's a good chance they will include varieties that will pollinate your trees.

Getting manure to the roots If you simply spread manure around the base of your trees, most of the nutrients will remain concentrated on the surface of the soil and only a small part will be absorbed quickly. To prevent this from happening, use a crowbar to make a series of holes, 20cm deep, at regular intervals at the base of the crown. Throw one or two handfuls of manure into each hole and water well.

Quince varieties

Champion ❶ A fertile tree, which fruits at a young age. Its medium-size, apple-shaped fruits ripen in midseason, have a delicate flavour and set rapidly.

Portugal An early variety with a bushy habit. It will flower again if the blossom is damaged by frost. Fruits are relatively large and pear-shaped.

Vranja A fertile, vigorous tree that will grow in a wide range of climatic conditions. The large yellow, pear-shaped fruit are strongly scented when ripe.

Protecting your fruit

Thin out at the right time

If they have been pollinated, all the flowers on an apple or pear tree can set, or form fruit. This will produce lots of tiny apples or pears, so it is essential to remove all but one of the fruitlets in a cluster to achieve good-sized fruits. Keep the fruitlet in the centre of the cluster for apples (left), and one on the edge of the cluster for pears.

Thin out in stages

Always thin out in two stages so that you do not traumatise the tree – a surge of sap to the remaining fruits could make them drop.

▶ Thin out pears first when the fruitlets are the size of hazelnuts and a second time when they are the size of walnuts.

▶ For apples, the fruit should be thinned out about a month after the tree has flowered, and then a second thinning should follow about a fortnight later.

▶ If you only thin out once, do it at the 'walnut' stage. Do not remove the fruit at the peduncle, or stalk, but cut the pear or apple in half, leaving part of the fruit on the tree (left).

▶ Quinces will fruit well without thinning out.

Preventing 'corky' apples There's nothing more unpleasant when you bite into an apple than coming across brown 'corky' patches in the middle of the fruit. These blemishes are caused by a lack of the trace element boron. Using completely natural manure or organic fertiliser will help to prevent these patches, which are often the result of adding large quantities of lime and potassium to the soil.

▶ If the deficiency is already apparent, try a rescue remedy of seaweed, which is rich in boron. It is available in powder and liquid form, the first for spreading around the base of the tree and the second for spraying on the leaves.

Say goodbye to canker Some varieties of apple tree are susceptible to a disease known as canker, which is particularly virulent in damp conditions and on badly drained soil. The telltale signs to look out for are brownish patches on young branches in winter, followed by the shrinking and cracking of the bark on the larger branches. The edges of the affected areas are transformed into a ridge and, eventually, the branches wither and die.

▶ Cut off and burn any affected young branches and use a pruning knife or well-sharpened knife to cut out the cankers on the larger branches until you expose the healthy wood. Apply a wash made from a mixture of garden soil and water, a product known as pine tar or an anticanker wound sealant.

Weigh down branches to get more apples The formation of fruit buds depends on the circulation of sap, which is in turn dependent on the angle of the branch. A vertical branch is more likely to make new wood than fruit. To reduce the circulation of sap and encourage fruit buds to form, reduce the angle of vertical branches by attaching weights to them such as baskets filled with pebbles or by tying them down with string attached to tent pegs. Try to get them as close to the horizontal as possible.

THE GARDENER'S CHOICE

Apples, pears and quinces ▶

Worcester Pearmain ❶ This apple fruits early and freely in September, producing bright red, sweet apples with firm, juicy white flesh. It is often used as a pollinator for 'Cox's Orange Pippin'.

Laxtons Fortune ❷ A self-fertile and strongly growing apple, with yellow fruits streaked with red and a flavour similar to that of a Cox. Trees can be susceptible to canker and may only produce fruit every other year.

Egremont Russet ❸ This apple crops heavily from late September to early October, producing golden yellow fruit with broken russet skin. Has a rich, sweet nutty flavour and crisp texture. Keeps for two or three months.

Conference ❹ The most widely grown late pear, it is a reliable cropper in October, and keeps well. The medium-sized fruits have a long neck and firm flesh.

Fertility Improved ❺ A self-fertile pear, producing a heavy crop of medium-sized, crisp, juicy and sweet pears in October. Can also be used for cooking.

Portugal ❻ A strongly growing quince tree, with early ripening, large yellow-orange pear-shaped fruit that turn red when cooked. Outstanding flavour.

'Bagging' your pears is a gentle, natural alternative to chemical treatment for protecting the fruit.

An anti-caterpillar belt In May and June, the codling moth lays its eggs on the leaves or young fruit of apple and pear trees. Its larvae – tiny caterpillars that tunnel into the fruit to eat the seeds – will leave your crop incurably worm-eaten.

▶ Prevent a second infestation by tying a strip of corrugated cardboard around the trunk of each of your apple, pear and quince trees. After feasting on your apples, the caterpillars will make their way down the trunk towards the ground where they will nestle in the cardboard, an ideal place for the larvae to turn into moths. In March or April, before the moths emerge from their chrysalises, remove the cardboard and burn it. In this way, you will destroy the next generation of codling moths.

▶ Another method of attracting and trapping codling moths is to hang sticky traps in the trees. These are available in various colours which attract different pests, and some have a pheromone scent which makes them even more effective. These sticky traps attract the codling moths, which then get stuck and can be disposed of.

Support the branches In heavy-cropping years, apples, pears and quinces can be quite literally weighed down with fruit. When this happens there is a risk of some of the framework branches breaking.

▶ You can prevent this by carefully lifting the branches and propping them on forked supports pushed into the ground (see page 242).

Preventive spraying for quinces In damp conditions, quinces are susceptible to fungal diseases that can cause the leaves and fruit to fall prematurely. Give your quince trees a

preventive spray of the organic Bordeaux Mixture – a mixture of copper sulphate and hydrated lime – just before they flower, and another just afterwards.

How to get perfect fruit In the early 20th century, before the introduction of chemical treatments, 'bagging' was widely used by commercial growers to protect their fruit. The method involves encasing each apple and pear – as soon as they reach the size of a walnut – in a paper bag or cone fastened around the stalk with an elastic band. This may be a laborious task but it is worth while.

▶ Fruit protected in this way isn't usually attacked by grubs and caterpillars, doesn't tend to have blemishes, ripens more quickly and is generally larger. Save up paper bags or make paper cones from old newspaper.

Storing fruit

Pick at the right time It is time to pick your fruit when the first few ripe apples or pears fall, not counting the ones that fall prematurely because they are caterpillar-eaten. Fruit is ripe when it comes away from the branch if twisted slightly.
▶ Quinces are ripe when their downy covering can be rubbed off easily by hand.

A useful gadget The fruit picker is a handy piece of equipment. It will save you having to climb or use a ladder when picking apples, pears and quinces at the end of the tallest branches of your fruit trees. Available from garden centres, it consists of a canvas or plastic bag that is fitted onto the end of a 3–4 metre handle. These bags have pliant prongs around the edge which catch the fruit stems, and with a gentle pull the fruit drops into the bag.

Handle with care Pick apples and pears carefully to avoid bruising them – otherwise they will not keep. Cup the fruit in your hand as you twist it from its branch.

Top tips for long-term storage Always harvest apples and pears in dry weather. Pick all the fruits before the first frosts as they cannot withstand temperatures below –3°C.
▶ **Discard damaged fruit** Examine apples carefully and put aside for stewing any damaged fruits.
▶ **Pack carefully** Place apples stalk down in a waxed cardboard tray. Make sure they do not touch.
▶ **Keep cool and dry** Put the trays in a well-ventilated, sheltered place for a few days so the fruit can really dry out, then store in a cool place such as a garage, cellar or outhouse.
▶ **Inspect regularly** Remove any that are beginning to rot.

Making preserves Since they are not eaten raw, quinces do not need to be stored as carefully as apples and pears. Use them soon after harvesting to make jellies and jam.

Composting damaged apples Fallen and damaged fruit usually contains larvae or bacteria, which become active after a few months spent on the surface of the soil and can be a welcome addition to the compost heap.
▶ Collect these apples, stamp on them to squash them, and then add them to the heap. The organisms already present in the heap will neutralise any harmful fungi and insects in the fruit, and you will be able to spread your well-rotted compost at the foot of your fruit trees the following autumn.
▶ Adding fruit to the compost heap also helps to accelerate the rate at which the material breaks down, as the sugar in the apples promotes fermentation of the compost.

Traditional autumn clear up As soon as the leaves begin to fall from your apple, pear and quince trees, run the lawn mower over the grass beneath the trees, leaving the cuttings. The shredded leaves will be a real treat for earthworms and will soon disappear into the soil. This is an ideal way of getting rid of all the scab bacteria – a disease that causes unsightly marks on the fruit and leaves – and reducing the following year's contamination.

To encourage your apple tree to produce abundant blossom, do not overprune it.

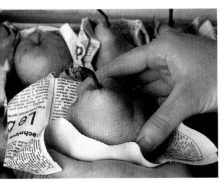

Storing pears After harvesting pears, place them in fruit crates and leave them to 'sweat' for a few days in a well-ventilated place. Then wrap them individually in paper and place carefully on fruit trays, in a cool, airy spot. Pears can be stored at a slightly higher temperature than apples, and keep well in an unused room in the house.

▶ For added protection, when the fruits have dried out completely dip the stalks in melted wax and leave them to dry. Removing the fruit stalk opens the way for disease; leave it in place to make the pear keep better and last longer.

Dried apple for winter snacks Drying fruit is an old-fashioned way of making the apple harvest last even longer and providing a rich source of vitamin C for the winter.

▶ Remove the core of the fruit and slice into rings about 5mm thick, without removing the peel. Dip each ring into a mixture of water and lemon juice, pat dry and thread onto a cane cut to fit between the shelf rests in your oven. When the cane is full, but not too tightly packed, place it in the oven on a low heat overnight. When they are dry, the rings can be removed from the cane and stored in paper bags.

Plenty of choice There are more than 2300 varieties of apple, 500 pears, 300 plums and 300 fruit bushes available. To ensure you buy the right variety of fruit for your needs, look out for local fruit-tasting days in your area. It is a good idea to visit specialist fruit nurseries as they will have a far wider choice than general garden centres.

Seasonal pears

There are three types of pear, based on the season when they are ripe and ready to eat, and their keeping qualities. Summer and autumn pears don't store well. Winter pears are picked in autumn, but will keep until January or February.

Summer pears These ripen in August and September. The best-known varieties are 'Docteur Jules Guyot' and 'Williams Bon Chrétien' ❶ (old variety).

Autumn pears These are ripe in October and November. This is the largest group and includes 'Concorde', 'Beurré Hardy' ❷ (old variety), 'Joséphine de Malines' (old variety) and 'Doyenné du Comice' (old variety).

Winter pears These ripen in October and November, but keep through winter if stored well. 'Conference', 'Winter Nelis' and 'Olivier de Serres', are all old varieties of dessert pear; 'Catillac' ❸, a culinary pear, keeps until May.

New plants from old

Before the rise of garden centres, a self-sufficient, old-fashioned gardener took it as a point of pride – if not necessity – to propagate new plants himself. All that is required to do the same is a little know-how and some patience. Here are a few traditional tips to make it simpler.

Cuttings take root

What is a cutting? Generally a cutting is a 15–30cm section of young stem taken from just above a leaf joint or node on the parent plant, then trimmed just below a node.
▶ A heel cutting consists of the young stem plus a strip of bark from the parent branch.

Natural rooting hormone Whether cuttings take root or not depends most of all on vegetable hormones. To help the roots to grow, make a notch in the base of your cuttings and insert a seed of corn or any other cereal. This seed will germinate on contact with the soil and spread growth hormones into its immediate area, which will help the cuttings to produce new roots.

A watery start in life Putting the base of a softwood cutting into a jar of water is a good way to make it sprout roots. This method also allows you to keep an eye on how the cutting is developing, so that you can plant it out as soon as the first roots show.
▶ To keep the water fresh, put in some pieces of charcoal – they will 'trap' the micro-organisms and stop them from multiplying.
▶ When placing the shoot in the jar, make sure no leaves are immersed in the water or they will rot and contaminate it.

Bury dormant cuttings upside down Hardwood cuttings are usually taken outside the growing period, which is not the best time to plant them. Keep them until spring by burying them completely in the ground. An old trick for encouraging future root growth is to bury them vertically, upside down. Mark the spot so you can dig them up and plant them in spring.

Plant at an angle If you have room, designate part of your garden a nursery bed. When you plant cuttings in the bed, position them at an angle with only the topmost bud above ground. This will ensure they have a good start.

Disentangle in water If the roots of cuttings growing in the same pot become entangled, remove as much earth as possible and soak the mesh of roots in a bowl of water. Once the soil has fallen away, you will be able to see the roots better and untangle them without causing damage.

Propagating by layering, suckers and division

A quick start for runners To ensure that your runners establish themselves quickly, do not leave them attached to the mother plant for too long. If you do, they will have developed too many roots and you will find it difficult to dig them out without damaging them. Runners produced in spring should be severed and planted out in October.

Do not layer with leafy stems Remove all the leaves from the section of runner to be buried or they will rot in the soil. This will delay, if not prevent, the formation of roots and new plants.

DID YOU KNOW?

The basics of asexual propagation

Asexual, or vegetative, methods of propagation produce exact replicas of the parent plant, unlike sowing, which is the sexual method of propagation.

Cuttings Planting a piece of young stem, or other part, taken from the mother plant so that it will take root. Nothing could be easier, but the procedure is not suitable for all species.

Layering Partially burying a young shoot still attached to the mother plant by runners, which produces roots.

Suckers Using a small tree or shrub that is attached to the underground stem of the mother plant and ready to develop.

Division Removing and replanting part of a clump, consisting at least of a bud and roots.

Propagating plants

Do not use old branches To be suitable for layering, a branch must be healthy and not the product of a rootstock that has been used for grafting. It also needs to be not more than two years old, otherwise its bark is likely to be too thick for the roots to pierce.

New hazelnut and raspberry bushes for free In winter cut the hazelnut or raspberry plant you want to propagate down to soil level. Then build a ridge of soil up over the remaining stump. When spring arrives you will find several shoots beginning to take root in the ridge. The following winter simply level out the ridge and cut all the runners and their roots from the mother plant and plant in position.

Suckers will create suckers
A sucker is merely a new tree or bush developing from the roots of an older one. Don't be confused by the idea that suckers suck the goodness out of the plants. In fruit gardening, suckers are desirable – they ensure your plant keeps fruiting.
▶ Dig up the sucker complete with some roots and replant it where you want it to grow. It will reproduce the characteristics of the tree or shrub that created it, unless the mother plant was grafted. Propagation with suckers is usual for morello cherry, hazelnut, strawberry and raspberry.
▶ Plants produced from suckers will tend to produce suckers themselves, which can make them invasive. Grow such plants in a tub or a corner of the garden on their own.

Divide to multiply Division means separating a mother plant into pieces, each piece complete with roots, so that you can replant separate, smaller plants. Division should take place in

Methods of propagating fruiting plants

Sowing	Cuttings	Suckers
Apricot (some)	Currant	Cherry (Morello)
Walnut	Fig	Hazelnut
Passion fruit	Vines	Strawberry
Peach (some)	Kiwi	Raspberry
Plum (some)	Passion fruit	

Division	Layering	Shield grafts
Currant	Blackberry	Apricot
Raspberry	Blackcurrant	Almond
	Fig	Apple
	Gooseberry	Cherry
	Hazelnut	Citrus fruits
	Vines	Medlar
	Loganberry	Peach
	Passion fruit	Pear
	Kiwi	Plum

the dormant period between October and March, but not in frosty weather. This technique is particularly suited to currant and raspberry bushes.
▶ Take a flat spade and drive it down between the young shoots emerging from the earth and the rest of the mother plant. Dig out one part of the divided clump with your spade and replant it, preserving as many roots as possible.
▶ Alternatively, lift the entire root from the ground and split it.

Willow water For centuries, old-fashioned herbalists have known of the amazing properties of the willow. The easiest of all woody plants to root, it produces powerful hormones that also help other plants to grow and develop.
▶ To make a willow water solution, in spring collect tender tips and leaves from a willow, cut them into 2–3cm pieces, and steep a few handfuls in a litre of water for a week. Strain the mixture into jars and store in a cool place.
▶ When propagating plants, dip fresh cuttings or roots in the solution for a few minutes before planting. Then water with the willow solution to give new plants an extra boost.

Healthy suckers have grown into a promising row of 'Glen Cova' raspberry canes.

Grafting fruit trees

What is rootstock? Rootstock is simply the stem and roots into which you implant a bud or fragment of stem – the graft – taken from a variety you want to reproduce. Amazingly, a rootstock can accept grafts that do not even belong to the same botanical species. For example, you can graft lilac onto ash, or a peach tree onto an almond or a plum tree. The rootstock will pass on some of its characteristics to the tree that results from the union. The new tree might, for instance, become better suited to chalky or dry soils because of the favourable characteristics of the rootstock, which is the reason it is selected. A rootstock's compatibility with a graft varies, just as with the transplanting of human organs, but most apple, pear and stone fruit trees are propagated in this way.

Grafting equipment

Traditionally, grafting was done with a special knife called a budding knife and the binding was raffia. Some gardeners now simply use a craft knife and adhesive or special polythene grafting tape. Wipe your knife with methylated spirits to prevent the spread of infection.

Buying stock to graft Winter is the best time to obtain your stock. A half standard or standard apple or pear tree is the most practical option for grafting onto.
► When buying rootstock, tell the nurseryman what form you wish to grow it in and the soil and growing conditions you have so that he can supply a suitable tree.
► When deciding where to plant a newly grafted tree, remember that it must remain in this interim position for one to three years before it is moved to its permanent home.

YESTERDAY & TODAY

Family trees ready to fruit

Today we are fortunate in having many specialist fruit nurseries that produce fruit trees on the correct rootstock. This means we can plant a tree and produce fruit faster than growing our own from scratch.

It is now even possible to buy an apple tree with two to four different but compatible varieties grafted onto one tree, meaning that you could pick the apple 'Cox's Orange Pippin' from the same tree as 'Spartan'. These are known as 'family trees'. This type of tree allows those with the smallest garden to plant just one tree and enjoy a range of different fruit. Cross-pollination is also ensured.

Only buy family trees from experts, as some varieties such as 'Golden Delicious' can take over a family tree – putting the right varieties together is an art.

Easy graft If you have not done grafting before, try shield-budding, sometimes known as T-budding. This involves inserting the graft – a strip of bark with a dormant 'eye' or bud on it from the variety of tree you wish to propagate – under the bark of the rootstock. This is one of the easiest grafts to carry out as long as the stock is compatible.

Shield-budding a pear tree

1 Cut a young branch from the tree and select a healthy bud. Detach the leaf, leaving the leafstalk, and slice under the bud, cutting a strip of bark without penetrating the wood.

2 Choose a place on the stock 5–10cm from the ground where the bark is smooth. With your knife, cut a T-shaped slit no deeper than the bark.

3 To enable the graft to be slipped inside the T, lift up both sides of the cut bark with the rounded tip of your knife.

4 With one hand lift the bark with a knife and with the other introduce the shield graft into the T so that the bud is pointing upwards, as it would naturally.

5 Gently ease the graft right into the slit, then fold over the two flaps of bark to enclose it.

6 Wind raffia several times around the cut area. If, ten days later, the leafstalk on the graft comes off easily, this shows that the operation has been successful.

Stone fruit – the taste of the sun

By growing an apricot, cherry, peach or plum tree you are bringing to your garden some of the most succulent summer delicacies. These luscious fruits were commonly grown in the past and deserve room in the modern garden.

Choosing a stone tree for your garden

The right growing conditions Plum and cherry trees grow well all over the country but require a sunny spot. Both prefer a moisture-retentive, free-draining soil, though cherries are not very successful in dry, sandy ground. Peaches and apricots, however, do require higher temperatures. Both can be grown in East Anglia and the South East of England trained as a fan against a sunny, protected wall, but rarely do well in the North unless protected areas of the garden or under glass. In the grand houses of the past, gardeners guaranteed success by growing them in large, unheated, 'lean-to' greenhouses, built against a south-facing wall in a kitchen garden.

Fruiting cherries are just as attractive as purely ornamental species and often have colourful foliage and bark as well.

The temperamental apricot Even in the most favourable soils, the quantity and quality of an apricot tree's production tends to be unpredictable. It does, however, self-fertilise, so you only need one.

▶ The apricot tree can blossom as early as February or March, depending on where it is planted, and therefore its flowers are liable to frost damage. If possible, plant a tree facing south, south-east or south-west but certainly not east: if you do, blossoms frozen during the night risk being roasted in the morning sun.

▶ If a frost is forecast, cover the trees with horticultural fleece.

A potted cherry As our gardens get smaller, there is a demand for small cherry trees. The most dwarfing rootstock is Colt, which reduces the height of most varieties to five metres. It isn't common to grow cherries and apricots in pots, but they can be happy in a large container with drainage holes, and rooted in a mixture of slightly clayey garden soil and a fairly sandy compost. You may have to bring apricots into a greenhouse or conservatory for winter.

Apricots to suit slightly cooler climates

Gold Cott A self-fertile variety with golden-yellow August fruits. It will cope with wet and cold British growing conditions.

Moorpark Large juicy apricots with late July fruits. It is not as hardy as 'Gold Cott' and needs an unheated greenhouse or a sunny, south-facing wall if grown outside. A good choice if you want to grow an old variety: it originated in 1760.

Alfred ❶ Medium to large apricots that are orange with a pink flush. Fruit in late July to early August. A vigorous tree.

The cherry tree – family matters

There are three types of cherry tree, which differ considerably in their fruit and overall appearance. Do you want to make jam, or to eat fruit straight from the tree? Make sure you know the difference to avoid planting the wrong type.

▶ **Sweet cherries** The descendants of the wild cherry tree produce sweet, large fruit which taste delicious straight from the tree. The trees are often far too large for modern or town gardens, but if you have room they are very decorative.

▶ **Sour or culinary cherries** These acid-tasting fruits with pink, red or white flesh are excellent for jam. They are descendants of the Morello (self-fertile) cherry.

▶ **'Real' cherries** Hybrids of the two types mentioned above, these cherries are quite large with a moderately acid flavour and tend to ripen late in the season. 'May Duke' is the most well known of this type.

Too tall for picking A cherry tree grafted onto a standard tree, one with a trunk 1.8–2 metres high, will be more likely to grow tall than the same tree grafted onto a half standard tree with a trunk 1.2–1.5 metres high. This is something to consider with future harvests in mind, since it is not always easy to pick the cherries growing at the end of high branches.

A smaller cherry tree

When grafted onto a wild cherry tree, a cultivated cherry will adapt to most kinds of soil, except excessively chalky ones. However, it will grow as tall as if it had been grafted onto a standard tree, and you could still have trouble reaching some of the branches, even with a ladder.

▶ To get a smaller tree, no bigger than seven metres in height, ask in the nursery for a cherry tree grafted

onto a Gisela 5 rootstock. In addition to its reduced size, grafts like this will take well in dry, poor, chalky soils.

Soil for stone fruit trees	
Fruit tree	**Preferred soil**
Apricot	Moisture-retentive, well-draining soils with a pH of 6.5–7.5
Cherry	Almost all, with a preference for good, well-draining soils 60–100cm deep with a pH of 6.5–7.5
Peach	Deep, well-drained medium-heavy loam with a pH of 6.5–7
Plum	A heavy clay loam, 60cm deep, with a pH of 6–6.5

Peaches in a pot The blackthorn is a thorny bush very common in the countryside. Years ago gardeners would use it as a rootstock for peach trees. They would shield graft onto it a bud taken from a healthy peach tree, and the result would be a very small tree, which could be cultivated in a large container on a terrace.

A hedge made of plum trees In some regions the plum tree is traditionally used in mixed rural hedges. The variety usually chosen is a wild one called *Prunus cerasifera*. Small and slightly thorny, it produces a mass of blossoms as winter draws to a close, which result in a multitude of perfectly edible small plums. If you are planting an informal mixed hedge in your garden, adding a few of these could make a tasty difference to the landscape.

Self-fertilising plum trees Some varieties of plum tree can be planted in isolation and produce plums without having to be pollinated by other varieties. These include the large-fruiting 'Jubilee', the cooking plum 'Marjorie's Seedling', the dessert 'Victoria' and the disease-resistant 'Purple Pershore'.

THE GARDENER'S CHOICE

Self-fertile cherries

Celeste A naturally smaller plant with really tasty fruits in early July. Its compact habit is ideal for a smaller garden.

Morello ❶ A favourite with the cooks. It fruits in August and, unlike many other fruits, will grow on a north-facing wall. It will pollinate nearly all other cherries.

Stella Tasty dessert fruits ripe for picking in July. This is another variety that will pollinate many other cherries.

Summer Sun The cherry to grow in the North, as it is very hardy. With its tasty fruits in July, this variety is becoming a popular choice for today's gardeners.

Getting the best fruit

How many years must you wait? Once planted, a stone fruit tree will not produce fruit immediately. It needs to develop its framework of branches before its young shoots can become fertile. You will have to wait three to four years before the first fruit appears, but it will take five to ten years, according to the species, before you obtain a substantial yield.

Juicier apricots Your apricots will be bigger and juicier if you give your tree four to six thorough waterings between 15 May and 15 September during dry weather.
▶ Water in line with the active roots, which means in a circle under the outer extent of the foliage.

Rainy day blues If the weather is consistently rainy as cherries ripen, there is a risk that they will burst as water is absorbed into the fruit. In rainy areas, choose varieties that are known to be less liable to burst.
▶ 'Early Rivers', as well as numerous varieties of Morello and other acid cherries are all resilient to this problem.
▶ To avoid causing bursting yourself, never water cherries just as they are ripening, nor afterwards.

How to ensure an abundance of cherries Think of the trunk of your cherry tree as a pipe transporting sap to the branches and the fruit. This sap flow is impaired by the bark of the tree, because its circular fibres tighten around the trunk.
▶ An old-fashioned tip for improving the flow of sap up the trunk of a young cherry tree is to cut four vertical slits around the trunk about halfway up. This will cause the bark to swell and rapidly form a new surface, but it will have relieved its stranglehold on the trunk.

A cherry-picking tip The first cherries ripen about 40 days after the tree has blossomed, and for a single variety the harvest lasts for about three weeks. When picking them, avoid tearing off the stalk the cherry hangs on, because that is where the buds will grow that will produce next year's fruit.

Planning your plum harvest

When you are choosing plum trees for your garden it is worth bearing in mind when they fruit. If you regularly holiday during August (when most plums ripen) you'll need to plant early or late fruiters, as the fruit won't wait to be picked and you'll lose your crop.

An early fruiter is the very old variety 'Mirabelle de Nancy', ripening in early August. The well-known, self-fertile 'Victoria' fruits in late August. Another old favourite, introduced in 1830, is 'Kirke's Blue', which fruits in early September. This old-timer is pollinated by another old variety, the cooking plum 'Czar', which fruits at the same time.

Fruit trees for all occasions ▶

Peach A fruit tree that was traditionally grown in kitchen gardens. 'Rochester' ❶ produces medium-sized fruit at the start of August. 'Peregrine' ❺ ripens in mid-August and has large, highly flavoured fruit.

Cherry Best in a large garden, unless grown on a dwarf rootstock or trained as a fan on a sunny wall. One of the best varieties is 'Stella' ❷.

Plum For a taste of the countryside, the plum has long been a favourite, as is this self-fertile 'Victoria' ❸ variety. Gages are also a type of plum. They are generally sweeter but cultivated in the same way. Merton Gage ❹ is a lesser known variety; it is self-fertile and ideal for use in desserts.

Nectarine Grown in the same way as a peach tree, 'Lord Napier' ❻ is a highly flavoured nectarine with pale green flesh that ripens in early August. Can be grown outdoors.

Barren plums If your plum tree is not producing plums, the first thing to consider is whether it is bearing blossom, as there can be no fruit without flowers.
▶ If your plum tree is not producing blossom, it is either because it is still too young – less than three or four years old – or because it is growing too vigorously. If the latter is true, 'calm it down' by sawing off one or two large roots growing just below the surface. To find them, dig a trench part way round the tree beneath the outer edge of the foliage. This is called root pruning.
▶ If there are flowers, the lack of fruit might be caused by the absence of a pollinating variety nearby. If that is the case, plant a good pollinating plum tree such as 'Oullin's Golden Gage', close by. The absence of fruit, however, might also be the result of bad weather when the tree was in blossom.

Thinning for perfect fruit If the branches of your plum tree are overloaded with fruit, you will need to consider thinning out the overloaded parts to ensure that the remaining fruit develops normally.
▶ Do not thin out until after June, which is when the fruit naturally drops. Sometimes things can safely be left to nature.
▶ Any fruit that is awkwardly placed or particularly small should be the first to be thinned out. Only keep six to ten fruits per metre on the main branches.

Pruning stone fruit trees

The limits of pruning If your cherry is growing to a giant size, you will not force it to stay small by repeatedly cutting it back. This will just limit the cherry crop and permanently harm the tree. You need to replace the tree with one that is naturally smaller.

The right time to prune a cherry If you cut large branches off your cherry tree, you risk exposing it to pests and diseases.
▶ Help the wounds to heal by pruning from July to the end of September, after the harvest, when the sap is descending. Never prune in winter as silver leaf disease may enter the tree via pruning cuts.
▶ If you forget to loosen the ties attaching a young cherry tree to its support, the trunk may look quite deformed. Loosen the tie and the trunk will gradually return to its normal shape. If you leave it for years the trunk will be scarred for good.

It is easiest to prune peach trees when they are in blossom.

Autumn clearance
After the leaves have fallen, remove all fruit 'mummified' by disease and still on the trees. These shrivelled fruits carry disease and are potential sources of further contamination.

Top tips for pruning peaches When you buy a new peach or nectarine tree, select a well-balanced specimen with at least four healthy laterals. This will make it much easier to perform the essential early pruning, and you will end up with a much better-shaped tree.
▶ **After planting** In the first spring cut back the main leading shoot just above a strong lateral, leaving at least four healthy laterals. This will prevent a very tall, spindly tree developing and encourage a neat rounded tree instead.
▶ **Removing shoots** Take out any shoots that have grown below the main head of the tree, cutting flush with the trunk.
▶ **Shortening lateral shoots** Cut back by two-thirds to an outward-facing bud. Remove any weak or damaged laterals.
▶ **Annual pruning** In the second spring, prune the main laterals and sub-laterals by half to an outward-facing bud. Hard annual pruning keeps the tree's growth in check and ensures the tree doesn't become bare in the centre.

Prune your peach trees when they are in blossom With a mature, fruiting tree (usually more than three years old), this is the best way of seeing where to prune, since it is the presence and number of blossoms that determines where to cut. As you cut away sections of branch with blossom on it, you are thinning out the future fruit, so the fruit that remains will be bigger and better. This late pruning also reduces problems from diseases attacking your tree.

Cruel to be kind To ensure that fruit doesn't grow at the ends of the stems on a peach tree, making them spindly and weighing them down, always cut off the early buds that appear at the tips of the previous year's shoots. Spare the fruit-bearing buds at the base of the shoots and you'll get a good crop of peaches and a tidy tree.

The easy-care plum tree The plum does not need to be pruned to produce plenty of fruit and does not like having its branches cut back, because this causes it to discharge gum.
▶ Prune lightly to keep the tree in shape when the sap is falling, between harvest and leaf fall.

Propping an overladen branch In a year when your tree is fruiting heavily, the branches may become bowed down with the fruit. Unless supported, they are liable to break under the weight.
▶ Rest the branch on a forked piece of wood (right), or strap it to the top of a support, and prop it up against level ground.
▶ For a branch on a low tree an inverted rake makes a good improvised support.
▶ Props are not very secure, so watch they don't collapse when the branches are being buffeted by strong winds.

Growing healthy trees

A bitter taste Rue has a reputation for being bitter. Take advantage of this characteristic by planting the perennial at the foot of your stone fruit trees. It will protect them from aphids, which establish their colonies on young shoots. It is thought that a bitter constituent from the rue passes into the tree's sap through its roots, and repels the aphids.

Spotting silver leaf Silver leaf is a common problem for plums and cherries: it is a fungal infection that turns the leaves silver. In advanced cases, the branches may be dead and the bark a home to growths of purple fungi. If the bark of a tree looks healthy but the leaves are silver, the tree may simply be showing signs of needing a general-purpose garden feed.
▶ There is no effective treatment for silver leaf, so remove badly blighted branches, preferably in summer, and burn them. Disinfect your pruning knife or secateurs afterwards. If the whole tree is affected it should be felled and burnt. Plums with the 'Pixie' rootstock have resistance to silver leaf.

A barrier against ants
Did you know that it is usually ants that bring aphids to fruit trees? Ants actually 'import' aphids so that they can consume the sweet honeydew that the aphids secrete when sucking the sap from their host plant.
Wrap grease bands, available from garden centres, around the tree trunks to keep the ants and other pests at bay.

Use a trap for plum-eating larvae

 To deal specifically with codling moths, whose larvae tunnel into fruit, professional tree growers put pheromone traps in their orchards. A sticky strip, covered with a substance that attracts the males, traps the larvae. These traps are now available to amateur gardeners. The traps kill the moths and so you avoid the need to spray.

▶ Check the manufacturer's information for the age of the tree the grease can be used on; young trees may absorb the substance through their developing bark.

Precious calcium Calcium helps fruit stones to form, which is why apricot, cherry, peach and plum trees always benefit from fertiliser rich in the substance, unless the soil is naturally chalky and already rich in calcium carbonate.
▶ Make a series of holes 25–30cm deep around the base of the tree, and pour into each hole one or two handfuls of a calcium or lime-rich fertiliser, such as powdered bone, natural phosphate or ground chalk. Water well. Most modern plant feeds have calcium as an ingredient.

Beware of broken branches Often, large branches will break off at the base, particularly on cherry and plum trees. This is usually because too many large branches were left on the tree when it was young, a problem made worse by the branches rubbing against each other. Prune a tree into shape during the first three years of its life: keep only those branches growing at an angle away from neighbouring ones.

Protect peaches from leaf curl Certain plants have a protective effect on fruit trees. Plant garlic, nasturtiums or tansy (right), a yellow-flowered member of the *Compositae* family, at the foot of your peach trees. This will help to overcome attacks of leaf curl, a very common disease caused by a microscopic fungus.
▶ Some trace elements help trees to stay healthy. Zinc, for example, is good for peach trees. Gardeners of old would spread a few zinc filings around the foot of their peaches, and rainwater would draw the beneficial metal down to the roots.
▶ Choose the variety 'Hylands Peach', which has tasty white flesh and was bred to be resistant to peach leaf curl. 'Rochester' has some resistance and offers a late crop of fruit.

Control whitefly naturally Plant tobacco plants among your fruit trees to attract whitefly. The sticky flowers and foliage are a natural trap.

Protect your apricot trees Apricot trees are prone to verticillium wilt. To help prevent this problem, do not plant them close to vegetables or dahlias, which can harbour the germs. In case of attack, which produces a sudden withering of the leaves, cut off and burn the affected branch or branches as soon as you notice the symptoms.

Are whole branches of your apricot tree failing? This often happens, and it does not mean that your tree is lost. To help it recover, cut back the old branches so that only a few centimetres are left, and preserve any suckers. The stumps will soon start growing again and will produce new branches.

Old-fashioned fruits full of charm

Fig, medlar, mulberry and citrus trees were 19th-century favourites that are now enjoying something of a revival. To be successful with these fruits you must take a little extra care, but there are some tried-and-tested techniques to help you establish them in your garden.

Growing a fig tree

A successful crop The good news about growing figs is that they do not require a pollinating partner and they can grow in nearly all British soils, as long as they are free-draining. Also, pests and diseases rarely affect them. Growing figs only gets complicated when you want to harvest fruit every year rather than growing them simply as an ornamental plant.
▶ To produce a good crop of fruit the roots need to be restricted by either growing the tree in a pot or by lining the planting hole with paving slabs.
▶ In the South of England figs will grow happily against a sunny wall, while in the Midlands you can have success if you find a really sheltered, sunny spot. Figs will need protection from the frost to avoid damage – nowadays this can easily be done by covering with horticultural fleece.

Varieties to look for The most commonly sold fig for outdoor use is the very hardy 'Brown Turkey', a variety that ripens in August to September. Another hardy fig is 'White Marseilles', which has early fruit with white flesh and an excellent flavour. This fig is often successfully grown in a pot. In the greenhouse opt for 'Rouge de Bordeaux', which has purplish-green fruits. Figs are commonly sold already fan-trained for planting against a wall.

UNDER GLASS

A greenhouse giant

In the past, it was quite common for figs to be grown under glass. However, as they have very large leaves they may cast too much shade over other crops in a domestic greenhouse filled with mixed plants. But if you have room for a plant and you can keep the temperature constant, your fig tree should produce abundant fruit.

Wear gloves when picking figs: the sap in their leaves and leafstalks irritates the skin.

Dry and chalky soil for a fig tree Although it is particular when it comes to climate, the fig tree, once settled, grows happily in the most barren of city garden soils.
▶ The best time to plant is in early spring when the risk of heavy frosts has passed. Plant in a deep hole with a layer of stones at the bottom and paving slabs to the sides to restrict root growth. Water copiously in its first summer.

Low-maintenance pruning Mature figs need little pruning – simply remove any shoots that are crowding each other and preventing a good airflow around the branches.
▶ After the first crop on a new tree, pinch out the lateral shoots, leaving a shoot with four leaves on. This will encourage replacement fruit-producing stems.

Growing figs in a barrel If you intend to move house in the near future plant your fig in a barrel so it can go with you. The barrel should have a capacity of at least 50 litres and be filled with ordinary soil. It also needs to have handles so you can move it about, and drainage holes drilled in the bottom.
▶ Place the barrel with its plant in a cool, well-aired, frost-free place as soon as the leaves start to fall, and keep it there until the following May before moving it to a sheltered spot.
▶ Make sure that the soil in the barrel does not dry out.

Winter protection As long as it is not too big, you can protect the branches of your fig tree from heavy frosts. Draw the branches together, tie them with rope and cover for winter with corrugated cardboard, plastic bubble wrap or garden fleece. Pile up leaves as a warming mulch around the base.

Taking cuttings from a fig tree In winter cut off one of the previous year's shoots complete with its heel – a fragment of bark – and a terminal bud. Plant out the cutting, protecting it from frost with dead leaves or straw.

Victorian fancies

Citrus trees need winter warmth These trees are the least hardy species grown in Britain and cannot tolerate temperatures below zero. Don't try to plant them outdoors.

Planting in pots Citrus trees were once the speciality of gardeners who worked in stately homes and had access to an orangery, where these delicate plants could spend the winter. However, a conservatory can be just as effective.
▶ Plant your citruses in large pots or tubs with 50cm sides and fill with appropriate compost (see below). Bring them indoors in September and keep them there until the end of May so that they escape the frosts.
▶ Water citrus trees twice a week with soft water (rainwater is ideal) until the warm, dry weather returns.

The right fertiliser for citrus trees Old gardening manuals discuss at great length which are the best soils and composts for these potted trees, but a balanced mixture of clayey soil, river soil, fine sharp sand, coarse sand and very well-rotted manure does the job admirably. It is not always easy to find all these different ingredients, however. These days, there are special citrus fertilisers available commercially as well as soluble fertilisers for use when watering.

Treatment for falling leaves If the leaves of your container-grown orange or lemon tree shrivel up and fall, it could be the result of too much water, lack of light, a sudden change in temperature or a very dry atmosphere. Place the pot on a bed

Citrus trees to grow indoors

Some varieties of orange and lemon trees can grow in a large pot on a veranda or in a room where there is plenty of light, such as a conservatory.

The Calamondin orange tree A hybrid of a kumquat (*Fortunella*) and a bitter orange. The oranges are small but perfect for jam. The tree requires a temperature of 13–15°C in winter and 18°C when the fruit is growing.

The Meyer lemon tree One of the most common varieties, with fruit the size of an egg. It needs a minimum of 10°C.

The kumquat A very decorative shrub, which is fairly resistant to the cold. It produces small, elongated fruits that can be eaten raw, skin included.

of wet gravel, only water when the compost has dried out, and spray the leaves as often as possible with lukewarm water. The fallen leaves will soon be replaced by new ones.

Getting a sterile orange tree to bear fruit An old-fashioned treatment was to give it zinc, a vital trace element sometimes lacking in the soil.
▶ To enable the beneficial metal to pass into the tree's sap, cut a slit in the bark with a very sharp knife and insert a pinch of zinc filings. Your orange tree will be encouraged to develop flowers and will eventually fruit.

Fruiting trees from another age Your great-grandmother might have had one of these trees in her garden.

▶ **Medlar** A thorny bush, the medlar has a cultivated cousin called the large-fruited medlar. It is a beautiful tree of modest dimensions, growing slowly and with a rounded head of branches. It is self-fertile, so fruits readily without cross-pollination. The flowers are borne in May or June and the hardy-looking fruit (left) follows in autumn. Wait until the first frosts have softened the fruit before picking. Medlars make delicious jellies.

▶ **Mulberry** The mulberry tree has been grown in Britain for hundreds of years. Before planting, bear in mind that many varieties are vast trees with a height and spread of over six metres, and that you will have to wait up to seven years for fruit. If you have a very large lawn and want a specimen tree then opt for the black mulberry rather than the smaller, but less tasty white. A self-fertile tree that suffers little from pests or diseases, it produces fruit in late summer, which can be eaten fresh or frozen. Pick the fruit when fully ripe, or lay plastic sheeting weighed down with stones under the tree and let the fruit drop. But be warned: mulberry juice stains clothes and is impossible to remove. It does, however, make good jam and is very high in vitamin C.

Nuts for the harvest

Once, no well-stocked garden would be without a nut tree. They have fallen from favour, but you can revive this tradition by planting a tree that will yield a hearty crop for decades to come.

The mighty walnut

An act of faith in the future A walnut does not produce its first nuts for 15 to 20 years and achieves its best yields only after about 60 years. It can live to the grand old age of 300 – quite a legacy for any gardener to leave behind. Trees grafted onto the American walnut tree, or hickory, produce nuts more rapidly but their life expectancy is no more than 30 years.

Harvesting walnuts For pickling, gather the nuts in autumn, before they harden. Otherwise, gather nuts after they drop, remove the husk, clean the nuts carefully and dry in an airy room. Store in containers, between layers of sand or sprinkled with salt.
▶ To avoid getting stained by the husks when you harvest walnuts, spread sacking under the tree then knock down the nuts with a pole. You will then be able to carry away the crop without touching it.
▶ The time-honoured way of removing walnuts from their husks is to pile them on hard soil and rake through them every day. It will not be long before the husks split and fall off. Then simply spread the walnuts out in the sun to dry.

The walnut tree takes time to produce its first fruit, but it can live for three hundred years.

A grand old tree If you inherit an old walnut tree that's in bad shape, remove damaged branches with a sharp saw to avoid introducing pests and diseases. It is important to note, especially in a small garden, that walnut tree roots produce a toxic chemical that will poison nearby fruit trees. This explains why, in very old gardens, it may be the only tree remaining. But this is no reason to cut down such an ancient tree – walnuts were roasted in the Neolithic period 8000 years ago, and the dark juice of the nut has been used to dye wool for centuries. Just site other fruit trees at a distance.

Well-timed pruning Choose the right time, and prune only lightly. If branches are cut off in autumn or winter, the wounds heal badly and start to rot. If the tree is pruned in spring, its wounds weep large amounts of sap. But there is a 'window' between June and August when pruning is possible.

Growing from seed Believe it or not, one of the easiest ways of propagating walnuts is by seed – that is, by sowing the nut itself (see opposite). However, the tree produced is very often not quite the same as the tree that bore the fruit, although the new one usually provides good crops.

Take care of fragile roots The walnut tree grows well and it seems that only high altitude and extreme summer drought can trouble it. However, it is seldom a good idea to transplant a tree grown from a seed, because its taproot system means that it is not certain to recover. It is better to leave seed-grown trees in place, so the taproot can dig deep down into the soil.

Hazelnuts and almonds

Winter hardy Whether you call them hazelnuts, cob-nuts or filberts, only hazel trees that are resistant to frost should be planted in areas where winters are hard. They will develop catkins in the middle of winter, sometimes even in December.
▶ The best varieties to choose are 'Cosford Cob', 'Gunslebert' and 'Ennis'. Wild hazel is more hardy than cultivated varieties, but it produces smaller nuts.

Prune your hazel tree now and again
In winter, saw off one or two large branches at the base to allow younger ones to grow stronger. Stand on a firmly placed ladder to cut the top off vertical branches just above a lateral shoot.

No more maggots The grubs of a tiny weevil, a kind of beetle, eat the kernel of the hazelnut (below) just as it is beginning to grow, causing the nut to fall prematurely. This insect is very difficult to deal with. Unless you have hens to peck under the trees, you will have to hoe the surface of the ground during winter to destroy the grubs.
▶ In May and June, paint sticky strips around all the branches of your hazel tree to trap insects as they climb into the tree – car grease is ideal for the purpose.

Safe keeping To prevent the residual dampness in the shells from causing mould that would spoil the taste of hazelnuts, remove their little cuplike shells (left) after harvest. Then every day for at least a week, spread the nuts out in the sunshine on a piece of canvas, bringing them in at night. When fully dry, store them in a dry place.

Plant two hazel trees for a plentiful harvest A good crop of hazelnuts depends on cross-pollination. Be sure to have two complementary varieties of the tree close together so the pollen from the catkins is carried from tree to tree by the wind. 'Cosford Cob' is a good pollinator for most other trees, and 'Gunslebert' pollinates 'Cosford Cob'.

Almond in blossom Almond trees can be bought and grown in Britain but they won't do as well as in Mediterranean countries. The reason for this is that *Prunus dulcis* has very early spring blossom, which is often damaged by frosts and if that happens you're unlikely to get fruit. The other common problem is that, even if they produce fruit, British gardens don't often have enough sunshine to ripen the fruits. But the blossom is so stunning that they are still worth growing if you live in a milder southern county.

Success with almonds Most almonds will produce more fruit if they are planted with another almond nearby. Avoid planting in ground that gets very wet in winter and choose the sunniest spot in the garden for success. The most popular variety is 'Phoebe', which has stunning pink blossom and is resistant to peach leaf curl.

Germinating by stratification

1 In autumn, take walnuts, hazelnuts or almonds out of their shells. Put slightly wet sand or light earth in a pot and place the nuts on it.

2 Cover them with a layer of sand or earth. You may be able to make several layers of nuts and sand.

3 Bury the pot at the foot of a north-facing wall, so that the sun does not heat it. The cold will start the process of germination.

4 Cover with a piece of board and set a large stone on it to deter rodents. By May the seeds will sprout and you will be able to plant them up in separate pots.

Enemies in the garden

Like all living things, plants have their enemies. The gardener's job is to prevent and cure problems to ensure a healthy garden, without harming the environment – and there are some interesting old techniques to try.

Bird boxes will encourage tits into your garden: a welcome feathered pest patrol.

Insect pests

Wash off aphids If small plants or shrubs are infested with aphids, sprinkle them with wood ash or talc. The next day hose down the plants that have been treated.

Prevent pests from climbing tree trunks Grease bands placed around trunks at 30cm from the ground, prevent climbing pests, such as the wingless females of the winter moth, from reaching the branches. Apply the bands from October to January, when the moths emerge to lay their eggs.

Welcome useful insects Beneficial insects, such as ladybirds and lacewings, which feed on aphids and other pests, cannot prevent these insects from proliferating but they ease the problem by keeping their numbers at a manageable level. Most helpful insects need flowers to feed on when they reach the adult stage, so offer them the ones they prefer: *Compositae* (sunflowers, marigolds, asters, cosmos, and oxeye daisies) or *Umbelliferae* (wild carrots, fennel and angelica).

A bird box for tits is a must Did you know that just two tits can keep apple maggots in check? Encourage them into your garden by putting up at least one nesting box in a quiet, sheltered spot in the garden. Its main features should be an opening 3cm in diameter and wooden walls 2cm thick.

Aphids on the run Aphids are discouraged by the extreme bitterness of aloe, a plant from hot desert regions. Dissolve 1g of aloe resin (available from a herbalist or hardware shop) in one litre of water and use a large paintbrush to cover the trunk and branches of vulnerable trees with the mixture.

A sex trap for codling moths The caterpillars of codling moths can decimate your pear, apple and plum trees by burrowing into the mature fruit. You can buy traps baited with capsules that give off pheromones – synthetic sexual substances similar to those given off by the females – capable of attracting male codling moths from a great distance. Use these from April to August to catch the male moths and reduce the mating chances of the females.

Trap flies If a swarm of tiny flies billows up as soon as you approach your pelargoniums, gerberas or busy lizzies (*Impatiens*) then white flies have probably been up to no good! The young larvae of these tiny insects eventually weaken plants by feeding on their sap. An alternative to using insecticides is to put out sticky yellow cards to trap the flies.

Weed out nuisances

Combating a persistent weed The convolvulus is perhaps the most difficult of all weeds to remove, especially in shrubberies as it is impossible to pull up its deep rhizomes. One solution is 'spot', or very precise, treatment. Wait until there is no wind, and then, with a small paintbrush, dab a little systemic weedkiller on as many leaves as you can.
▶ To get rid of convolvulus in the vegetable garden, use the false sowing technique: after one crop has been harvested, allow the weeds to grow and then hit them hard with systemic weedkiller. Repeat the operation after the next crop to kill off the tough ones that survived the first treatment.

Pull them up at the right time Thistles and brambles are prime examples of intrusive plants. There is a moment in their life cycle after they have flowered when their vital reserves are low. This is the time to pull them up if you want to get the better of them. Deal with thistles between mid-August and early September. As for brambles, it is best to remove them in the last week of June.

In hot water To get rid of weeds between paving stones and in the cracks of cement, there is nothing more effective and environmentally friendly as boiling water. Pour the water used to cook your potatoes, pasta or artichokes over these weeds while it is as hot as possible, taking care not to burn yourself.

Water the ground the day before weeding The roots will be easier to pull up and it will be less disruptive for nearby plants you want to keep.

Stifle couch grass with nasturtiums Plant climbing nasturtiums for three consecutive years where couch grass is a problem and let them grow along the ground. The couch grass, deprived of air and light, will eventually die.

Weedkilling plants There are some plants in the vegetable garden that help to kill weeds. The potato has a reputation for doing this, and the pumpkin makes a good ally because of its dense foliage. However, it is the tomato that most deserves to be a called a weedkiller: wherever it grows, it drives away convolvulus and couch grass.

You can't beat hand weeding Not many weedkillers can do a better job than hand weeding. Keep on top of weeds and hoe them off as soon as they appear. Remove the roots of very vigorous weeds from the soil with the help of an old-fashioned soil sieve. The tiniest section of convolvulus root can create a new plant. Remove perennial weeds before they flower and set seed to produce yet more plants to plague you the following year.

Combating plant disease

Use flour against honey fungus Clumps of yellow, shiny mushrooms, which suddenly appear at the foot of a tree indicate a case of the often fatal disease honey fungus, or *Armillaria mellea*.
To combat it, spread plenty of flour or starch (available from chemists and hardware shops), at the foot of your trees. The starchy substance will encourage the proliferation of another fungus, called *Trichoderma*, which is hostile to the honey fungus and will help to destroy it.

Make sure you choose a suitable climate Fruit tree diseases are particularly common in years when we have a cool, damp summer. If you live in an area with these climatic conditions, there is no point in struggling to grow tender trees like the apricot, unless you can offer them a very sheltered position.

Good hygiene and stress relief Apple trees are susceptible to scab and mildew. Good hygiene is vital in the control of these and most other diseases. Collect up and remove all leaves, fallen fruit and prunings from around the plants. Make sure they get enough water and boost their defences with plenty of nutrients by applying a generous organic mulch and fertiliser over the plant roots.
▶ Feed regularly to produce strong, healthy disease-resistant growth. Liquid nettle manure (see page 255) is rich in soluble nutrients that will be a tonic to most plants.

Pests and diseases of fruit

There is nothing more satisfying than growing and eating your own fruit. However, this satisfaction is considerably compromised if there is a bug inside!

Roots

CROWN GALL This bacterial disease causes whitish swellings on the roots of trees and at the base of the trunk. The swellings can grow as large as footballs, then turn black and rot. The vigour of the tree is not affected and there are no signs of disease on the leaves or shoots. The bacteria enters the tree through a wound. See page 150.

Trunks and branches

ANTHRACNOSE

This fungal disease affects currants and raspberries as well as trees. The bark splits and white patches with purple-tinged edges appear. The canes and branches eventually dry up. Precise symptoms vary slightly with the host plant and the particular fungus involved. See page 150.

BARK BEETLES The larvae of the bark (or engraver) beetles (insect family *Scolytidae*) bore into several species of fruit tree and can be extremely destructive. Their presence is indicated by a series of tunnels beneath the bark, running in all directions from a central point. These tunnels are formed by the newly hatched larvae as they bore away from the egg chamber. See page 150.

CANE BLIGHT
▶ **Symptoms** Fruit canes turn brown at the base and the extremities wither. The entire cane is soon affected by the disease and becomes brittle, making it easy to snap. This blight is caused by a fungus, *Leptosphaeria coniothyrium*, which usually enters the cane through frost cracks. It can also contaminate surrounding soil.
▶ **Plant affected** Raspberry, particularly 'Norfolk Giant' and 'Lloyd George'.
▶ **Treatment** Depending on the seriousness of the attack, one or several sprayings with a copper-based fungicide may eliminate the disease. However, it can be more effective to cut back the infected cane to below ground level and burn it. Disinfect your pruning tools afterwards. Plant a resistant raspberry variety.

CANKER

Cracks form on the bark, which become gradually wider, sometimes forming raised edges. The diseased tissue from underneath appears and a whitish gum oozes from the cankers. The diseased branch, and sometimes the entire tree or bush, withers and dies. See page 150.

CLEARWING MOTH

▶ **Symptoms** Shoots become brittle and, when broken, reveal a hollow, black interior. This is because the pith has been eaten by the white caterpillar of the clearwing moth (*Synanthedon tipuliformis*). The adult moth looks rather like a wasp. The larvae burrow into the shoots and pupate the following year; exit holes can be seen on stems in early summer.
▶ **Plants affected** Red, white and blackcurrant, apple.
▶ **Treatment** There is no effective control as the caterpillars cannot be reached inside the stems. In winter, cut back the affected shoots to where the pith is no longer discoloured and burn them.

FIREBLIGHT This serious disease affects apples, pears and quinces, causing the foliage and then the branches to dry up completely. It is highly infectious, and the bacteria that causes the disease is easily spread by rain splash or on pruning tools. See page 152.

GUMMOSIS
▶ **Symptoms** A sticky, viscous, yellowish brown gum oozes from a wound on the trunk or branches. Stem and leaf lesions may also develop but these are less common. The fungal disease may be caused and spread by a simple insect sting, and the affected trees and bushes gradually wither and die. The oozing gum is the tree's response to an attack. This disease is encouraged by cool, damp conditions.
▶ **Trees affected** Apricot, cherry, peach, plum.
▶ **Treatment** Avoid damaging the tree. Prune at the height of the growing season. Scrape off the gum and paint the wound with a product that protects the healing scar. Prune out infected growth to healthy wood. Spray with an approved copper-based fungicide and feed with liquid nettle manure (see page 255) to strengthen new growth.

LEOPARD MOTH
▶ **Symptoms** The creamy yellow caterpillars of the leopard moth (*Zeuzera pyrina*) bore into the trunk or branches making a network of tunnels where they stay until they pupate. The branches become brittle and may easily snap on a windy day. Another sign of infestation are pellets of compacted sawdust, which are the caterpillar's excrement, coming from one of the entry or exit holes. The infestation often consists of only one

caterpillar, but this can still be disastrous if present in the trunk of a young tree.

▶ **Trees affected** Apple, birch, hawthorn, maple, oak, sorbus, sycamore.

▶ **Treatment** Preventive measures are not possible as the attacks are sporadic. If caterpillars are found, prune and burn the infected branch. Alternatively, insert a piece of wire into the tunnels to skewer the caterpillar.

SHOT-HOLE BORER

▶ **Symptoms** The branches and trunk are riddled with tiny holes, each marked by a pile of sawdust, surrounded by a reddish brown canker. The tree gradually withers and dies. This is caused by a small brownish black insect (*Xyleborus dispar*), whose larvae burrow into the tree to pupate. Attacks usually only occur on trees growing under stressful conditions and should not be a problem on vigorous fruit trees.

▶ **Trees affected** Cherry, sweet chestnut, apple, pear, plum.

▶ **Treatment** Destroy the larvae by pushing wires into the tunnels or, more effectively, cut out and burn the infested branches. Insecticides are ineffective as the larvae are protected by the bark.

SPUR BLIGHT

▶ **Symptoms** Purplish blue patches appear around young shoots and buds. The blight then spreads down to the canes, which turn a silvery grey colour and are covered with prominent black spots. The canes will produce virtually no fruit the following spring. Caused by a fungus, *Didymella applanata*, this blight is active during hot, wet summers.

▶ **Plants affected** Loganberry, raspberry.

▶ **Treatment** Cut out and burn the heavily infected canes and spray with an approved copper-based fungicide at regular intervals from leaf bud burst to blossom time.

WOOLLY APHID

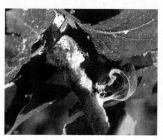

▶ **Symptoms** The bark is split and swollen and a cottony, white 'wool' appears on the trunk and branches. The reddish brown aphids (*Eriosoma lanigerum*) are about 2mm long and are sometimes visible. The aphids first appear in spring and suck sap from cracks in the bark and from young shoots. Their ability to reproduce by parthenogenesis (without fertilisation) means that a single aphid can produce as many as 100 offspring, which hibernate inside crevices in the bark.

▶ **Tree affected** Apple.

▶ **Treatment** Encourage natural predators such as ladybirds, lacewings and birds, who feed on this aphid, into

the garden. Use a forceful water jet to wash off the woolly cover, then spray with an approved treatment as soon as the aphids appear in spring.

Leaves

BLACKCURRANT RUST

▶ **Symptoms** Yellow-ochre blisters appear on the undersides of the leaves, which wither and fall, leaving bare branches. This is caused by fungus that hibernates on conifers in the form of orange blisters that burst and release its spores. These spores contaminate currant bushes causing more blisters, which in turn release spores that reinfect conifers and thereby perpetuate the cycle.

▶ **Bushes affected** Red and blackcurrant.

▶ **Treatment** Avoid planting conifers and currant bushes in close proximity. In the event of contamination, treat with an approved copper-based fungicide. The disease is spread through rain splash and the spores need a moist condition to germinate and infect, so make your plants less susceptible by preventing damp, warm conditions where a film of moisture can develop on the leaves.

BLACKFLY This aphid's dark colour makes it easily visible against foliage. Colonies tend to collect at the ends of branches on a number of fruit

trees, feeding on sap and distorting growth. Spray with a combined solution of derris and pyrethrins. See page 97.

BUFF-TIP MOTH Branches are quickly stripped as the leaves are systematically eaten by caterpillars of the buff-tip moth, with their distinctive black-and-yellow chequered markings. See page 151.

CAPSID BUG The leaves of affected trees and shrubs look as if they have been riddled with shot. See page 97.

CORYNEUM BLIGHT

▶ **Symptoms** This fungal disease is characterised by the appearance of small patches – about 1mm across, purplish red in the centre and edged with brown – on the leaves. These patches die and leave numerous little holes, and the leaves eventually fall. The disease can also affect the shoots, causing cankers and gum ooze, as well as flower buds, which dry up and drop. Patches on the fruit have a grey or black centre, which sometimes becomes pitted, revealing the stone. This is caused by the *Coryneum beijerinckii* fungus.

▶ **Trees affected** Apricot, peach, almond, cherry, plum.

▶ **Treatment** Spray with a fungicide containing copper. Remove all the affected branches when pruning. Build up the trees' vigour by spraying them with liquid nettle manure

Pests and diseases

(see page 255) during the summer and water thoroughly in dry weather.

CURRANT APHID

▶ **Symptoms** The leaves turn from green to yellow and then red. They become deformed and blistered, and eventually wither and die. The disease is caused by the yellow currant aphid (*Cryptomyzus ribis*), which becomes active as the buds open.
▶ **Bushes affected** Red and blackcurrant.
▶ **Treatment** Encourage natural predators or spray with derris or pyrethrins.

DOWNY MILDEW This fungal disease widely affects vines and can completely destroy several vine stocks. See page 206.

ERMINE MOTH

▶ **Symptoms** Tents of silken webs can be seen woven around clusters of leaves. These are made by the ermine moth to house its small yellowish caterpillars that feed on the juicy foliage.
▶ **Trees affected** Apple, apricot, peach, plum, quince.
▶ **Treatment** Hang sticky cardboard traps in the branches to catch the adult moths. Prune and burn infested branches to kill the caterpillars.

FIREBLIGHT This serious disease affects apples, pears and quinces, causing the foliage and then the branches to dry up completely. Lift and burn affected trees. See page 151.

GREENFLY

▶ **Symptoms** Although its colour allows this aphid to blend with the green of the foliage, the effects of its presence are unmistakable. Afflicted leaves become deformed, curl up, turn yellow and fall. However, there is usually time for the leaves to grow back, as greenfly generally attack in early spring.
▶ **Plants affected** Most fruit.
▶ **Treatment** Use predators, such as ladybird larvae, which are widely available by mail order. Keep these predators in your garden by building a ladybird shelter from hollow sticks or a bundle of thorny prunings to protect them during the winter. If aphids become a problem, remove quickly by spraying with derris or pyrethins. Feed with liquid nettle manure (see page 255) to aid recovery.

HAWTHORN RUST

▶ **Symptoms** Orangey yellow patches appear on the surface of the leaves while the undersides are covered with lattice-like swellings. This variety of rust is caused by a fungus (*Gymnosporangium globosum*), which hibernates on junipers, developing kidney-shaped galls. Light brown gelatinous blisters then appear and release spores that contaminate nearby fruit trees. Swellings develop on the leaves of these trees and, when mature, release spores that reinfect junipers.

▶ **Trees affected** Apple, crab apple, juniper, pear, quince.
▶ **Treatment** Avoid planting pears, apples, crab apples and quinces near junipers. Spray with a fungicide containing copper.

MEALY PLUM APHID

▶ **Symptoms** As the pale green mealy plum aphid (*Hyalopterus pruni*) bites into the leaves on which it feeds, it secretes a honeydew on which a fungus develops. This mould prevents the leaves from breathing, so they wither and die. Each aphid's body is covered in a waxy substance that gives it a 'mealy' appearance. Colonies of aphids are found on the underside of leaves or on shoot tips.
▶ **Trees affected** Most fruits with stones.
▶ **Treatment** From late spring, spray with a fatty acid, oil or derris-based product if the aphids build up.

PEACH LEAF CURL

▶ **Symptoms** The leaves curl up and change from green to yellow and then to bright red or purple. These symptoms are accompanied by the appearance of characteristic blisters. The leaves drop and young shoots become deformed. Gum will ooze from the affected area. Peach leaf curl is caused by a fungus of the genus *Taphrina*. It develops in early spring when the weather is cold and wet after a mild winter.

▶ **Trees affected** Almond, cherry, nectarine, peach.
▶ **Treatment** Spray with a copper fungicide in late winter. As soon as the buds begin to swell in early spring, spray with Bordeaux mixture to prevent spores from entering the buds. Repeat two weeks later and again just before the leaves drop. Erect polythene covers over fan-trained trees to keep off rain.

PLANT SUCKERS

▶ **Symptoms** The leaves curl upwards, becoming deformed and stunted before dropping. Affected buds do not develop. The symptoms are caused by a yellow sap-sucking insect that is about 4mm long. Its larvae appear in spring. The most common are the apple sucker (*Psylla mali*) and the pear sucker (*Psylla piricula*).
▶ **Trees affected** Apple, fig, pear.
▶ **Treatment** In early summer, when the pest becomes active, spray the tree with a fatty acid, oil or an approved, bifenthrin-based product to prevent damage to the plants.

PLUM POX

▶ **Symptoms** The leaves become deformed and a light-coloured mottling appears along the veins. The fruit also becomes misshapen and covered with mottling, and sometimes oozes gum. This viral disease, also known as Sharka, is transmitted by an aphid, which may be accidentally introduced into your garden on new plum rootstocks.

▶ **Trees affected** Peach, plum.

▶ **Treatment** There is no known treatment for this serious disease. In Britain, suspected outbreaks must be reported immediately to DEFRA (the Department for the Environment, Food and Rural Affairs). It's best to destroy the crop to avoid spreading the virus.

POWDERY MILDEW

▶ **Symptoms** The upper surface of the young leaves, shoots and flower trusses are covered with the characteristic white powdery mould of this fungal disease. The foliage becomes deformed, growth is stunted and diseased flowers do not set. Affected fruits may crack and split because they are unable to expand normally. They may also develop brown patches and the leaves fall.

▶ **Trees affected** Apple, grape, gooseberry, melon, peach, quince, vine.

▶ **Treatment** Remove and burn affected leaves and shoots. Spray infected plants with Bordeaux mixture at the first sign of the disease and repeat treatment several times, once a fortnight. Space plants well to prevent them being overcrowded and to avoid humid conditions.

RED SPIDER MITE

These tiny mites, easily recognised by their bright red colour, are found on most species of fruit tree in hot, dry weather. Affected leaves turn yellow and become covered with greyish mottling. The leaves eventually wither and fall. See page 153.

SCALE INSECT

▶ **Symptoms** A number of spots can be seen on the shoots and undersides of the leaves. These are accompanied by an accumulation of waxy or cottony threads and large amounts of soot-like fungus (genus *Apiosporum*), which develop on the leaves of infested plants.

▶ **Trees affected** Apple, fig, pear, plum, vine.

▶ **Treatment** Spray the infested plants with an approved fatty acid or oil-based insecticide.

SILVER LEAF Silvery grey patches appear on the leaves of a few branches and gradually spread to the rest of the foliage. The tree withers and dies. This fungal disease mainly attacks plums, but can also affect trees in the family *Rosaceae* (apples, cherries,

plums and peaches). See page 153.

WINTER MOTH The winter moth caterpillar attacks soft fruit bushes as well as most types of fruit trees, especially cherries, plums, apples and pears. See page 153.

Flowers

APPLE-BLOSSOM WEEVIL

▶ **Symptoms** The flower buds fail to open, turn brown and wither. Inside are tiny white grubs. On raspberries, the peduncles (fruit stalks) are cut. The apple-blossom weevil (*Anthonomus pomorum*) has a brown and white shell with a characteristic 'V' on its back. This tiny insect lays its eggs in the flower buds, which are then killed by the grubs.

▶ **Trees affected** Apple, pear, raspberry.

▶ **Treatment** Protect buds at risk by spraying with an approved insecticide at regular intervals as the young growth develops in the spring and early summer.

FRUIT MOTH

▶ **Symptoms** The flower buds are eaten as well as woven together with silken webs, which causes them to dry up and wither. This pest is a green, brown-headed caterpillar.

▶ **Trees affected** Most fruit, including fig, lemon.

▶ **Treatment** Treat infected trees with an insecticide containing pyrethrins or rotenone (derris).

MONILIA BLOSSOM BLIGHT

▶ **Symptoms** The flowers bloom and then wither, closing together to form a fairly compact, brown mass. This wilt is caused by a fungus of the genus *Monilia*, which can cause extensive damage to trees if left untreated.

▶ **Trees affected** All trees bearing fruit that contain pips or stones.

▶ **Treatment** Remove and burn affected parts to prevent the blight from spreading. Spray with copper or sulphur as soon as the tree begins to flower. Fungicides containing mancozeb are effective if applied in autumn, and in spring at bud burst.

WINTER MOTH The winter moth caterpillar attacks a number of plants and particularly the flowers of fruit trees. See page 153.

Fruit

ANTHRACNOSE

▶ **Symptoms** This disease affects stored fruit. Blisters appear on skin lesions, caused by a fungus, *Glomerella cingulata*, which enters the fruit via the pores on lesions.
▶ **Trees affected** Apple, pear, quince.
▶ **Treatment** Avoid storing damaged, marked or bruised fruit. At the first sign of anthracnose, remove and burn affected fruit to prevent the disease from spreading.

APPLE SAWFLY

▶ **Symptoms** The skin of the fruit has a long scar running from the peduncle (fruit stalk), while insect excrement pellets fall from a round hole. Inside are foul-smelling tunnels containing caterpillars of the apple sawfly (*Hoplocampa testudinea*) as they bore through the skin of the fruit to feed on the flesh. The larvae hatch out of cocoons in the soil in spring and burrow into the young fruit, often causing them to drop prematurely.
▶ **Trees affected** Apple, plum.
▶ **Treatment** Remove and burn any infested young fruit to prevent the caterpillars causing further damage. If the pest becomes a problem, spray with a bifenthrin or pyrethrin-based product.

BOTRYTIS Also known as grey mould, this disease causes fruit to become covered with a whitish furry fungus, while the flesh becomes soft and then dries up. The fruit eventually rots. See page 97.

BROWN ROT

▶ **Symptoms** The fruit (on the tree or in storage) bears signs of rot in the form of concentric circles with pale beige blisters. The rot gradually spreads and eventually affects the whole fruit. This rot is caused by a fungus of the genus *Monilia*, which is carried by rain, wind, birds and insects. The mycelium (a strand of fungal growth) enters the fruit via an insect bite or blemish.
▶ **Trees affected** All trees whose fruit contains pips or stones.
▶ **Treatment** Burn rotten fruit and, to avoid re-infestation, do not put the dead leaves on the compost heap. Treat infected trees with an approved fungicide spray in the spring and repeat as directed.

CODLING MOTH

▶ **Symptoms** The fruit ripens prematurely and falls from the branches. The flesh is riddled with tunnels made by the larvae of the codling moth (*Cydia pomonella*). The openings where the caterpillars enter the fruit are marked by small piles of dark brown, sawdust-like insect excrement pellets. The pale pink, brown-headed caterpillars bore into the centre of the fruit and feed on its flesh. When it is time to pupate, they leave the fruit and burrow under the bark.
▶ **Trees affected** Apple, sweet chestnut, pear, walnut, peach, plum.
▶ **Treatment** Hang pheromone traps in the branches to attract the moths and reduce attacks. The moths are attracted by the smell of the sticky boards, get too close and become stuck and die. Treat with an insecticide containing bifenthrin, spraying several times at three-weekly intervals.

FRUIT FLY

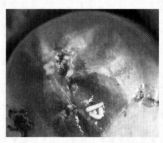

▶ **Symptoms** The fruit contains tiny larvae that feed on the flesh and reduce it to pulp. The fruit rots whether it is being stored or is still on the tree. The larvae of several types of flies are responsible for the devastation after they emerge from eggs laid in the developing fruit.
▶ **Trees affected** Most fruit.
▶ **Treatment** If the problem becomes a nuisance, spray with products containing derris or pyrethrins.

GRAPE VINE MOTH

▶ **Symptoms** Vines are attacked by two generations of reddish, black-headed caterpillars, about 1cm long, laid by the grape vine moth (*Eupoecillia ambiguella*). The first devours part of the flowers and uses the rest of them to form a silky nest. The second bores into the grapes, which turn purplish brown, wither and rot.
▶ **Plant affected** Vine.
▶ **Treatment** Spray with an organic insecticide containing pyrethrins or rotenone (derris).

HAZELNUT WEEVIL

▶ **Symptoms** Each infected hazelnut is pierced by a small hole, 1–2mm across, and the shell is empty. This condition is caused by a weevil (*Balaninus nucum*), which lays an egg inside the developing fruit. The larva feeds on the flesh of the hazelnut as the shell hardens. It exits the fruit in order to pupate by boring through the shell and then dropping onto the ground.
▶ **Tree affected** Hazelnut.
▶ **Treatment** Insecticides are ineffective against this pest owing to the hard hazelnut shells. However, since the larvae pupate in the ground at a depth of only a few centimetres, rotavating or deep digging around the base of the affected tree tends to bury them deeper and destroy them.

PLUM POX

This serious disease is caused by the plum pox virus. It affects the fruits of stone fruit trees, such as peaches, apricots, nectarines and plums, which become misshapen and mottled, and sometimes ooze gum. It also affects the leaves. In Britain, you are obliged to report this disease to DEFRA (the Department for the Environment, Food and Rural Affairs) at the first sign of an outbreak. There is no known treatment. See page 253.

POCKET PLUM

▶ **Symptoms** The fruit does not develop but becomes wrinkled and elongated without swelling. It has no pulp or stone, but instead a hollow pocket, and becomes covered with a light, pinkish down. The fruit stays green, then drops prematurely. This disease is caused by a fungus (*Taphrina pruni*), which affects developing fruit.

▶ **Tree affected** Plum.

▶ **Treatment** There is no successful treatment. Although this fungus overwinters in the twigs on the tree, it may not attack the tree every year. To minimise damage, remove any affected plums promptly, preferably before they become covered in down. Fortunately, it is unusual for the entire tree to be infected.

SCAB

▶ **Symptoms** The fruit becomes cracked, allowing parasitic infestations to enter, and covered with dark brown scabs. In addition, the fruit is sometimes deformed, and the infected part is harder to the touch. The leaves can also be affected as well as the fruit. This disease is caused by a fungus of the genus *Venturia*.

▶ **Trees affected** Apple, pear.

▶ **Treatment** Treat with an approved fungicide based on copper or sulphur.

HOMEMADE PREVENTION

Yesterday's gardeners used gentle but effective herbal remedies to discourage pests and diseases from attacking their plants. It is not always necessary to resort to chemicals in the garden.

GARLIC INFUSION AGAINST COMMON GARDEN PESTS

▶ 25g garlic cloves
▶ 1 litre water

Chop the garlic and place it in a heatproof bowl. Boil the water and pour it over the garlic. Cover the mixture and leave to infuse for 15 minutes. Strain the liquid through a large sieve. Spray the garlic infusion undiluted on plants susceptible to aphids every two to three weeks.

HORSETAIL DECOCTION FOR FUNGUS

▶ 500g fresh horsetail 'needles' and stems
▶ 5 litres water

Chop the horsetail and place it in a large bucket. Pour in the cold water. Leave the mixture to infuse for 24 hours, then pour into an old cooking pan and simmer over a low heat for 15–30 minutes. Leave the brew to cool. Strain the liquid through a fine sieve, pressing the herbs through with the back of a wooden spoon. Dilute this decoction with water (1:5). Spray plants infected with fungus on three consecutive days.

STINGING NETTLE EXTRACT (NETTLE MASH)

▶ 200g fresh stinging nettle leaves
▶ 2 litres water

Chop the leaves and place them in a bowl. Pour the cold water over them and keep them submerged by placing a weighted plate on top. Leave to infuse for 24 hours. Strain the liquid through a large sieve. Dilute the extract with water (1:5) and spray on your plants as soon as you notice a pest.

LIQUID NETTLE MANURE FOR STRONGER PLANTS

▶ 1 kg fresh stinging nettle leaves
▶ 2 tbsp fuller's earth, or 2 tbsp talcum powder
▶ 10 litres water

Chop the stinging nettle leaves and place them in a bucket. Add the fuller's earth or talcum powder, then pour in the cold water. Leave to infuse, stirring once a day. After three days fermentation should begin. The liquid manure will be ready to use after 10 days, when the liquid darkens and the solids have settled at the bottom. Pour the liquid through a fine sieve into plastic bottles with caps. Dilute the manure with water (1:10) and pour it on the soil around the plants or spray the leaves. Use it every two weeks or more frequently if there is heavy rain. This manure will strengthen your plants and make them less susceptible to attack. Always wear gloves when handling stinging nettles.

Garden basics

The life of plants

Without the benefit of modern science yesterday's gardeners had to develop an intuitive understanding of how their plants grew and what they needed to thrive. By combining a basic knowledge of plant biology with tips from the past, you can learn to work with nature to grow a garden full of healthy specimens.

Ensure success by choosing plants to suit the conditions in your garden. In acid soil and semishade, grow rhododendrons.

The more you know, the better they grow

Sleeping beauties All seeds need very specific – and often different – conditions to trigger their germination: warmth or cold, moisture, air and, in some cases, light. Without these, seeds can lie dormant for centuries, buried deep in the soil and only springing to life when the right conditions occur, like the poppy seeds stirred up by warfare in the fields of Flanders.
▶ To stimulate germination of large seeds such as walnuts and hazelnuts, store them in cool, damp sand over winter before sowing (see page 247). This treatment is called stratification.

Leaves breathe too Plants absorb air through minute pores on the underside of their leaves. Rainfall washes off any dirt and dust from plants in the garden, but indoor plants need regular cleaning to prevent blocked pores impeding growth.
▶ Beer and milk are often recommended for cleaning and shining the leaves on indoor plants, but these leave a sticky surface that will trap dust instead of giving a clean fresh leaf. Use plain, soft water, possibly mixed with a tiny amount of

washing-up liquid. Alternatively, stand your plants outside in the rain – or in the shower with the temperature on cool.

All plants need light Without light, plants cannot produce the energy they need to sustain life, a process called photosynthesis. Some plants need lots of light while others – indoor plants such as ferns and the indestructible aspidistra – can survive in the shade. A loss of green colour indicates that a plant is getting insufficient light.
▶ **Artificial light** Special 'daylight' bulbs are available to help to foster photosynthesis, but an ordinary 100-watt bulb works just as well.
▶ **Reflected light** You can boost the light for sun-loving garden plants. Paint exterior walls white and plant up adjacent borders to create a Mediterranean-style courtyard garden.

Kill weeds with darkness A simple but effective way of controlling unwanted plants is to stop their growth by blocking out their light. Cover them with a piece of old carpet, cardboard or black plastic sheeting.

A thirst for water Plants take up water from their roots. It moves up through the stems and, on reaching the leaves, evaporates from the surface, so drawing up more water from the soil. This process will continue as long as there is water in the soil. If the ground becomes dry and roots cannot take up enough water, the stems and leaves will wilt and photosynthesis will cease. Some plants, however, are well adapted to survive in very dry conditions – cacti and succulents can store water, and have prickly spines or hairy leaves that reduce water loss.

DID YOU KNOW?

Photosynthesis

The green pigment in a plant's leaves – chlorophyll – uses light to produce sugars, which plants consume as fuel. During this process, called photosynthesis, water combines with carbon dioxide from the air, releasing oxygen back into the atmosphere. The gases are exchanged through pores called stomata on the underside of leaves. At night, the process is reversed and carbon dioxide is given off. Traditionally, plants were discouraged in bedrooms because of this – especially if anyone was sick – but the amount of carbon dioxide given off by a few plants is much too small to do any harm.

Plant food Plants need a balanced diet. A lack of food will result in poor growth, and leaves may become yellow, stunted and drop off. Plants growing in containers are particularly at risk and depend on you to replenish the nutrients in the soil at regular intervals. Leafy plants need high levels of nitrogen (N), root crops need high levels of phosphate (P) and flowering and fruiting plants need extra potassium (K). Use a fertiliser that offers the best balance of nutrients for each type of plant. The product label will give you the NPK balance.

▶ The acidity or alkalinity of the soil affects the uptake of plant nutrients via the roots. You can help neutralise the pH of the soil by balancing the acidity of the water used. Add manure or leaf mould to make alkaline water more acidic, and steep crushed eggshells in 'acid' water for 48 hours to make it more alkaline.

Top tips for watering pot plants Mains water is not ideal for plants as its fluoride salts interfere with the absorption of nutrients. If possible, use rainwater collected in water butts linked up to guttering from the house, shed or greenhouse. Alternatively, there are several old recipes for protecting and nourishing container-grown plants – in the home and garden – as you water them.

▶ **Vinegar tonic** Every month, mix one spoonful of cider vinegar in a litre of water and give your plants a good soak to counteract the effects of fluoride salts.

▶ **Leftover tea** Add stewed tea or used tea bags to the watering can to make a nitrogen-rich feed for foliage plants. Camomile tea is antibacterial and fungicidal and so counteracts mildew, and green or black tea is good for acid-loving plants.

▶ **Coffee perk** Acid-loving plants also appreciate a top-dressing of coffee grounds every month or so.

Acidifying water for indoor plants

1 If the water where you live is very hard, fill a thin cotton bag with leaf-mould. You can also add oak leaves or pine needles to boost the acidity.

2 Tie up the bag and suspend it from a stick. Leave the bag to soak overnight in a bucket of water. You will then have acidic water for your plants.

Plants that tolerate dryness

Many plants that originate from dry areas of the world need less water to help them absorb the nutrients they require.

Trees Albizia, eucalyptus, fig, koelreuteria, mimosa ❶, olive, pine, *Pistacia lentiscus*, rhus, *Tilia tomentosa*, yew and ziziphus

Shrubs Callistemon, ceanothus, *Cercis siliquastrum*, cistus, coronilla, cotinus, escallonia, genista, hypericum, *Lagerstroemia indica*, lantana, lavender, photinia, pittosporum, rosemary, tamarix ❷ and *Ulex europaeus*

Perennials, bulbs and annuals Acanthus, achillea, agave, cleome, cortaderia, euphorbia, gaura, helianthemum, iris, kniphofia, narcissus, nepeta, pennisetum, phlomis, portulaca, ruta, santolina, sempervivum, valerian ❸, verbascum, verbena and yucca

▶ **Vegetable broth** Cool the water in which you have cooked your vegetables and water your plants with it.

▶ **Fish stew** Smelly aquarium water is full of nutrients and trace elements. Whenever you clean the aquarium, use the water to feed your plants.

Healthy roots The root system takes up minerals dissolved in water in the soil. Without water this process stops and the plants fail. However, too much water can have the same effect by saturating the soil, driving out the air and suffocating the roots. Good drainage is vital to keep the soil aerated.

▶ Many house plants die from overwatering. Stand pots on feet or on gravel to allow them to drain.

The ideal environment Bear in mind the origins of plants before introducing them into your garden. There is no point trying to cultivate a tropical plant out of doors in a chilly British garden. It may survive a hot summer but will need cosseting indoors in winter. Plants are very adaptable, however, and many that have been introduced from around the world are now regulars in our gardens.

Plants need a rest! Plants naturally go through a period of dormancy during the winter, when growth slows down or stops altogether.

▶ Indoor plants also benefit from a rest at this time, during which they need little water and no feeding. Start feeding again when growth resumes in spring.

▶ 'Resting' outdoor plants can be lifted and moved during winter, at times when there is no risk of severe cold.

Buying the best

Successful gardening starts with strong healthy plants. While the old way was to raise plants from seeds and cuttings, the variety of plants that can now be bought from nurseries and garden centres, by mail order and over the Internet gets wider every year. Here are a few tips to help you to make the right choice and buy only good plants from the best sources.

Where to buy

Use your local nurseries and garden centres Nursery people are passionate about plants and how they are grown, and they will always be pleased to give you good advice. Discover what grows well in the area – and therefore what will be ideal for your own garden situation – by visiting local nurseries and garden centres and talking to the experts.

Get the freshest plants Look for nurseries and garden centres that renew their stock frequently, and find out when they get their deliveries. The plants in such places will be fresher, and there will be a greater choice available.

Make the most of mail order Ordering by mail or over the Internet is an ideal way to buy special and unusual plants that you cannot find locally. It is also a good solution if getting to a nursery or garden centre is difficult. But catalogues aren't always accurate so, to avoid being tempted by misleading photos and descriptions, look up the true plant details for yourself – preferably in an illustrated gardening book – before placing your order.
▶ Contact the supplier to check the availability of the plants you want, and the best time of year to order them. Check the suitability of the plants for your own garden, soil type and conditions. Find out when and how the plants will be delivered.
▶ Unpack your delivery as soon as it arrives, water the plants and place them in a light spot to overcome transport shock. Once they have recovered, plant out as soon as you can.

Avoid weekend crowds in the garden centre if you can – staff will have more time to answer your queries.

Guarantee equals security Reputable companies will guarantee the quality and success of their plants, as long as the planting and aftercare instructions have been followed.

Buying small plants as plugs This is a very cost-effective way of buying large quantities of plants, particularly annuals and biennials for mass planting. Plug plants are grown from seed in containers divided into compartments. They are available in various sizes with a root system ready for transplanting. Although they are not very impressive at first, they will quickly grow on to full-size plants.

Understanding plant labels Read the label carefully before you buy. Labels contain the key information you need to achieve the best results from the plants you want – including when they will flower or produce a crop, the ideal growing conditions and lots more.
▶ Make sure you note the size a plant will eventually grow to and mark out the extent in your garden so that you can avoid overcrowding.
▶ Some plants, such as fruit trees, need a pollinating companion to produce fruit or berries. Others are self-fertile and will produce a crop on their own – check the label for this type of detail.

When to buy and plant out Wait until a plant's dormant period so it can recover from the shock of planting before the growing season begins.

▶ **November to March** These are the best months to buy good-value bare-rooted deciduous trees, shrubs and roses. However, try to avoid taking delivery of plants in periods of severe cold, when planting out is difficult.

▶ **October or March** Plant conifers, evergreen trees and shrubs in these months. The moist soil will encourage them to root and establish quickly.

▶ **Early autumn or spring** This is the ideal time for planting herbaceous perennials and biennials. However, if your soil tends to be heavy in winter, don't choose autumn. Wait for spring when the soil has warmed up and dried out, particularly for more delicate plants such as summer and autumn-flowering anemones and some grasses.

▶ **Spring** When the risk of frost has passed it is time to plant summer annuals and plants for baskets and containers. Do not be tempted to buy these plants too early in the year – they will have been forced in warm conditions and will struggle to grow when they are planted out into cold soil.

Check the roots A poor root system will produce a weak plant. Before buying any plant, if possible check the condition of the roots. A healthy root system will almost fill the container that it is growing in with loose, white, fibrous growth. Do not take a chance – avoid plants with roots that show any of the following symptoms.

▶ Small, underdeveloped roots that come away from the compost when removed from the pot will not sustain the plant. The rootball should hold the surrounding compost together in a unified clump.

▶ 'Pot-bound' roots, where the root growth is a solid, tangled mass, indicate that the plant has been kept in the container for too long. Particularly avoid any plants where the plastic pot has actually burst with the amount of root growth (left).

▶ Roots escaping from the drainage holes in the bottom of the pot – and sometimes growing into the soil beneath – are also pot-bound (left). Do not try to untangle the roots or cut them out of the container. These plants have also been in their container for too long and are unlikely to do well.

Tip-top bedding plants Annuals and biennials are useful as colourful bedding plants and can be bought in plugs and small pots. When buying bedding plants look for:

▶ Plants with sturdy green growth, with plenty of shoots and flower buds.

▶ Well-rooted plants, which can easily be removed from the plug or pot in one piece.

▶ Plugs or pots that are not too wet and not too dry – just moist is ideal.

▶ Trays of the same colour – mass planting has more impact than a mixture of colours.

▶ Clean compost. Don't buy plants that have algae and moss growing on the surface – these are old stock.

Interim care While waiting to plant out bedding plants, keep them cool, moist and draught-free. Small plugs and pots dry out quickly, so water frequently without saturating the compost.

Bare roots can save you money Dormant plants with bare roots are sold by specialist nurseries (sometimes mail-order) during the autumn and winter months. They are an inexpensive way of buying deciduous trees and shrubs, fruit trees and bushes, roses and hedging stock. Here are a few tips to keep in mind.

▶ The root structure should be well branched and fibrous, and the largest root should be no thicker than your thumb.

▶ Do not allow the bare roots to dry out completely. To avoid this, wrap the roots in damp newspaper or a similar covering and transport in a plastic bag.

▶ Plant out within three days of buying or receiving them. If this is not possible, you can 'heel them in' (above). Dig a trench with one sloping side, lay the plants in the trench so they are supported against the slope, then refill the trench with moist soil, covering the roots. Firm the soil, then cover the plants with straw to protect the roots from severe cold. They can be kept in this way for weeks or even months before planting in their final position.

▶ Before planting, soak the roots in a mixture of soil and water for a couple of hours.

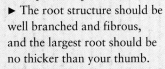

YESTERDAY & TODAY
Buying plants via the Internet

The Internet is a convenience yesterday's gardeners could never have dreamed of. With a few clicks you can browse through a catalogue on line, fill up your virtual shopping trolley, pay by credit card and have your plants delivered a few days later. More and more nurseries now have their own web sites where you can often see photos of the plants in situ, ask advice from plant experts and check the availability of what you want. As with all mail-order companies, you should not hesitate to reject the goods if they are not good quality or if the package has been damaged during transit.

Feeding the soil

Gardeners have a saying: 'A clay soil will break your back, but a sandy soil will break your heart.' Each soil type has its benefits and drawbacks, but there is a lot you can do, using traditional methods, to balance and enrich your soil to provide the right conditions for most plants.

How to identify your soil

Soil types Garden soils vary considerably, but all will be a mixture of ingredients such as clay, sand, limestone and humus in varying proportions. You can identify the composition of your own garden soil type by observing and feeling it. Dig out soil samples from several areas around your garden, at a depth of 20–30cm below the surface, and mix them together. Rub wet and dry samples between your fingers and note the difference.

Garden soil is made up of a mixture of ingredients. The ideal soil is loam – a fertile mix of sand, chalk and clay.

Clay soil This looks shiny and feels smooth, sticky and slippery when wet. It is either brown, yellow or grey in colour.
▶ Its fine particles bind together to form solid, heavy clods. In summer the surface hardens and cracks.
▶ In wet weather, puddles remain on the surface and take time to drain away. These soils become muddy, heavy and sticky to work with.

Chalky or lime soil A yellowish white soil, this is also sticky to the touch, although it has a crumbly texture and does not bind together when wet.
▶ It contains fragments of limestone and can be stony. Chalky or lime soil drains freely and dries out in summer.

Peaty soil This black and crumbly soil contains high levels of organic matter and humus and does not clump together.
▶ Peaty soil soaks up water like a sponge but also dries out and crumbles rapidly.
▶ It is fibrous to the touch, with a spongy texture, and does not stick together.

Sandy soil Between yellow and red in colour, sandy soil is gritty to the touch.
▶ Light and easy to work with, it is well drained and does not hold water, making it dry out rapidly and lose nutrients.
▶ Sandy soil breaks up easily and feels coarse and gritty.

Analysing your soil

A balanced, nutritious soil is essential for healthy plant growth. Modern home-testing kits give you a reliable indicator on the health, nutrition and level of acidity, called pH. The ideal level for most plants is 6.5. Once you have the test results you can take the appropriate steps to improve your soil and correct any imbalance. Test your soil every three or four years.

Sampling the soil Collect 8–10 samples of soil from each area you wish to analyse. For lawns, sample at a depth of 5–15cm, for cultivated areas at 10–30cm and for trees at 60–80cm. Depending on the type of kit you buy, you will either need to add the soil samples to demineralised water and then test with a strip of indicator paper, or add the soil to a chemical solution supplied in the kit, which changes colour according to soil type. In both cases, check the colour against the reference scale provided to identify the soil's acidity, its pH value. If you don't want to do the test yourself, you can send the mixed samples to a laboratory for professionals to analyse.

Chalk soil test Place a handful of dry soil on a clean, dry cloth and gather the edges of the cloth together to enclose the soil. Hammer the soil into small fragments then tip it into a dark-coloured bowl. Cover the sample with white vinegar, which will start to bubble. The greater the frothing and the longer it lasts, the more chalky the soil is.

Clay soil test Moisten a handful of soil, squeeze it into a ball and then roll it into a sausage shape, about 1cm in diameter (top). The longer the sausage can be stretched, the greater the clay content. If you can bend it into a ring without cracking it, this is a very clayey soil. If the sample breaks up when rolled (right) it is likely to have a high sand or possibly peat content. Many gardens have a mix of different soil types.

Plants will tell you Check the weeds and wild plants that grow well in your garden. These will give you an excellent idea of what the soil type and condition is.
▶ **Heavy clay soils** Here grow coltsfoot, dandelion, creeping buttercup, sorrel, love-lies-bleeding, thistles, goutweed, camomile and black bindweed.
▶ **Waterlogged soils** In this soil type you will find buttercup, field horsetail, wild mint, comfrey, coltsfoot, lady's thumb, meadow saffron, silverweed and lesser celandine.

If you have acidic soil then ferns are an excellent choice. They thrive in soils with a low pH.

▶ **Chalky or lime soils** These soils are perfect for growing mustard seed, poppy, cornflower, thistles, clover, camomile, elder, mountain ash, old man's beard, pale toad flax, scarlet pimpernel and bladder campion.
▶ **Acid soils** Here you can grow ferns, heathers, gorse, broom, foxglove, sorrel, field pansy and creeping buttercup.
▶ **Mineral-rich soils** These soils, especially those rich in nitrogen, are good for growing nettles, fat hen, comfrey, chickweed, couch grass, thistles, petty spurge, speedwell, purple dead nettle, camomile, dandelion, lesser celandine, shepherds purse, black nightshade, fumitory, stitchwort, mugwort, mustard seed and goosegrass.

Improving the soil

Improvement has its limits It is generally preferable to match your plants to your soil type, rather than trying to modify your soil to suit the plants you want to grow. It is still possible to cultivate plants that will not tolerate your garden soil by growing them in containers with the right soil mix.

Heavy clay soil Clay can be very fertile, but it is dense, gets very cold and wet in winter and heats up slowly in spring, which can retard plant growth and prevent good root activity. This kind of soil is also difficult to work.
▶ **Add lots of organic matter** Lime and gritty material will improve and break up the heavy structure of the soil. Each year, ideally in autumn, dig in and incorporate 3kg per square metre of well-rotted manure, garden compost, mushroom compost, or similar composted plant waste. Spread a 2–3cm layer over the soil and dig it in well.

▶ **Green manure crops** These are a good way of adding organic matter to the soil in areas of the garden that are unplanted. Sow rye grass, clover, comfrey or mustard seed onto bare soil in autumn. Dig it in when it has grown to about 20cm in height but before it flowers.
▶ **Add lime** This will reduce the acidity of clay soil. Spread 150g per square metre over the bare soil every two or three years and dig it in. This will keep the soil acidity at an ideal level for growing most types of plants. Allow at least a month before planting or sowing.
▶ **Mushroom compost** As this contains a lot of lime it can be used instead of lime to boost soil alkalinity.
▶ **Horticultural gravel or pea shingle** Either of these can be incorporated to improve drainage. Spread a 2–3cm layer over the soil and dig it in. Do not use fine sand as it will not break up clay. Dig in a layer of crocks when planting shrubs.

Feeding the soil

Chalky or lime soil With a pH over 7, chalk's high alkalinity can cause a yellowing of leaves, known as chlorosis, on plants intolerant of lime. It can also be shallow and lack nutrients.
▶ **Lower the pH** Do this by incorporating acidifying materials, such as well-rotted manure, garden compost, leaf-mould or flowers of sulphur and acidic fertilisers.
▶ **Add organic matter** This should be done each year to replenish nutrients and improve the soil's water-holding capacity. Dig in rotted manure or compost, or grow a green manure crop in uncultivated beds. Mulching the surface of the soil around plants will also incorporate organic matter, but without disturbing the planting.

Peaty soil This humus-rich soil retains water well but has a poor structure and can be poorly drained. Dig in coarse, sharp sand or pea shingle to improve the drainage. If it becomes acidic, add garden lime or chalk.

Sandy soil A light soil that warms up quickly in spring, sand is excellent for growing early crops. It has a very open, free-draining structure, however, which allows water and nutrients to be lost quickly, so that fertility drops rapidly if water and nutrients are not replaced regularly.
▶ **Well-rotted manure** This manure, garden compost or any other composted green waste should be incorporated each year. They will act as a natural sponge to soak up and retain water. Dig in a 2–3cm layer of manure or compost.
▶ **Green manure** Dig this in on empty beds and use as a surface mulch around plants to help to conserve water.

Soil that is too acid Few plants do well in an overly acidic soil with a pH of 4 or less, although heathers, azaleas, camelias and hydrangeas need a soil with a pH of 4–5.5.
▶ **Add garden lime or chalk** To counteract acidity add garden lime or chalk in autumn. The amount you need to add will depend on how acid the soil has become. If the pH of the soil is 6–6.5 add 150g of garden chalk or other lime-rich products per square metre. For pH 5–6 add 200g per square metre, and for pH 5 or less, add 300g per square metre.
▶ **Add plenty of organic matter** To improve the soil's nutrients, feed well, and dig in organic matter in spring. Do not apply manure at the same time as lime as they react together to produce ammonia – a pungent gas.

Giving feed the right way

Choosing the correct fertiliser Whether you are using a natural fertiliser, or an artificial one, make sure you are treating your plants properly. For example, are you remedying a general soil problem, or feeding a particular plant to make it flower more profusely? Once you've decided which fertiliser to use, you have several ways to apply it.

Feeding trees The spread of tree roots is more or less equivalent to the spread of the branches, which means that the absorbent roots will usually be well away from the trunk, at a point directly below the outer limits of the branches. Apply feed in this area. If the soil is compact, make fork holes in the ground (right) and water in the application.

Feeding shrubs Spread the fertiliser around the base of each plant and rake it into the top 2–3cm of soil. Unless the soil is very wet, always water in the feed.

Foliar feeding Spraying a dilute liquid fertiliser onto the leaves of plants is a quick and effective way of direct feeding, particularly during

---

The ideal soil

The right balance The ideal soil is called a 'loam' and is a mixture of approximately 20–25 per cent clay, 30–35 per cent lime or chalk and 40–50 per cent sand. It is also rich in humus, such as compost or leaf-mould. This mixture combines large and small particles of clay, lime and sand that, with the humus, bind together, holding on to moisture and nutrients while also draining freely.

Porous and open A well-aerated soil allows strong, deep plant root growth. It also encourages healthy micro-organism activity that decomposes organic matter into humus, releasing nutrients into the soil. Excess water can drain away freely, avoiding waterlogged conditions that can damage roots, inhibit growth and cause plant failure.

pH preferences The majority of plants grow best in a slightly acid soil, around pH 6.5. Azaleas, hydrangeas, conifers and other acid-loving plants need a soil below pH 5.5. Asters, forsythia and cotoneaster are examples of plants that prefer an alkaline soil, above pH 7.

Digging in green manure

1 Green manure is ideal for use in the vegetable patch. Once it has flowered, cut it down with shears or a strimmer.

2 Leave the cut crop lying on the ground to dry for several days.

3 When the crop has dried, go over with a rotary mower without the grass box to chop up the dry remains.

4 Dig in the manure to a depth of 10–15cm. Allow a week before planting seedlings and three before sowing seeds.

periods of dry weather when the roots are less active. Foliar feeding is a great tonic for struggling plants and will give them a quick boost, but don't do it when the plant is in direct sun.

Flowerpot special Flowers in pots need extra nutrients to grow and bloom well, as the plant quickly uses up the goodness in the small amount of soil in the container. Feed regularly or push modern, controlled-release fertiliser pellets into the soil around plants (left). This will provide all the nutrients the plant needs for up to six months.

Natural fertilisers You can buy natural fertilisers, such as the fish, blood and bone meal used by our forefathers. These substances are broken up in the soil, which encourages good microbial activity and improves the health and texture of the soil. That's an advantage they have over a straight inorganic fertiliser, which is a compound of the pure nutrients nitrogen, phosphate and potassium plus trace elements. Inorganic fertilisers are absorbed immediately by the plants for instant success, such as bigger blooms, but do little to improve the soil.

NPK – initials to remember Nitrogen (N), Phosphates (P) and Potassium (K) are the essential chemical nutrients that all plants need. Proprietory fertiliser packs display the amount and ratio of N:P:K they contain. For example, an 18:8:8 fertiliser contains 18 parts of Nitrogen and 8 parts each of Phosphate and Potassium. Choose a fertiliser with the best balance for your plants, looking out for ones that also contain essential trace elements, such as magnesium and copper.
▶ **Nitrogen** This promotes the growth of green leaves and stems, and is ideal for lawns and leafy plants.

▶ **Phosphates** Use to stimulate the growth of roots, flower buds and general plant health.
▶ **Potassium** This will boost a plant's resistance to pests and diseases and encourages good fruit and flower development, ripening and colour.

Liquid feed When using proprietory liquid fertilisers, follow the directions carefully. In general, feed every two weeks in the growing season, reducing to half the amount in the first and last months.
▶ To avoid burning the roots, make sure the compost is moist before applying the feed. Water plants 15–30 minutes before feeding if the compost is dry.

DID YOU KNOW?

Organic matter and fertilisers

Organic matter Bulky organic material is the lifeblood of any soil and must be replaced regularly, whether it is applied as manure, garden compost or green manure. By improving the structure and water content of the soil, it encourages root growth and increases a plant's uptake of nutrients from the soil. At the same time, earthworms and micro-organisms in the soil digest the organic matter into humus, slowly releasing nutrients in the process, which plant roots can draw on over time as they need them.

Fertilisers Yesterday's gardener depended on the quality of the soil for the abundance of his crop. Now, natural and artificial concentrated fertilisers can be used to supplement the nutrients released by organic matter in the soil. Vegetables, fruit crops and many ornamental plants that put on a lot of growth in a short period of time will benefit from these fertilisers, which provide a balanced diet. Plants in containers and baskets must be fed regularly to sustain strong growth.

The gardener's black gold

Well-made garden compost is the best source of organic matter: the lifeblood of a fertile soil. It breaks down slowly, releasing a steady supply of nutrients for strong, well-fed, disease-resistant plants. A boon to gardeners in years gone by, it has just as important a role today, enabling us to recycle waste for the good of the garden.

Making compost is the natural, ecologically friendly way to recycle your 'green' domestic waste.

Making and using compost

The ideal compost bin Good compost-making is not difficult if you follow a few golden rules, starting with the design of the bin.
▶ Build or buy a good-sized bin – a one metre cube is ideal. This volume allows high temperatures to develop inside the heap, which are needed to start the breakdown process.
▶ The traditional bin is made of treated wooden slats with 2cm gaps between the slats to allow air into the heap. The top is left open for adding material but must be covered to keep off the rain. One side can be opened to dig out the compost.
▶ Bins constructed from sections of reinforced chicken wire, or modern plastic bins can be equally effective.
▶ If you have space, use two or three bins for different composts at varying levels of maturity.

Making your own traditional wooden compost bin

Recycle old wooden pallets, or use new treated timber to build a structure that lasts.
▶ You will need four uprights for the corners and planks cut to one metre lengths for the slats. Screw the slats between the uprights, leaving 2cm gaps, until you have a box shape.
▶ Unscrew the bottom planks for access to the compost. Cover the top with a piece of old carpet to keep the rain off.

Golden rules for successful compost-making The secret of good composting is to produce a high temperature that breaks down a variety of plant waste from the garden and kitchen. Mixing moist, soft plant waste with drier, more fibrous material helps to keep the heap well aerated and damp, which encourages decomposition.
▶ As you make the heap, activate the compost by adding small amounts of soil between the layers and watering with nettle-manure solution, made by steeping chopped nettles in water. Add a handful of garden chalk or lime to balance acidity.
▶ Tread the heap from time to time, to firm it down and to remove any large air pockets.
▶ Test the temperature of the heap by inserting a wooden stick into the centre. It should feel hot to the touch.

Shred woody waste

Chopping or shredding material for composting – particularly woody cuttings – speeds up the process of breaking down. Recycle newspapers and plain cardboard by shredding them before adding to the heap.

What not to put on your compost heap Do not add weeds with strong roots or seed heads which will sprout. Coloured paper or cardboard and painted wood shavings will all contaminate your compost, and anything too solid, such as citrus peel, won't rot down at the same speed as the other waste. Meat or fish scraps will attract vermin, and bread, pasta and rice can form moulds that attack the bacteria responsible for decomposition. In the old days, these would have been used to feed the dogs or chickens.

Quick action To accelerate the breakdown process and maintain the temperature, turn the heap every few months to move the less-rotted material to the centre.

Too dry or too wet Spray the heap with water if it becomes dry – keep it moist but not soggy. If a white mould appears on the outside of the heap, it is too dry.
▶ If the compost has a nasty smell of ammonia, it is too wet and not aerated enough. Remake the heap, adding more absorbent and fibrous material, such as sawdust or shredded paper, which will increase aeration, and turn more often.

The best way to use your compost Dig a liberal amount of well-rotted garden compost into the soil in early spring, around 5kg per square metre. Spread a further 5cm layer as mulch over the soil's surface in late spring. This will help to control weeds, conserve soil moisture, protect roots against frost and add more organic material to the soil.
▶ Partially rotted compost will burn the roots and stems of most plants, but you can use it safely with potatoes, tomatoes, cucumbers, courgettes, gourds and pumpkins. Mix a few forkfuls with soil in the planting hole and spread more over the soil surface around the plant – but not touching the stem.

Natural propagator Place trays or pots of seedlings and cuttings on the surface of a half-made compost heap, but not a very hot new heap. The extra warmth will encourage growth.

An ideal planting mix Make an excellent planting mixture, to use for pricking out or potting on, by sieving equal parts of compost and soil through a fine wire-mesh sieve. You can make your own garden sieve by removing the base from a wooden box and fixing fine wire mesh over the area.

Making a compost heap

1 To ensure good ventilation at the bottom of the heap, spread a layer of branches at ground level.

2 Cover this with a layer of decomposed organic matter. This will activate decomposition in your heap.

3 Make up the third layer from garden and kitchen waste. It should be about 30cm thick.

4 Alternate soft wet waste (grass clippings, peelings) and dry waste (dead leaves or straw) or make a mixture.

5 Water regularly. Moisture evaporates as the heap warms up, and this can affect the decomposition process.

6 Do not add too many loads of grass cuttings at first. Mix with drier material to keep the process working.

7 Activate the heap with manure, comfrey leaves, or a nettle-manure solution (see page 269) every 7cm.

8 Cover to prevent the heap from drying out or being rained on. Rain washes away nutrients and cools the heap.

A well-prepared soil

Preparing the soil is the indispensable first stage for a successful garden. Although we tend to dig less today than gardeners used to do, the time and effort expended will bring ample rewards.

The importance of digging

How often should you dig? Digging breaks up and aerates the soil, it buries the weeds and exposes soil pests to be eaten by the birds or killed by frost. However, digging too often can upset the ecological balance of the soil by interfering with micro-organism activity, which helps to break down organic matter and aids the absorption of nutrients by plant roots. Thorough digging once a year is generally all that is needed.

The best time to dig Ideally, dig in autumn to bury old weed growth, incorporate organic material and expose the clods of soil to frost, which will break them up. If a green manure crop is to be grown over winter, dig the soil during late summer and sow the crop immediately.
▶ Avoid digging when the soil is too wet, which can damage its structure and cause it to compact. A simple test is to squeeze a handful of the soil. If it crumbles it is all right to dig, but if it sticks together it is too wet.

Digging techniques Simple digging – lifting out a spade's depth of soil and turning it over – is adequate when working on cultivated beds, but if you are preparing a new bed or digging in a lot of organic matter, single or double digging is preferable. These traditional techniques involve digging a

Spiking the soil with an aerator assists surface drainage.

series of trenches to a single or double spade's depth, and filling each empty trench with soil from the next as you dig. All this hard work will increase the depth of the topsoil, break up compacted layers in the soil and improve drainage.
▶ On shallow soils, dig down to the subsoil and incorporate small amounts of topsoil into the subsoil to increase the depth of cultivated ground.

Watch your back Do not overreach yourself by tackling too large an area or by attempting to take up too much earth with each spadeful – you should be able to lift it without difficulty. Bend knees and elbows rather than your back while lifting the spade. Spread out the work – two hours a day, or digging about 20 square metres of soil that is neither too heavy nor too stony, is enough. Any more and you will wear yourself out.

Spring digging and weed control Digging in spring can bring thousands of weed seeds to the surface, which will then germinate.
▶ To avoid a mass of weeds among your seedlings, hold off sowing until the weeds have grown and you have cleared them to produce a clean seedbed for your crops and flowers. If the soil is dry, watering will stimulate weed growth and speed up the process.

The lazy no-digging method When conditions are dry, digging on a light soil can cause valuable moisture to be lost. Instead of setting to the hard work of digging, an alternative is to cover the soil with a thick layer of well-rotted compost or manure. This layer protects the soil from water loss and

Easy digging with a rotavator

For breaking up, aerating and cultivating large areas of soil, powered rotavators take the strain out of the task. Rotavators are available in different sizes and come with a range of attachments. The smaller hand-held models are ideal for the average garden. They are not strenuous to use and are powered by petrol motors. Hire shops will have a range for hire at reasonable rates.

compaction, and is gradually drawn into the soil by worms. Their busy activity helps drainage and aeration.
▶ If you do not make your own compost, buy some soil-conditioning organic material such as composted bark, composted wood or famyard manure from a garden centre, or contact your local authority composting centre for a supply of recycled green waste.

Getting ready to plant

Controlling weeds Bare, weed-free soil is much easier to cultivate than ground covered with growth. Weeds will take nutrients out of the soil, encourage pests and diseases and make the garden look untidy. Preventing weeds from taking hold is an important job to keep on top of.
▶ Keep freshly cultivated soil clear of weeds by covering the area with old carpet. Leave it in place until you are ready to use the ground. On small areas, recycle flattened cardboard boxes covered with a layer of soil. The cardboard controls the weeds and slowly rots to add organic matter to the soil.
▶ If weeds have been allowed to develop, mow them down right after they flower. If you let them go to seed, you will have to contend with generations of hardy survivors.

Making nettle manure

1 Half-fill a bucket with chopped nettles and add rainwater (10 litres of water to 1kg of chopped nettles).

2 Cover the bucket and then leave to infuse for around 3–4 weeks.

3 Filter the mixture – it will now have a strong odour. To use, dilute 1 part infusion to 4 parts water.

4 Use the diluted solution to water the roots of plants, to enrich the soil or spray as a foliar feed.

Which green manure crops?

There are many plants you can grow as a green manure. Each one has its particular benefits.

To enrich the soil and add nitrogen Grow fodder plants such as alfalfa, clover and spring vetch.

As winter ground cover Grow rye, which is very helpful in eliminating couch grass.

In a dry climate Grow phacelia – its pretty blue flowers also attract bees.

For rapid growth Grow mustard seed – it thrives when sown at the end of autumn.

Before you sow or plant Dig only well-rotted compost and manure into the soil. Fresh material should be left in a heap to decompose before it is dug in, while partially broken-down material can be spread over the soil surface as a mulch that will gradually rot and be taken into the soil by worm activity.
▶ You can enrich a mulch with wood ash, poultry manure, phosphate-rich bone meal, nitrogen-rich dried blood, or blood, fish and bone meal, a balanced general feed. You can also use nettle manure (left) to improve the soil.

Don't forget green manure Green manure crops can be used at any time of the year to improve and enrich the soil. These quick-growing crops (above) are cut down and dug in at the height of their growth, just before flowering. Their top growth protects the soil surface from erosion and prevents weeds, and the roots improve drainage and aeration. When the crop is dug into the soil, it adds organic matter, which slowly breaks down to release valuable plant nutrients.

Rake over the soil Before sowing seeds or planting out small seedlings, it is important to break up the soil surface into a fine crumbly texture so that plant roots will establish quickly. Rake over the surface with a soil rake until large clods are broken down to a fine, level finish – called a fine 'tilth'. Remove large stones and any remaining weeds.
▶ **The best way to rake** Hold the rake like a broom, as upright as possible. The teeth should be almost parallel to the soil, so they do not go too deep. Work evenly back and forth in small sections.

Hoe lightly Avoid hoeing more than 5cm deep. This shallow action will cut off new weed growth near the soil surface and avoid bringing up more seeds from lower down. Weed seeds buried below 5cm are unlikely to germinate and grow.
▶ Keep a hoe in a handy spot, ready to take with you whenever you walk around your garden, so you can 'worry away at the weeds'.

Sowing seeds and planting out

There are as many tips and tricks for sowing, thinning, potting on and planting out as there are gardeners to recommend them. Everyone has their own sure-fire favourite, discovered by trial and error or passed on by word of mouth.

Successful sowing

Testing the seeds The capacity of seeds to germinate diminishes over time and the expiry date on the pack can be optimistic if the seeds are not stored correctly. Once the packet has been opened and the seeds exposed to heat and humidity, the seeds' condition will deteriorate rapidly. Try these traditional tests for success.

▶ To sort the viable seeds from the others before sowing, soak them in a glass of water. Within half an hour the good ones will sink and the others will remain floating on the surface.

▶ To test germination, place 10 seeds on a couple of layers of moistened kitchen towel on a saucer and seal them in a plastic bag. Put the bag in a warm, but not hot, place and wait for the seeds to sprout. If eight or more sprout, the germination chances for the rest of the batch are good. Seven or less is a poor result; the seeds can still be sown, but you should add a few more to compensate.

A chilling experience
Nuts and shrub seeds such as walnuts, cob-nuts, cotoneaster, euonymus and viburnum need to be exposed to cold for up to four months before they will germinate.
▶ Pierce the base of a plastic container to make drainage holes, and add the seeds between layers of sand, making sure they do not touch. Cover with fine chicken wire to keep off cats and rodents and bury the pot at the foot of a north-facing wall. In March, dig up the pot, recover the seeds from the sand, and plant up in pots.

Early sowing tips Most seeds need a night-time temperature of at least 13°C to germinate. Some will sprout at less, including carrot at 9°C, and radish and lettuce at 10°C.
▶ Warm the soil by a degree or two before sowing to get an early crop. Cover it with a cloche or a piece of old carpet or ground sheet weighed down at the edges with bricks or soil.

▶ After sowing, cover the seeds with a cloche or a homemade mini-greenhouse made out of a large plastic bottle with the base cut off. Leave the top open. This protection will also prevent mice, snails, rabbits and pigeons from nibbling the young shoots.
▶ Do not sow in frozen or very wet ground.
▶ Sow cold-sensitive plants that need a longer growing period, such as melon, tomato, aubergine, begonias and geraniums, in pots or trays and put in a cold frame for an early start.
▶ Speed up germination indoors by placing seed trays or pots on a plank of wood on top of a radiator or other warm place.

The apple tree and the lilac Follow the rhythms of nature and read the signs around you. Sow vegetables and cold-resistant flowers when the apple blossom opens. With more delicate species, wait for the lilac to flower.

The friendly mole The fine, rich soil from mole hills is excellent as sowing and potting compost or for using as a top-up for pot plants. To make your own fine soil, pass soil from your borders through a 2mm mesh sieve.

Waste not, want not If you buy your eggs in old-fashioned cardboard boxes, you can separate the sections and use them as plant pots. Put them directly in the soil when the seedlings are ready to plant out – the cardboard will gradually decompose in the ground, adding organic matter.

UNDER GLASS

The heated mini-greenhouse: a trump card for tender seedlings

The more exotic a plant's origins, the more likely it is that the seeds will need extra warmth to germinate. A heated mini-greenhouse, or propagator, is the perfect answer. Essentially just a seed tray with a transparent cover, a propagator provides a sealed humid environment and heat via soil-warming cables to encourage germination and rooting. Mist propagators supply the extra moisture needed by softwood or greenwood cuttings, such as ceanothus, forsythia, hydrangea and viburnum, while their root systems develop. Both types of propagator are economical to buy and run, and easy to use.

A piece of chicken wire placed over the seed tray makes an excellent template for sowing large seeds evenly.

Sow with the rising moon
When the moon is in the ascendant, plant energy is said to be drawn upwards, making germination more likely. On the other hand, planting out should take place in the descendant phase, when the lunar energy in the soil will encourage the growth of new roots.
▶ Sow in the morning when the warming conditions will benefit seed germination.

Avoid backache
A seed dispenser will help you to sow rows of seed without bending. Improvise with a piece of plastic tubing about a metre long. Drop the seeds down the tube and into the drill (left).

Sowing small seeds
Fine seeds, such as petunia, begonia and lobelia, may stick to your fingers and be difficult to spread out. Mix the seeds with dry sand or coffee grounds in an old flour shaker and shake the mix lightly over the soil. Or use a piece of folded card and tap it gently to keep the mix flowing. Don't go back over already seeded areas.

A pencil tip
Spread moistened seed compost in a seed tray, take an ordinary pencil and dip the lead tip into the soil to make a small hole. Then use the moistened tip to pick up a tiny seed – the moisture makes it stick – and poke it into the hole. Use the blunt end to cover the seed with compost.

Sowing large seeds evenly
When sowing broad beans, peas, French beans and other large seeds, place a piece of chicken wire over the seed tray and sow one seed per hole.

Good insurance
Sow seeds in pairs to avoid blank pots and to make sure you have enough plants. If both seeds grow, cut out the weakest one at soil level.

Do not sow too deeply
In nature seeds fall to the ground and, generally, nobody buries them. Remember this if you do not have instructions for the sowing depth of seeds. Small seeds should be close to the surface and only just covered with soil. This used to be done using a feather, but an artist's paintbrush works well, too.
▶ Bury large seeds, such as nuts and acorns, at twice the depth of their largest dimension.
▶ In lighter soils, bury the seed a little deeper to encourage better rooting.
▶ In less fertile soils, sow seeds more thickly to allow for poor germination and development. Thin growth can encourage the invasion of weeds, which might smother tender seedlings.

Help hard-skinned seeds to germinate
Although soaking hard seeds often works (right), you may have to break into the seed coat on very tough seeds to let in enough water for germination to take place. Making a small nick in the outer shell of the seed with a clean sharp knife or small hacksaw is a tried-and-tested technique. Another one is scarification, which involves rubbing the seeds against sandpaper or another rough surface. Seeds that benefit from scarifying include camellia, ceanothus, hawthorn, sweet pea and wisteria.

Soak hard seeds Plants of the Leguminosae family such as haricot beans and peas – and even lupins and mimosa – have very thick skins. To aid germination, soak them for 24 hours in warm water or overnight in a cup of hot tea so they swell and soften before sowing.

Protect seeds from hungry birds by covering them with netting, or newspaper kept moist. Keep an eye on the seeds and once they begin to germinate remove the newspaper.

Sowing and planting

Sowing seeds in trays

1 Mix 1 part fine sand with 2 parts sterilised seed compost and fill a seed tray with the mixture.

2 Level the compost then tamp it down with a block of wood to 12mm below the lip of the seed tray.

3 Moisten the compost thoroughly with a spray or fine rose without displacing the mixture.

4 Sow the seeds evenly over the surface using a seeder or folded card. Mix fine seeds with dry sand.

5 Cover the seeds with a fine layer of sifted soil.

6 Then cover the tray with glass and put it in a well-lit room out of direct sun. Wipe the glass clean occasionally.

New forms of seed for greater success Coated or pelleted seeds are covered in a layer of clay that contains agents such as bird and animal repellent and fertiliser that stimulate growth and protect from diseases.

Selfish genes F1 hybrid seeds are more fertile than those bred by more traditional selection methods. They do not pass on this genetic potential so the seeds produced by F1 hybrid plants will not be as fertile as the parent plant. To grow hybrid varieties, it is necessary to buy the specially bred seed each time you need it.

Marker seeds When sowing outside, plant stronger, faster-germinating seeds next to tiny ones to break the soil crust and help the little ones push through. Victorians used radishes as marker seeds for poppies, evening primroses and carrots.

On edge Melon, marrow, courgette, squash and cucumber seeds like to be planted edgewise, not flat on the soil.

Collecting your own seed In days gone by, collecting seed from flowers and vegetables was often the only means of guaranteeing more plants the following year. Today, it still makes sense to save seeds from annuals and biennials, and from salad crops, but you will need to purchase new seeds every few years to maintain quality. To obtain healthy seed:
▶ Collect seed only from the best, disease-free plants.
▶ Keep the plant well-watered while flowers and seed heads are forming and stake if necessary to keep them off the ground.
▶ Allow the seed to dry naturally on the plant.

Sterilising compost The microbes in compost can be lethal for seedlings. The most damaging soil-borne microbe causes damping off, a fungal disease that most gardeners will have experienced. Mix small pieces of charcoal with the compost to decontaminate it, or sterilise small quantities by baking the compost at 80–90°C in the oven. Buy fresh compost each year.

Discouraging birds To keep birds at bay, cover seed beds with netting, fleece or a single layer of pegged-down damp newspaper. Or cover the soil with a thin layer of fine gravel.
▶ Prickly branches such as holly, rose and berberis, tied to strings suspended across the seeded area, can also deter birds.
▶ Threading foil milk bottle tops on string stretched across the bed is a tried-and-tested deterrent. If you don't have milk bottle tops, use strips of kitchen foil or unwanted CDs instead.

Problem paws Prickly prunings or a mulch of gravel may also deter cats from digging in your beds. Anything that is uncomfortable on their paws should keep them away.

Transporting seedlings Many gardeners like to swap plants with their friends, which sometimes means that seedlings and cuttings must make long journeys.
▶ Sow seeds in whole egg boxes (right) so you can transport the seedlings easily. Closing the box for the journey will give the young plants extra protection.
▶ For short journeys, cuttings can be pushed into holes made in a half potato (right), which will keep them moist. Wrap the potatoes in damp newspaper to ensure they don't dry out.

'Pots' made of rolled newspaper decompose in the soil, so you can plant the seedlings without disturbing their roots.

Looking after seedlings

Healthy seedlings All seedlings will grow towards the light. Turn the tray each day to ensure their growth is balanced.
▶ Do not put seedlings in full sunlight, especially in a large window where they may be scorched.
▶ Give plants a good watering at least one hour before you lift them out of the compost for transplanting. They will retain the water and survive the shock of being moved much better. Keep transplants in a plastic bag as you plant them out.
▶ Plant out in the cooler part of the day.

Thinning for stronger plants Thin out seedlings when they have two or three well-formed leaves. Larger seedlings will become crowded and will be harder to separate. They may grow tall and spindly and turn pale: all signs of weakness in young plants that cannot be rectified.
▶ If seedlings become overcrowded, do not thin them out by pulling on their stems. It may damage the roots of the seedlings that remain. Instead, cut the unwanted seedlings off at the base with pointed scissors and they will die naturally.

Nature and nurture

Victorian and Edwardian nurserymen certainly lived up to their name. They were enthusiastic breeders who produced many of the important varieties of plants we know today. Their plant-breeding efforts often took many years to produce new varieties which, if they showed promise, were multiplied by grafts from the mother plant.

Occasionally pure chance played a part. The famous Granny Smith apple came from a pip that sprouted on a manure heap belonging to an Australian grandmother by the name of Smith.

Harden off seedlings for planting outside When the temperature outside is still low, place trays of seedlings into cold frames or an unheated greenhouse for a week or two, to harden them off. For small numbers of seedlings, dig a trench in the ground to hold the tray and cover with a pane of glass. Remove the glass whenever conditions are warm. You can then transplant seedlings out into the garden, but cover them with fleece or a tent of newspaper if there is a risk of frost.

Damping off To avoid this seedling disease, make sure the top centimetre of the compost contains at least 50 per cent good drainage material, such as sharp sand. The lower layer should be straight compost, which is more nutritious and encourages the seedlings to form a strong root system. Avoid letting the compost become waterlogged.
▶ Keep the compost around the seedlings well aerated, and provide plenty of light and fresh air. Lightly watering the seedlings with camomile tea is an old herbal remedy used to prevent damping off.

Never let the soil dry out
Seedlings need to be kept moist but not wet. The difference is small, but by observing when they droop, and testing the compost with your finger, you will soon learn through experience how much water they need. The best way to avoid damping off disease is to spray the compost lightly or to dribble water from a sponge to moisten but not drench the surface.

Sow into the soil Californian poppy (*Eschscholzia californica*), cornflower (*Centaurea*), love-in-a-mist (*Nigella*), clarkia and many plants of the *Leguminosae* family such as broom and lupin do not transplant well. Once all danger of frost has passed sow these directly into the garden soil where they are to be grown.

Protecting young plants Seedlings and small plants can be damaged by harsh weather or even hot, direct sunlight. When they are at risk, cover the plants with fleece or a dampened dustsheet draped over a frame. This allows rainfall and light to pass through, but gives protection.

Handling seedlings Lift out seedlings carefully with a dibber, a notched strip of wood or an old pencil or pen, and hold them by the leaves rather than the stem or roots. Plants such as radish, beet and other root vegetables may be set back by transplanting.

Watering your garden

We take our modern plumbing for granted, but water has not always been available at the turn of a tap. No wonder gardeners have learned to guard it jealously and use it wisely, devising all sorts of strategies for coping with both floods and drought.

Two golden rules for watering – never water in the heat of the day, and water a lot but not too often.

Watering wisdom

The best time to water Never water during the heat of a sunny day. The water will evaporate before it can soak into the soil and benefit the plants. A plant's leaves may also be scorched by the magnification of the sun's rays through any droplets of water that are resting on them.

▶ Also avoid watering in early evening after a hot day, as the cool water will vaporise on the warm surface of the soil, creating a humid atmosphere around the plants that can encourage fungal diseases.

▶ If the weather is very hot, it is better to water in the cool of the early morning or later on in the evening when the soil temperature has dropped.

Not too little and not too often It is better to soak the soil from time to time than to water sparingly every day.

▶ Soaking the soil to a good depth will encourage your plants to grow deeper, stronger root systems, capable of tapping reserves of water during periods of drought.

▶ Light watering does not penetrate down into the soil, and

encourages roots to seek water at the surface, producing a shallow-growing root system that is vulnerable to drought: one that will suffer if you forget to water when it is hot.

Water delivers nutrients Water carries soluble nutrients to plant roots deep in the soil. However, excessive rainfall or heavy watering can wash away nutrients from the soil's surface, especially on sandy soils and slopes. Replace nutrients regularly by adding garden compost or similar organic material to the soil and by applying fertilisers when needed.

Seasonal watering
In spring, autumn and winter, make sure you water your plants in the morning rather than in the evening. This will help to protect them from the cold when the temperature drops at night, which could cause droplets of water on the leaves to freeze.

Preventing soil erosion

Heavy rainfall or excessive watering on sloping ground can wash away topsoil and create furrows in the surface. Stabilise slopes by building level terraces to plant into.

▶ A retaining wall at the foot of a terrace is the best way to hold soil in place. It will encourage water to soak into the soil and benefit the plants too. Planting a low hedge along the wall line is an attractive way of edging the terrace.

▶ As an alternative to terracing, you could sow a ground cover of plants to hold the soil in place. Good ground-cover plants for banks and slopes are ground ivy, periwinkle (*Vinca minor*) and rose of Sharon (*Hypericum calycinum*).

▶ Another, more modern, way of holding the soil in place, is to use a synthetic semipermeable ground-cover fabric. Lay the fabric at an angle to the slope to reduce the risk of it being dislodged by downward drag, and peg it securely to the ground at intervals along its length.

▶ Once the fabric is in place, it will absorb water and help to prevent the soil under it from washing away. You can then plant shrubs and ground-cover plants through the fabric, and in time their roots will also help to stabilise the surface.

Hoeing to reduce water loss

Hoeing not only controls weeds, which compete with other plants for water, it also makes the soil surface crumbly, allowing water to soak in quickly to nourish the roots. Take care not to hoe too deeply to avoid damaging surface roots and stems.

Mulching to conserve water

By mulching the surface of the soil when it is moist, you can reduce the loss of moisture through evaporation. A mulch also prevents weeds growing, which means that your plants get all the moisture there is available.

A homemade water reservoir For thirsty vegetables or any plants that need a lot of water, sink a terracotta pot, or a large plastic bottle with drainage holes punched into the bottom, into the soil next to the plant. When you make your watering rounds, fill the container with water, which will then slowly soak into the soil without any waste.

Hosepipe know-how

Gently does it Water with a gentle spray. Better still, use a perforated hosepipe, which will automatically produce a constant light spray, or a seep hosepipe (below) which will apply a trickle of water where it is needed. These systems are traditionally left in place all summer. Seep hoses can even be disguised under a mulch around permanent plantings so that they can get their water to the base of plants unnoticed. If you attach either of these simple systems to a time clock, it will make watering the garden all the more discreet and easy.

▶ To improvise your own seep hose, take an old hose and make small holes along its length using a bradawl to puncture the surface. Clamp or block one end of the pipe and attach the other to a tap. Turn on the tap gently to achieve a 'seep'.

A coordinated system Wherever possible, buy your hose, attachments and component parts from the same manufacturer to make sure they fit together well. Invest in a thick, durable, good-quality hose that will not kink. A coloured wall reduces the amount of light that penetrates the hose, preventing algae growth on the inside.

Avoid pressure Do not use a strong, forceful spray when watering your garden plants. The weight of water can cause stems and branches to break off and flower petals to be damaged. Water at the base (right) or keep to a light spray, arching the water over the plants so that it falls naturally from above.

▶ The same technique is a quick way of oxygenating ponds with fish during the heat of summer. Play the hose at least 60cm above the water to carry oxygen into the pond.

Creating a watering well

1 To concentrate water where it is needed, build up a ring of soil 30–50cm away from the stem of the plant.

2 Scoop out some soil from around the stem to create a well. Firm the edge, sloping it towards the stem.

3 Gently fill the well with water, avoiding damage to the retaining wall. Repeat until the soil is soaked.

4 The water will seep into the soil around the roots, ensuring the shrub or tree is kept well watered.

Well-behaved hoses Use old small terracotta pots to make sure your hoses behave properly. Stack two pots on the ground at the edge of a flower bed, with the narrow bases facing to make an hourglass shape, then push a dowel through the centre holes into the soil. This makes a good-looking hose guide that will prevent your hose dragging over vulnerable flowers in the border and damaging them.

▶ You can also use a large, up-ended terracotta pot to wind your hose around for storage and to keep it from kinking. Once wound, push the nozzle end in the pot drainage hole to keep it in place. There are convenient hose-reel winders you can attach to the wall of your house next to the outdoor tap or ones you can wheel around the garden.

Automatic drip-feed watering To save time watering, install an automatic drip-feed system (below). Unlike a seep hose, which delivers water all along its length, automatic drip-feed and trickle systems consist of a tube and individual nozzles which can be positioned to direct water where it is most needed – to individual plants, for example, that need more water than others. A variety of nozzles are available to produce sprays or trickles, and the system can be expanded using connectors and additional tubes.

▶ Use to water individual containers on patios and balconies, window boxes, hanging baskets and plants in inaccessible parts of the garden.
▶ Do not be ambitious – keep the system compact and manageable. The nozzles need regular cleaning to prevent blocking with lime scale. Soak the nozzles in vinegar overnight to keep them clear.
▶ An automatic timer will complete the system. It makes it easy to water regularly at the best time of day and means your garden gets watered when you are on holiday.

Garden sprinklers Less efficient than seep hoses or drip-feed systems, sprinklers are still useful for delivering a fine spray over a specific area of the garden, such as a lawn or vegetable patch. However, they do use a large volume of water and some local authorities will permit their use only if you have a water meter. Use in the cool of the evening to reduce evaporation.

Dust off leaves When it is dry and dusty, conifers and evergreens that are not in bloom will benefit from a regular spray with water to clean the leaves and help to deter pests, such as red spider mites, which hate getting wet.

Watering plants indoors and under glass

Containers, planters, pots and troughs Potted plants can dry out rapidly, particularly in warm weather, and need regular watering to keep their roots healthy. There are also a few simple rules to remember.
▶ **Water twice** Water once and then wait for 15 minutes to allow the water to soak through the compost, then water again. This will ensure that the complete rootball and compost is moist throughout.
▶ **Use warm water** Let water warm up to ambient temperature before use. Applying cold water from the tap to a warm root system can cause the plant to go into shock and suddenly wilt. If you are in a hurry, add a little hot water to the watering can to warm up the contents.
▶ **Get good drainage** Check that the drainage holes in the base of pots are kept clear to allow excess water to drain away. Make sure that all containers are raised off the ground using pot feet or bricks, or are standing on gravel or clay beads if they are in saucers. This will prevent water from building up in the pot and avoids damage to the roots. Clay beads retain moisture and will help to humidify the air around house plants and in greenhouses.

Rule of thumb It is not always easy to gauge when and how much water pot plants really need. One way is simply to insert a finger into the compost – if it feels moist, do not water. If it is dry, water well to moisten all the compost, but allow excess to drain out of the pot.

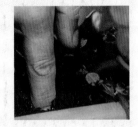

▶ The weight of the pot is also a good guide. Pick it up – if it feels heavy it will still be moist, if it is light then water well.

UNDER GLASS

Automatic watering in the greenhouse

There are several systems you can employ, some comparatively low-tech, others highly sophisticated.

Sand bench The simplest is a tray of sand, connected to a water tank that feeds it via drip-feed nozzles. Pots are set on the sand and take in water through their drainage holes.

Trickle irrigation This consists of a plastic pipeline with nozzles that drip water into pots, or feed misting jets that moisten plants from overhead. The flow of water from a small tank is usually controlled by a hand-adjusted valve.

Photo-electric control This system automatically switches on when the light reaches a certain intensity and runs for a set period. It can be used to run either of the systems above.

To prevent water loss through evaporation, the best time to water the garden is early morning or late evening.

Rainwater for your garden

Nature's gift Do not waste valuable rainwater. Instead, collect it in well-placed water butts around the garden. The earliest water butts were simply barrels or other containers placed wherever water would be needed for plants. They allowed the water to warm up as it stood, and many gardeners believe that warm water is best for plants.

Rainwater from the roof Purpose-built water butts can be connected to the drainage pipes and gutters of your house, greenhouse or out-buildings so that you can collect the run-off from the roofs. They are durable and hold a good volume of water, which can be tapped off from the bottom. Make sure

you raise the butt off the ground on bricks or a platform sold with the butt, so that you can get your watering can under the tap.
▶ Disguise the water butt by growing shrubs or climbing plants around it (left). Avoid rampant plants or those with thorns or needles – remember that you need to be able to get to it easily year after year.

▶ Keep the water clean by putting a lid on the butt to exclude light and to prevent small creatures and leaves from falling in.
▶ At regular intervals, add a little charcoal, available from garden centres, to keep the water clean and fresh.
▶ Place a plug of fine wire mesh at the top of the downpipe to stop debris getting into and polluting the water butt. Clean the wire filter from time to time to prevent debris from building up and blocking the downpipe.
▶ Make sure you have an overflow pipe from the top of the butt or you'll have to drain off some water from time to time.

Water butts for small areas For small gardens and patios, choose a compact water butt that will not look an eyesore. It should have a strong, durable design that will not leak.
▶ If you live in a flat, ask the Residents Association or property managers if you can divert rainwater from a downpipe into a butt for you and others to use.

Most plants prefer rainwater
If your tap water is hard, use rainwater to keep your lime-hating plants healthy.
▶ If you must use tap water, then add ericaceous compost or leaf-mould to the soil surface from time to time to increase its acidity. Alternatively, make acid water (see page 259) or add a small amount of vinegar to the water in the watering can (right). These measures will all help to create the acid environment that the plants demand.

Unpolluted rainwater When it rains after a dry spell, the first flush of rainfall is likely to be laden with dust and pollutants. You can divert the polluted rainfall by attaching a small bypass pipe to the end of your drainpipe, a temporary measure that will dispose of unwanted rainfall down the drain. Do not forget to remove the bypass after the first flush of rainfall so that you can continue collecting the clean rain.

Tools for gardeners

Many of the tools we have today were familiar in Roman times. But modern, lightweight, long-lasting materials make them more effective and easier to use than ever before. Invest in the best quality you can afford and look after your tools well.

A well-stocked tool shed

Spades, shovels and forks Choose your spade carefully, as you will use it more than any other implement. It's said that you can do every job in the garden with a good spade so you need one you can use comfortably but efficiently. Select one with a relatively short blade to make light work of digging. A 'Lady's Spade' is perfect for many gardeners – small and light, it puts less strain on the back – but those who have the strength for heavier work will want a heavier duty tool.
▶ **Spade or shovel?** A spade has a flat, sharp blade; a shovel has curved edges and is used for scooping up material. It tends to be larger and heavier.
▶ **The fork** Choose one to suit your strength. You will need a fork for breaking up heavy and stony ground, preparing the soil, turning a compost heap and forking up debris.

Sharp shears Straight-edged shears are best for cutting through soft growth. For woody material, shears with a serrated blade will grip and cut more effectively.

The days of large teams of hired gardeners are long gone, but tools still need to be stored well, however many you have.

▶ Angled, long-handled edging shears make edging lawns an easy and satisfying job, but check the handles are the right length for you before you buy. They can be as short as 90cm or as long as 110cm. On large lawns, cordless electric edge trimmers make short work of this regular task.

Quality secateurs This is a hard-working tool where quality is important. Strong, sharp secateurs cut through plant growth cleanly without causing damage and are effortless to use. Invest in the best, with hard steel blades that can be sharpened easily and replaced when worn.
▶ There are secateurs available with self-sharpening blades, which should always give a clean cut.
▶ Sharp scissor-action secateurs are the best for pruning soft growth with a clean cut. Anvil-action blades, which cut down on a soft metal plate, are best for cutting through hard, dry woody material. Invest in a good-quality sharpening kit to keep blades razor-sharp at all times.

Hand hoes and cultivators Available in various designs, the hoe is one of the most useful tools in the garden.
▶ The digging hoe is used for controlling weeds and breaking up small areas of hard ground.
▶ The Dutch hoe is perhaps the most familiar, with a flat, thin blade that is pushed and pulled through the soil to loosen the soil crust and chop off weeds without damaging plant roots.
▶ The angled draw hoe is used for chopping off heavy weed growth, for earthing up and for making seed drills.
▶ The hand cultivator (see box, top right) has three curved, narrow prongs that are dragged through compacted and clogged soil to break it up.

The indispensable trowel

A trowel is the best tool for setting out small plants and seedlings without damaging their roots. It is convenient, easy to use and ideal for carrying out small jobs in restricted spaces. Trowels are often sold in sets with a small fork and hand hoe, which are designed for gardening on balconies and patios, and in all types of containers. They come in a variety of materials, including very durable plastic, and coated steel and carbon steel. If you use these tools frequently, think about investing in a stainless steel set – they are attractive and will never rust.

Improvised ruler On the handle of a wooden rake or hoe, make small notches every 5cm and highlight them with coloured paint. Then you'll always have a ruler for measuring distances between drills and seeds after raking or hoeing soil.

Ready to hand Stand large flowerpots at key places around the garden to put your tools in when working. This avoids misplacing them when they're not in use and finding the rusty remains months later. Alternatively, wear a belt that holds the small tools you are working with, or invest in a tool caddy or trug to keep all your small tools to hand as you work.

A manicured lawn It is said that the English manicure their lawns with nail scissors. While it is true that the lawn can be a source of pride, it is a pair of long-handled lawn shears you need, not scissors, for cutting grass in areas that are inaccessible to a lawn mower, such as along edges and under shrubs. These give a neat result and are easy to control – the alternative of a strimmer is speedy but may damage shrubs and tree trunks.

Improvised kneelers Really get down to it and garden on your knees, but take care to avoid straining your back and making your knees sore. To make a comfortable, soft kneeling pad, fill an old hot-water bottle with sawdust or sand and cover it on one side with a piece of old carpet.

Raking and sweeping There are two types of rake. A soil or garden rake has a head about 40cm wide with short fixed tines. Use it to break up the soil surface. A spring-tine rake is for clearing lightweight debris, such as leaves, and is essential for raking lawns clear. Find one with wooden rather than metal tines as it will be much springier and lighter to use.
▶ **A good stiff brush** That well-tended look to paths and patios is achieved only with a thorough sweep.

A sharp edge A half-moon edging iron with a sharp blade set into a straight handle gives a military neatness where a lawn meets a hard surface or border.

Off to the heap Treat yourself to a good-sized wheelbarrow with an inflatable tyre. Pneumatic tyres ride over irregular garden surfaces more easily than solid tyres and spread the weight of the load, reducing soil compaction. Buy the biggest wheelbarrow you can for fewer journeys, but don't overfill it with heavy material.

From the kitchen cupboard Use old spoons, ladles, forks and whisks to transplant tiny seedlings and mix up homemade solutions. An apple corer is an excellent dibber for tiny bulbs, and a colander makes an inexpensive trug.

A tool for every task

PREPARING THE GROUND

Flat spade	Digging, edging borders, making large planting holes
Fork	Digging in hard and stony soil. Moving and piling up plant material
Mattock	A pickaxe for breaking up heavy ground, loosening soil at the base of planting holes
Cultivator ❶	Loosening soil surface and breaking up clods
Rake	Levelling the ground, removing clods and stones
Digging hoe ❷	Controlling weeds, loosening soil, making furrows, working soil in small areas
Shovel	Removing earth from planting holes, moving heaps of material such as compost, gravel and manure

SHAPING, CUTTING, PRUNING

Loppers	Cutting inaccessible branches up to 3cm thick
Pruning knife	Taking cuttings from woody plants
Pruning saw	Cutting out medium-sized branches
Secateurs	Cutting stems up to 1cm thick; long-handled secateurs or loppers ❸ cut high branches 3cm thick
Shears	Trimming hedges and grass edges

WEEDING

Dutch hoe	Chopping off weeds, loosening and ridging up soil
Draw hoe	Chopping out strong weeds and roots, earthing up
Pronged weeder	Removing individual strongly rooted weeds.

PLANTING

Bulb planter ❹	Planting bulbs, tubers and corms, planting naturalised bulbs in grass
Dibber	Making planting holes for small plants, seedlings and potato tubers
Trowel	Digging small holes to plant out or dig up young plants

Make your tools last a lifetime

Protecting your secateurs Plant sap and rotting vegetation corrode the blades of secateurs. Each time you use them, wipe the blades with an oily rag to remove any residue and protect the metal. To sterilise the blades so diseases aren't passed on as you work, wipe them with methylated spirits.
► Sharpen shears and secateurs regularly by rubbing the cutting edge, round side down, with a sharpening stone dampened with water or oil. Blunt blades cause damage and possible die-back.

Clean tools To maintain your tools in good condition and to prolong their life, wash or wipe off soil and other residues with newspaper or a rag after using them. Use a small piece of wood to scrape off earth; never use metal, which can scratch. With a rag or fine steel wool, soaked in engine oil, wipe all metal parts. Do this after every use, or at least several times each season.
► Keep oil in a hand-soap bottle with a plastic plunge dispenser for ease of use.

Take care of tool handles Protect wooden handles by treating them once a year with linseed oil. Before you put the tools away for the winter, smooth the wood with fine sandpaper to remove rough areas and dirt, rub on the oil and leave it to soak in.

Natural rust control
Use a cut onion sprinkled with castor sugar to rub down rusted metal parts. Change the onion when it gets dirty.
► If you can afford it, invest in polished stainless steel spades and forks, which are easier to use and to clean, and do not rust.

Instant protection Keep the metal parts of your tools from rusting by plunging them into a bucket, at least 30cm deep, filled with a mixture of sand and a little lubricating oil. The abrasive sand will remove harmful residues and the oil coating will prevent rusting. Do this after each use.

In plain view Wrap brightly coloured tape around the handles of all your garden tools. This will not only protect the handle and give you a smoother, more comfortable grip but it will help you to see any tools you may have mislaid in the garden.

New uses for old tools When they are past their best in practical terms, old tools can be decorative too. Fix an old trowel to the door of your shed to make a good-looking and easy-to-grasp handle. Don't throw away 'antique' wooden spades, forks and hoes that are too heavy and worm-infested to use. Paint them and hang them along a fence.

Hard-wearing handles Traditional gardening tools such as rakes and hoes are mounted on strong, hard-wearing ash or beech handles. Unlike plastic, woods stays cool and dry in your hands. When choosing a wooden handle, look for one with a straight grain. A grain that is crooked or knotted will make the handle less durable.
► Cheaper, varnished, softwood handles will not last long.
► Some modern tools are attached to strong polypropylene handles that will be long-lasting and worth the money.
► Choose the right length of handle. If it is too long it will feel unbalanced, too short and it will leave you with a backache. Long-handled spades and forks are generally more comfortable to use and give greater leverage.
► However, never use a handle as a lever – it might break and cause injury.

Looking after your cutting tools

1 After each time you use secateurs or shears, clean and sterilise the blades with alcohol or methylated spirits.

2 Sharpen blades regularly with a stone to maintain a clean cutting edge that will not damage plants when pruning.

3 Before putting secateurs away for winter, oil all parts making sure oil flows around the blade and mechanism.

Comfort tips Try out the different shapes of handle before buying tools: many people find a D-shaped handle more comfortable than a simple T. And if any handle feels too hard, wrap it in flexible rubber tubing, such as the kind used to insulate pipe work.

Empty pipes and hoses At the end of autumn, do not forget to drain all water out of garden pipes and hoses. Water left in these can freeze and cause a rupture.

Using power tools

Safety first Always wear protective equipment when using any power tools. Goggles, gloves and steel-capped boots are essential when operating rotavators and strimmers. Even when using a power mower you should wear leather boots or shoes.
▶ When you work with any electrical equipment in the garden, guard against shock by using a circuit breaker.

Operation ground clearance
Powered strimmers and brushwood cutters are invaluable modern tools for quickly cutting down light and heavy plant growth, particularly weeds.
▶ A range of models is available, powered by electric, 4-stroke and 2-stroke petrol motors. You don't have to buy your own – simply hire one when you need it.
▶ Strimmer and brushwood cutter heads have a rotating thread or wire for cutting down soft growth. For tougher jobs, a solid cutting disc with saw teeth can be used to cut down hard wooden growth up to 1cm thick. Take great care when using this blade.
▶ Larger models come with a body harness to take the weight and make working more comfortable.

Making a mower choice A manual cylinder mower is ideal for a small lawn, but for most people the powered mower is a quick and less-strenuous way of mowing.
▶ Powered cylinder machines, with a roller at the back, mow to a very precise finish and produce a striped or 'coloured' effect. They need to be used regularly as they don't work well on long grass.
▶ A rotary mower cuts with a scythe action. It will cut all kinds of grass, including rough and long growth. Electric or petrol-driven models are available. Some incorporate a roller to give a striped finish.
▶ The hover mower, like the rotary type, cuts with a spinning blade. These are very light and make easy work of difficult-to-mow areas, such as slopes.

A reliable mower
For 4-stroke petrol mowers, record the time the machine is in use so that you know when to change the oil. Do the first oil change after 2–5 hours of use, thereafter every 25 hours or at least once a year.
▶ Keep the inside of the mower clean and free of grass and soil residue which might block the blade. Sharpen the blades at the beginning of the season and at regular intervals to maintain a sharp cutting edge.
▶ Clean the spark plugs at least once a year and replace every 100 hours. Change air filters every 50 hours.
▶ For safety's sake, deactivate the mower by disconnecting the spark plugs before cleaning or working on the machine.

Winter storage For a problem-free start-up in spring, clean everything scrupulously before storing for winter, as dirty metal parts can corrode very quickly.
▶ Provide dry shelter under canvas or an oilcloth. Avoid plastic covers, which can lead to condensation.

For a traditional striped finish to your lawn, you need a mower with a heavy roller.

> ### Mower service
> The best time to service your mower, or any other garden equipment, is in the winter when you do not need it and mechanics are less busy. In spring there is likely to be a long wait and you may not have your mower when you want to use it.

Gardeners' friends

Hedgehogs, frogs, toads and birds feed on many of the pests that attack our plants. They are valuable allies, as are worms that work hard in underground burrows. Bees and butterflies pollinate many flowers, and ladybirds are the sworn enemy of greenfly.

The birds and the bees

Welcoming hedges and bushes Hedgerows are a favourite habitat of birds: elder, dogwood, rowan, wild cherry, blackthorn and sea buckthorn all produce edible berries, while hazel trees, alder, viburnum and shrub roses have thick branched growth that can hide and protect nests.
▶ Use several of these species to create a bird-friendly native hedge, or dot them around the garden. Train climbing plants (such as ivy and creepers) up walls and fences. This will attract numerous insects – and the birds that feed on them.

Winter feeding Coarse-ground sunflower seeds, wheat, corn, barley, millet and peanuts will be dined on by most garden birds, including robins, wrens, sparrows, thrushes, tits and finches. Some birds relish a feast of worms and insect grubs, while others – such as the blackbird and thrush – prefer pieces of apple, pear and cherries. Try making a fat ball containing millet, barley and sunflower seeds – a favourite winter treat – and hang it in the garden.
▶ If you do not have a bird bath, place a few shallow, flat-bottomed pot saucers on the ground and fill them with water. Defrost water in winter for birds to drink.

Nest boxes Tits, treecreepers and other birds are very partial to fruit tree pests such as greenfly and codling moth. Put nest boxes in your orchard and these birds will protect your trees and fruit, while raising their brood. The box hole must be around 3cm in diameter to attract these species and not other types of birds.
▶ When building nest boxes, they must be designed to be secure, so that predators such as cats, squirrels and other birds cannot take the eggs or fledglings.
▶ The entrance hole must be positioned at the top of the box so that cats cannot reach in to attack young birds. Attach a slender perch that will just support the nesting bird. Place the box at least 1.5 metres from the ground, in dense bushes with slender branches that won't support the weight of predators.

Ensure a good harvest Bees and butterflies are valuable to the gardener. They feed on nectar and pollen from flowers, and in so doing pollinate numerous plants, particularly fruit trees, ensuring a good harvest. Attract pollinating insects by growing plants that yield a rich nectar source.
▶ **Perennials** Mallow, catmint, heather, yarrow, St John's wort and candytuft.
▶ **Aromatic plants** Thyme, rosemary, lavender, as well as sage, savory, marjoram, hyssop, lemon balm, camomile and garden myrrh. In the vegetable garden, dill, fennel, angelica and sunflower, or trefoil and phacelia as green manure.
▶ **Trees and shrubs** Lime, chestnut, acacia, common privet, buddleja, lilac with single or double flowers; shrubs bearing small fruit, particularly climbing raspberry bushes.

Building a nest box

Only use untreated wood. You will need: 12mm-thick wood for the roof and base, 23x28cm for the roof and 15x12cm for the base; 35x15cm of 12mm-thick wood for the back; 57cm of wood with the bark on, cut into 3 pieces 15cm wide for the sides and front (see step 1). Fix the roof with a 15cm length of 12x12mm beading. Make the entrance hole 3cm in diameter.

1 Cut bark wood in three pieces: one 15x16.5cm for the front, two 15x20cm for the sides, cut at a slant.

2 Bevel the top edge of the front section to match the sloping edges of the sides, and drill the entrance hole.

3 Glue the front and sides together, then screw in place. Fix on the back in the same way.

4 Fix the base section in the same way as the back. Screw on the roof and add beading to make it watertight.

A blue tit feeds from a ball of fat filled with wheat, nuts and seeds – a winter feast for hungry birds.

Planting nectar-rich flowers The ideal places for growing nectar-rich shrubs and perennials are ornamental flower beds and hedges bordering your garden, and alongside garden walls. Do not attract bees to borders alongside paths or areas of the garden used for relaxation and sports.

Other friendly creatures

Earthworms Earthworms are vital for fertile soil: they bury and digest plant waste such as leaves, stems and dead roots, drain the soil by digging tunnels, and strengthen soil structure. They're usually found in the top 15cm of the soil, but they can dig down to 1.8 metres. In winter, they burrow below the level of soil affected by frost and break up dense layers. Their aeration of the soil supplies oxygen and encourages bacteria. A million or more earthworms can be found in just one acre. Avoid cutting up worms with equipment by working in the middle of the day when they are deeper in the soil, and using a fork rather than a spade.

Free plant food Earthworms eat the equivalent of their body weight every day. They produce mounds of material on the soil surface called worm casts, which are highly nutritious and can be collected to feed your pots, window boxes and tubs.

The redworm These worms, also called manure worms, are smaller than earthworms and can be recognised by their bright pink-and-white ringed bodies. They play a vital role in a compost heap, converting plant material into brown, crumbly humus. There is no need to add them to your compost heap, they will find their own way there. When the earthworms take their place, you will know your compost is ready.

A home for hedgehogs Hedgehogs are very partial to slugs, snails, worms, insects, and small vertebrates, which they hunt

at dusk. Make sure they stay in your garden by providing a shelter in the winter, which they can also use as a hiding place for the rest of the year. Safe access to a pond or a large saucer filled with water is also necessary. Do not put out milk for hedgehogs – it is not good for them.

▶ Build a pile of logs and branches, 30–50cm high, leaving an entrance and a cavity in the centre. Line the cavity with dry leaves. Make sure that the retreat is positioned under the shelter of a leafy tree or against a sheltered wall – hedgehogs like to keep warm and dry. Reward your hedgehog for its hard work by putting out chopped-up apple close to its home.

Encouraging ladybirds
Ladybirds are one of the best allies the gardener has against insect pests, including aphids, scale insects and red spider mite. Encouraging them will reduce the need for other control measures. Colonies of ladybirds will build up in your garden and soon devour large numbers of aphids, up to 50 per day, each.

▶ Allow several clumps of nettles to grow in your garden. It may be an unpopular weed, but it harbours an aphid that will not attack your other plants and is an excellent food source for ladybirds. Ladybirds will build up and attack other aphids on your flowers, vegetables and fruits.

> *Ladybirds for sale*
> Ladybird larvae and other beneficial insect predators can be bought from specialist suppliers, often listed in gardening magazines. Place the larvae near to aphids and other pests and let nature take its course.

Where do ladybirds go in the winter? Ladybirds hide in cracks and crevices around your home and garden, to shelter from cold winter temperatures. They burrow into piles of leaves, stone walls, garden sheds, garages and any other hideaway they can find. Some are lured into the warmth of the house and take refuge on house plants. Try not to disturb hibernating colonies of ladybirds. In spring, the long black yellow-spotted larvae emerge and will start to eat aphids. They look nothing like the adults. Do not kill them as they will change into the familiar red spotted beetle.

Attracting frogs, toads and other wildlife There is nothing better than a pond for attracting wildlife into your garden. Frogs, toads and dragonflies will flock to water, and will eat insect pests and grubs that can be damaging to your plants.

Mosquito control Goldfish and other fish are welcome additions to any pond or lake, as they eat mosquito and other insect larvae that live in the water. Koi carp have even bigger appetites, feeding not just on these larvae, but also on slugs and other undesirable pests. However, these fish can become very large, so seek advice from your aquatic centre on the maximum number for the size of your pond.

SPRING

Buds are bursting, seeds are ready to be planted, green shoots are everywhere, and gardeners can't wait to pick up their tools. But though spring days are mild, beware of frosts at night.

JOBS FOR SPRING

Warm the soil with horticultural fleece This was not available to previous generations of gardeners, but nowadays fleece enables us to start gardening earlier than was possible in times gone by, and to expand the varieties of plants we grow. Sow seeds outdoors in early spring then cover the ground with a single layer of fleece.

Eradicate slugs and snails As the weather warms up, take precautions to protect young shoots from slugs and snails.

Tried-and-tested solutions include scattering crushed eggshells, bran or sharp grit around the base of plants or installing traps, such as a hollowed-out grapefruit or a jar of beer sunk in the ground.
► Hand-pick slugs and snails at night, but be prepared to stamp on them: they will return if you don't.

Thin excess oxygenating plants Rake floating plants from the pond, taking care not to puncture the plastic liner with the metal prongs. Lift out containerised plants and trim back a few stems

before replacing them. This will prevent the plants from becoming invasive.

Prepare the soil for early planting In the kitchen garden, spring is a good time to replenish the soil. Clear up perennial weeds, then dig in organic fertiliser, such as rotted manure or compost.
► Or grow green manure over winter and dig in the plants in spring.

Control moss in lawns Moss is most common in wet, shady lawns and in underfed grass. Treat it with lawn sand in spring, then rake out the dead moss. This is much more ecologically friendly than using moss killer.
►If the problem recurs, aerate the soil to improve drainage and feed regularly for strong growth. In dense shade, replace the lawn with ground-cover plants.

UNDER GLASS

Start off begonia tubers

Start tuberous-rooted begonias into growth in spring if you have a greenhouse. You will have large well-developed plants to put in the garden, and they will flower much earlier in the season than if you plant the tubers directly into the soil.
Fill a seed tray with seed-and-potting compost containing a peat-substitute rather than peat itself. Place the tubers with a small gap between each, pressing them into the compost and making sure that the slightly hollow side is facing upwards.
Do not water them in. Keep the tray in a warm, light position until the plants are strong enough to plant out.

March

TREES AND SHRUBS

Water young trees and shrubs
To retain moisture when you water, mulch the soil with well-rotted manure, bark or an attractive layer of gravel or stones (above).

Prepare sites for rhododendrons You will need to fill planting holes with ericaceous compost to give the shrubs a good start. Plant them before late May.

Propagate heathers Layer established heathers, or root heel cuttings of side shoots in a cold frame.

Plant bare-rooted deciduous trees Make sure the roots don't dry out before planting by soaking them in a bucket of water.

Hard-prune dogwoods Cut the stems to 5cm from the base.

Protect new shrubs Erect temporary windbreaks, such as netting or sacking.

Prune miniature roses Reduce the main stems by half and cut out any dead and frost-damaged shoots.

Plan a new hedge For a new hedge, plan out the area and dig a trench. Fill it with well-rotted manure or compost and plant the new shrubs at the end of the month when the soil is not waterlogged.

LAWNS AND PONDS

Sow new lawns if the weather is warm Rake the surface lightly to cover the seeds. On sandy soils, use a roller to firm the seedbed (above).

Aerate established lawns Rake thoroughly to remove dead grass and moss. Spike the soil with a garden fork to aerate it.

Mow for the first time Set the lawnmower blades on high. Mow when the grass is about 7.5cm tall.

Watch for fusarium patches in the lawn These are irregularly shaped areas of grass that turn brown in spring due to poor drainage. Treat with an appropriate fungicide, then take action to improve the drainage of the lawn.

Remove algae from ponds Use a net or rake.

Top-dress baskets of water lilies Use a good soil mixed with fertiliser. Mulch with a layer of grit.

Cut back marginal plants Remove any faded top growth.

KITCHEN GARDEN

Plant onion sets and early potatoes Do this from the middle of March, so long as the winter was not too wet.

Chit seed potatoes Place tubers in a tray or open egg box in a light position. They are ready to plant out when shoots are about 2cm long (above).

Dig potato trenches Add a generous quantity of manure to the bottom of each trench.

Plant out asparagus crowns Do this as soon as they arrive. Top-dress established asparagus beds with well-rotted manure.

Sow aubergines, basil, peppers, tomatoes and summer cabbages Place seed trays in a heated greenhouse at a temperature of 18°C.

FLOWERS AND BULBS

Top-dress established beds Sprinkle with a general organic fertiliser.

Plant out hardy perennials

Sow hardy annuals where they are to grow Half-hardy annuals should always be grown under glass.

Plant out summer-flowering bulbs in mild areas (above).

Deadhead daffodils Repeat for other flowering bulbs and winter-flowering plants.

Divide overgrown clumps of snowdrops

Sowing a new lawn

Powered cultivators can be hired to prepare an area of soil ready for planting a lawn in spring. However, many people are now returning to traditional methods of digging, and adding well-rotted compost. Digging is good exercise, and a form of stress busting.

April

TREES AND SHRUBS

Plant evergreen trees and shrubs Climbers, heathers and pot-grown wall shrubs can also be planted in April.

Transplant rhododendrons They do not like their roots disturbed too often, so only transplant if they have totally outgrown the space.

Prune winter-flowering heathers Remove the flower spikes as they fade.

Lightly prune shrubs that have finished flowering These include early-flowering clematis and Japanese quince. Hard-prune forsythias after flowering (above). Hard prune *Buddleja davidii* and *Hydrangea paniculata* to give more flowers in the summer.

Trim lavenders to shape

Deadhead early-flowering azaleas by hand Repeat for rhododendron bushes.

Sever rooted layers of forsythias Replant immediately where you want the new bushes to grow.

Feed established roses Use a rose fertiliser and mulch with well-rotted manure. Water and mulch new roses but do not feed.

Prune the stems of frost-burnt rose tips Cut them back to undamaged buds.

Tie in new shoots of ramblers and climbing roses Make them as horizontal as possible to produce more flowers. These shoots will replace last year's flower stems.

Top-dress container-grown trees or shrubs Replace the top 5cm of compost. Add a handful of water-retaining granules and slow-release fertiliser as necessary. Finish off with a decorative mulch.

LAWNS AND PONDS

Aerate, scarify and feed established lawns

Remove persistent weeds Dig out perennial weeds by hand, pulling out the roots. Use a chemical spot treatment as a last resort.

Sow new lawns and lay turf

Re-seed patches suffering from damage Top-dress with loamy soil or handfuls of spent potting compost.

Roll new lawns lightly This will help to firm the surface. Mow when necessary (usually about six weeks after sowing, depending on the weather) with the blades raised high.

Prepare new ponds for planting Cover the base and marginal shelves with a layer of rich, neutral to alkaline soil. Do not plant up until the soil has settled.

Sow seeds of bog primulas and mimulus in boxes

Plant deep-water and marginal aquatics Do this at the end of the month. Weight floating underwater oxygenators with stones and gently drop them into the pond. Place floating plants on the surface.

Divide and replant marginal aquatics Do this at the end of the month, finishing each basket with gravel to weigh down the soil (above, left).

Transplant self-sown seedlings Many deep-water floaters and marginal plants self-seed, so transplant the new plants to avoid overcrowding.

Propagate water lilies Lift, divide and replant overgrown water lilies. Cut the rhizomes into pieces, each with a growing point.

Mid-spring is a good time to plant water lilies, as the water begins to warm up.

Traditional garden structures

Spring is a good time to examine the bare bones of a garden and identify places where a new structure, whether a pergola or just a tub, would give it a lift. Reclamation yards are good sources for an old sink or traditional half-barrel, and many suppliers offer summerhouses and pergolas with antique appeal.

KITCHEN GARDEN

Hoe the vegetable patch
Frequent hoeing helps to keep weeds down. Work in between rows to avoid digging up seeds and disturbing seedlings.

Water seedlings Remember to water the vegetable patch during dry spells.

Earth up potatoes Do this as they grow and cover the leaves with straw, newspaper or horticultural fleece if a hard frost is forecast.

Thin vegetable seedlings sown last month Plant out summer cabbages (above).

Continue to plant onion sets In the north or colder areas, plant early potatoes.

Sow salad crops Grow these outdoors as well as in the greenhouse to stagger their harvest times.

Sow brassicas These include purple-sprouting broccoli, winter cabbages and late-summer cauliflowers. In colder areas wait another month until the soil has warmed up.

Plant tomatoes in growbags in the greenhouse

Plant out hardy herbs These include bay, hyssop, lavender, mint, rosemary and sage.

Sow annual herbs These include dill, fennel, parsley and pot marjoram. If basil was not sown last month, sow now under glass.

Propagate thyme Layer creeping stems and sever the new plants when the roots have fully developed.

Remove rhubarb flowers This must be done as soon as they appear, before they rob the plants of energy.

Harvest asparagus You will probably get your first crop at the end of the month. Cut the stems when they are 10–15cm high.

Check newly planted fruit trees Make sure that tree ties are secure and firm the ground if any trees or bushes have been lifted by spring gales.

Ventilate strawberries Remove cloches when the weather is fine. This will prevent the plants from becoming leggy, stop pest build-up and allow bees access for pollination. Remove flowers from young plants to prevent fruiting in their first year.

Prune stone-fruit trees Pruning is especially important with morello cherry trees. Cut out crossing branches first. On fan-trained stone fruit, remove those branches that are growing towards or away from the wall.

Mist open peach flowers Spray the flowers with water. This helps the fruit to set.

Protect open flowers on fruit trees and bushes If a heavy frost is forecast, place a layer of horticultural fleece over susceptible plants.

FLOWERS AND BULBS

Keep down weeds Hoe regularly between established plants, avoiding root damage. Water during dry weather.

Stake tall, weak-stemmed perennials Especially delphiniums and peonies.

Feed chrysanthemums Sprinkle a general fertiliser around each plant, raking it into the soil. Position stakes.

Begin to check for lily beetles Remove and squash all adults and any young that hide under the leaves in a layer of brown excrement.

Plant out tubers In mild areas at the end of the month, plant out chrysanthemums, dahlias, arum lilies and gladioli.

Plant late-flowering perennial plants

Sow half-hardy annuals under glass These include busy lizzies and petunias.

Set out spring-raised sweet pea plants

Propagate perennials Lift, divide and replant healthy outer sections of perennials such as heleniums, Michaelmas daisies and rudbeckias (left).

Deadhead faded blooms Remove dead flowers from early-flowering bulbs and spring bedding plants to promote continued flowering and prevent seed formation.

Pot up rooted dahlia cuttings Gradually harden them off by placing them in an open cold frame during the day. Pot up tuberous begonias.

Bring out container plants from their winter shelters

Prepare for summer colour Sow seeds of hardy annuals under trees and shrubs.

Awaken dormant plants Increase the watering of fuchsias and pelargoniums. Give a liquid feed to each plant every fortnight.

As spring bulbs finish flowering, remove faded flowers from daffodils, tulips and hyacinths.

May

TREES AND SHRUBS

Water in hot weather Spray the leaves of newly planted evergreens and hedges. Give the roots a thorough water.

Conserve moisture Spread a thick layer of shredded bark around young rhododendrons and heathers. This will keep weeds at bay and lock in the moisture.

Plant tender young shrubs and climbers Plants such as arbutus, choisyas, *Clematis armandii*, hardy fuchsias and hydrangeas are tender when young. Do not plant them out before the end of the month.

Tidy up spring-flowering shrubs Deadhead faded flowers, shorten long shoots and thin out old wood from spring-flowering shrubs, such as ribes, kerrias and spiraeas.

Prune hedging plants Cut back any newly planted hedges to encourage bushy growth. Clip privet and *Lonicera nitida* hedges into shape.

Halt invasive lilac Cut out suckers at the growing point from the bases of lilac trees.

Check new growth on rose bushes for aphids At the first sign of pests, spray with an insecticide that does not kill beneficial insects. Individual green fly can be removed by squashing them.

Boost rose beds Underplant formal rose beds with both bedding plants and annuals for summer colour.

Clip topiary to shape Trim bay and yew topiaries as soon as the growth begins to appear uneven (above).

Mulch rhododendrons to conserve moisture, and remove the dead flower heads to ensure a good show next year.

LAWNS AND PONDS

Water new lawns in dry weather (above)

Remove weeds Prick out perennial weeds using an old kitchen knife.

Start regular mowing Fine lawns need mowing at least once a week, and coarser grass once a fortnight.

Mow areas naturalised with early-flowering spring bulbs Mow the grass as soon as the bulb leaves die down.

Neaten lawn edges Prevent border plants from flopping over the lawn and creating bare patches. Support plants with sticks or canes, or edge the lawn with stones or bricks.

Feed poorly growing turf Winter rain leaches nutrients, making turf look yellow. Apply a high-nitrogen fertiliser.

Continue to plant up ponds Plant deep-water aquatics, bog and marginal plants in and around the pond. Collect and plant turions, the swollen buds of plants such as *Hydrocharis morsus-ranae*.

Propagate marginal pond plants Divide and replant overcrowded clumps of plants.

Maintain the bog garden In dry weather, flood the bog garden to keep plants moist.

KITCHEN GARDEN

Prepare beds for planting Early in the month, prepare the soil for courgettes, cucumbers, marrows, squashes and tomatoes. Sow the relevant seeds in pots or seed trays ready for planting out next month.

Erect supports for runner bean seedlings Use erect stakes with cross bars, or make a teepee.

Remove cloches Broad beans, carrots and early peas no longer need protection from harsh frosts.

Sow summer crops Towards the end of the month, sow French and runner beans, long-rooted beetroot, sea kale, salsify and sweet corn. In the north, sow runner beans under glass.

Prolong your harvest Make further sowings of salad crops and summer spinach.

Plant seedlings Plant out late-summer cauliflowers and, in colder areas, Brussels sprouts.

The herb garden Thin out herb seedlings sown last month. Plant out or pot up basil seedlings. Take cuttings of pot marjoram, rosemary (above), sage and thyme. Divide mint and thyme plants that are becoming straggly.

Use straw to cover the soil between strawberry plants to discourage weeds, slugs and grey mould.

Tie in greenhouse tomatoes

Spray and feed fruit trees and bushes Make sure that they are well watered in dry periods as the fruit is swelling.

Thin fruit on wall-trained stone fruit Remove a number of morello cherries, nectarines and peaches from each tree to obtain large, evenly sized fruit. Remove any shoots that are growing directly towards or away from the wall.

Protect strawberries Place straw or black polythene around the base of each plant to lift the fruit off the soil.

Summer prune outdoor vines Grape vines fruit on the current season's growth. Prune in the summer to ensure one bunch of grapes from each spur.

Strengthen newly planted fruit trees Remove the blossom from new trees to direct the plant's energy into producing strong new wood that will subsequently bear fruit.

Thin out raspberry canes

FLOWERS AND BULBS

Regularly water newly planted perennials

Mulch cordon-grown sweet peas Tie in the stems. Pinch out the side shoots and tendrils on each plant.

Prepare for summer bedding Lift spring-flowering narcissi and tulip bulbs if an area is needed for summer bedding. Heel in the bulbs until the foliage has withered.

Plant out At the end of the month, plant out and stake chrysanthemums and dahlias.

Add support Continue to stake tall-growing perennials, such as delphiniums (above) and border carnations, before they flower in summer.

Plant out lilies potted up in the greenhouse

Finish sowing annual seeds outdoors

Transplant half-hardy annual seedlings If there is no danger of frost, plant out seed-raised half-hardy annuals after hardening off.

Refresh window boxes Towards the end of the month, empty window boxes and other containers of spring bulbs and other plants. Replant with summer bedding and place outside.

Move over-wintered plants outdoors Plant out fuchsias and pelargoniums that have been over-wintered and hardened off.

Plant up hanging baskets Use a water-retaining polymer and add slow-release fertiliser. Protect the baskets in a greenhouse for three to four weeks before hanging outside.

YESTERDAY & TODAY

Beneficial manure

Before artificial fertilisers were developed, gardeners relied on wholesome, organic manure to enrich the soil in their gardens. People used horse, cow, pig and chicken manure although it was always left to rot down thoroughly before being dug into the soil. Cattle dung was the most popular variety used as it was said to make the earth mild, fresh and robust. Nowadays, pelleted chicken manure and spent mushroom compost are more easily available. They are also more pleasant to handle, being sold in clean tubs rather than arriving in a huge smelly heap by your front door, as cattle dung used to do.

SUMMER

Early summer is a busy time. Weeds grow rapidly and tender species can be planted out. By mid to late summer, you can enjoy the results of your efforts; just make sure plants don't go short of water.

JOBS FOR SUMMER

Train climbers The long, flexible stems of climbers grow at their fastest during the summer months and often need support. Wrap self-supporting tendrils around wire supports, spiralling the stems upwards. Tie more substantial stems against posts or trelliswork using garden twine or raffia.

Watch for pests and diseases Warm, wet British summers encourage pests and diseases to multiply rapidly. Treat aphids, blackspot and powdery mildew before they take hold. Avoid problems in the first place by choosing disease-resistant plants and starting them out well.

Propagate softwood perennial cuttings New summer growth is perfect propagating material. Look for strong, pliable stems and cut off the top 10cm or so below a leaf joint. Trim off all but the top two pairs of leaves, then insert into pots of compost. Water the cuttings lightly and keep the compost moist by placing a plastic bag over the top.

Water the garden As the summer gets hotter and drier, it is essential to water well – but sensibly. Water in the early morning and evening to minimise evaporation. Water precise areas thoroughly rather than giving the whole garden a sprinkling. If you water in the day, avoid wetting the leaves as the sun may scorch them. Installing water butts wherever you have a downpipe means you will have more water if there is a water shortage.

Damp down the greenhouse floor When watering greenhouse plants, spray a fine mist over the benches, paths and windows. On hot days open doors, windows and vents to aid ventilation. This prevents overheating and deters red spider mite.

June

TREES AND SHRUBS

Weed out seedlings Remove self-sown seedlings of ash and sycamore before they become established.

Prune deutzias Cut out flowered shoots.

Laburnums and lilacs Remove faded flower clusters and thin out weak shoots.

Hard-prune broom Cut back plants hard after flowering, avoiding old wood.

Clip hedges Trim berberis, escallonia, hawthorn and privet hedges.

Take softwood cuttings Use softwood or semiripe side shoots of cotoneasters, deutzias, fuchsias and philadelphus. Root in a cold frame.

Disbud large-flowered bush roses Remove all the buds adjacent to the main bud at the end of the stem to give extra-large blooms for cutting (above).

Keep the area around trees and shrubs clear of grass

Reduce water-loss from the soil Mulch moisture-loving plants with garden compost or shredded bark.

LAWNS AND PONDS

Spike lawns Make small but deep holes to enable rain to penetrate to the roots.

Mow regularly During dry spells, raise the mower blades and leave the clippings on the grass. This will help to conserve moisture.

Lay turf This is a good time to lay turf as it will settle down quickly, but water continuously throughout the growing season.

Dry-weather strategies Stop all weedkiller treatments and feeding during dry spells, unless you can water the lawn regularly.

Top up ponds Maintain the water level in ponds with fresh, clean water.

Reduce floating plants This will allow light to filter through to the deep-water plants below.

Flush out aphids Water lily buds can be attacked by aphids. There is no need to spray. Instead, use a mesh net to immerse the afflicted plant in the water for several days (above) and drown the pests.

KITCHEN GARDEN

Earth up maincrop potatoes Lift early varieties that are ready for harvest.

Set out tomato plants Provide stakes for all but bush varieties. Keep them well watered and feed regularly with liquid tomato fertiliser.

Start planting out Plant leeks and make a watering well at the base to retain water. Plant self-blanching celery. Make sowings of chicory, spinach beet and swedes. Sow chervil and dill, and thin out seedlings.

Pick herbs regularly This includes annuals such as chervil (above). Regular picking keeps them bushy.

Tie in long, vigorous shoots of cane fruits The shoots are soft, so be careful not to damage or snap them.

Protect bush and cane fruits from birds Use fine netting or a wire cage.

Prune outdoor vines Cut new shoots back to 60cm. Tie in two replacement shoots to carry next year's side shoots.

FLOWERS AND BULBS

Finish planting half-hardy annuals

Pinch out growing tips on chrysanthemums, dahlias and modern pinks Disbud border carnations. This encourages larger flowers.

Sow hardy perennials in an outdoor seedbed

Propagate pinks Take side-shoot cuttings and root in a cold frame.

Move planted-up hanging baskets outdoors Turn them regularly so plants develop evenly on all sides.

Promote bushy plants Pinch out growing tips of annuals to induce side-branching (above).

Pinch-prune container plants Nip out new shoots with your fingers to encourage new leaves. Stop a month or so before you want the plants to flower.

Maintain thriving containers Fill gaps with annual plants lifted from the garden.

July

TREES AND SHRUBS

Remove suckers from grafted rhododendron bushes

Prune deciduous shrubs Cut back long stems of choisya, jasmine and philadelphus after flowering. This will help to maintain a good shape and stop spreading.

Propagate shrubs Root semi-ripe cuttings of *Buddleja alternifolia*, callicarpa, cotoneaster, deutzia, euonymus and viburnum in a cold frame. Take heel cuttings of choisya, hibiscus and *Jasminum officinale*.

Feed roses Use an organic rose fertiliser. Spray against black spot, greenfly, mildew and rust at the same time if necessary.

Deadhead faded roses Remove the flowers on modern bush roses and climbers as they fade. Cut back to a leaf bud. Deadhead hybrid tea and floribunda roses (above) to encourage a second flush of flowers.

LAWNS AND PONDS

Aerate compacted lawns Water thoroughly during prolonged dry weather.

Maintain regular mowing Continue to mow the lawn at least once a week, except during drought.

Neaten lawn edges After mowing, use long-handled edging shears to trim the grass overhanging the edge of the lawn.

Watch out for fungal diseases These are prevalent during hot, humid weather and must be treated immediately.

Limit damage to scorched lawns Avoid walking on grass that has been scorched. You may damage the healthy shoots that remain and create bare patches.

Remove excess leaf growth from water lilies (above)

Weed the bog garden Water regularly and make sure that the soil does not dry out.

KITCHEN GARDEN

Plant late-summer crops Sow globe beetroot, round-seeded peas, calabrese, chicory, endive and other salad crops, winter radishes and Swiss chard.

Harvest greenhouse cucumbers and tomatoes

Lift shallots Spread them out to dry in a shed before storing. Lift onions at the end of the month and leave on the ground to dry.

Limit wind damage In windy gardens, earth up or stake broccoli, Brussels sprouts and calabrese.

Limit leaf growth on tomatoes Pinch out the side shoots on outdoor tomatoes, but leave bush varieties intact.

Cut down fruited raspberry canes to ground level Remove weak and surplus new shoots.

Thin out apples and pears Remove all but one of the fruitlets in a cluster – the one in the centre for apples (above), and one on the edge of the cluster for pears.

Prevent branches from snapping Support heavy fruit trusses with forked sticks.

Feed hungry plants Apply a general fertiliser around plants that lack vigour.

FLOWERS AND BULBS

Keep borders looking tidy Cut back early-flowering perennials and tie in plants with tall flower spikes.

Plant autumn-flowering bulbs Plant *Amaryllis belladonna*, autumn crocuses, nerine and sternbergia for prolonged border colour.

Disbud dahlias Pinch out the side buds growing below the terminal bud on each young dahlia plant (above). The remaining bud will develop into a larger bloom.

Cut back perennials for a second flush of flowers Prune achilleas, delphiniums, hardy geraniums, lupins and *Salvia* 'Superba' to the ground.

Divide rhizomatous plants Lift irises, then divide and replant the best pieces.

August

TREES AND SHRUBS

Trim hedges (above) Give privet hedges their second trim and clip beech and yew.

Prune shrubs after flowering Shorten the stems and thin out old wood on ceanothus, escallonias and lavenders.

Prune wisterias Pinch out young shoots beyond three or four leaves.

Take semiripe cuttings Propagate deciduous and evergreen shrubs. Root the cuttings in a cold frame.

Stop applying rose fertiliser Too much fertiliser will encourage the development of soft growth in autumn.

Watch out for mildew on roses In prolonged dry weather, watch for mildew on ramblers and roses grown against walls in sunny dry positions.

LAWNS AND PONDS

Prepare the ground for turfing and sowing Fork over the soil, tread it down well, then rake in a low-nitrogen lawn fertiliser. A week after feeding, sow lawn seed, ensuring that it is sown evenly and protected from birds by netting.

Continue to mow established lawns regularly

Watch for red thread Improve your lawn maintenance to prevent red thread in the first place. Make sure that the soil contains plenty of nitrogen and is well aerated. If necessary, you can control this disease with a fungicide.

Replenish the pond Maintain the water surface at a specified level (above) to avoid causing stress to either pondlife, such as fish and newts, or plants.

KITCHEN GARDEN

Stop greenhouse tomatoes Remove at least 50 per cent of the foliage to allow the fruits to ripen. Stop feeding the plants and reduce watering. Stop outdoor tomatoes when four or five trusses have set. Harvest when ripe (above).

Take cuttings of herbs Root herbs, such as bay, lavender, mint, rosemary, rue and sage, in a cold frame or sheltered, outdoor nursery bed. Lift, divide and replant chives.

Harvest ripe crops Pick sweetcorn cobs. Harvest self-blanching celery in plenty of time to avoid the first frosts. Pick early apples and plums. Eat the apples now as they are not suitable for storing.

Protect ripening outdoor grapes Cover with netting.

Prune plum trees Cut out dead, diseased, broken and crossing branches when the harvest has finished. On fan-trained plums, cut lateral branches back by half.

Keep herbaceous borders looking their best through the summer by watering and feeding them well. Remember to deadhead and trim fading plants, and keep the beds free of weeds.

FLOWERS AND BULBS

Maintain border plants Tie in and feed chrysanthemums and dahlias. Keep late-flowering perennials well watered and weed-free. Deadhead faded flowers (above).

Plant bulbs Plant madonna lilies, crocuses and narcissi in late August ready for early spring colour.

Propagate iris Lift, divide and replant clumps with over-crowded rhizomes.

Prune untidy plants Pinch back trailing plants, such as ivy-leaved pelargoniums, that are becoming straggly.

Propagate half-hardy plants to ensure winter survival Take cuttings of fuchsias, pelargoniums and other tender container plants that cannot be raised from seed.

AUTUMN

As temperatures change, be vigilant and watch the weather to protect half-hardy plants from surprise frosts. Enjoy late flowers, ripe crops and golden colours before winter sets in.

JOBS FOR AUTUMN

Collect and store seeds

Choose a sunny day to collect seeds, and make sure they are dry before storing. Place them in envelopes or paper bags (do not use plastic bags). Label each item and store in a cool, dry, dark place. Seeds tend to lose their reliability to germinate after a year.

Prepare the pond for winter
As leaves fall from the trees, they clog up ponds. They sink to the bottom and decompose, causing harmful by-products. Gather up leaves regularly and remove any that have dropped into the pond using a rake. To prevent leaves from falling in, place fine-mesh netting across the top of the pond and secure it at the edges with bricks. Remove the netting every fortnight, collect the fallen leaves and replace the net securely.

Move, divide and transplant perennials

Early autumn, while the soil is still warm, is a good time to move perennials as the plants prepare for the dormant season. Water roots well before planting, soaking them in a bucket for about an hour. Prepare the planting hole by forking over hard soil to create a crumbly texture that the roots can easily penetrate. Add plenty of organic matter to get the plant off to a good start. Give shrubs an initial prune after planting and stake if needed.

Harvest crops when ripe
Most vegetables are ready for picking from early autumn onwards. Harvest onions on a dry day. Once pulled, lay them on the ground, or hang in a shed, for 10–14 days with the leaves intact. Onions will rot if not dried before storing. Dry garlic the same way but do not harvest until the leaves have faded.

Greenhouse hygiene

The greenhouse is a cosy place for pests and diseases to sit out the winter. If you only undertake one clean-up in the year, autumn is probably the most important time. Remove used growbags and plants, then use a stiff brush to go all over the interior framework and staging. Get right into the corners, where pests like to hide. Rake and brush up the debris from the floor. Wash down the whole structure with disinfectant, taking care not to splash too much water about, as this will create a damp atmosphere. Clean both the inside and outside of the glass to remove algae and grime. Finally, dig over the greenhouse border, if you have one, and dispose of any weeds.

September

TREES AND SHRUBS

Prepare the soil Autumn is the best time to plant evergreen and deciduous trees, shrubs and hedging. Dig in well-rotted manure or compost and a handful of bone meal.

Transplant rhododendrons and azaleas Fill the planting hole with ericaceous compost (above) or plant in a container.

Lightly trim hedges Give established hedges a final cut.

Propagate shrubs Take hardwood cuttings of deciduous and evergreen shrubs. Root the cuttings in pots in a cold frame.

Divide suckering shrubs Thin the top growth of suckering shrubs, such as philadelphus, to promote root growth.

Check supports and ties Early autumn gales can cause damage, so make sure that the ties and supports are secure on young trees and climbers.

Fertilise roses Top-dress rose bushes and climbers with a handful of sulphate of potash. This will protect late shoots by helping the new wood harden.

Prune rambling roses and climbers Cut back flowered shoots to ground level. Prune flowered shoots of weeping standards back to a main stem.

LAWNS AND PONDS

Scarify established lawns Remove the dead grass by raking vigorously with a spring-tine rake.

Improve drainage Fork deeply over the lawn with a hollow-tined fork. Fill the holes by brushing in sharp sand or old potting compost.

Lay turf Water it in thoroughly and make sure that it does not dry out.

Re-seed worn and damaged patches of lawn Add sandy loam to level the damaged part with the rest of the lawn. Sow grass seed over the damaged section and water well.

Continue to mow (above) Raise the blades on the mower for a lighter cut.

Clear and tidy the bog garden Remove decaying foliage from bog plants that die back naturally after frost.

Feed fish sparingly Use a high-protein fish food.

Propagate pond plants Collect winter-resting buds of bladderwort and frogbit before they sink to the pond's base. Keep them in a large jar of pond water on a cool windowsill until spring.

KITCHEN GARDEN

Sow spring-cropping herbs Sow chervil and parsley seeds outdoors in the soil and in frost-proof containers.

Plant out spring cabbage In the north, plant out spring cabbage towards the end of the month.

Sow seeds for early crops next year Sow broad beans, spring cabbages, carrots and lettuces under cloches.

Cut down outdoor tomato plants Bring the unripe fruit indoors and place with a banana to ripen fully.

Harvest apples for storing Pick apples (above) and pears before they are fully ripe.

Pick autumn raspberries

Order new trees and bushes

FLOWERS AND BULBS

Tidy up the borders Clear beds of summer annuals and cut back fading perennials.

Plant bulbous irises (above) Choose a sunny, well-drained spot with an alkaline soil.

Plant hardy spring bedding plants Include forget-me-nots, wallflowers, pansies and polyanthus. Plant out hardy biennials.

Pot up bulbs for forcing Buy prepared bulbs, such as hyacinth. Plant in bulb fibre and place in the dark until the flower spikes are visible.

Sow hardy annuals Sow drifts of candytuft, cornflower, larkspur, love-in-the-mist and poppy seeds in blank spaces left from clearing the borders. Sow marigolds in containers.

Blanching vegetables

Excluding daylight as plants mature in autumn produces pale-coloured, or blanched, vegetables. This process prevents chlorophyll from forming, and makes the edible stems and leaves more tender. Plants traditionally blanched are chicory, rhubarb, endive, cardoons (left) and celery.

October

TREES AND SHRUBS

Top-dress rhododendrons Add a thick layer of leaf-mould or a lime-free mulch around the base of each plant.

Plant container-grown trees and shrubs Stake and tie in trees to prevent movement in autumn gales.

Transplant evergreens Spray conifers against needle drop. Soak the roots in water before replanting to prevent them from drying out.

Plant new hedges Enrich the planting holes with organic matter. Space 30–60cm apart and mulch after planting.

Prune deciduous trees and shrubs Cut out crossing and badly placed branches.

Propagate deciduous and evergreen shrubs Continue to take hardwood cuttings.

Plant shrubs to attract birds Plant red-berried shrubs such as holly (above) to provide food for birds in winter.

Autumn-prune roses Cut the stems back by half to prevent wind rock during winter.

Plant containers for winter colour Choose plants with winter interest, such as aucubas, dwarf conifers, winter-flowering heathers and skimmias.

LAWNS AND PONDS

Lay turf This is the ideal month for laying turves for a new lawn (above).

Rake up fallen leaves and stack for leaf-mould This is particularly important on newly sown lawns as fallen leaves raise the humidity around young grass shoots. High humidity will lead to fungal infections which will kill the grass.

Scatter wormcasts These are ideal sites for weeds to germinate. Brush them into the soil with a stout broom.

Mow with the blades raised This is especially important if you intend to naturalise bulbs in the lawn.

Keep ponds clear Scoop out any fallen leaves and secure netting over the pond to catch further leaf-fall. Thin out underwater oxygenating plants. Cut off any dead water-lily leaves.

Lift, divide and replant bog garden plants

Continue to feed fish sparingly

KITCHEN GARDEN

Prepare the soil for winter Dig vacant ground and incorporate well-rotted manure or garden compost. Leave the soil rough to be broken up by frosts.

Harvest the end of the crop Pick any remaining marrows and store in a frost-free place. Lift and store beetroot and winter radishes. Lift maincrop potatoes (above). Pick the last greenhouse tomatoes.

Plant out cabbage seedlings In the south, plant out seedlings for an early spring crop. Make sure that they have sufficient moisture until they are well established.

Plant winter and spring vegetables Plant lettuce and pea seedlings and cover with a cloche. Sow broad beans outdoors in the south, and under cloches in colder areas. Sow spinach to overwinter for an early crop in spring.

Force rhubarb Cover the dormant buds with straw or leaves inside a forcing pot.

Cut down bean and pea haulms Leave the roots in the ground.

Plant out strawberry runners

Take hardwood cuttings of healthy gooseberry bushes Root in an outdoor trench.

FLOWERS AND BULBS

Cut down and lift frost-blackened dahlias After drying off the tubers, store in a frost-free place.

Plant up borders for next year Plant hardy perennials and biennials. Plant hyacinth and tulip bulbs.

Sow sweet peas Sow the seeds directly in the soil under cloches, or in sweet pea tubes, and place in a cold frame. A good alternative to a sweet pea tube is an empty yogurt pot.

Propagate perennial plants Lift, divide and replant overgrown clumps.

Keep an eye on bulbs being forced Water the compost if it is dry.

Protect tender bulbs Move tubs of agapanthus, amaryllis, crinums and nerines to a frost-free position, such as an unheated greenhouse.

Lift and pot up tender fuchsias and pelargoniums (above) Bring the plants indoors for winter flowering, or rest in a cool greenhouse.

Bring plants in containers into a protected space

November

TREES AND SHRUBS

Protect tender trees and shrubs Erect protective windbreaks of sacking or stout polythene around newly planted shrubs.

Cover the bases of tropical trees with straw or sacking

Plant bare-rooted deciduous trees and shrubs Continue to plant container-grown specimens. Water in well.

Take heel cuttings of winter jasmine Root cuttings in frame.

Plant bare-rooted roses (above) Use a planting mixture of garden compost and bone meal. Prune out twiggy side shoots and cut back damaged roots to healthy tissue.

Prevent wind damage Trim back bushy top growth of clematis grown in tubs. Finish pruning in spring.

LAWNS AND PONDS

Prepare the ground for sowing a new lawn in spring Dig over the soil and leave it to be broken up by frost.

Continue autumn lawn care Aerate, improve drainage and rake leaves from both new and established lawns. Finish laying turf as soon as possible.

Continue to mow This depends on the warmth of the weather and how much the grass is growing.

Maintain pond hygiene Continue to remove fallen leaves and thin out oxygenators in the pond.

Continue feeding fish until the end of the month (above).

KITCHEN GARDEN

Lift chicory plants (above) Place in boxes of moist soil and force in a greenhouse at 10–18°C.

Protect tender crops Protect overwintering root crops against frost by covering them with straw. Place cloches over late-sown chervil and parsley.

Detach suckers from globe artichokes Pot up and overwinter in a cold frame.

Prepare holes for new fruit trees and bushes Plant bare-rooted trees and bushes during mild, dry weather. Insert support stakes before planting. Mulch afterwards.

Prune soft fruit Shorten leading shoots by half, and side shoots to 5cm on gooseberries and red currants.

Inspect fruit cages Check that there are no tears in fruit-cage netting and that it is secure against birds.

FLOWERS AND BULBS

Tidy up for winter Finish digging new borders, leaving the soil rough. Continue to tidy flower beds and borders by deadheading and cutting back unsightly top growth to ground level. Remove, clean and store stakes and canes.

Condition soil Mulch with green waste or leaf-mould to improve the soil condition without encouraging plants to start into growth.

Prepare tubers for storing Check chrysanthemum stools and dahlia tubers. Discard any that are rotting. Clean gladioli corms, discarding old corms and separating bulbils for storing and growing on in the following spring.

Mulch nerines for winter protection In cold areas, protect tender nerines with a thick layer of coarse grit.

Bring forced bulbs into the light Move forced bulbs that have made sufficient top growth (above) to a cool, well-lit position on a windowsill, where they will bloom.

Provide warmth for tender plants Greenhouse plants and tender specimens in tubs should be kept at temperatures of 7–10°C during the autumn and winter months.

YESTERDAY & TODAY

Grow traditional apples

Many old apple varieties are too large to grow in today's small gardens. However, when these are grafted onto dwarf root stocks, gardeners can enjoy their wonderful flavour without the spreading boughs. Traditional varieties include 'Laxtons Superb' and 'Worcester Pearmain' (left).

WINTER

There are always jobs to be done in the garden, but winter is a good time for planning and leafing through catalogues and gardening books. Prepare now and your garden will never lack interest.

JOBS FOR WINTER

Plant bare-rooted roses Soak the roots in water for an hour. Cut out damaged growth and remove crossing stems. Dig a hole wide enough to hold the roots and deep enough for the bud union to be 2.5cm below ground level. Add compost and a handful of blood, fish and bone. Set the plant in the hole and spread out the roots. Refill the hole and firm the soil to remove air pockets. Finish this job by early winter, or before the ground becomes too cold.

Plan for next year Order seed catalogues so that when the weather is not suitable for going out into the garden, you can make up a list of crops to purchase for sowing in the new year.

Winter-prune wall shrubs Shape evergreen shrubs, such as flowering quinces or pyracanthus, to keep them flat against a wall. Prune out any outward-facing shoots and those growing towards the wall. Remove unwanted stems at their point of origin. Space out the other shoots, pulling them down horizontally and tying them in. Prune back the longest stems by two or three buds to keep the shrub balanced.

Sow seeds in the greenhouse Start sowing seeds in mid-winter if you can provide sufficient warmth for germination, and a well-lit position to put the seedlings in afterwards. Make sure that the glass is clean to let in plenty of light. Wait until later on in the winter to sow seeds of bedding plants and pot plants.

Clear away snow Don't let snow weigh down conifer branches. Brush it off immediately or tie the branches together with twine to preserve the plant's shape.

Traditional timings

Some people today still plant and harvest their fruit and vegetables according to a traditional timetable. These seasonal dates were handed down through families or passed from professional gardeners to their apprentices. Broad beans, for instance, should be sown on Boxing Day because early sowings are said to be less prone to aphid attacks.

December

TREES AND SHRUBS

Limit frost damage Firm in newly planted trees and shrubs loosened by frost.

Renovate deciduous climbers and hedges Hard prune old and congested shrubs while they are dormant. Mulch heavily afterwards.

Protect tender wall shrubs Place fleece over climbers if very cold weather is forecast.

Prune established trees and shrubs In frost-free weather, prune dead, damaged and diseased branches. Cut back to healthy wood.

Stop colour reversion Cut out totally green or yellow reverted shoots on variegated evergreen shrubs (above).

Reduce shade over borders Prune deciduous trees whose long branches overhang herbaceous borders.

Propagate shrubs Take root cuttings of clerodendrum, aralias and *Rhus typhina*.

LAWNS AND PONDS

Treat turf against leatherjackets The larvae of crane flies can create unsightly brown patches in newly laid lawns. Deter the adults from laying eggs by double digging the soil to improve drainage.

Continue to mow occasionally Set the mower blades at high, and mow only if growth demands it.

Protect the grass Constant walking over a lawn during the winter when the soil is waterlogged causes compaction and impedes drainage. Avoid walking across the lawn by the same route every day. Alternatively, build sunken stepping stones or a path (above).

Clean and overhaul machinery Clean and oil all moveable parts before storing under a waterproof cover or in a shed. Empty the fuel tanks of petrol-driven lawnmowers.

Protect ponds from freezing over Place an inflated ball on the surface to absorb expansion that could damage pond walls.

Melt pond ice Place containers of boiling water on the surface of frozen ice to melt it slowly.

KITCHEN GARDEN

Lift or protect winter crops In the north, lift and store swedes and turnips. In the south, where temperatures are milder, earth up the plants for protection.

Clear away annual herbs from beds and containers

Harvest winter vegetables when ready These include Brussels sprouts (above), winter cabbages, cauliflowers, leeks and parsnips.

Protect mediterranean herbs In colder gardens, protect marjoram and rosemary with straw, leaf-mould or shredded forest bark.

Feed all fruit trees Top-dress wall-trained trees with well-rotted manure.

Prune newly planted apple and pear trees Reduce leading shoots by up to two-thirds.

FLOWERS AND BULBS

Winter maintenance Finish tidying beds and borders. Check stored tubers.

Firm the soil around plants loosened by frost Remove air pockets by firming the soil with your feet.

Encourage early flowering Place cloches over Christmas roses to bring them on quickly (above). This will also protect the flowers from mud splashes.

Create bushy seedlings Pinch out the growing tips of sweetpea seedlings when three pairs of leaves have developed. This will encourage further side shoots to grow.

Protect winter baskets Move hanging baskets into a porch or greenhouse when severe frosts are forecast.

Plant up early colour Cram window boxes and containers with winter pansies and ornamental cabbages.

January

TREES AND SHRUBS

Prune established trees and shrubs Remove any dead wood or diseased branches. Prune wisterias, cutting back all but extension shoots.

Check for wind damage Firm trees and shrubs that have been loosened by the wind; stake if necessary (above).

Prune vines in tubs This is your last chance, as leaving it until next month may cause the cut surfaces to bleed. Hard prune outdoor vines to leave live shoots, then train these horizontally along support wires.

Take chrysanthemum cuttings Mid-winter is the best time to take hardwood cuttings, as they root easily.

LAWNS AND PONDS

Be ready for the spring Order top dressings and seed mixtures for spring sowing.

Improve aeration and drainage Note where water remains on the surface of the lawn after a heavy rainfall. Continue to spike if the weather permits.

Clear fallen leaves from ponds and water courses

Clean garden tools Disinfect pots and hand tools ready for spring planting. Sharpen spades, secateurs and cutting implements. Make sure all tools are cleaned, oiled and in good repair (above).

KITCHEN GARDENS

Force established rhubarb Cover the crowns with pots or boxes filled with straw to exclude the light. Plant out new rhubarb crowns.

Spray fruit trees and bushes Use a tar-oil winter wash to eradicate aphid eggs.

Gather winter crops Harvest Jerusalem artichokes, Brussels sprouts, winter cabbages, leeks and perpetual spinach (above).

Check all vegetables and fruit in store Discard any that show signs of rot before diseases spread.

Prune fruit trees Prune established trees except stone fruits, such as damsons and cherries. Newly planted fruit trees should be lightly pruned to shape them, reducing all leading shoots by half.

Prune soft fruit Cut back new cane fruits, such as raspberries, to within 25cm of the ground.

FLOWERS AND BULBS

Mulch alpine plants Place a mulch of grit or stone chippings around small alpine flowers to prevent the crowns from rotting.

Weed borders In mild weather, fork over the soil between established perennials to remove weeds. Use a hand fork around smaller plants.

Plant out forced bulbs Transplant hyacinths and narcissi that have finished flowering indoors (above).

Use your greenhouse Take basal leaf cuttings of large-flowered chrysanthemums. Sow carnation and sweet pea seeds in a frost-free greenhouse. Plant lily bulbs in pots of moist compost ready to transplant in spring.

Deadhead winter-flowering pansies This will ensure they continue to flower freely.

UNDER GLASS

Propagate plants by seed

Most seeds are sown between late winter and early spring. It is too cold to keep them outside, so a greenhouse is essential. Use a 9–13cm pot and fill it with moist seed compost. Firm the surface gently to remove air pockets. Sow the seeds as thinly and evenly as possible on the surface of the compost. Cover the seed to its own depth with a layer of sieved compost or vermiculite. Label the pot and water with a rose nozzle. Place a sheet of glass, or a plastic bag, over the pot until the seeds germinate. Remove the cover and transplant when the seedlings have developed two leaves.

February

TREES AND SHRUBS

Prepare sites for spring planting of evergreens

Prune crab apple trees to shape Remove inward-growing shoots and badly shaped branches.

Thin out weak shoots from climbing shrubs Hard prune shrubs such as celastrus and solanum if they are neglected and misshapen.

Commence hedge trimming Give deciduous hedges their first trim by the end of the month, provided the weather is frost-free.

Propagate shrubs by seed Sow seeds of broom and Spanish broom in a propagating unit with bottom heat.

Protect tender, early-flowering shrubs and trees Drape horticultural fleece over rhododendrons and magnolias if severe frost is forecast.

Cut back established hamamelis after flowering (above) Remove straggly branches to reshape the shrub and encourage next year's flowers.

LAWNS AND PONDS

Aerate an established lawn Go over it with a spiked roller or shoes (above). If moss is a real problem, reduce shade cast on lawn, improve drainage and reduce compaction rather than applying moss killer.

Avoid walking on the lawn when there is frost or snow Do not mow if the grass is completely waterlogged.

Feed birds on the lawn If you do not have cats, feeding birds on the lawn will encourage them to eat lawn pests. However, watch how much food you scatter, as too much could attract rats.

Propagate bog plants Sow seeds of bog primulas in boxes of compost. Leave the boxes outdoors to expose the seeds to frost, but protect them from heavy rain.

Winter pond care Continue to protect ponds from freezing over completely. Begin to feed fish, if the weather is mild.

KITCHEN GARDEN

Continue the winter harvest Cut savoy cabbages (above) and other brassicas.

Warm up the soil At the beginning of February, cover the ground with polythene ready for early sowings of vegetables.

Plant shallots in the open Delay the planting until the end of the month in cold and northern gardens.

Sow early carrot seeds in a cold frame

Prune newly planted fan-trained stone fruit Cut shoots back to 30–45cm.

Put cloches over strawberries This will advance ripening by two to three weeks.

FLOWERS AND BULBS

Check tuber stores Discard chrysanthemum stools and dahlia tubers that are rotten.

Plant out indoor bulbs

Transplant bulbs Plant in a sheltered border outside once they have finished flowering.

Prepare the soil for sowing Complete digging and manuring sites for sowing annuals and biennials (above).

Sow half-hardy annuals Sow begonias and lobelias under glass at a temperature of 18–21°C.

Protect early-flowering crocuses against the birds Criss-cross white cotton thread around the flowers.

Flowering house plants outdoors

The Victorians were enthusiastic plant hunters and encouraged plants in the home. Bowls of forced hyacinths are still popular at Christmas time. Instead of throwing the bulbs away when the flower spikes have faded, plant them outside in the border with plenty of grit.

Glossary of gardening terms

Acid soil Soil with a pH below 7. Suitable for most plants, but particularly good for growing rhododendrons and heathers.

Adventitious roots Roots that grow from the aerial stems of plants, not from other roots.

Aeration Loosening the soil to allow air and water to penetrate. Spike a compacted lawn with a garden or hollow-tine fork to a depth of about 7.5cm. A large area of compacted soil can be aerated using a spade or rotavator.

Aerial roots Roots that grow above the ground straight from the plant's stem. They absorb moisture from the air and help to support climbers, such as ivy, against walls and fences.

Alkaline soil Soil with a pH level above 7. Most plants and vegetables grow well on slightly alkaline soils.

Alpine A small plant suitable for growing in a rock garden. Botanically, the term refers to plants that grow in mountainous areas between the tree line and the snow line.

Annual A plant that has its entire life cycle within one growing season. It germinates, grows, flowers, sets seed and then dies.

Aquatic A plant that grows in water, either totally submerged or with just its roots under water and its flowers and leaves on the surface.

Axillary A bud that grows in between the stalk and stem or branch, rather than at the tip.

Bark ringing Removing a complete ring of bark from around the trunk of an apple or pear tree, a technique used to encourage new buds to form. Not suitable for stone fruit trees, such as cherries or plums.

Biennial A plant that lives for two years. It germinates and forms leaves in the first year, and then produces a flower stem, flowers, sets seed and dies in the second.

Blanching A technique for excluding sunlight from vegetables in order to maximise tenderness and flavour. Earth up the vegetables, wrap them in thick paper or cover with up-turned clay flowerpots. Stems of celery and leeks, and leaves of chicory are all commonly blanched, (see **Earthing up**).

Bog garden An area in the garden where the soil is waterlogged, either naturally or artificially. Plants that prefer their roots to be around water or in moist soil, such as primula or lysichiton, grow best in this position.

Bolting When vegetables prematurely run to flower or seed. Bolting can often be caused by poor soil or lack of water. Lettuces, spinach and coriander are prone to bolting.

Bract A modified leaf at the base of a flower or flower cluster. Bracts can be brightly coloured, large or small and scale-like.

Bud A condensed shoot that is protected by overlapping scales. Leaves or flowers develop from inside the bud.

Bulb A modified stem, which acts as a storage organ. Usually found underground and produces roots, shoots and flowers every year. It is made up of fleshy scales wrapped around each other.

Bulb fibre The perfect compost for growing indoor or outdoor potted bulbs. Bulb fibre contains peat, oyster shell and charcoal, which keeps the compost 'sweet' and helps to prevent the bulbs from rotting. If you prefer not to use peat, buy coir or peat-free multipurpose compost and add charcoal and oyster shell.

Bulbil A small immature bulb that forms at the base of a mature bulb. It can be removed and potted up to form a new plant. In some lilies, the bulbils form on the stems above ground.

Calyx The name given to the outer protective covering of a flower. It is made up of a number of green sepals, fused together to form a bowl, funnel or tube-like structure (see **Sepal**).

Cane A tough, thin woody stem with a hollow centre, such as that of bamboo or raspberries. Dried bamboo canes can be used for staking and supporting other garden plants.

Catch crop A fast-growing crop that is planted between slower-maturing crops. Alternatively, a catch crop can be grown in the interval between harvesting one crop and planting another.

Chalk A soft type of limestone. When ground into powder form, chalk is used to neutralise acid soil.

Chlorophyll The green pigment responsible for light absorption and photosynthesis in plants.

Chlorosis A condition that arises when a plant cannot produce sufficient amounts of chlorophyll, resulting in the leaves losing their green colour and, in some cases, turning brown and dying.

Clamp A device made up of thick layers of straw and soil for storing harvested root vegetables. Pile up the crop, such as carrots or potatoes, on the soil, then cover with a 30cm-deep layer of straw followed by a 25cm-thick layer of soil. Firm and smooth the soil so that rain will run off, then make a hole in the top and fill it with straw to provide ventilation.

Clay soil A heavy soil that is predominantly made up of tiny mineral particles, forming a sticky mass when wet, and hard, compacted sods when dry. To improve clay soil, dig in plenty of organic matter.

Cloche A shelter, traditionally made from glass or tough clear plastic, that protects early crops outdoors or warms up the soil prior to planting.

Clone A plant raised from a single parent plant by means of vegetative propagation (cuttings, division, layers or grafting) and not sexual propagation (seeds). A clone is identical to the parent plant and other plants raised from the same plant in this way.

Coir Processed coconut fibre that is used in seed and potting composts to completely or partially replace peat. By using coir compost, gardeners will help to lessen the destruction of wetland habitats due to excessive peat harvesting (see **Peat**).

Compost A term that describes two different materials: garden compost and commercial potting compost. Garden compost is brown and crumbly humus. It is formed by rotting down garden clippings and kitchen waste, and is used to improve and nourish the soil. Commercial seed and potting compost or multipurpose compost is a specially formulated soil-based or soil-less mixture that is used for raising seedlings and growing plants in containers.

Conifer A tree or shrub that bears its seeds in cones. Conifers are usually evergreen.

Cordon A restrictive pruning technique used to train fruit trees into one main stem.

Corm A rounded underground storage organ and stem, which looks similar to a bulb. A bud at the top of the corm produces shoots and new roots. Crocuses and gladioli grow from corms.

Crocks Small pieces of broken clay pot used to cover the drainage holes in planting containers and facilitate soil drainage. Place one or two crocks, concave side down, at the bottom of a container before filling with compost.

Crop rotation An organic technique for growing vegetables on different sections of a plot on a three or four-year cycle. Crop rotation helps to reduce the build-up of pests and diseases in the soil and prevent the soil from being stripped of particular nutrients by one crop.

Crown The base of a herbaceous perennial. The roots and shoots grow from the crown.

Cultivar A plant variety that originates from cultivation, not from the wild. The term cultivar is actually an abbreviation of 'cultivated variety'.

Damping down A technique used to increase the humidity and lower the temperature in a greenhouse on a hot day. To damp down, spray the floor and staging with water using a hose or watering can.

Deadheading Removing dead or faded flowers from plants to tidy them up. Deadheading will also promote further flowers by preventing seed formation. Plants that need to be regularly deadheaded are roses, peonies and pansies.

Deciduous A plant, usually a tree or shrub, that sheds its leaves in winter.

Dibber A pointed tool, traditionally carved from wood, used for making holes in soil when transplanting seedlings. The end of a pencil makes a good alternative to commercially available tools.

Disbudding A technique to remove all but one bud on a stem. This concentrates a plant's energy into producing fewer, but larger blooms and high-quality fruit.

Division A form of propagation where the roots and stems of a herbaceous perennial are teased or cut apart to make more than one plant. Each division of the separated clump will form a new plant.

Dormant A state in which a plant's growth slows down or ceases temporarily. This usually occurs in late autumn and winter.

Double-digging A cultivation technique that improves soil drainage, aeration and fertility, and allows plant roots to penetrate more deeply. When double-digging, make sure that the soil is dug at least two spits deep (see **Spit**).

Drill A shallow, straight and narrow furrow in the soil in which seeds are sown or seedlings planted.

Earthing up A technique for protecting plants, especially potatoes, from frost, sun or disease. Gently draw the surrounding soil up around the base of the stem using a spade. This technique is also used for blanching vegetables.

Espalier A pruning technique for training fruit trees or ornamental shrubs against walls or fences. To create an espalier, trim the branches and train them horizontally to form matching pairs on either side of the main stem.

Evergreen A tree or shrub that retains its foliage throughout the year.

Fan A pruning technique used to train a fruit tree or ornamental shrub into a fan shape against a wall or fence.

Fern A nonflowering plant that reproduces by way of tiny spores that form on the undersides of the fronds.

Fertiliser A mixture that provides one or more of the major plant nutrients such as nitrogen, phosphorus or potassium, plus important trace elements, to the soil.

Forcing A technique for encouraging plants to grow, flower or fruit before their natural time. To force a plant, place it in a dark place, such as under a large clay pot, or stand the plant in a heated greenhouse. Early crops such as lettuces or rhubarb, or indoor pot plants, are all commonly forced.

Fumigate To use poisonous fumes to eradicate pests and diseases in a greenhouse.

Fungicide A chemical that kills fungi, which are flowerless plants that possess no chlorophyll. Fungi need to be eradicated because they are parasitic and are responsible for various plant diseases.

Genus (pl. genera) A group of closely related plants that are linked by a range of common characteristics. For example, all species of horse chestnut are grouped under the genus *Aesculus*.

Germination The first stage of a plant's development, when a shoot sprouts from a seed.

Grafting A propagating technique for joining a stem or bud of one plant onto the root or stem of another, forming a new plant. Grafting is often used by rose or fruit-tree specialists.

Half-hardy A term to describe plants that can be grown outdoors during the summer only. They are usually killed by the first frosts. It is also applied to shrubs and herbaceous perennials that can survive average winter temperatures outdoors in sheltered positions.

Hardening off Gradually accustoming tender and half-hardy plants that have been raised under glass to outdoor conditions. To harden off a plant, move it in late spring from the greenhouse to a cold frame. Increase ventilation gradually over two to three weeks until the plant can be placed outdoors.

Hardwood Fully ripened wood of trees and shrubs, from which cuttings are taken.

Hardy A term to describe plants that are able to withstand normal winter temperatures, including frosts.

Heel The expanded base of old wood or a small heel of bark on a side shoot when it is pulled away from the main stem of a plant.

Herbaceous A term for a plant that does not form a woody stem. Herbaceous plants usually die down in winter and grow up again in spring from basal shoots. The term herbaceous is usually applied to perennial plants, although botanically it also applies to annuals and biennials.

Humus Dark brown, sweet-smelling, crumbly vegetable matter that has decayed, such as compost or leaf-mould.

Hybrid A plant that is derived from crossing two different species, varieties or cultivars, often of the same genus. The new plant has some of the genetic characteristics of each.

Inorganic A chemical compound that does not contain carbon, which is derived from animal matter, such as excrement or dead plants. Inorganic fertilisers are mined or chemically produced.

Insecticide A substance that is used to eliminate garden insect pests. Insecticides are available as liquids or powders, or in smoke form.

Intercrop A fast-growing vegetable crop that is raised between rows of slower-growing crops.

Joint The part of a plant's stem from which leaves, buds and shoots grow. The joint is sometimes slightly swollen, as on rose bushes. A joint is also known as a node.

Lateral A side shoot or stem growing from a bud on a larger stem.

Layering A propagation technique where a plant's stem is induced to form roots by laying the stem on the soil. This technique is particularly good for making new plants from honeysuckle and rhododendrons.

Leaching The washing away of soluble plant food and trace elements from the topsoil by water drainage.

Leaf-mould Compost made from dead or decaying leaves.

Lime A soil conditioner that is sprinkled over acid soil to neutralise it, and over heavy clay soils to improve the texture. Calcium, the chief chemical element of lime, is also an essential plant food.

Loam A soil that contains a mixture of clay, sand, humus and silt. Loam is well aerated and free-draining.

Marginal A plant that requires a constantly damp or wet soil, such as at the edge of a pond, to thrive.

Mulch A layer of material that is spread over the soil around plants in order to conserve moisture, enrich the soil, suppress weeds or warm the ground. Manure, garden compost and bark chippings all make beneficial organic mulches.

Municipal compost Composted green waste produced by local councils and sold as a soil conditioner.

Naturalise To grow bulbs or other plants in a simulated natural environment in the garden, such as growing daffodils in a lawn.

Neutral soil Neither acid nor alkaline, with a pH level of about 7.

Nitrogen A natural element, occurring in the soil and air, which is absorbed by plants primarily to make green foliage.

Node See **Joint**

Organic Substances such as manure and compost that are derived from animal or vegetable remains. Organic fertilisers contain carbon and are made from formerly living matter.

Oxygenator A submerged aquatic plant that releases oxygen into the water in a pond.

Parasite A plant that lives on another plant, and takes all its nourishment from its host. A good example of a parasite is mistletoe.

Peat Organic matter that is formed when dead plants from bogs (sphagnum peat) or heathland (sedge peat) are prevented from decaying past a certain point through lack of oxygen. Peat is traditionally used for growing plants and improving soils. However, gardeners are now turning to peat-free alternatives because they realise that peat is not an infinite resource.

Perennial The name given to a plant that lives for at least three seasons. The term can refer to trees and shrubs, but it is mainly applied to herbaceous plants that die down in winter and emerge again the following spring, such as phlox and peonies.

pH A scale running from 1–14, used to measure the acid-alkaline balance of soil. A reading of 7 is neutral, while those below mean that the soil is acidic, and those above are considered to be alkaline. Most garden soils are within the range of pH 4.5–8.

Pinching out A technique for removing the tip, or growing point, of a stem to encourage branching or to induce bud formation.

Pollarding A pruning technique for cutting a tree back to its trunk and the stubs of the main branches. Willow trees are often pollarded to provide young shoots for basket-making.

Potting on Transferring a plant to a larger container. Plants are usually potted on when their roots become pot-bound and need more soil space to grow.

Potting up Placing a plant and compost in a container.

Pricking out Transplanting seedlings from their initial containers into larger ones. To avoid plant damage when pricking out, do not touch the seedlings by their stems, but gently hold the leaves.

Propagation The increase of plants, either by seeds or vegetatively, by means of cuttings, such as division, grafting or layering.

Pruning The technique for controlled cutting back of plants to restrict their size, train or shape them, promote the growth of flower or fruit buds, or remove damaged, diseased or dead wood.

Pruning is usually carried out on plants with woody stems, such as roses, fruit bushes or trees (see also **Pinching out** and **Thinning**).

Repotting Transferring a plant to a similar-sized pot after reducing the soil ball and roots to make space for fresh compost.

Resting period A time in the annual cycle of many plants when they are dormant and do not put on any growth.

Rhizome A thickened underground horizontal stem with roots and leaves or shoots. A rhizome acts as a storage organ when a plant, such as a geranium or an iris, is dormant (see also **Bulb**, **Corm** and **Tuber**).

Rootstock A propagation term for a rooting plant onto which another plant is grafted. The graft takes on some of the attributes, in size and vigour, of the rootstock plant. Fruit trees are often grown on rootstock.

Runner A stem that roots at the tip on contact with moist soil and forms a new plant. Runners are commonly found on strawberries.

Scion A shoot or bud cut from one plant to graft onto a rootstock of another.

Seedling A young plant after germination, with a single, unbranched stem.

Self-fertile A term applied to a plant that will set fruit and seed when fertilised with its own pollen. This term is usually applied to fruit trees.

Self-sterile A term applied to a plant that requires a pollinator of a different clone to produce fruits.

Sepal Derived from modified leaves, these surround and protect a flower in bud.

Softwood The young shoots of half-hardy perennials and house plants, from which cuttings are taken between spring and early summer.

Soil improver Organic matter such as manure and leaf-mould, and inorganic material such as chemical fertiliser dug into the soil to improve drainage, structure and fertility.

Spit A term used to denote depth of digging. It is the length of a spade's blade, or about 25–30cm.

Staking Supporting top-heavy plants with canes or wooden supports. Some young trees also need to be staked until they are established. This prevents the tree from rocking in the wind and becoming up-rooted.

Stolon See **Runner**

Stratification The period of either warmth or cold (depending on the plant) required by some seeds to trigger germination.

Subsoil The layer of soil that lies below the topsoil. It is easily recognised by its marked difference in texture and colour from the layer above, although its depth may vary.

Sucker A shoot sprouting from below ground at the base of a plant. If the sucker has sprouted from a grafted plant, it must be torn off at source to prevent the rootstock from taking over the scion. Roses frequently produce suckers (see also **Rootstock** and **Scion**).

Systemic insecticide A chemical compound that is sprayed onto the foliage of a plant and enters the sap in order to poison sap-sucking insects.

Taproot The main anchoring root of a plant, particularly in trees, which grows vertically down into the soil. The term taproot also applies to long root-formed vegetables, such as carrots and parsnips.

Tender A term to describe plants that are vulnerable to frost damage.

Tendril A thin, curling stem-like growth that twines around supports in order to help a plant to climb.

Terminal A bud that grows at the tip of a stem or branch.

Thinning The removal of some seedlings in a batch to improve the growth of the remaining plants. The term thinning also describes the removal of a number of flower or fruit buds on a plant to prevent overcrowding and to encourage better results.

Treading Firming recently cultivated soil by walking on it before preparing it for sowing or planting, such as when planting a lawn. This technique is also used when transplanting shrubs or trees to remove air pockets from the soil and to make sure that the soil can be packed around the plant's roots.

Trenching A deep-digging technique where soil is cultivated to a depth of three spits, or 75–90cm (see **Spit**).

Tuber A thickened fleshy root or an underground stem that serves as a food store and produces shoots.

Variegated Leaves and flowers marked decoratively in a contrasting colour. Variegated foliage is usually green mixed with yellow, gold, cream or white.

Weed A plant that is growing where you do not want it. The term commonly refers to non-ornamental species that are fast growing and will take over an area if not removed. Perennial weeds are more difficult to eradicate than annual weeds.

Windbreak A hedge, fence or wall that shelters plants by diminishing or diverting the wind.

MEASUREMENTS

LINEAR

Metric	Imperial
2mm	⅟₁₆in
5mm	¼in
10mm/1cm	½in
15mm	⅝in
2cm	¾in
5cm	2in
5.5cm	2¼in
10cm	4in
20cm	8in
30cm	12in
40cm	16in
50cm	20in
75cm	2ft 6in
100cm/1m	3ft 3in
1.5m	5ft
2m	6ft 6in
5m	16ft 6in
10m	11yd
20m	22yd
50m	54yd 2ft

VOLUME

Metric	Imperial
30ml	1fl oz
50ml	2fl oz
75ml	2½fl oz
90ml	3¼fl oz
100ml	3½fl oz
125ml	4fl oz
150ml	5fl oz
175ml	6fl oz
200ml	7fl oz
250ml	9fl oz
500ml	18fl oz
750ml	1 pint 7fl oz
1 litre	1¾ pints
1.2 litres	2 pints
1.5 litres	2¾ pints
2 litres	3½ pints
2.5 litres	4½ pints
5 litres	8¾ pints
7.5 litres	13¼ pints
10 litres	17½ pints

WEIGHT

Metric	Imperial
5g	⅛oz
10g	¼oz
15g	½oz
20g	¾oz
50g	1¾oz
100g	3½oz
150g	5½oz
200g	7oz
250g	9oz
500g	1lb 2oz
750g	1lb 10oz
1kg	2lb 4oz
1.25kg	2lb 12oz
1.5kg	3lb 5oz
1.75kg	3lb 13oz
2kg	4lb 8oz
2.5kg	5lb 8oz
5kg	11lb
7.5kg	16lb 8oz
10kg	22lb

TEMPERATURE

Celsius	Fahrenheit
-10°C	14°F
-5°C	23°F
0°C	32°F
5°C	41°F
10°C	50°F
15°C	59°F
20°C	68°F
25°C	77°F
30°C	86°F
35°C	95°F

Index

Figures in *italics* refer to illustrations; glossary terms are in **bold** type. Plant variety names follow any other sub-headings.

Index

Index

Index

Index

Index

Index

Acknowledgments

Abbreviations:
HSC = Harry Smith Collection
HS = Horizon/A.Schreiner
M&JCL = M. & J. C. LAMONTAGNE
MD = MAP/A. Descat
ML = MAP/F. Lamarque
MM = MAP/N. & P. Mioulane
RD = Reader's Digest
b – bottom, l – left, m – middle, r – right, t – top

10 M&JCL 12 tr MAP/F. Marre bl ML 13 br HS 14 tr SRD/J.P. Delagarde 15 tl M&JCL bl MAP/N. & P. Mioulane/Design : Sonny Garcia mr MAP/C. Nichols/Design : Sonny Garcia 16 tr © Marcus Harpur/Wendy Wetherick, Croydon, S London bl MAP/A. Guerrier 17 tl M&JCL ml MM r MM br HS 18 tl HS 19 tl HS br ML 20 bl MAP/C. Nichols 21 tl MD tr MAP/C. Nichols ml MM mr MD bl MAP/A. Guerrier br MD 22 tl MD ml MD br MAP/C. Nichols/Eastgrove Cottage 23 bl S & O Mathews tr HORIZON/V. Vitis 24 bl ANNESS PUBLISHING 25 bl © RD tr M&JCL mr MD br Howard Rice - GPL 26 bl RUSTICA/M. Faver-Maltaverne 27 tl MAP/F. Didillon tr M&JCL ml MAP/Noun/Jardin de Luré mr MAP/Y. Monel/Jardin de curé de Wy dit Joli village (Val d'Oise) bl MD br MD/Jardin privé - Rémelard (Orne) 28 tr © Jerry Harpur mr © John Glover 9610 29 bl (r1, l) M&JCL bl (r1, m) GWI/HSC bl (r1, r) M&JCL br (r2) M&JCL tr (1) MD tr (2) © RD tr (3) © RD/Richard Surman tr (4) MAP/F. Didillon 30 bl MM/'Danse avec les carpes' - Festival des jardins - Chaumont, 1997 30 tr MAP/C. Nichols/Brook Cottage, Oxon 31 br MM 32 tl (1) GWI/HSC tl (2) M&JCL tl (3) HORIZON/M. Viard bl HORIZON/P. Glemas mr RUSTICA/V. Klecka/La Tour Marliac 33 tl M&JCL tr GWI/HSC ml MAP/C.

Nichols/Chelsea mr MM/Roots and Shoots, Hampton Court 01 bl MAP/F. Didillon br © John Glover 967 34 tl (1) MD tl (2) MM tl (3) MM tl (4) MAP/J. Y. Grospas tl (5) HORIZON/V. Vitir tl (6) MM tl (7) M&JCL tr MM 34 br M&JCL 35 ml MM 35 tr M&JCL br ANNESS PUBLISHING Ltd © 1999 36 bl (1) MD bl (2) MAP/F. Strauss bl (3) MAP/F. Strauss bl (4) MAP/F. Strauss tr © Lynne Brotchie/GPL 37 ml (1) MM ml (2) M&JCL tr MM 38 tl © John Glover 91 mr MM 39 tl © Jerry Harpur br (1) © RD br (2) © RD br (3) © RD br (4) © RD 40 bl MAP/F. Strauss tr GPL/John Glover mr Photos Horticultural/Michael and Lois Warren 41 tl Photos Horticultural (Picture Library) mr © Mel Watson/GPL br (1) GWI/HSC br (2) © Brian Carter - GPL br (3) GWI/HSC 42 bl (1) S & O Matthews bl (2) © RD/Richard Surman bl (3) © RD bl (4) © RD mr MAP/F. Strauss 43 tl © RD 44 bl (1) M&JCL bl (2) M&JCL bl (3) M&JCL tr GPL/Linda Burgess 45 ml MAP/F. Strauss br © J S Sira - GPL 46 tr © Jerry Harpur 47 ml M&JCL tr MM br © RD 48 bl HS 49 tl Photos Horticultural/Michael and Lois Warren ml MAP/Noun & Gaëlle br © Jerry Harpur 50 tr MM b © RD 51 ml MM 52 ml © Martin Cameron, Andrew Long and Malkolm Warington for RD br (1-6) SRD/J.P. Delagarde 53 tl HORIZON/Lamontagne mr MAP/F. Gager br M&JCL 54 MAP/F. Didillon 56 bl (1) MD bl (2) MD bl (3) MAP/C. Nichols bl (4) MAP/F. Strauss 57 bl MM mr MM 58 bl RUSTICA/F. Marre/Jardin Le Bois Pinard/Stylisme M. Marcat mr M&JCL 59 tl (1) M&JCL tr (2) MD ml (3) MM mr (4) M&JCL bl (5) M&JCL br (6) MAP/F. Strauss 60 bl © RD tr HS 61 bl MM tr © RD 62 tl © John Glover 992 b (1-3) MM b (4) MD 63 tl RUSTICA/J. P.

Praderes ml MM tr MAP/Noun & Gaëlle br MAP/Noun & Gaëlle 64 bl MAP/F. Didillon tr MAP/Noun & Gaëlle mr © RD 65 l (1) M&JCL l (2) MD l (3) M&JCL l (4) MAP/F. Didillon tr M&JCL 66 l (1-5) MM l 6 GWI/HSC 67 tl (1) MAP/F. Strauss tr (2) MD ml (3) MD mr (4) M&JCL bl (5) M&JCL br (6) M&JCL 68 l MM tr M&JCL mr M&JCL 69 bl M&JCL tr (1) MD tr (2) MAP/N. & P. Mioulane tr (3) MM tr (4) SRD/J. P. Delagarde 70 ml MM tr Photos Horticultural 71 ml MAP/F. Strauss tr M&JCL (1) © RD br (2) MM br (3) MD br (4) HORIZON/M. Viard br (5) MD 72 bl MAP/Noun & Gaëlle tr MD 73 bl MAP/Noun & Gaëlle r (1) MAP/A. Guerrier r (2) MD r (3) MAP/F. Didillon r (4) MD r (5) MD r (6) © RD r (7) MM r (8) MAP/F. Strauss 74 bl (Steps 1-3) RUSTICA/F. Marre bl MAP/Noun & Gaëlle tr MD 75 tl MD mr MAP/F. Strauss br MAP/Y. Monel 75 tl MD mr BIOS/G.P.L/W. Watson 76 ml MD tr MAP/F. Strauss br MAP/F. Strauss 77 tl M&JCL tr M&JCL 78 bl MAP/F. Strauss tr MAP/F. Didillon mr SRD/J. P. Delagarde 79 tr MAP/F. Didillon br (1) M&JCL br (2) MAP/Y. Monel br (3) MM br (4) HS 80 ml (1) MAP/C. Nichols/RHS Garden, Wisley, Surrey ml (2) MM ml (3) MAP/F. Didillon tr MAP/F. Didillon 81 r (1) MAP/Noun r (2) M&JCL r (3) MAP/Noun & Gaëlle r (4) MAP/Noun & Gaëlle r (5) M&JCL r (6) GWI/HSC 82 bl HS tr © Jerry Harpur 83 tr MAP/Noun & Gaëlle mr M&JCL 84 l (Steps 1-6) MAP/Noun & Gaëlle 85 tl (1) M&JCL tr (2) MD ml (3) MD mr (4) M&JCL bl (5) MAP/Globe Planter bl (6) M&JCL 86 tl © RD bl MAP/Noun tr MM 87 tl MAP/Noun br M&JCL 88 tl M&JCL bl MM/Paul Dyer, Hampton Court (Grande Bretagne) r (1) RUSTICA/Boucourt/Jardin de Miromesnil r (2) MM r (3) MAP/Noun & Gaëlle r (4) MM 89 tl Photos Horticultural bl

© John Glover 91 tr MM 90 tl HORIZON/A. Guerrier ml M&JCL tr MM br GWI/Harry Smith Collection 91 tl MAP/C. Nichols br M&JCL 92 bl RUSTICA/E. Brenckle/Le Bois Pinard/Stylisme Marie Marcat tr HS mr © Jerry Harpur 93 tl HS tl HS br (1) MAP/Globe Panter br (2) MD br (3) MD 94 tl (Steps 1-4) MAP/Noun & Gaëlle br MAP/F. Strauss 95 tl MAP/Y. Monel ml HORIZON/M. Viard br (Steps 1-3) MM br (Steps 4) Heather Angel/Natural Visions 96 bl © HSC tr © HSC 97 ml MM tml © A. Breuil mvr © HSC mbr MM 98 bl MAP/M. Duyck mtr © HSC tr MAP/M. Duyck br MAP/A. Descat 99 ml MAP/A. Breuil mvr MAP/E. Ossart mr Horizon/G. Ken 100 Horizon/J. P. Soulier 102 tl HS © John Glover 006 103 ml HS tr HORIZON/M. Viard br (Steps 1-4) HS 104 bl (1) M&JCL bl (2) HORIZON/Lamontagne bl (3) M&JCL bl (4) MM 105 tl (1) MD tr (2) MD ml (3) RUSTICA/A. Petzol/Roseraie de l'Hay-les-Roses (Val de Marne) mr (4) MD bl (5) MD br (6) MAP/F. Didillon 106 bl Photos Horticultural/Designer: Lady Xa Tollemache tr HORIZON/V. Vitis tr M&JCL 107 b (Steps 1-4) MAP/Noun & Gaëlle tr (1) Photos Horticultural tr (2) MD tr (3) M&JCL tr (4) M&JCL 108 l (Steps 1-6) M&JCL tr M&JCL br M&JCL 109 tl Andrew Lawson tr RUSTICA 110 tl RUSTICA br RUSTICA/F. Marre 111 tr MM mr M&JCL br (Steps 1-2) MM br Step 3 MD 112 ml HS bl © Howard Rice/GPL tr Photos Horticultural, Michael & Lois Warren br © RD 113 bl ML tr MAP/C. Nichols 114 ml RUSTICA/F. Boucourt/Le Bois Pinard tr MD br (1) RUSTICA/Hebe br (2) RUSTICA/Hebe 115 br (Steps 1-6) MM 116 bl 'GWI/Harry Smith Collection, © Charles Hawes' mr MM 117 tl (1)

MM tr (2) MD ml (3) HORIZON/V. Vitis mr (4) MD bl (5) MD br (6) HORIZON/V. Vitis 118 tl M&JCL bl (1) MD bl (2) MD mr MAP/P. Nief br GWI/Harry Smith Collection 119 tl MM tm MAP/C. Nichols tr MD br MAP/Y. Monel 120 tr © RD tr M&JCL br MAP/Noun 121 tl MD/Création Timothy Vaughan br MM 122 tl ML bl MM br MD 123 tl MAP/Noun br (Steps1-3) MM 124 tr MAP/F. Didillon 125 bl MD tr M&JCL br (Steps 1-4) MM 1261 (1) © RD l (2) © RD l (3) Richard Surman/RD l (4) Richard Surman/RD l (5) © RD 127 tl © Alec Scaresbrook/GPL mr RUSTICA/Ph. Asseray br MM 128 tl RUSTICA/Boucourt mr MM 129 tl (Steps 1-4) MM mr MAP/F. Strauss br MAP/Y. Monel 130 ml © HARRY SMITH COLLECTION 130 tr MD/Jardin de Bagatelle 131 tl SRD/J.P. Delagarde ml HS br (Steps 1-4) MAP/Noun & Gaëlle 132 t (1) © RD t (2) Adrian Gadsby © t (3) MD t (4) RUSTICA/V. Klecka 133 tl (1) © John Glover 994 tr (2) Andrew Lawson ml (3) © RD mr (4) © RD bl (5) GWI/Harry Smith Collection mr (6) GWI/Harry Smith Collection 134 tl MD/Jardin privé à St Helier (Jersey) bl (1) RUSTICA/J. Creuse bl (2) RUSTICA/C. Hochet bl (3) MD bl (4) MM mr MD 135 tl M&JCL br (1) MAP/Y. Monel br (2) MM 136 tl MM ml MM tr MAP/Y. Monel 137 bl (1) © JS Sira/GPL bl (2) © John Ferro Sims/GPL bl (3) © Clive Nichols 138 ml MAP/Y. Monel bl (Steps 1-2) MM tr Andrew Lawson: Haseley Court, Oxford 139 ml © Clive Nichols/GPL mr M&JCL br MM br M&JCL/Prieuré d'Orsan (Cher) 141 tl MAP/C. Nichols/Sleightholme Dale Lodge, North Yorkshire br (Steps 1-6) HS 142 bl MM tr © Clive Nichols/Launa Slatter 143 bl M&JCL tr HS 144 bl (1) HS bl (2) MD bl (3) HS tr HORIZON/A. Guerrier 145 tl (1) M&JCL tr (2) M&JCL tml (3) © RD tmr (4) M&JCL bml (5) HORIZON/V. Vitis bmr (6) M&JCL br (7) MAP/Y. Monel br (8) MAP/Y. Monel 146 b (Steps 1-8) HS tr HORIZON/V. Vitis 147 bl RUSTICA/Ph. Asseray mr (t) M&JCL mr (b) M&JCL br (m) HS br (r) RUSTICA/Ph. Asseray 148 bl (Steps 1-2) MAP/Noun & Gaëlle tr (Steps 1-2) MM 149 tl MM ml © CHRYSALIS br Steps 1-4 MAP/Noun & Gaëlle 150 tl MAP/A. Breuil tr MM mr HORIZON/M. Viard br MAP/F. Nief 151 tl © Harry Smith Collection ml MAP/P. Averseng tr MAP/A. Breuil 152 mr MM br MAP/P. Averseng bl MM ml MM mvr MAP/F. Didillon mbr © HSC tr © HSC mr HORIZON/g. Ken 153 tl MAP/P. Averseng bl M&JCL mml MAP/Noun mvr © HSC br MAP/A. Breuil 154 © Eric Crichton

Photos 156 bl MAP/F. Didillon/Jardin de la Lande Chevrier (Cher) br MAP/C. Nichols/Ivy Cottage Dorset 157 ml M&JCL bl RUSTICA/V. Klecka tr M&JCL 158 br RUSTICA/F. Marre/Le Bois Pinard/Styliste Marie Marcat 159 tl RUSTICA/Le Potager de Grand Papa, Miromesnil br MAP/Noun/jardin privé, Belgique 160 ml MD bl MAP/Noun tr M&JCL br MM 161 tr Steps 1-3 MAP/Noun & Gaëlle 162 ml M&JCL br M&JCL 163 tl (1) MD tr (2) MD ml (3) MAP/F. Didillon mr (4) M&JCL tr MAP/Noun & Gaëlle 164 bl MAP/Noun tr M&JCL br RUSTICA/Ph. Asseray/Jardin du Feyel 165 ml M&JCL b Steps 1-3 MM b (Steps 4) M&JCL 166 ml M&JCL bl BIOS/O. Frimat tr (Step 1) RUSTICA/G. Cotonnec tr (Steps 2-6) RUSTICA/G. Cotonnec 167 bl HS tr MD mr (top) HS mr (mid) MAP/C. Nichols mr (below) M&JCL 168 ml M&JCL tr Photos Horticultural mr M&JCL br Steps 1-4) MAP/Noun & Gaëlle tr © Eric Crichton Photos 170 ml M&JCL br (Steps 1-3) MAP/Noun & Gaëlle 171 tl M&JCL bl MAP/Noun & Gaëlle tr MAP/Noun & Gaëlle 172 bl (top) M&JCL bl (below) M&JCL tr M&JCL mr M&JCL 173 ml M&JCL tr (1) © RD tr (2) MAP/F. Didillon tr (3) MD tr (4) M&JCL tr (5) MD 174 tl M&JCL bl © GPL/Jane Legate mr M&JCL 175 tl Photos Horticultural br M&JCL mr M&JCL tr (1) RUSTICA/Ch. Hochet bl M&JCL 177 tl (1) M&JCL tr (2) © RD ml (3) HORIZON/M&JCL mr (4) M&JCL bl (5) MD br (6) © Philippe Bonduel/GPL 178 tl © John Glover/GPL br RUSTICA/A. Petzold/Les Jardins du Feyel tr M&JCL br MD 179 bl M&JCL tr (1) M&JCL tr (2) MD tr (3) M&JCL tr (4) M&JCL br M&JCL 180 bl (Steps 1-3) M&JCL tr M&JCL 181 ml MM tr MD br RUSTICA/Thobois 182 bl MAP/Noun tr MAP/F. Didillon br RUSTICA/D. Lerault 183 bl (top) © Howard Rice/GPL bl (mid) MAP/Noun bl (below) M&JCL tr MAP/F. Didillon mr MAP/Noun & Gaëlle 184 tl MAP/Noun bl M&JCL br (Steps 1-2) MAP/Noun & Gaëlle mr MAP/Noun & Gaëlle br RUSTICA/Ph. Asseray 185 ml Garden World Images, HSC bl © Harry Smith Collection mr MD 186 bl (1) M&JCL bl (2) MAP/Noun bl (3) MAP/Noun bl (4) M&JCL tr Garden World Images, HSC 187 tl M&JCL bl M&JCL br © Jerry Pavia/GPL 188 ml (top) MAP/F. Didillon ml (below) MAP/F. Didillon mr MD 189 tl (1) M&JCL tl (2) MM mr (top) MAP/Noun mr (below) MAP/Noun 190 bl HS tr HORIZON/V. Vitis 191 bl MM mr (top) M&JCL mr (mid)

M&JCL mr (below) M&JCL br MM 192 ml MAP/Noun & Gaëlle tr © Clay Perry/GPL bl MM bm MAP/Noun br MM 193 ml MAP/Noun br Photos Horticultural, Michael & Lois Warren 194 ml M&JCL bl MAP/Noun tr © Eric Crichton Photos 195 tl M&JCL mr (1) RD 06464 mr (2) RD 06463 mr (3) RD 06462 196 bl MAP/F. Didillon tr M&JCL br RUSTICA/Ch. Hochet 197 tl M&JCL bl MM br SRD/J.P. Delagarde 198 bl © RD tr © Steven Wooster/GPL mr MAP/Noun 199 ml RUSTICA/V. Klecka/Les Jardins du Feyel tr HORIZON/M. Viard mr M&JCL 200 tl M&JCL ml M&JCL 201 tl (1) MAP/F. Strauss tr (2) M&JCL ml (3) M&JCL mr (4) M&JCL bl (5) MD br (6) MAP/Noun 202 tr MAP/Noun 203 ml MAP/F. Strauss br M&JCL tr Steps 1-4 M&JCL 204 bl Step 1 MD bl Steps 1-4 MAP/Noun & Gaëlle tr MAP/C. Nichols 205 mml © HSC mvr © HSC br © HSC tr © HSC 207 tl © HSC bl MAP/P. Nief mbr © M&JCL MD br. Bernadin 208 bl MAP/S. Bonneau mtl © HSC br © G. BLONDEAU 209 bl © P. AVERSENQ mbr © HSC mr MM 212 tl (1) © Liz Eddison bl (2) Howard Rice mr M&JCL mr MAP/Noun & Gaëlle 213 tl M&JCL bl MAP/Noun & Gaëlle mr M&JCL 214 ml M&JCL bl RUSTICA/J. Creuse tr M&JCL br (1) GWI/HSC br (2) MD 215 tr MAP/F. Didillon 216 bl © MAYER/LE SCANFF/GPL tr MAP/Noun mr M&JCL 217 tl (1) GWI/HSC tr (2) Photos Horticultural ml (3) MD mr (4) MD bl (5) MD br (6) GWI/HSC 218 tl Photos Horticultural tr M&JCL 219 bl M&JCL tr (1) Photos Horticultural tr (2) Neil Holmes 220 bl MM tr M&JCL br M&JCL 221 bl (1) Neil Holmes bl (2) Neil Holmes bl (3) Photos Horticultural tr M&JCL 222 ml MM bl (Steps 1-4) MM tr Photos Horticultural 223 bl (1) © Rita Coates bl (2) Photos Horticultural, Michael & Lois Warren tr Photos Horticultural mr MM 224 b SRD/J.P. Delagarde tr © Steve Wooster 225 br M&JCL 226 tl M&JCL tr HORIZON/M. Viard mr M&JCL br M&JCL 227 r MAP/F. Didillon 228 tr M&JCL br M&JCL 229 tl Poirier tm Pommier en cordon tr Andrew Lawson br GWI/HSC 230 tl RUSTICA ml MM mr MAP/Ph. Fauchere 231 tl (1) Neil Holmes tr (2) Andrew Lawson ml (3) © Garden Matters mr (4) GWI/HSC bl (5) GWI/HSC tr (6) Holt?? 232 tl RUSTICA br (1) RUSTICA/F. Marre br (2) RUSTICA/F. Marre br (3) RUSTICA/J. Creuse br (4) RUSTICA/J. Creuse br (5) RUSTICA/J. Creuse 233 tl MM 234 t MAP/Y. Monel ml (top) MM ml (below) RUSTICA br (1) MAP/F. Didillon br (2) RUSTICA/V. Maisons br (3) GWI/HSC 235 ml

M&JCL bl HS tr MM 236 tl MM bl © GWI/Jo Whitworth 237 ml M&JCL r (Steps 1-6) HS 238 bl Photos Horticultural tr © John Phipps br M&JCL 239 l MAP/Noun & Gaëlle br Photos Horticultural 240 mr Photos Horticultural 241 tl (1) © Jacqui Hurst/GPL tr (2) GWI/HSC mr (3) © Jerry Harpur mr (4) Photos Horticultural, Michael & Lois Warren bl (5) © Eric Crichton Photos br (6) © Eric Crichton Photos 242 ml MM tr MD br MAP/Noun & Gaëlle 243 ml © RD bl M&JCL mr MAP/Noun 244 tr M&JCL br M&JCL 245 tr © Friedrich Strauss-GPL br HORIZON/M. Viard 246 ml © GPL/Mayer/Le Scanff br HORIZON/M. Viard 247 ml MAP/P. Averseng bl M&JCL tr HORIZON/M. Viard br MAP/Noun & Gaëlle 248 tr M&JCL mr M&JCL ml M&JCL bl M&JCL mr SRD/J.P. Delagarde 250 ml MM br MM mr © G. Blondeau 251 tl © OPIE/R. Coutin tr M&JCL mr MM 252 tl © Harry Smith Collection tm MAP/P. Averseng mr MAP/P. Averseng 253 tl MAP/P. Averseng ml M&JCL tml MD bml M&JCL br © A. BREUIL 254 ml MM bml M&JCL mr MAP/P. Averseng tr © HSC mr RUSTICA/V. Klecka/Les Jardins du Feyel 255 ml (3) MAP/P. Averseng 256 INSIDE/L. Terestchenko 258 tr © RD 259 tl MAP/E. Strauss bl Steps 1-2 MAP/F. Strauss tr (1) MAP/Ph. Fauchere tr (2) MM tr (3) MD 260 ml © RD tr HORIZON/P. Glemas br M&JCL 261 bl (above) M&JCL tl (below) RUSTICA/Ph. Asseray mr M&JCL 262 bl MAP/Noun rtl MM rtr MM rbl MM rbr MM 263 tr MAP/Noun & Gaëlle mr MAP/Noun & Gaëlle bl Clive Nichols Garden Pictures mr RUSTICA/Boncourt 264 ml MAP/F. Strauss tr M&JCL br MAP/Noun & Gaëlle 265 t (Steps 1-4) MAP/Noun & Gaëlle ml MM mr MM 266 bl M&JCL tr MAP/Noun 267 tl MM r MAP/Noun & Gaëlle 268 bl Paul Hart–G.P.L. tr MAP/Noun mr MAP/Noun 269 bl (Steps 1-4) MAP/Noun 270 bl M&JCL br M&JCL 271 tl M&JCL ml MAP/Noun & Gaëlle mr M&JCL 272 tl (Steps 1-6) MAP/Noun & Gaëlle mr M&JCL br (above) M&JCL tr (below) M&JCL 273 tl © RD mr M&JCL br © RD 274 tr MAP/F. Didillon 275 bl RUSTICA tr © RD br (Steps 1-4) MAP/Noun & Gaëlle 276 tl G.W.I. ml HORIZON/P. Glemas mr MAP/Noun & Gaëlle 277 tl RUSTICA/F. Marre/Le Bois Pinard - Styliste Marie Marcat bl G.W.I. mr MAP/Noun & Gaëlle 278 bl MAP/F. Strauss tr MAP/Y. Monel 279 ml M&JCL r (1) MAP/Noun & Gaëlle r (2) MAP/Noun & Gaëlle r (3) MM r (4) MAP/F. Didillon 280 ml MAP/Noun tr M&JCL br (Steps 1-3) HS 281 br G.W.I. ml Paul Hart–G.P.L.

Secrets and Tips from Yesterday's Gardeners was published by The Reader's Digest Association Limited, London
First edition copyright © 2004
The Reader's Digest Association Limited,
11 Westferry Circus, Canary Wharf, London E14 4HE

The book was adapted from **Secrets et Astuces des Jardins d'Autrefois**, published by Sélection du Reader's Digest (France).
First edition copyright © 2003

Adapted by Craft Plus Publishing Limited,
53 Crown Street, Brentwood, Essex, CM14 4BD

FOR CRAFT PLUS PUBLISHING LIMITED
Project Manager Sue Joiner
Writers Vincent Gradwell, Katharine Gurney, Kay Maguire, Paul Patton, Barbara Segall, Jean Vernon, Tamsin Westhorpe
Indexer Diana Lecore
Editors Sue Churchill, Gisela Roberts
Sub Editor Bea Agombar
Design Kerrie Blake

Colour origination Colour Systems, London
Printing and binding Maury Imprimeur SA, Malesherbes, France

Oracle code 250005404H.00.24
Concept code FR1577/G
Book code 400-095-01
ISBN 0 276 42844 7

FOR THE READER'S DIGEST ASSOCIATION LIMITED
Editor Alison Candlin
Art Editor Julie Bennett

READER'S DIGEST GENERAL BOOKS
Editorial Director Cortina Butler
Art Director Nick Clark
Executive Editor Julian Browne
Managing Editor Alastair Holmes
Picture Resource Manager Martin Smith
Pre-press Account Manager Penny Grose

We are committed to both the quality of our products and the service we provide to our customers. We value your comments, so please feel free to contact us on **08705 113366** or via our web site at:
www.readersdigest.co.uk
If you have any comments or suggestions about the content of our books, email us at **gbeditorial@readersdigest.co.uk**